THE SCOTT AND LAURIE OKI SERIES IN ASIAN AMERICAN STUDIES

WILLIAM WEI

ASIANS IN COLORADO

A History of Persecution and
Perseverance in the Centennial State

UNIVERSITY OF WASHINGTON PRESS
Seattle and London

Asians in Colorado is published with the assistance of grants from the Scott and Laurie Oki Endowed Fund for Publications in Asian American Studies and from the Charles Redd Center for Western Studies at Brigham Young University.

© 2016 by the University of Washington Press
Printed and bound in the United States of America

20   19   18   17   16   5   4   3   2   1

UNIVERSITY OF WASHINGTON PRESS
www.washington.edu/uwpress

LIBRARY OF CONGRESS CATALOGING-IN-PUBLICATION DATA
Names: Wei, William, 1948–   author.
Title: Asians in Colorado : a history of persecution and perseverance in the
   Centennial State / William Wei.
Description: Seattle : University of Washington Press, 2016. | Includes bibliographical
   references and index.
Identifiers: LCCN 2015041094 | ISBN 9780295995434 (hardcover : alk. paper)
Subjects: LCSH: Asian Americans—Colorado—History. | Colorado—Race
   relations—History. | Colorado—History.
Classification: LCC f785.a75 w45 2016 | DDC 305.8009788—dc23
LC record available at http://lccn.loc.gov/2015041094

The paper used in this publication is acid-free and meets the minimum requirements of American National Standard for Information Sciences—Permanence of Paper for Printed Library Materials, ANSI z39.48–1984. ∞

For Susan Cherniack Wei

白鷗沒浩蕩

萬里誰能馴

―杜甫

A white bird vanishes in the vast expanse

Ten thousand miles off, can you call it back?

―Du Fu

CONTENTS

ILLUSTRATIONS

ACKNOWLEDGMENTS

Historians know that their research rests on the work of a legion of librarians, archivists, and specialists who collect, organize, and make accessible the information and materials that are the foundation of their work. These individuals are the unsung heroes of the scholarly community. Among the many such experts who have assisted with this book, I am pleased to acknowledge the following and their affiliated institutions, in alphabetical order: Auraria Library Special Collections and Digital Initiatives: Matthew C. Mariner; Colorado State Archives: Kevin Luy; Colorado State Demography Office: Barbara Musick; Denshō, Japanese American Legacy Project: Caitlin Oiye; Denver Public Library, Western History and Genealogy Collection: Coi Drummond-Gehrig and Abby Haverstock; Denver Regional Census Office: Kimberly Ann Davis; Fallen Heroes Project: Eric Herzberg; History Colorado (formerly Colorado Historical Society), Stephen H. Hart Library and Research Center: Patrick J. Fraker, Megan K. Friedel, Sarah Gilmore, and Melissa VanOtterloo; Japanese American National Museum: Lauren Zuchowski; National Archives and Records Administration: Eric Bittner and Cody White; Pueblo City-County Library District: Maria Tucker; University of California at San Diego: Lynda Claassen; University of Colorado at Boulder, Norlin Library: Susan Guinn-Chipman, Erika Kleinova, and Leanne Walther; and US Census Bureau: Stephen Baugh. In addition, I wish to express my appreciation to the anonymous volunteers who compiled indices of information about Asian Americans in Colorado for both the Colorado Historical Society and the Denver Public Library, continuing a Civil Works Administration project begun in 1933.

In the course of writing this book, I also received assistance from the following individuals: Frank Abe, filmmaker, who provided me with photographs of Jimmie Omura; Roger Baker, Blackhawk historian, who sent me excerpts from Central City newspaper articles related to Chinese Coloradans; Tom Dickinson, University of Colorado, Institute of Behavior Science, who produced the Colorado maps in the book; Steven Grinstead, managing editor at History Colorado, who provided me with the photographs that accompanied my articles in *Colorado Heritage*; Christian Heimburger, who sent me a copy of his doctoral dissertation; Jennifer A. Kuehner, executive director of the Aurora History Museum, for the tour of the exhibit "An Epic Journey: Aurora's Asian/Pacific Communities"; Carolyn G. Kuhn, who provided me with pictures of her uncles Edward and William Chin; Reverend Kanya Okamoto, Tri-State Denver Buddhist Temple, who shared his knowledge about Denver's Japanese Americans; Luke Meagher, Wofford College Library, who provided me with the picture of the Shitara sisters; Joe Wismann-Horther, coordinator of the Integration Partnerships, Colorado Refugee Services, CDHS, who talked to me about recent refugees to Colorado; and Holly Yasui, who provided me with pictures of her father, Min Yasui.

Portions of this book are based on my previously published articles: Chapter 2 is a revision and expansion of "The Anti-Chinese Movement in Colorado: Interethnic Competition and Conflict on the Eve of Exclusion," *Chinese America: History and Perspective* (1995): 179–197; Chapter 3, "History and Memory: The Story of Denver's Chinatown," *Colorado Heritage* (Autumn 2002): 3–13; and Chapter 4, "Representation of Nineteenth-Century Chinese Prostitutes and Chinese Sexuality in the American West," in *Enduring Legacies: Ethnic Histories and Cultures of Colorado*, ed. Arturo Aldama et al. (Boulder: University Press of Colorado, 2011), 69–86. Chapter 8 is based on "'Simply a Question of Patriotism': Governor Ralph L. Carr and the Japanese Americans," *Colorado Heritage* (Winter 2002): 3–15; "A Profile in Courage: The Story of Gov. Ralph L. Carr and Japanese-Americans," Center of the American West series, *Sunday Daily Camera*, December 5, 1999; "The Internment of Japanese Americans in the United States," *Everyone's War* 8 (Autumn/Winter 2003): 52–58; and "'The Strangest City in Colorado': The Amache Concentration Camp," *Colorado Heritage* (Winter 2005): 3–21. Chapter 10 is an expansion of "Asian Americans," in *Encyclopedia of Military Science*, ed. G. Kurt Piehler (New York: Sage, 2013), 1:181–186.

I want to take this opportunity to express my thanks to Professor Linda Tamura, Willamette University, and Professor Liping Zhu, Eastern Washington University, for serving as external reviewers of the manuscript for the University of Washington Press. They provided constructive comments and detailed suggestions, which improved the work considerably. In addition, they gave me sound advice on how to shorten a text that was too long by half.

I also want to convey my appreciation to the University of Washington Press staff, especially Jacqueline Volin, editing, design, and production manager, and Emily Park, copy editor, for their fine work.

I am indebted to two individuals. The first is Ranjit Arab, the dedicated acquisitions editor at the University of Washington Press. During the Western History Association meeting in Denver in 2012, Ranjit invited me for coffee to talk about my recent research. He listened patiently as I described my work and interest in local history, and the need for historical monographs on Asian Americans in the Interior West. Ranjit encouraged me to submit a prospectus to the University of Washington Press. Afterward, he expertly shepherded the book through the acquisitions process, providing encouragement and feedback.

Last but not least, I wish to express my heartfelt gratitude to Susan Cherniack Wei, PhD, my loving wife and best friend. She has always been there for me. At no time was this truer than during the writing of this book. Much to my delight, in the course of my research, Susan developed in keen interest in the history of Asians in Colorado even though her own field is Chinese literature. She understood what I was trying to say better than anyone else. Besides providing unwavering moral support, she served as a researcher and editor, making the completion of this work possible.

ASIANS IN
COLORADO

FIG. P.1. On November 9, 1868, a reporter from the *Alta California* concluded that the Chinese laborers working on the Central Pacific Railroad were the "vanguard of the construction forces." He judged them to be "systematic workers, competent and wonderfully effective because [they are] tireless and unremitting in their industry." From Stephen E. Ambrose, *Nothing Like It in the World: The Men Who Built the Transcontinental Railroad, 1863–1869* (New York: Simon and Schuster, 2000), 314–315. Denver Public Library, Western History Collection, Z-3335.

ONCE UPON A TIME
IN THE WEST

A SIANS ROAMED THE AMERICAN WEST. THEY CAME LOOKING FOR work, found jobs, and settled in ethnic enclaves. Along with other immigrants they formed part of the multi-ethnic landscape of the region until they were driven out by ethnic cleansing campaigns. Once gone, it was as if they had never been there.

Anti-Asian agitation forced Asians to leave the West, and anti-Asian legislation kept them from coming back. While in the region, they performed essential work that made the place viable for others. But their accomplishments generally went unacknowledged or underreported. They remained largely invisible in the public record until recent decades. A case in point is their absence from the famous Andrew J. Russell photograph of the joining of the Union and Central Pacific Railroads at Promontory Point, Utah, on May 10, 1869. Looking at this historic scene, one would never know that Chinese workers had played a crucial role in the construction of the western half of the Transcontinental Railroad, which extended the horizon of the nation. They had even been the ones to place the last section of rail joining the two railroads. Chinese completed the railroad, and in a sense, without their story the nation's history remains incomplete.

POPULAR MYTHS

Although Asians have played a significant role in the development of the United States, they have usually been relegated to legends about the Old West. Perhaps the most powerful purveyor of such myths in modern times has been the Western, especially the Western film. This globally influential genre tells tall tales set in the American West during the latter half of the nineteenth century. Besides providing entertainment, these narratives serve a political purpose. They justify "western expansion," a euphemism for the colonization of the North American continent. In classic Westerns, American pioneers are portrayed as the standard-bearers of civilization, in contrast to "others," the backward people who are in the way and require subjugation. Thus, Westerns also serve to reinforce racial boundaries. While the central "others" of Westerns remain Native Americans, Asians are also viewed as others.[1]

Westerns serve as a bellwether for how Asians have been and continue to be perceived or misperceived by society. Chinese, who initially made up the majority of the Asians in the American West, regularly appear in such stories, but their representations are fictional constructs bearing little resemblance to the real Chinese who populated the region. As a matter of convention, Chinese characters play minor roles and generally stay in the background as local color to lend the setting a degree of verisimilitude. They are depicted in a limited set of situations, exhibit rote behaviors (often comical or negative), and are presented in a decontextualized fashion. In other words, Westerns are powerful vehicles for perpetuating Asian stereotypes.

There is, for instance, the character Chen Lee in the 1969 movie *True Grit*, directed by Henry Hathaway and based on the 1968 novel by James Portis.[2] As portrayed by H. W. Gim, Chen is a thin, slightly stooped character straight out of central casting. He wears a skullcap and sports a wispy beard. Chen is a study in contrast to the film's main character, "Rooster" Cogburn, played by John Wayne, the iconic Western movie hero. Although Cogburn is a wreck of a man, he dwarfs the diminutive Chen physically in their short scenes together and dominates him psychologically.

In Hathaway's film and in Portis's novel, Chen serves as a foil to Cogburn. His role implicitly perpetuates popular perceptions of Chinese in the American West. Though Chen and Cogburn are friends, theirs is an anomalous relationship. Since they live together in a room behind Chen's store, Chen is probably the landlord, though he acts less like a proprietor than a servant, preparing food for Cogburn and Mattie Ross, the story's narrator. Mattie's observations disclose aspects of Cogburn's character as well as Chen's.

The first revelation occurs during dinner, when Ross comments on the differences between the two men. Cogburn eats his beef stew with a spoon in one hand while sopping up the juice with a piece of bread in his other hand, while Chen uses chopsticks. Mattie comments: "What a contrast to the Chinaman with his delicate chopsticks! I have never seen them in use before. Such nimble fingers."[3] Chen's nimbleness is underscored by his dexterity in dealing with customers during the meal. His ability to adapt to circumstances is indicated further by the fact that he prepares an American meal, though he eats it in the Chinese way.

In an equally telling anecdote, after dinner, when Cogburn is drinking whiskey and losing money to Chen in a card game, Cogburn explains his losses to Mattie by blaming it on the Chinese: "You cannot tell what a Chinaman is thinking. That is how they beat you at cards."[4] Here Cogburn evokes the image of the inscrutable Oriental. Cogburn implies that the Chinese, as fundamentally unfathomable and hence unpredictable competitors, have an unfair advantage. This was a common criticism.

In the scene, Chen comes across as a refined, assured, and intelligent individual with an aversion to violence. Cogburn may lack these qualities, but he has true grit, which in this context means that he is sufficiently intrepid and tenacious to find and kill the man who had murdered Mattie's father. True grit is the attribute that allows men like Cogburn to win the West.

Among other things, my book shows that Asian Coloradans did not lack true grit. On the contrary, they displayed a dogged perseverance and refused to be discouraged by setbacks. They demonstrated the daring to pursue their goals and the inner drive necessary to attain them. They were courageous folks with initiative and the willingness to take risks in an unknown region, where they were likely to incur substantial costs—emotional, financial, and physical. Except for their racial background, they were the epitome of the rugged individualists pursuing the American Dream admired in folklore. Their continued presence in the country after repeated attempts to expel or exclude them is a testament to the human spirit.

ACROSS THE PACIFIC TO AMERICA

During the latter half of the nineteenth century, Asians came to the United States for a variety of reasons, mainly as immigrants, though a few came as refugees fleeing internal conflicts. Most of them settled in the Pacific Coast states, particularly California, where they constituted 10 percent of the population, and Hawaii, where they became the majority. Later they migrated to the Interior West, eventually making their way to Colorado—the Centennial State.[5] By the end of the century, three-quarters of

Asians lived in the American West, the vast region west of the hundredth meridian.

Then, as now, their status as people of color from the far side of the world differentiated Asians from other immigrants. They entered a society structured along a white-black fault line and found themselves on one side or the other of the divide. Their position was problematic. Asians fell between whites, who belonged to various European ethnic groups, and blacks, who were either slaves or freedmen. White Americans perceived Asians in the terms familiar to them. This was hard on Chinese workers, who were widely condemned as "coolies." At a time when antislavery sentiment was at its height, Americans saw them as slaves in the thrall of the Six Companies, a Chinese consortium that supplied laborers for US employers. For those with abolitionist sentiments, ending Chinese immigration to the United States was one way to free exploited Chinese laborers from their bondage. The stigma of coolieism was subsequently passed on to Japanese workers who followed the banished Chinese.

Meanwhile, Asians, blacks, and Europeans were all struggling for a place in a race-based society riven with an inequality at odds with its professed ideals of equality and justice for all. Asians were at the bottom of the heap. Initially, Americans viewed some European groups as non-whites, considering them culturally inferior, morally depraved, and physically dangerous. Over time, Europeans managed to redefine their racial identity and overcome objections to their presence, ultimately assuming their place in American society as whites. These formerly despised immigrants accomplished this transformation by interacting with members of mainstream society and acquiring an education in public schools. This facilitated social mobility and allowed them to cross class, religious, and ethnic barriers. Unfortunately, Europeans also embraced American prejudices. They took their cues from the dominant society and viewed Asians with scorn and suspicion, treating them as an invasive species in the labor market against whom they had been unfairly made to compete.

Among the maligned Europeans, the Irish were the most vociferous opponents of the Chinese. The sociologist Rose Hum Lee finds that throughout the Intermountain West, "the Irish immigrants regarded the Chinese as their strongest competitors in the placer mining industry, in manufacturing, in hand laundries, in domestic services and in railroad construction."[6]

Given their own experience of discrimination, the Irish might have been expected to sympathize with the Chinese. During Ireland's terrible potato famine (1845–52), many Irish fled to America, where they too were greeted with scorn and suspicion. On the East Coast, Americans considered the Irish inferior and only above blacks. The Know-Nothings, a nativist secret society, treated the Irish with distrust because most were Catholics. The Irish were also saddled with a reputation as drunks and criminals, a degrading stereotype that resulted in various forms of discrimination in housing and employment. Some critics even compared them to the Chinese. In 1857, the diarist George Templeton Strong wrote, "Our Celtic fellow citizens are almost as remote from us in temperament and constitution as the Chinese."[7]

However, after the Irish migrated to the American West, they were able to raise their position in society and enjoy more privileges. They no longer occupied the lowest social and labor stratum, which was reserved for the Chinese and other racial minorities. As historian Reginald Horsman observes, "An Irishman might be described as a lazy, dirty Celt when he landed in New York, but if his children settled in California they might well be praised as part of the vanguard of the energetic Anglo-Saxon people poised for the plunge into Asia."[8] In other words, their status depended on social context. The Irish were seen as "other" until compared with Italians, Poles, and Jews—who appeared more alien—or with people of color—who appeared more threatening.

As whites, the Irish were accorded a higher rank in the region's social hierarchy. They became naturalized citizens and translated their right to vote into political power. They attained political positions in part by vilifying Chinese and other people of color and supporting a system of institutionalized racial subordination.[9] Through their endorsement of white supremacy, the Irish sought to become accepted members of society in the American West.[10]

Today, whites appear to be more willing to share their superior position in the racial hierarchy with Asians, but this willingness requires distinguishing Asians from other people of color. Asians can no longer be placed easily alongside other minority groups given their comparatively high socioeconomic status. In terms of material and educational attainment, Asians are right behind or even ahead of whites, and like whites, they are commonly contrasted with blacks, Latinos, and Native Americans. However, it would be a mistake to take this as evidence that Asians have managed to cross the color line to become whites, like some of the formerly non-white Europeans, or that the line itself has disappeared in what some critics claim is now a post-racial society. The color line remains in place and will continue to hold until demographic changes now under way either greatly reduce its significance or render it irrelevant.

PATTERN OF PERSECUTION

During the nineteenth century, Asians faced discrimination throughout the United States in general and in the American West in particular. Successive Asian ethnic groups experienced a common cycle: as soon as members of one Asian group arrived in the United States, they became targets of local hostility. Then the federal government stepped in to arrange treaties with their home countries or to enact legislation to restrict or prohibit further immigration to the United States. But workers were still needed to build the country, so another Asian ethnic group came to replace them.

As my analysis of Asian Coloradans shows, the root cause of anti-Asian feelings was racism. Discrimination against people because of their skin color and other physical features has been around since time immemorial. It has been part of American life since the founding of the republic. From the beginning, the United States had a racial ideology that led to the creation of a bifurcated society, one that justified white dominance. The assumption of white superiority was implicit in the US Constitution, which treated Native Americans as aliens in their own land and defined blacks as inherently unequal—as the equivalent of three-fifths of a white person, to be exact. Ever since, race has permeated all aspects of US society. Indeed, racism was an inherent feature of the American way of life, sustained by the highest law of the land as well as local laws and practices.

A year after enacting the Constitution, the US Congress passed the 1790 Naturalization Act, which restricted the right of citizenship to any alien who was a free white person. From 1790 until 1870, Congress ordained that only whites were eligible to apply for naturalization. In doing so, Congress made it known what kind of people it considered worthy of being American and what kind of nation America was to be, at least racially. Until relatively recently, whiteness was a prerequisite for being an American. The exception to this was blacks, who became eligible for naturalization after the Civil War. But citizenship failed to confer equality on blacks. At best, they were considered second-class citizens. Given this history of denying citizenship to people of color, it is hardly surprising that blacks were presumed to be something less than 100 percent American and Asians were regarded as non-American despite their naturalization or birth.

While the definition of whiteness was debated in various forums, especially the legal arena, the value placed on it was always very high. To cross the threshold of acceptance and to attain a prominent place in the US social hierarchy, one had to be white or eventually be considered white. With the arrival of each new European group, the definition of who was white was adjusted. But there was never much doubt that Asians were a people of color, with all the attendant inferior physical and cultural qualities, at least in the popular mind. This constituted the framework for interaction between whites and Asians that was passed down from one generation to another in Colorado and elsewhere.

As the first populous group of non-white immigrants to the United States, the Chinese inherited the prevailing prejudice against people of color. Moreover, they became the ethnic group that everyone, both white and non-white, felt superior to. In fall 1879, in an article aptly titled "Race Antipathies," the *New York Times* observed that every group in America had some other group it looked down on, but ultimately, everyone looked down on the Chinese: "All representatives of the white race look down upon the poor Chinaman . . . in his turn, the negro [*sic*] puts the Chinese far down below himself in the social and political scale. In California, where, as one would suppose, the Digger Indian, the lowest form of man on this continent, would represent the social substratum, the proud aborigines look upon the Chinaman with inexpressible contempt. . . . There may be a race yet lower than the Mongolian, but it has no representative in this Republic."[11]

In spite of strenuous efforts to avoid it, the Japanese inherited the same treatment that had bedeviled the Chinese because in the eyes of many, they belonged to the same race and therefore shared the same moral and intellectual characteristics. According to British travel author Alleyne Ireland's influential assessment in 1900, bias against the Chinese was due to the general misconception that the Chinese were a colored "tropical people" like the "Filipino, the Bengalese, and the Negro," and thus had deficient "physiological and psychological make-up."[12] Such ill-founded conceits gave peoples' anti-Asian biases the illusion of scientific objectivity.

As this last point suggests, questionable characteristics were attributed to Asians to give substance to white ambivalence about Asian Coloradans and to justify antipathy toward them. One such assigned trait was the so-called Asian inability or unwillingness to assimilate into American society. This served as a rationale for discriminating against those who were here already and prohibiting others from entering the country. In effect, this criticism blamed the victimization of Asians on the Asians themselves.[13] As such, it is typical of anti-Asian claims.

Whites believed that the enclaves (ghettos, really) where Asians lived gave them the opportunity to disregard normative American values and perpetuate their own undesirable characteristics. As cultural geographer Kay Anderson points out, the irredeemably alien quality of Asian communities, such as Chinatowns, was a reflection of Western perceptions. Of course, the Chinatown conceived by whites never existed outside their imaginations, though it has been endowed with "a cultural history and a tradition of imagery and institutional practice that has given it a cognitive and material reality in and for the West," as Anderson says.[14] For the West, the construction of Chinatown as a locus of Asian "alienness" or "otherness" helped establish a boundary between normal white communities and aberrant Asian ones, which were portrayed as hives of pestilence and corruption. As a self-reflective concept, Chinatown provides insight into how whites saw themselves as much as how they saw Asians. Essentially, whites used the notion of Chinatown to define themselves in opposition to the Chinese and to promote their own interests.

Unscrupulous journalists, ambitious politicians, and opportunistic labor leaders encouraged animosity toward Asians. This triumvirate exerted a powerful influence on shaping public discourse about Asians. They defined the struggle against Asians in racial terms and emphasized cultural differences to spread anti-Asian sentiment throughout the country. These anti-Asian proponents coalesced first in California, where they spewed attacks against Asians that spread like a contagion throughout the Interior West. Long before Chinese appeared in Colorado in the 1860s, Coloradans knew mostly malevolent things about them from stories in California newspapers. Local publications recycled these stories to shape, if not predetermine, how the people of Colorado would receive Chinese. As a result, before there were any Chinese in Colorado, many Coloradans already disliked them.

Occasionally, Colorado newspapers also reprinted informative stories about China's ancient culture and sympathetic articles about the persecution that Chinese suffered in California and elsewhere.[15] By describing the contributions of Chinese civilization and by depicting Chinese as hard-working yet harmless individuals, these articles tried to allay popular fears. Nevertheless, outweighing these favorable reports were many more that depicted Chinese as curiosities or mocked them because they were racially and culturally different.[16]

Through the 1870s and 1880s, newspaper coverage of Chinese Coloradans came to be dominated by alarmist reports predicting economic ruin and social disruption from the growing Chinese population on the West Coast and elsewhere. A typical treatment, "Caucasian against Mongolian—The Survival of the Fittest," asserted that the "white man cannot compete with the Chinese [who] have practiced for two thousand years what amount of fatigue the human body can undergo on the smallest allowance of food."[17] Critics deplored that "fields of labor cannot be thrown open to our own poor white citizens, instead of a class of beings that are but the scum and offscouring of a great pagan nation."[18] These stories stoked fears about the danger that Chinese moral and physical attributes posed to Coloradans' livelihoods and their way of life, instigating citizens to take action.[19] As historians Carl Abbott, Stephen Leonard, and Thomas Noel have concluded, "Asians [in Colorado] suffered more than any other immigrant group from the hostilities of economically insecure Caucasians."[20] In holding the Chinese responsible for the low wages and the unemployment of others, newspapers stoked tensions that led to violence against the Chinese community. Later, newspapers published similar stories about the Japanese. For decades, publications like the *Rocky Mountain News* used the Chinese as convenient scapegoats, blaming them for economic distresses, and the *Denver Post* directed harsh attacks against the Japanese imprisoned in the Amache concentration camp in southeast Colorado during World War II. By promoting the persecution of Chinese and Japanese, these newspapers bear a major responsibility for what happened to these groups in Colorado.

Contrary to popular perceptions, Asians actively opposed the prejudice and discrimination described above. They rejected the hierarchy that relegated them to the bottom of American society. As representatives of esteemed cultures and even countries with extensive empires, they thought of themselves as equal if not superior to the whites they encountered. They arrived in the United States with a certain amount of cultural self-confidence, which ran afoul of American ethnocentrism.

Asians actively tried to protect themselves individually and collectively from those that would do them harm, rather than passively accept the abuse.

Their efforts to defend themselves were actually quite impressive considering the severe handicaps under which they labored. Perhaps the most significant problem was that they were prevented from becoming citizens. As aliens, they were automatically deprived of the legal rights accorded to their adversaries in judicial proceedings, and they lacked access to the voting franchise necessary to secure their interests. Given this state of affairs, the expression "not a Chinaman's chance" (originally, "not a Chinaman's chance in hell"), meaning "no chance at all," aptly describes the difficult situation of the Chinese as well as other Asians. A ruling by the famous judge Roy Bean, justice of the peace of Pecos County, Texas, illustrates their predicament. In 1884, when an Irish worker who had killed a Chinese man was brought to his court, Judge Bean reportedly looked through "two or three dilapidated law books from stem to stern" and declared that "he'd be d——d if he could find any law against killing a Chinaman," and then released the suspect.[21] Nevertheless, Asians fought back. They employed attorneys to contest local and federal laws that discriminated against them and used whatever other means were available to seek justice.

Given these disadvantages, it is little wonder that some Asian Americans believed that even if they were born in America, they were not of America. At best, they were Americans in disguise, remaining forever foreigners. But there were inexorable demographic and other forces at work that would in time redefine America's national identity, making it more inclusive.

THE ASIAN COLORADAN EXPERIENCE

This book explores how the nation has sought to resolve the tension between its aspirational ideals and its hard realities through a history of Asians in one place in the American West—Colorado. This work tells the story of Asian Coloradans beginning with their arrival in the mid-nineteenth century and extending through modern times. However, it is not simply an Asian Coloradan story; it is also an American story, for the two stories are inseparable. This study fills in a gap in our understanding of Coloradan as well as US history by placing the Asian Coloradan experience in larger historical and cultural contexts wherever possible. In so doing, this work engages concerns that go beyond those conventionally addressed in state or regional histories. My argument here is that Asian Coloradans are important for reasons apart from any achievement attributed to them, and beyond setting the historical record straight, as important as these are for historiography. Asian Coloradans are worth considering because they help us better understand who we are as Americans.

An investigation of this nature is a complex inquiry, in that it needs to examine both macro and micro issues—in other words, both ends of the scale. This book focuses on events of the moment in Colorado as they played out against the transgenerational rhythms of the Asian diaspora, the vicissitudes of American–Asian relations, and ongoing developments in American society. One aim is to reconstruct the trajectory of individual lives against a backdrop of the socially sanctioned alternatives available to members of the Asian American community to which these individuals belonged.

The sources for research on this subject presented another challenge. Such sources are often scattered and uneven, and must be retrieved from disparate sources spanning a long period of time. To take one topic, for example, it is difficult to ascertain the full range of reasons for Asian immigration to Colorado across ethnic and nationality groupings given the paucity of information for many groups. Also, the early Asians who came to Colorado were frequently illiterate, leaving little personal information behind. Public information about them is equally scarce and often colored by the prejudices of the period. What can be learned depends heavily on the history of the period and its unfolding.

For all that, this is still a story worth telling because it is about real people with eventful lives, diverse interests, grand dreams, and unusual talents. Asian Coloradans overcame a formidable set of obstacles to make a life for themselves and their families in the state. In doing so, they have played and continue to play an essential role in the formation of America's identity. That identity has been defined in large part by the way the nation has tried to resolve the dynamic tension that exists between its ideals, as they were expressed in its founding documents, and the realities of the nation's evolution.

The nation's strength has always been derived from its founding principles and the continuous effort to live up to them. The most famous line in the Declaration of Independence states: "We hold these truths to be self-evident, that all men are created equal, that they are endowed by their Creator with certain unalienable Rights, that among these are Life, Liberty and the pursuit of Happiness." As we have seen, some men (and all women) were treated unequally and denied these unalienable rights, handicapping their pursuit of happiness. The new nation faced the problem of imagining a nation in civic terms that contradicted the nation it had created in racial terms.

The treatment of Asians constitutes a barometer of larger societal challenges and the political responses to them. These can best be understood in historical context. The treatment of Asians indicates how the country defined itself in different time periods, influencing the discourse on national identity. In the nineteenth century, Asians were considered marginal people incapable of being Americans; in the early twentieth-first century, Asian Americans are considered exemplars for other minorities to emulate. Paradoxically, in both instances, these views are a result of attitudes toward Asians' race and culture. This remarkable reversal in status from a persecuted minority to a "model minority" is also part of the story of Asians in Colorado.

A HISTORY RECONSIDERED

The story properly begins during the nineteenth century in Asia with a discussion of the reasons why Asians left their native lands to go to America. Leaving their homes because of dire circumstances was, of course, a difficult experience, but it was not unusual. Indeed, this happened to Asian peasants with unfortunate regularity. Going to America because of such an experience was extraordinary. The critical difference was the proactive role Americans played in the emigration from Asia. Chapter 1 explains in broad terms how this occurred. In spite of being a republic, the United States engaged in imperialist activities to establish an empire in Asia at the same time that it expanded its national borders to the West Coast, all the while believing it was its Manifest Destiny to do both. Asian immigration intersected with American nationalism to meet the demand for workers in the newly acquired territories.

Chapters 2 through 5 discuss the history of Chinese Coloradans, their efforts to earn a living, and the hostility they encountered during the Gilded Age (1870–1900). With little money but a lot of energy, they made a life for themselves in the Centennial State. Despite their small numbers in comparison with the rest of the state's population, they attracted a disproportionate number and a wide range of enemies. This examination explains why they were driven out of Nederland, banned from Leadville, embroiled in the so-called Chinese-Italian War in Como, and terrorized during the race riot in Denver. In spite of these brutal incidents, they refused to be intimidated and continued to live in Colorado as best they could.

The Japanese were the next significant group of Asians to follow in the wake of the Chinese. They arrived toward the end of the Gilded Age to meet the chronic need for workers, especially in the burgeoning agricultural sector of the state's economy. Chapters 6 through 9 discuss the Japanese Coloradans. Like the Chinese Coloradans, they too came to make a living, establishing local communities and encountering animosity in the process. And they too were eventually banned from the country. With their exclusion from the United States, anti-Japanese sentiment shifted from the Japanese in America to Japan itself. Both Japanese Americans and Japan were viewed as a "Yellow Peril" that threatened the security of the United States.

While the Chinese population declined, the Japanese population increased, in part due to unforeseen circumstances. During World War II, West Coast Japanese Americans seeking to avoid incarceration in America's concentration camps—as they were called by President Franklin D. Roosevelt and other government officials, and also the Japanese American prisoners themselves—augmented the Japanese Coloradan community.[22] They included those freed from the Amache concentration camp in southeast Colorado.

World War II was a watershed event for both Chinese and Japanese Coloradans. As chapter 10 discusses, their actions during and after the war showed that most Chinese and Japanese Coloradans never lost faith in the nation even when it had betrayed their trust. They were part of Asian America's "greatest generation," to borrow Tom Brokaw's term, not only by virtue of their wartime service but also because they served in spite of painful prejudice. They never stopped believing that America would one day deliver on the promises embedded in its ideals, if not to them then to future generations. Their participation in the war changed how they perceived themselves and their place in the nation, and changed the nation's perception of them as well. They came home to Colorado with heightened expectations for themselves and their families. Asian American veterans, however, did not immediately receive the coveted equality that they had earned through service to the country. Still, World War II set in motion changes that would make American society more equal.

The most significant change to follow was the gradual liberalization of America's immigration laws, allowing Asians to enter the country once again. From 1965 to the present, over forty million immigrants have been admitted into the United States and over eighteen million, or 45.8 percent, of them have become naturalized citizens.[23] Of the forty million immigrants, almost twelve million, or 29.2 percent, emigrated from Asia, resulting in a dramatic increase in the Asian American population. The recent arrival of Asians has played an important role in developing the information economy of the nation and the state of Colorado. Many Asians have become successful in business and as professionals, taking advantage of the opportunities afforded them in the United States. Some of them, however, have not done so well and are struggling to make it in America.

Finally, the epilogue considers how contemporary Asian Coloradans are faring in a multiracial and multicultural America. While the problems of the past persist, there are reasons to be hopeful about the future.

A PERSONAL NOTE

I was drawn to this study by reflections on my family's history and by a desire to answer the question: what makes an American? Two family experiences prompted this work among the many that inform it. The first was the story of how my family emigrated from China to America, and the second was what my older brother told me just before he went off to the Parris Island recruit depot to become a US marine.

According to my family's history, our journey to America began when my father, Ling Ching-wei, was serving as quartermaster aboard a German vessel that found itself stranded in New York Harbor after the Japanese attack on Pearl Harbor on December 7, 1941. Afterward, my father and his entire Chinese crew joined the US Army, where he attained the rank of sergeant. When the war was over, he went back to China, where my mother, Lee Cha-wei, and my older brother, William Ling, had been patiently waiting for his return. My mother asked my father about life in America. Since my father was one of those enthusiastic immigrants who loved the country and everything it stood for, he delighted in telling her about it. In the midst of his long narrative, my mother interrupted to ask one question: were there wars in America? Father said, "No, Americans do not fight wars unless they have to." With that, my mother decided my family should leave for America because it promised to be a place where there would at least be peace, if nothing else. Having lived through decades of turmoil in China during the Warlord era, the Japanese occupation, and the

Chinese Civil War between the Communists and Nationalists, she had had enough of conflict and could imagine a better life in America.

Life *was* better in America, but it was not without its difficulties. Living in the tenements in the Lower East Side of New York City had its trials, which we faced like the immigrants before us. We were the only Chinese family in a neighborhood that consisted of mainly Eastern European Jews, who had come a generation earlier, and newly arrived Puerto Ricans, all of whom were striving to make a go of it in America. Seeking to escape the confines of the neighborhood, where prospects for the future were bleak, my older brother enlisted in the US Marine Corps. Before he left, he told me something I have never forgotten. First, he told me that with our father away working as a seaman to support the family, I was the man of the house and now responsible for taking care of my mother and younger brother. Being only seven at the time, I found that to be a heavy responsibility. He also told me that, a long time ago, the government had put Japanese Americans in camps because they were Asians and that the same thing could happen to us. He wanted me to always remember that we were Americans and not to let anyone tell me otherwise. I have tried to do just that.

I realize now that I became a historian in part to learn what it was that made me an American or, to be more precise, an Asian American. It has been a circuitous journey that began with my becoming a scholar of modern Chinese history, participating in the Asian American movement (one of the social movements of the sixties), and finally settling in the Centennial State. At an early age I knew that being asked whether I was Chinese or American was a false choice. Intuitively, I knew I was a Chinese American with a distinct history and culture, even though that history and culture were barely known or documented. I have come to learn that being a Chinese American is part and parcel of being an Asian American, so I have made it a point to write and talk about Asian Americans. This has confused those who prefer that historians limit themselves to one field. Adding to their bewilderment is my decision to write a book about Asian Coloradans, whose history seems all the more peripheral because it is local. Perhaps a way to end their wonderment is by paraphrasing Hillel the Elder: If I do not do it, who will? And if I do not do it now, when will it be done?

ONE

IMPERIALISM, NATIONALISM, AND THE COMING OF ASIANS TO COLORADO

A SIANS CAME TO COLORADO AS THE UNEXPECTED CONSEQUENCE of a confluence of events. In the past, when Asians suffered from what the Chinese call *nei luan, wai huan* (literally, troubles within and without), they migrated to a different part of their country or immigrated to another country in the region. In the nineteenth century, Asians crossed the Pacific Ocean to the United States mainly because of economic push-pull factors. While the decision to do so was individualized, the circumstances were largely the result of the historical intersection of nineteenth-century Western imperialism and American nationalism.

AGE OF IMPERIALISM

In the nineteenth century, the main driving force behind imperialism was the capitalist system's need for low-cost labor, abundant resources, markets for the goods it mass-produced, and places to invest the profits it made. Asia promised to satisfy all these needs. By 1878, imperialists dominated 67 percent of the world; by the eve of World War I, they held sway over 84 percent.[1]

The imperialists embraced the ideology of Social Darwinism to justify their dominion over Asia, Africa, and Latin America, considering their activities an essential part of human evolution. Political domination was the natural outcome of living in a competitive world where nations were engaged in a perpetual struggle for existence and only the fittest among them survived. The conflict between nations (and by extension, races) was perceived as necessary if there was to be human progress. Imperialists assumed that it was their innate racial superiority that enabled them to conquer Third World nations and that qualified them to govern those

FIG. 1.1. "En Chine—Le gâteau des Rois et ... des Empereurs" ("China—the cake of kings and ... of emperors," a French pun on king cake and kings and emperors wishing to "consume" China), by Henri Meyer, *Le Petit Journal*, January 16, 1898. A pastry representing "Chine" (French for "China") is being divided between Queen Victoria of the United Kingdom, William II of Germany, Nicholas II of Russia, the French Marianne, and a samurai representing Japan, who is contemplating which pieces to take. A Qing official throws up his hands to try and stop them, but he is powerless. Denver Public Library, Western History Collection.

nations as colonies. In the case of semi-colonies like China, they presumed it also gave them the right to interfere in a nation's internal affairs.

In terms of effects on immigration to the United States, the most consequential expression of this ideology was the so-called unequal treaty system. The system began with Britain's defeat of China in the first Opium War (1839–42) and the signing of the Treaty of Nanjing. The unequal treaty system forced China to open its doors to international commerce, acquiesce to the presence of foreign troops on its soil, and endure Christian evangelism. The system placed China in an inferior position vis-à-vis the West (and later Japan). In so doing, it also engendered disdain in the West for Chinese people. The historian Harold Isaacs aptly labeled the nineteenth century the "Age of Contempt" for China.[2]

Having developed its own Sino-American trade, the United States was well placed to ride on Britain's coattails. Contrary to the conventional understanding, American imperialism did not begin with the Spanish-American War (1898–1901) and the subsequent annexation of the Philippine Islands. It had its origins a half century earlier, in the gradual development of an overseas commercial network based on America's trade with China and its subsequent opening of Japan to facilitate that trade. Later, when the United States acquired a territorial empire, it did so in part to safeguard its trade network. Guided by the strategic thinking of Captain Alfred Thayer Mahan (1840–1914) of the US Naval War College, American leaders believed that their nation's future depended on overseas markets, which needed to be protected from rivals and enemies. So, as a matter of national security, the United States established a naval presence along key trade routes, building military bases and refueling stations across the Pacific. By the end of the nineteenth century, the United States had one of the world's most powerful navies.

Ironically, it was British animus toward its former colonists that provided the initial impetus for American imperialism. Out of vindictiveness as well as self-interest, the British excluded Americans from their mercantile trade network in the Western Hemisphere, making it difficult for the United States to balance its international payments. This constraint drove American merchants and manufacturers to look for markets and suppliers elsewhere.

Asia was deemed the wealthiest part of the non-European world and China the wealthiest part of Asia. The development of Sino-American trade was intended to minimize the risk of American conflict with the British and other Europeans. In 1784, the *Empress of China* (aka the *Chinese Queen*) initiated the so-called Old China Trade with its historic voyage from New York City to Canton, China, via the Cape of Good Hope. It carried a cargo consisting of lead, animal skins, fine camel cloth, cotton, pepper, and, most important, thirty tons of ginseng, a root that grew wild in North America. The Chinese prized ginseng for its medicinal properties. These goods were valued at $120,000 and traded for tea, nankeen (Chinese cotton cloth), tableware, silk, and spices. The *Empress of China* returned a profit of better than 25 percent, encouraging others to participate in the trade.

By the early nineteenth century, Americans were making about fifty voyages a year to China, and to a lesser extent to other parts of Asia, such as the Philippines, Java, and India. Though the trade helped to bolster the relatively weak US economy, China never became the market for American products that businesses hoped for. China was for the most part self-sufficient and had little need for US manufactured goods, such as textiles that were being produced at the time. By the end of the century, China accounted for only 2 percent of American exports. But the dream remained. And though the China trade never yielded the profits American entrepreneurs expected, it provided something unexpected and more meaningful—Chinese laborers.

Chinese workers came mainly from the maritime province of Guangdong. As historian June Mei notes, during the nineteenth century the province was undergoing rapid and drastic socioeconomic change, with a large, impoverished peasantry who lived near treaty ports with well-established foreign trade.[3] Many lost their livelihoods through the commercialization of agriculture, the influx of cheap foreign cotton textiles, and the shift in export trade to competing treaty ports such as Ningbo and Shanghai. Exacerbating the situation were a series of social upheavals, the greatest of which was the Taiping Rebellion (1850–64), a revolt against Manchu rule that devastated Southern China and dislocated many peasants. Distressed peasants therefore became a potential supply of laborers to work in the Western empires being established around the world.

Under the protection of the unequal treaty system, Americans or their agents recruited Chinese workers with impunity and in contravention of Chinese law. The Qing dynasty forbade Chinese on pain of death to leave the country, mainly because it feared that they would become dissidents and conspire against the government. Nevertheless, through treaty ports such as Canton, approximately 370,000 Chinese eventually left the country, finding their way across the Pacific to such places as Hawaii, the West Coast of North America, and inland to Colorado.

In previous centuries, when Chinese were forced to immigrate, they went as settlers and colonizers with considerable autonomy to determine their own destiny. In underdeveloped regions such as Southeast Asia, they became an economic force in their own right. But in the racial hierarchy of nineteenth-century America's emerging industrial economy, they stood little chance of acquiring either status or power. Though Chinese were wanted as laborers, they were unwelcome as settlers. Even before Chinese arrived on American shores, traders, diplomats, and missionaries had already nurtured a Sinophobia, which was later promoted in the new mass medium of the penny press to create the conditions that eventually contributed to Chinese exclusion from the country in 1882.

Compared to the thirty-five million Europeans who came to the United States at the same time, Asians were few in number, perhaps about a million. But their work proved indispensable to the development of the western half of the country. They built the physical structures and worked in the extractive industries that made the American West viable.

AMBIVALENT IMPERIALISTS

Although America businesspeople were eager to extend US influence to open markets in Asia, an undercurrent of ambivalence about the compatibility of imperialist ambitions with American identity remained. Some critics warned that imperialism was inimical to free trade and contradictory to the ideals on which the country was founded. American ambivalence about imperialism was manifested in its treaties with China. On the one hand, these treaties abridged Chinese sovereignty. With the signing of the Treaty of Wanghia (July 3, 1844), Americans laid the cornerstone of the unequal treaty system by establishing the principle of extraterritoriality, which in effect excluded foreign residents from the Chinese judicial system and placed them under foreign jurisdiction.

On the other hand, with the Burlingame-Seward Treaty (July 28, 1868), the United States conferred on China equal status with other nations and sought to limit its own interference in Chinese affairs. In effect, the United States subverted the unequal treaty system to maintain China's administrative and territorial integrity. The Burlingame Treaty granted China most-favored-nation status in trade relations and recognized it as a diplomatic equal in accordance with the principles and practices of Western nations. Each country promised to protect the other's citizens and permitted access to education in the other's country. Perhaps most important, the Burlingame Treaty ended the Qing dynasty's restriction on immigration to allow Chinese to go to the United States.

The Burlingame Treaty ensured a steady flow of Chinese workers to help build the infrastructure of the American West and to work in America's newly developed industrial economy. For this reason, American capitalists greeted the treaty warmly. So did American liberals such as Mark Twain, who announced prematurely that with this treaty, discrimination and violence against Chinese would end. He predicted that persecutors "can never beat and bang and set the dogs on Chinamen any more. These pastimes are lost to them forever."[4] In fact, the abuses continued unabated. If anything, they got worse during the economic depression of the 1870s, when Chinese were blamed for rising unemployment. Western states passed ordinances to persecute Chinese. When Chinese officials complained that the mistreatment of their countrymen in America violated the Burlingame Treaty, the US government rationalized its inability to protect them as a matter of states' rights.

Shortcomings notwithstanding, the Burlingame Treaty was unprecedented in reflecting republican ideals. In 1901, on the occasion of Abraham Lincoln's birthday, Wu Ting-fan, the Chinese minister to the United States, used his celebratory remarks to praise the treaty—and by extension the man after whom the treaty was named—as enlightened and humane.[5]

ANSON BURLINGAME AND THE CHINESE

The person responsible for negotiating the favorable treaty that bears his name, Anson Burlingame (1820–70), is unique in diplomatic history as the only person to represent the United States and then China.[6] Burlingame had earned the respect and confidence of the Chinese officials for his fairness as the US envoy during the treaty negotiations. Once the job was over, the Chinese government turned around and appointed him envoy extraordinary and minister plenipotentiary to the American government in 1867.

Burlingame's early interests were representative of the period. A religious abolitionist from Massachusetts and a member of the nativist American Party (1853–56), popularly called the Know-Nothings, he was elected to the US House of Representatives in 1854. After the American Party collapsed over the issue of slavery, Burlingame worked with like-minded individuals, such as Abraham Lincoln, to establish the new Republican Party, and in July 1861, President Lincoln appointed him minister to the Empire of China.

As minister, Burlingame was responsible for furthering America's interest in China, particularly its commercial claims. To ensure American access to China's markets, he walked a fine line between opposing European colonialism and acquiescing to it. But he wanted to take a conciliatory approach rather than the coercive one used previously. In fact, Burlingame's sympathies for the Chinese were so strong that other diplomats considered him a Chinese partisan.

Burlingame made it a point to educate himself about China's history and culture. He traveled throughout the country, met the people, and learned about their struggles. Committed to American ideals, including anti-colonialism, he came to understand the unfairness of the unequal treaties imposed on China. He also came to realize that the Europeans were essentially colonizers intent on maintaining spheres of influence where they could exercise exclusive rights to extract profits from captive markets. After negotiating the treaty, Burlingame toured the United States, giving lectures about China in which he expressed compassion for its people. He advocated amicable Sino-American relations, equal treatment of the Chinese nation, and fair treatment of the Chinese in America. Anson Burlingame shows what a difference one person can make in history.

GUNBOAT DIPLOMACY, AMERICAN STYLE

Japan's involvement with the unequal treaty system was briefer than China's, but it too resulted in immigration to the United States. When Commodore Matthew C. Perry used gunboat diplomacy in 1853 to force feudal Japan out of two and half centuries of seclusion, he set in motion forces that disrupted the country politically and economically. Perry not only ended more than two centuries of Japanese isolation, he also upended the so-called baku-han equilibrium, the delicate political balance between Japan's central government and the provinces. His arrival unleashed forces that in 1868 led to a rebellion called the Meiji Ishin against the feudal Tokugawa shogunate that governed the country. Perry also unwittingly initiated a process that eventually compelled Japanese peasants to immigrate abroad.

As Japan made the transition from a feudal to a modern country, a diverse group representing virtually the entire spectrum of Japanese society made its way to the United States. The most important members were the large number of students who, with the encouragement of the newly established Meiji government, went to America to learn from one of the newest nations in the world about the modern age they had entered.

Japan's Charter Oath encouraged students to go abroad. On April 7, 1868, at the enthronement of the Meiji emperor, the government promulgated this inspiring document; the fifth clause states, "Knowledge shall be sought for all over the world and thus shall be strengthened the foundation of the Imperial polity."[7] Japanese students traveled abroad to learn from foreigners and bring what they had learned back home to assist in Japan's ambitious modernization program. At least, most did. An exception was Matsudaira Tadaatsu, a member of the Iwakura Mission (1871–73).

Matsudaira Tadaatsu was one the first Japanese students to study abroad. He was the first Japanese to live and work in Colorado. In 1872, Matsudaira enrolled in Rutgers University, in New Jersey, but he transferred to Harvard two years later, graduating in 1877 with a degree in civil engineering.[8] He then went to work in New York City for the Manhattan Elevated Railroad, where he invented the trigonometer, a reliable surveyor's tool for making calculations. Subsequently, he worked for the Union Pacific Railroad for three years as a surveying engineer in the American West before returning east to become a city engineer in Bradford, Pennsylvania. In Bradford, he married the daughter of the retired US Army general Archibald Sampson. This marriage was quite unusual, perhaps even scandalous, at the time, given the social opprobrium attached to interracial relationships. When Matsudaira contracted tuberculosis in 1886, he and his family moved to Denver, believing like so many others that the city's dry climate would be restorative.[9] Until his death in 1888 at the young age of thirty-three, Matsudaira worked for the state inspector of mines and also as a civil engineer for the state engineer's office. His life shows the extraordinary capacity of earlier waves of Japanese immigrants to find their place in American society.[10]

Matsudaira and other Japanese students made a positive impression on those they encountered in the United States—understandably, since they came with the aim of learning from Americans, whom Japanese considered to be the most progressive people in the Western world. As college students, they were well educated, well dressed in the Western fashion, and well versed in the English language. However, the only Asians most

Americans knew anything about were Chinese, and what they knew, they interpreted negatively. When two Japanese students stopped in Denver on their way to Yale, they were initially mistaken for Chinese. To justify treating them differently from Chinese, one newspaper reporter noted that the young men were tastefully dressed, spoke fluent English, and "had all of the virtues of the ordinary Caucasian . . . and closer inspection of their appearance showed them to be, though rather dark persons, of quite regular features and of rather an intellectual appearance."[11] This description suggests that the reporter saw race as a matter of both physical and behavioral differences. Here, as elsewhere, the acceptance of Japanese depended in part on their mastery of Western cultural norms, which provided a kind of protective coloration that made it easier for whites to accept them.

The Qing dynasty's approach was markedly different from that of the Meiji government. Blinded by acute ethnocentrism, the Qing dynasty believed it had little to learn from foreigners and agreed only reluctantly to send students abroad. Reformer Yung Wing, the first Chinese graduate of an American university (Yale), persuaded the Qing dynasty to sponsor the Chinese Educational Mission (1872–81) to the United States. Altogether, 120 young Chinese went to New England to study Western science and engineering. After the students' Confucian tutors discovered that they had readily adopted American customs, trading in their long scholars' gowns for trousers and even playing baseball, and Chinese officials learned that the graduates would not be allowed to attend American military academies as provided by the Burlingame Treaty, the Qing dynasty disbanded the mission. Once back in China, the students were briefly detained and interrogated. Many of the returned students had difficulty launching their careers. Years later, in the aftermath of the abortive Hundred Days of Reform in 1898, an effort to modernize Chinese political, social, and educational institutions led by the young Guangxu emperor and squelched by the Empress Dowager Cixi, Yung Wing fled Shanghai for Hong Kong when the Chinese government posted a reward of seventy thousand dollars for his capture. Adding to Yung Wing's woes, the American government revoked his citizenship, which he had held for fifty years, preventing him from returning to the United States.

The contrast in attitudes toward study abroad illustrates an essential difference between Japan and China. The early Japanese who went abroad did so for their country, while the Chinese left in spite of their country. China forbade its people from leaving out of fear that they would conspire against the government, while Japan encouraged select members of its society to go abroad as a way of strengthening the nation. Japan could do this in part because it had a tradition of sending its people abroad to learn from others and adapting what it had learned to its own needs. When it sent official missions to China between the seventh and ninth centuries, it consciously and selectively imported aspects of Chinese culture that enabled it to evolve as a nation.

At the start of the Meiji era (1868–1912), progressive Japanese leaders realized that, during their long period of seclusion, they had fallen behind and become vulnerable to other nations. In order to get out from under the unequal treaty system and to attain the larger goal of amassing wealth and power, they sought to emulate the West. Initially, they elevated Western culture above their own, accepting the single-alternative fallacy that if they were ever to become modern, it would be necessary to replace their stagnant Eastern culture with a dynamic Western one. Some extremists even proposed replacing the Japanese language with English and intermarrying with white women to improve Japan's racial stock. A more moderate proposal was to learn from the West rather than simply to imitate it.

Meiji leaders sent embassies abroad. The most famous was the two-year Iwakura Mission that traveled around the world. It departed from Yokohama in 1871 aboard the SS *America* to San Francisco. The mission sought but ultimately failed to renegotiate Japan's unequal treaties with the United States, Great Britain, and other European countries. It was, however, successful in gathering general and technical information from these countries that was useful in modernizing Japan.

In the wake of the Iwakura Mission, Japanese often passed through Denver by rail on their way to the East Coast or visited the city itself to learn about Colorado's manufacturing methods, railway systems, and mining industries.[12] Coloradans appreciated their deferential attitudes. As one of Japan's leading mining engineers respectfully observed, "We feel in relation of pupil to teacher when we think of this great country. It was the United States which first opened Japan to the travel and improvement of the world, and we are grateful."[13] Perhaps more important, Japanese visitors came with "money in their clothes" to spend in Colorado.[14] Coloradans were pleased when a group of Japanese capitalists, visiting the United States in 1896 to purchase steel and other materials for ships, leased oil fields in Florence in southern Colorado.[15]

The feverish efforts of the Japanese to rebuild their nation had a downside, one with repercussions in America. Modernization also caused considerable psychological tension and socioeconomic trouble in Japan, sufficient to compel Japanese peasants to become migrant workers within and then outside the country. These Japanese laborers constituted the majority of those who immigrated to the United States, and they were less welcome than their capitalist countrymen.

On their way to the mainland United States, Japanese workers stopped in Hawaii, where most of them remained. Hawaii, along with the Philippines, were America's most important colonial possessions in its Pacific empire. Annexed by the United States at the end of the nineteenth century to bolster its economy, both Hawaii and the Philippines played important roles in Asian immigration to the United States because they were way stations along the China trade route, links in the labor supply chain from Asia to America.[16]

THE MAKING OF A NATIONAL IDENTITY

For some, America's acquisition of overseas colonies was a continuation of the romantic nationalist vision of an empire of liberty encompassing the entire North American continent. Americans' sense of Manifest Destiny justified territorial expansion and, through a process of circular reasoning, the successful conquest of the frontier and the founding of an empire was seen to provide proof positive of the country's divine destiny.

According to this vision, the territory between both coasts was deemed a vacant or untamed expanse ready for American civilization, with its democratic institutions and ideals. The bringers of civilization were always white pioneers—mainly Anglo-Saxons descended from Germanic or Teutonic peoples, who were deemed adventurous, resourceful, and brave. According to the national narrative, these pioneers embodied the values, ideas, and institutions necessary to tame the Wild West. John Gast's famous painting *American Progress* (1872) captures this idealized version of the country's westward expansion. In his allegorical painting, the goddess Columbia, symbolizing America, floats across the continent with the Star of Empire emblazoned on her forehead. In her right hand, she carries a schoolbook to educate the people; in her left, she trails a telegraph line to unify the nation. Below her are the railroads that integrate the country economically and the white pioneers who settle it, while Native Americans, along with buffalo and other wildlife, flee before them.

FIG. 1.2. *American Progress*, by John Gast, 1872 (chromolithograph published by George A. Crofutt). Denver Public Library, Western History Collection, Z-8848.

To achieve this vision, the investment capital of East Coast entrepreneurs was essential—many of them supported the national ethos of westward expansion. From their base along the Eastern Seaboard, entrepreneurs promoted the colonization of the frontier in gradual stages, from the Appalachian West and the Old Northwest to the Far West along the Pacific Coast. Beyond the Far West lay the Far East, a source of Asian labor that could be used to exploit the resources of the frontier. But while the entrepreneurs needed Asian workers, they rejected Asian settlers. The presence of Asians in the West was a challenge to the national narrative, engendering a debate about who was an American and what was the American nation. As this study shows, one way to reconcile this contradiction was to exclude Chinese and Japanese from public discourse about American identity and to incorporate that exclusion into the nation's immigration policies and practices. This had the unintended consequence of undermining the American ideal of being a nation that was diverse and inclusive. Instead of emphasizing the humanity that settlers in America shared, whites emphasized what made them different. This was the dark side of romantic nationalism.

AMERICAN RACE RELATIONS

The presence of Asians became a divisive issue in American race relations as the state and society sought to resolve the contradictions between the ideal of being a land of freedom and equality and the reality of being a land of slavery and inequality. Asians continuously challenged Americans' assumptions about the nature of American society, focusing attention on the plight of the country's people of color.

During the Reconstruction Era (1865–77), the antebellum condemnation of black slavery gave way to sharp attacks on Asiatic coolieism, which was viewed as another form of slavery. Coolieism, the exploitation of involuntary Chinese labor for little or no wages, did exist in a trade that was active in the 1840s and 1850s, but not in the American West. In overcrowded, unsanitary ships, indentured Chinese laborers, who were dubbed *coolies* (from *kuli*, the Mandarin Chinese term meaning "bitter strength"), were transported to the Caribbean and South America. There they endured the harshest of work conditions. Many worked and died on the Cuban sugarcane plantations or in the guano pits of Peru under conditions so intolerable that they mutinied aboard the ships that transported them and rebelled on the plantations.

Enemies of the Chinese branded them all coolies. Indeed, for Sinophobes, *coolie* was a pejorative term for Chinese men in general. Coolies were equated with black slaves, the coolie trade with the African slave trade, and the Pacific Passage with the Middle Passage. In 1862, while the Civil War was still raging, the federal government prohibited American participation in the coolie trade as part of its antislavery crusade.

Most Asian American scholars differentiate coolies from the Chinese workers who came to North America, considering the latter to be voluntary immigrants and equating them with their white counterparts. Chinese workers usually borrowed money from brokers to pay for their passage to the United States and repaid the money plus interest through their wages. However, as historian Moon-Ho Jung observes, the term *coolie* symbolized something unique: "something between and beyond slaves and immigrants, an ideal noncitizen, migrant labor force for the age of emancipation, allowed to enter the United States for decades as tenuous 'immigrants' and racially excluded from naturalization and then immigration."[17]

Chinese were caught between blacks, who sought to free themselves from bondage, and whites, who depended on an enslaved labor force and tried to keep black freedmen in a state of servitude through Jim Crow laws. Through the notorious Black Codes, laws passed by southern states in 1865 and 1866, freedmen were essentially re-enslaved and leased to companies to labor in mines and factories.[18]

Southern planters, northern industrialists, and western capitalists hoped to use the threat of cheap Chinese laborers to control recalcitrant freedmen, as well as European workers and American workers. As a Colorado pundit observed: "A desire for cheaper and more steady laborers than the freedmen, or a disgust at the airs the negroes [*sic*] take on in their new estate, has prompted the planters to seek Asiatic laborers. . . . They are much more likely to supplant our southern negroes [*sic*] and drive them that way; and our skin deep Democracy ought to welcome the yellow men for the sake of getting [rid] of the blacks."[19]

Perhaps in recognition of this threat to freedmen, Frederick Douglass, the great African American social reformer and abolitionist leader, made common cause with the Sinophobes. He publicly declared that the Chinese were "destined to overrun [the] country with cheap labor and cripple the efforts of organized workingmen to secure fair living compensation."[20] In 1887, the *Rocky Mountain News* reported that Douglass's sentiment assured workingmen that "the masses of the American people will never submit to be degraded to the level of the Mongolian race."[21] Whether his objection to the Chinese was simply a matter of political expediency or an expression of his true beliefs is uncertain, but it did reflect the general opposition of freedmen to Chinese labor. As the *St. Louis Democrat* explained, freedmen "regard [the Chinese] as interlopers."[22]

In an attempt to find a place in American society, freedmen reminded whites of their shared Christian faith and newly acquired civic credentials by condemning the Chinese as idolatrous heathens and transient foreigners with no commitment to American government or society. In effect, freedmen appealed to the nativist traditions of mainstream Anglo-Protestant culture. Underlying their opposition to Chinese was the fear that planters and capitalists might use them to reduce freedmen's wages and return them to quasi-slave status.

After the Civil War, southern planters who needed agricultural laborers began recruiting Chinese workers to replace emancipated blacks. As freedmen began to exercise their newly acquired political rights to leave the South to seek higher wages, planters sought a cheaper and more pliable labor force, which they thought they had found in the Chinese.[23] Chinese workers were less expensive and more reliable than their European counterparts, who tended to leave whenever new opportunities appeared. In contrast, the Chinese were considered docile, thrifty individuals who took care of themselves and did their jobs without reluctance.[24]

Southern planters turned to labor contractors such as Cornelius Koopmanschap and Tye Kim Orr to recruit Chinese laborers. Koopmanschap was a Dutch merchant who had gone to California during the gold rush and entered the China trade in the 1850s, specializing in the importation of Chinese laborers to the American West. He claimed to be the nation's best-known recruiter of Chinese workers, having brought thirty thousand to California.[25] In 1861, he supplied several thousand to work on the Central Pacific portion of the Transcontinental Railroad.

Koopmanschap would not have been able to accomplish this without Chinese collaborators such as Tye Kim Orr, a charismatic Chinese missionary from the Straits Settlements of Southeast Asia, who had left his family behind in Singapore to found Hopetown, a community of Chinese in Guyana. Orr left Guyana after being accused of assorted crimes, such as embezzlement and extortion. Later he found his way to Cuba, where he allegedly participated in the coolie trade, and eventually to Louisiana, where he continued to work as a labor contractor.

In July 1869, at the Memphis labor convention, Orr told the five hundred assembled southern delegates that the Chinese were the solution to their labor needs, the right replacement for emancipated blacks who had become increasingly difficult to control and exploit. According to him, the Chinese were well adapted to plantation life, as the products of China (such as rice and cotton) were in many ways similar to those of the American South.[26] True, they were heathens, but the planters wanted "cotton and cane—and if [a Chinese worker] makes them you will not object very much to him."[27] Finally, Orr added that by employing the Chinese, the southern planters would be civilizing them in the process.

Koopmanschap, Orr, and others who characterized the Chinese as willing to submit to peonage were selling the planters a bill of goods; the Chinese proved more expensive and less pliable than was originally thought. As the *Daily Central City Register* noted about the Chinese working on the sugar plantations in Louisiana, they were "extremely jealous of the conditions of their contract, and most of the difficulties with them grow out of this fact."[28] Unwilling to be exploited, they left the plantations as soon as they could, usually after the expiration of their three-year contracts, whereupon they sought better-paying jobs. After leaving the plantations, they often founded small Chinese communities in nearby urban areas. It was reported that those who established themselves near New Orleans had prospered, married Irish women, and even voted in local elections.[29]

COLORADO TERRITORY

Difficulties with Chinese workers in the South did not stop promoters from seeing them as a way to overcome the obstacle of scarce labor in the Colorado Territory. Proponents appealed to California's experience, arguing that Chinese labor there had proved profitable to employers and increased the wealth of the country. They hoped that a rational argument based on the known facts, including statistical information, would counter predictions about hordes of Chinese invading Colorado. The *Rocky Mountain News* initially supported this effort by publishing articles offering information about Chinese contributions to the local economy as well as what Chinese had contributed to California, stating that they had paid over two million dollars in various taxes to city, state, and national treasuries and had spent six million dollars of their earnings in the state on various goods and services.[30] It added, "We believe no whiteman was ever crowded out of a place on account of a Chinaman. They generally work where whitemen will not, or can not; and if their 'invasions' are not to be encouraged, there is certainly no use of misprinting the facts or closing our eyes to the figures."[31]

However, given the Colorado Territory's ambiguous boundaries, uninviting geography, and reputation as a wild and woolly place, attracting Chinese, or anyone else for that matter, was a challenge. As the Chinese who ventured there would discover, Colorado was already a site of contention between various groups of people with strong identities and interests. Coloradans competed with one another for the territory's resources, and they did not hesitate to wage war against the state's weakest inhabitants, such as the indigenous Ute people. In campaigns conducted under the catchphrase "The Utes Must Go!" whites eventually forced them onto an Indian reservation in southwestern Colorado.

Initially, few Chinese went to Colorado, preferring Idaho and Montana, where they found greater economic opportunity. By 1870, there were about four thousand Chinese in the Idaho Territory and fifteen hundred in the Montana Territory.[32] Some Coloradans thought that more should be done to attract the Chinese, whose low wages and mining skills would make the extractive industries in the state a paying proposition, as elsewhere in the American West. Indeed, the Chinese were credited with producing nine-tenths of the yield of the placer gold–producing areas.[33] The boosters optimistically observed that it was only a matter of time before they began coming to Colorado.

The Chinese miners that the Colorado Territory eventually attracted were enterprising individuals willing to face loneliness and danger, as well as exposure to the elements, in exchange for a life of unbridled freedom and the promise of striking it rich. For their pains, they encountered hostility. Antagonism readily rose to the surface whenever there was an economic downturn and did not necessarily disappear when there was an economic upswing. Sinophobia was immune to boom and bust cycles because it was at heart racist and not merely an offshoot of the general xenophobia characteristic of American nativism. In Colorado, the racism that underlay the antipathy was obvious. In all the communities involved, the number of Chinese residents was far too few and their work too specialized to make them a serious economic competitor to white workers. Given their sparse numbers, the Chinese as well as the Japanese who came after them were hardly a real menace, merely a symbolic one. Though the threat they posed was imaginary, the violence they suffered was real.

TWO

CHINESE PIONEERS: LOOKING FOR WORK, FINDING VIOLENCE INSTEAD

H E WAS THE MAN WITH NO NAME. THE FIRST CHINESE TO ARRIVE
in Denver, Colorado, was identified simply as "John Chinaman." In
the June 29, 1869, *Colorado Tribune*, he was described as "a short, fat,
round-faced, almond-eyed beauty, dressed in a shirt, blue overalls, blouse
and hat, with his pig-tail curled up on top of his cranium as nice as you
please."[1] John, as he shall be called, was part of the Chinese diaspora,
pushed out of his homeland by dire poverty and pervasive strife and
drawn to frontier America by the opportunities it offered. He most likely
came with the intent of earning money to support his family and with the
ambition of saving enough to buy land when he returned. Such desires
gave him the psychological strength to endure hardships in America.
Meanwhile, his wife remained at home to maintain her side of a split
household, taking care of the children and fulfilling responsibilities to her
in-laws, with whom she lived.

After being in America for a while, John most likely decided to stay. He
became a transnational immigrant, moving between China and America.
He was like many other expatriates (Italians and Greeks, for instance) who
initially came as temporary workers and then decided to remain, returning home when they could. In John's case, shedding his sojourner status to
settle in America was a tough decision, since it involved not only long-term
separation from his family but also the prospect of living among people
who denied him civil rights, economic opportunity, and social equality.

John was probably among the first generation of Chinese who came to
the United States as part of the California gold rush (1848–55). He may have
heard the apocryphal story about a countryman who had found a 240-
pound gold boulder worth thirty thousand dollars near the Yuba River
and been moved to try his own luck.[2] Like most other would-be miners

FIG. 2.1. "Chinese emigration to America—sketch on board the Mail Pacific Steamship *Alaska*," *Harpers Weekly*, May 20, 1876. Denver Public Library, Western History Collection, Z-3281.

from around the world who came to the goldfields, John probably paid a hefty price for passage—$100 to $125 for a ticket worth half that much just to book passage across the Pacific—and endured crowded conditions on one of the minimally seaworthy vessels that carried human cargo from Hong Kong to San Francisco, a voyage of about seven thousand miles.

Like thousands of other prospectors, John discovered that the country was hardly a *Gam Saan* (Gold Mountain), the Cantonese name for America. After trying his hand at mining, he probably worked on one of the railroads being built at the time, perhaps the Central Pacific portion of the famous Transcontinental Railroad. In 1862, the Pacific Railroad Act chartered the Central Pacific and the Union Pacific Railroad Companies to build a railroad that would span the continent from west to east. Over the next seven years, the two companies raced toward each other from Sacramento, California, on one side and Omaha, Nebraska, on the other. Facing a labor

FIG. 2.2. Most Chinese Coloradans were anonymous. Charlie Hong (Liu Laohong) was an exception. This studio portrait of him was taken in Denver on February 28, 1887. History Colorado, Stephen H. Hart Library and Research Center, 10049335.

shortage, Charles Crocker, a construction contractor for the Central Pacific and former member of its board of directors, shrewdly hired thousands of Chinese workers. Crocker's "pets," as they were derisively called, had the more arduous task of negotiating the Sierra Nevada Mountains and making their way across Utah's Great Basin. Without John's participation, the railroad would have taken much longer to be built, if it was completed at all. It certainly would have delayed the development of the western half of the United States and its integration with the eastern half. Settlers were dependent on the railroad for the transportation of their products to distant markets in exchange for the goods and services that made life possible out West. With its completion, the Transcontinental Railroad facilitated cultural interaction and promoted the formation of a national consciousness.

In all likelihood, John was one of the discharged laborers who completed the Kansas Pacific Railroad and then went to Denver seeking

FIG. 2.3. Charles Gow, with a pit bull seated next to him in a two-wheeled cart drawn by a burro. Picture taken between 1875 and 1892, in Georgetown, Clear Creek County, Colorado. Denver Public Library, Western History Collection, X-6549.

gainful employment—founding its Chinatown in the process. In the Colorado Territory, he was an exotic, an object of curiosity. The local press kept track of his presence and that of other Chinese, noting that there was a Chinese in Golden, another in Cañon City, and still another in Pueblo.[3]

John would have been prepared for local suspicion and hostility. Upon arrival, he found the environment unfriendly. Critics derided him as a burlesque of humanity imported by capitalists who would have been just as happy to profit from shiploads of "long-tailed, horned and cloven hoofed inhabitants of the infernal regions."[4] What many dreaded most about John was his capacity to do work of all sorts, a quality that was often exaggerated by those hostile to the Chinese. As one Denver critic put it, Chinese workers' "aptitude in employments that require mechanical skill and inge-

FIG. 2.4. Chinese Coloradans: second from left is Wa Chin, who is wearing a long shirt and wide-brimmed hat; fourth from left is Tang Ya-shun, wearing a suit and watch chain with a charm. Studio portrait taken between 1890 and 1910, in Georgetown, Clear Creek County, Colorado. Denver Public Library, Western History Collection, X-21660.

nuity places them in the first rank among skilled workmen. . . . Thus in every trade they are able to distance all competitors."[5]

Ironically, the Chinese were well matched to the American ethos. From the beginning, work was and for the most part still is the principal basis for status in the United States, rather than caste or class, which may predominate in other societies. Energy, ambition, a willingness to take risks, resilience in the face of failure, perseverance, self-reliance, and above all an ability to do hard work—had the Chinese been white, these attributes would have commanded respect. But as American literature professor Renny Christopher observes, "The American virtue of hard work becomes a vice when practiced by a non-European race."[6] So it was for the Chinese pioneers as well as later Asian immigrants in Colorado.

Despite the mocking welcome, it is evident that some boosters saw Chinese as a way to solve the Colorado Territory's chronic labor shortage. Under the editorship of pro-growth proponent William N. Byers, the *Rocky Mountain News* (RMN) published supportive commentaries. In one letter to the editor, Boulder resident Joseph Wolff opined that the Chinese were the solution to the problem of expensive labor that was impeding the territory's development: "High wages eat up the profits of [Colorado] farms, put an embargo on thousands of lodes that might otherwise be profitable, hinder manufacturers, and act in general as an incubus on our efforts."[7] Indeed, Wolff hoped there would be "an organized effort . . . to send an agent to California and secure the immigration of a large number of them, as soon as spring opens."[8]

In its early years, the RMN sought to allay the fears that some Coloradans had about the risk that Chinese workers posed. As an 1869 editorial conceded, Coloradans were concerned that the Chinese might "reduce wages for every kind of work which they can do; and for a time, at least, they will come into unpleasant competition with some of our own laboring men . . . [who are concerned about being] reduced to the level of the pauper laborers of Europe and Asia."[9] In laying out a broad perspective on changes affecting the territory, the newspaper sought to assuage the anxieties of its readers by reminding them that "twenty-five or thirty years ago the most gloomy predictions used to be made about the degradation of American laborers by the influx of Irish and Germans," yet overall, American workers eventually found "higher grades of employment, and have gained more than they lost by the changes."[10] Besides, the country was benefiting from its trade with China, exporting to it a great variety of agricultural machinery and other appliances.

One optimist even predicted that "three fourths of our farmers and a large majority of our mine owners will not only favor the [importation of Chinese] but give material assistance to it."[11] Appealing to racial pride, these advocates observed that the "enterprise and self-respect of the Anglo-Saxon [i.e., the white] race" would be more than sufficient to protect them from Asian laborers.[12] Instead of being overwhelmed by the Asian "barbarians," the Anglo-Saxons would "elevate them, and through them all races, until 'liberty, equality and fraternity' prevailed everywhere."[13]

The RMN also supported Chinese immigration with appeals to American values. While conceding that the "evils and perils connected with this irruption from Asia cannot be denied," another editorial asked, "Will we evade the difficulty by denying our own first principles?"[14] Asians could be naturalized like other immigrants despite the risk to whites because to deny them equality would pose an even greater danger to American identity. In the RMN's view, enfranchisement brought with it the "risk that the original Anglo-Saxon stock will be out-voted and made subordinate. Not that there is reason to fear such a result, but it is one of the possibilities." But the editors argued, "We must apply our idea of equal rights to all, or we must . . . take the ballot from the negro [sic], and go for 'a white man's government.'"[15] Given the enormous cost to the country of the recent war against slavery, the latter alternative was unthinkable.

McCOOK AND THE CHINESE

Among local leaders, Major General Edward M. McCook was the highest official to welcome Chinese to Colorado. McCook served in the Civil War, professed abolitionist sentiments, and embraced radical ideas such as women's suffrage and more. As he declared to the Colorado legislature in 1870, "The logic of a progressive civilization leads to the inevitable result of universal suffrage."[16]

President Ulysses S. Grant, friend and former superior officer, appointed McCook governor of the Colorado Territory (1869–73 and 1874–75). McCook realized that a prerequisite for growth was the development of Colorado's infrastructure. Under his leadership, the territory expanded its railroads, built irrigation canals, and established smelting and mining operations.

To solve the seemingly intractable problem of insufficient labor, Governor McCook (Republican) turned to a proven solution—the importation of immigrants from elsewhere in the United States and also from abroad. He recommended that the territorial legislature institute an immigrant aid system to make the new arrivals feel welcome, from the moment they left their original homes until they were settled on their homesteads or found work in Colorado. As part of the immigrant recruitment effort, he recommended that the government disseminate accurate information about the area's climate, soil, and what it could produce. McCook believed that the territory could withstand close scrutiny. Such an effort would give Colo-

FIG. 2.5. General Edward M. McCook. Picture taken between 1860 and 1865. Denver Public Library, Western History Collection, US National Archives, Matthew Brady Photographs of Civil War–Era Personalities and Scenes, 111-B-1846.

rado an advantage over California, which complacently relied on its natural advantages and made no effort to attract immigrants.

McCook believed that immigrant workers would effectively address Colorado's labor shortage just as immigrant recruits had met the Union Army's manpower needs during the Civil War. He observed that "those new States of the West, like Iowa, Wisconsin and Minnesota, which have made organized efforts to secure European emigration, have increased in population and wealth beyond all precedent in the history of our country."[17] He also noted that Europeans were interested in coming to Colorado, citing the communications he had received from "two German colonies containing over two hundred families each, and from one containing forty families," inquiring about the agricultural and other resources of the territory.[18]

McCook hoped Coloradans would not be afraid of immigrants but would instead see their potential benefit: "No American should fear the competition of foreign labor, no matter what that labor may be. . . . Every man who comes here with strong arms and willing hands, no matter what his nationality, adds to the wealth of the community, and should be welcomed."[19] He believed that "holding out the hand of welcome to the impoverished of all nations, and the disheartened of all lands" would also contribute to the country's development.[20]

In this context, McCook encouraged Chinese immigration to Colorado. In his January 4, 1870, message to the Colorado Territory Council and House of Representatives, he advocated bringing in Chinese workers.[21] His willingness to recruit Chinese was probably influenced by his experience as US minister to the Hawaiian Islands (1866–68), where he had had ample opportunity to observe sugarcane plantations run on Chinese labor. Chinese would be easy to attract, he told the legislature in his address on immigration:

> There is one class of foreign immigration which I think will come to us without any other inducement than some assurance that they will be defended in life and property, and that around them will be thrown the full protection of the civil law; I mean the Chinamen! They may be of inferior race, and lower in natural traits than ourselves; they are undoubtedly pagan in religion; but notwithstanding all these moral disabilities, they are exceedingly muscular; and if we can first avail ourselves of their muscle, we can attend to their habits and morals afterwards. They will supply what this country eminently needs,—an abundance of cheap labor; and as they will come to us in the future anyhow, whether we will or not, we of this generation may as well welcome them, and derive what benefit we can from their labor and their numbers. They are persistent, saving, and industrious; and I firmly believe are the people destined to solve the great problems, as the future of that vast, unpeopled and unproductive country between the Missouri river and Pacific Ocean.[22]

McCook's argument in support of Chinese immigration is noteworthy in several respects. He anticipates the arrival of increasing numbers of Chinese, so he accepts their presence as a pragmatic matter. He believes that they can be acculturated to American society and that their "habits and morals" can be improved. He also predicts that they are destined to develop the American West. This prediction was never realized because of their later exclusion from the United States as a matter of national policy. McCook implicitly recognized this possibility when he acknowledged that Chinese laborers had previously suffered from a lack of protection, which was certainly the case on the West Coast.

McCook's remarks also reveal that, although he was in many respects an extraordinary man for his time, he was quite ordinary when it came to racial matters. He accepts the prevailing racialism of the period and considers the Chinese an inferior people. They are welcome to come as a subordinate group to provide cheap labor rather than as future citizens of the Colorado commonwealth.

McCook departs from the usual view in asserting that, while Chinese are handicapped by various "moral disabilities," they can be fixed and folded into American society. Most whites at the time believed the contrary, that Chinese were unassimilable, an inherent feature of their so-called sojourner mentality.

As a matter of fact, the Chinese were no more sojourners than their European counterparts, who also came as temporary workers. Indeed, the return rate of Chinese compares favorably with that of Europeans, especially when the obstacles the Chinese had to overcome in order to stay in the United States are taken into consideration. From 1848 to 1882, when Chinese were able to travel freely between China and the United States, their return rate was about 47 percent. By comparison, between 1861 and 1913, the return rate of the English and Welsh was approximately 40 percent, and during the early twentieth century, the return rate of the Italians was between 40 and 50 percent. Overall, it is estimated that between 1815 and 1930, about one-fourth of all Europeans returned to their native lands.[23]

The crucial difference between Chinese and Europeans was how they were perceived. Chinese were seen as migrants while Europeans were seen as settlers. Europeans were considered people who planned to stay and invest in the country rather than transients who intended to take something away from the country. After living in the United States for a decade or two, Europeans who came initially as sojourners shifted their focus to becoming permanent residents. Presumably, under the same circumstances, Chinese would have acted similarly had they been encouraged to do so. Instead, barriers were put in place to discourage Chinese (and later other Asians) from staying. The difficulties Chinese faced were formidable: they were forced to accept the most menial work, prevented from living where they wanted, compelled to live out their lives as bachelors, and subjected to hostility. Between 1850 and 1906, there were nearly two hundred roundups of Chinese intended to drive them out of the country.[24] Chinese were being expelled from many places in the American West even as Colorado was inviting them to come.

COME TO COLORFUL COLORADO

In 1870, by a vote of fourteen to six, the territorial legislature adopted Governor McCook's audacious recommendation to attract Chinese to Colorado, acting on a joint resolution introduced by House Representative A. D. Bevan. As Governor McCook had recommended, the legislature guaranteed the security of Chinese persons and property, in marked contrast to other parts of the country but specifically to Colorado's rival, California, where there was a virulent anti-Chinese movement.[25] Unfortunately, officials failed to take tangible steps to ensure the safety of the Chinese in the territory's increasingly Sinophobic environment, so the promise proved empty.

To entice Chinese to the Colorado Territory, an offer of free land rather than personal protection would probably have been more effective. After all, the main incentive for pioneers to brave the hazards of the frontier was simple—land, and lots of it. Land was something that Chinese peasants have wanted since time immemorial and something that they knew how to work with. Given their demonstrated resourcefulness in other endeavors and their experience with irrigation and other water-control techniques, Chinese settlers most likely could have adapted to the area's severe environment. As Utah senator Frank J. Cannon (Republican) noticed during his trip to China in 1896, "They are great agriculturalists."[26]

Giving Chinese land was hardly a novel idea and had even been considered earlier in California when the Chinese first arrived. In 1852, in order to increase the immigration of Chinese to California, Governor John McDougal (Democrat) recommended providing land grants, since he considered the Chinese "one of the most worthy of our newly adopted citizens."[27] However, with the subsequent rise of Sinophobia in California, this was no longer an option when the state's constitution was rewritten in 1879 to limit land ownership to whites and those of African descent. Around this time, most places in the American West enacted similar alien land laws barring Asians from ever owning or leasing land, essentially eliminating the main reason that had traditionally motivated people to settle the frontier.

Perhaps as farmers who fed the growing population in the American West, Chinese would have been more accepted. Furthermore, they would have been dispersed and therefore less visible in agricultural regions. As will be discussed in chapter 6, the experience of Japanese farmers suggests that while Chinese farmers would not have been spared animosity, their experience might have been less intense.

In spite of Governor McCook's efforts to attract Chinese to the Colorado Territory, they were slow to come. Many of them preferred to go to places like Boise Basin, Idaho, where they found greater economic opportunity. But as the Central City *Daily Miners' Register* astutely observed on August 2, 1867, it was only a matter of time before they began arriving in Colorado: "Within the last two years they have penetrated in considerable numbers in Montana and Idaho, and when the railroad shall be completed, or even advanced a few hundred miles further we shall have them here."[28]

Chinese eventually came to Colorado, as they did to other areas of the West, looking for work. They came along the railroad lines that they helped to build. When the Kansas Pacific Railroad was completed at its terminus in Denver, which served as a supply station for the mining business in the Rocky Mountain region, some of the discharged Chinese workers settled in Colorado. Documents show that by 1870, there were between seven and forty-two Chinese in Colorado.[29] By 1875, there were seventy-five Chinese in Denver and several hundred scattered in mining camps throughout the state, according to Edward L. Thayer, a labor contractor who recruited Chinese for various companies.[30]

Some Chinese found employment as common laborers, helping to build the railroads, clear the forests, and raise cattle. Others worked in boardinghouses and laundries, and at least one for an express company. By 1876, when gold was discovered at Boulder Creek, independent Chinese miners came to try their luck. By the end of the decade, their numbers had increased to 612, with most living in Denver's Chinatown or in the small mining communities in Gilpin and Park Counties. Later, during

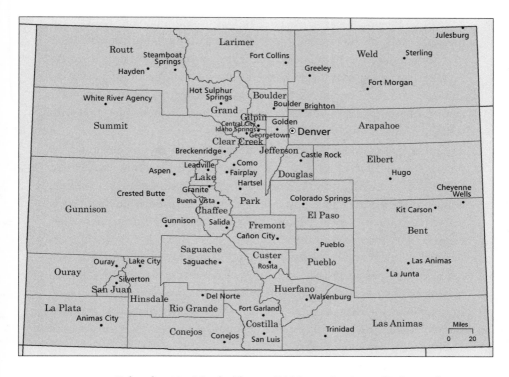

MAP 2.1. Colorado, 1880. Map by Thomas Dickinson, Institute of Behavioral Science, University of Colorado, Boulder, "1880 U.S. Census County Borders: Minnesota Population Center 2011," Minnesota Population Center. National Historical Geographic Information System: Version 2.0. Minneapolis, MN: University of Minnesota 2011.

the 1880s, the decline in the Chinese populations in these two counties and their increase in Arapahoe County suggests that those who had been expelled from the smaller mining communities went to Chinatown for greater security.

CHINESE PLACER MINERS

Most Chinese who went to Colorado worked as placer and gulch miners, while most white miners worked as underground miners.[31] Utilizing their knowledge of water management, the Chinese specialized in placer mining. A placer was created when a stream eroded gold-embedded rock, depositing the precious portion in a sandbar or gravel bank near a river or mountain stream. The gold was extracted by washing the gravel with water and using quicksilver to isolate it. This type of mining was a labor-intensive activity avoided by most other workers. For that reason, some Coloradans considered the Chinese an asset to the area. Contrary to allegations made against Chinese miners, they were usually not in direct competition with American and European miners.

Chinese miners scoured the gulches of the Arkansas, Platte, and Blue Rivers seeking "water-washed" gold. Under the supervision of Ah Say, formerly of the Union Pacific, a group of forty from Evanston, Wyoming, equipped themselves in Denver, leased land, and engaged in mining activities on their own in July 1873.[32] When self-employed, Chinese were at their best, according to the *Fairplay Sentinel*.[33] While Chinese miners hardly became wealthy, they were able to make a living gleaning the gold left behind by earlier prospectors, in effect proving correct those who had advocated their recruitment. Proponents had claimed that even though the mines had been worked earlier, the white miners had only skimmed the surface, taking in most instances the best pay but leaving enough gold to pay handsomely for ground sluicing.[34]

Some people believed that the Chinese were suited only for this type of mining. Writing in 1880, Frank Hall, mining editor of the *Denver Inter-Ocean*, expressed the common opinion that "the talk about Chinese to work in other than gulch or gravel mines, is simply hogwash. Anyone familiar with the subject, knows that they are utterly unfit for service in the quartz lodes."[35] Hall was advancing a popular image of the Chinese as qualified for only the most menial kinds of labor. Contrary to Hall's assertion, the Chinese who labored in Colorado's extractive industries were quite capable of performing various types of work and proved to be more than satisfactory to those willing to hire them.

In the summer of 1873, the brothers Robert and Alexander Cameron were among the first Coloradans to employ Chinese miners, hiring forty-five former Texas Pacific Railroad graders. They paid the Chinese workers thirty-five dollars a month, without board, to work in their placer mines in North Clear Creek Canyon, near Central City in Gilpin County. They were so impressed with their Chinese workers that six months later, they hired more of them. By the beginning of 1874, there were approximately 150 Chinese working for them, making $1 to $2.50 per person.[36] The Camerons' profitable employment of Chinese prompted others to consider doing the

FIG. 2.6. Chinese miners contributed significantly to Colorado's economy through their work in placer and gulch mines, c. 1880s. History Colorado, Stephen H. Hart Library and Research Center, 10028086.

same. This gave rise to concerns about Colorado being inundated by Chinese. As one commentator humorously observed, "Possibly the alarmists are right in professing to look forward with dismay to the prospect of our wearing pigtails and eating our rice and beans with chopsticks a few years hence."[37]

The Camerons' employment of Chinese became a controversial issue. The prejudice against Chinese gave rise to threats of physical violence against them. But the authorities dismissed such warnings out of hand. Most believed that the Chinese would have no trouble. As one reporter noted, it was well known that "white labor has not been found to be remunerative on this property [the Cameron placer mine in North Clear Creek], and are only too glad that Chinamen are coming, conceding the right of Asiatics to be as good here as that of Europeans. There is ample room for everybody."[38]

There were a few Chinese in Black Hawk and some in nearby settlements. But most preferred to be near where they worked, in what became known as Cameron's Chinese colony, living peacefully in small huts or in a railroad section house that they later acquired. Heaps of mail from their families in China began arriving at the local post office, causing some puzzlement for the postmasters, who could not read the Chinese addresses.[39] The Chinese community became a source of local curiosity. Interest focused on habits that made them different from white people. These differences were a source of entertainment, as shown in one reporter's description:

> An inspection of one of their huts will show that what is stinted room for two Americans is spaciousness for a dozen Chinese. . . . Privacy is not one of John's luxuries—he wants a houseful. . . . They are not nice about their houses. Smoke has not horrors for them, and soap they keep entirely for their clothes and bodies. Floor and wall-washing are things never hinted at. The chattering in these huts, in the evening, after work ceases, and during meal times, is incessant. They often sing, during evenings, in a monotonous caterwaul, which serves first-rate to awaken the echoes. There are two or three string instruments in camp, whose sounds are a modified species of saw-filing.[40]

Other aspects of Chinese behavior, such as diet and use of pidgin English, also lent themselves to mockery. Another reporter noted that Chinese miners' preferred "Melican [American] chicken" to their customary fare of "Chinese rats."[41]

In general, views of Chinese were mixed. Along with derogatory remarks were those that showed a grudging admiration of their work ethic. But both views shared a fundamental perspective: that the Chinese were a race apart. Difference was always foregrounded in such descriptions even when the Chinese were observed acting unexceptionally. One commentator discovers, "They work steadily and faithfully, yet talk incessantly. But they have learned the trick of working and talking at the same time."[42] Frequently, the emphasis on difference obscures the view of Chinese as members of the human race. Thus, a prominent Central City physician declares that Chinese are the only people in Gilpin County who do not suffer from the heat because "the Chinaman is a nerveless, unimpassioned animal and doesn't let anything worry him."[43] This sort of comment made employers want to hire Chinese workers and made white workers despise them.

This image of the phlegmatic but industrious Chinese automaton become so well established that challenges to this view were a source of comedy. One Coloradan critic jibed that, while Chinese labor had materially reduced mining expenses, "the idea that a Chinaman is a continuous worker and does not require watching" was sheer nonsense.[44] He went on to say that "unless they [the Chinese] are continually under the vigilant eye of a foreman, they are the most adroit shirkers that ever went into a mine," declaring for better effect that he did not know whether this was simply a natural tendency or whether the Chinese had learned it from the Cornish miners.[45] The humor of this comparison is that Cornish miners were valued as expert, highly disciplined workers, not shirkers, and those who lived in the Cripple Creek district were quick to go after the Chinese because they regarded them as their chief competitors. As American West historian Richard White points out, "The Cornishmen attacked the Chinese not for what they had done but for what others might do with them."[46]

However, the combination of modest success and lack of protection often made Chinese targets for robbers who stole their hard-earned money or claim jumpers who tried to take away their leases. When three masked, armed robbers held up two Chinese miners near Nevadaville and made off with $1,700, the incident was regarded as hardly unusual.[47] Robbing Chinese was commonplace enough that after dispossessing a Chinese miner of his savings, two discharged railroad workers decided to arrest him and march him to the town of Black Hawk. To their surprise, the townspeople took exception and rectified matters and then drove the robbers out of town. As the *Central City Register-Call* reports with wry humor, when the railroaders left, "they counted the ties at a lively rate towards Golden."[48]

To protect their persons, their homes, and their property, Chinese armed themselves, as others did. Such was the case at Frederick Gulch near Leadville, when Chinese miners mistook a group of hunters for a gang of robbers. According to the RMN report, the tables were turned when the hunters were confronted by about twenty "knights of the cue [*sic*] armed with pistols, shotguns, and rifles."[49] No one was hurt.

In at least one instance, a Chinese decided to become an outlaw himself. This was Mi Gow of Central City, dubbed the Chinese "desperado." Two years before he was captured, he had shot another Chinese, barely avoiding a stint in the penitentiary due to a mysterious escape. When Mi Gow was down on his luck, he assumed the role of a gunslinger, presenting himself in gambling parlors in Denver's Chinatown in full dress with gun drawn and robbing his fellow countrymen. Alternately, he made a living as a cat burglar, lifting valuables from the homes of wealthy whites elsewhere in Denver. If discovered by the owners while still in the house, he claimed to be their new "washee" boy who was just looking for the laundry.[50] In so doing, Mi Gow showed an astute awareness of the power of stereotypes as camouflage for his criminal ventures. This enterprising maverick illustrates one type of adaptation that Chinese could make to life in the Wild West.

CHINESE AND THE "CRIME OF 1873"

The arrival of the Chinese in Colorado was ill timed because it overlapped with the Panic of 1873, a severe financial crisis that led to a prolonged economic depression. After the Civil War, railroad construction in the United States boomed. By 1873, railroad mileage had doubled, causing many investors to engage in rash speculation. Nearly a hundred of the nation's railroads collapsed within a year, discharging their workers, including the Chinese who had moved on to build other railroads following the completion of the Transcontinental Railroad.

The Crime of 1873, as the Panic of 1873 was called in Colorado, precipitated the Long Depression (1873–79), a worldwide crisis that adversely affected the industrial nations of Europe and the newly industrialized United States. Domestically, the panic halted building construction, caused real estate values and corporate profits to plummet, decreased wages, and increased unemployment to a staggering 14 percent in 1876. Workers engaged in strikes to protest wage cuts and poor working conditions. In Colorado, class conflict intersected with racial antagonism as nativists took advantage of workers' discontent to place the onus on the Chinese for the workers' problems.

Using the Chinese as scapegoats for economic distress was a tactic largely imported from California. Coloradans were warned to avoid at all costs the ruin attributed to the Chinese in California, where citizens were said to "groan under the millstone that [was] grinding her citizens to pauperism, withering up her industries with dry rot and scattering her bone and sinew to distant fields of labor [caused] by the cursed presence of the almond eyed, cancer-breeding pests to her civilization."[51] They convinced themselves that such a fate awaited Colorado.[52] Demagogues sounded the alarm that the "Chinese are coming!" in very large numbers. Economic pundits, who predicted that Colorado would be flooded with cheap Chinese laborers to replace white workers, joined them.[53]

The image of countless Chinese engulfing the sparsely settled area worried white workers, stirring up resentment that was just below the surface. It fueled Sinophobic activities throughout the 1870s and afterward. Rather than wait for the imagined hordes to descend on them, white miners acted against the few Chinese among them, often ruthlessly. Such was the case at the Caribou Mine.

ANTI-CHINESE VIOLENCE IN NEDERLAND, LEADVILLE, AND COMO

In the spring of 1874, white miners evicted Chinese from Nederland even before the latter had a chance to start work. The Nederland Mining Company of Boulder County had recruited twenty-five Chinese laborers to work at the Caribou Mine, one of the most profitable in the area, producing approximately $350,000 worth of bullion in 1874 and 1875. Even though the Chinese were hired to chop wood, transport dirt, sort ore, and act as "roustabouts" at the mill rather than to extract the minerals from the underground mines themselves, the RMN erroneously claimed that they were being hired to replace white miners.[54] That was enough to move the white miners to vigilantism. Claiming that they were merely protecting the interest of American workers, a mob of fifty men in disguise forcibly entered the building where the Chinese were housed, ordered them to leave, and threatened violence if they ever returned. Meanwhile, the local sheriff tried to muster a posse to intervene only to discover that his men supported the mob, so he was compelled to stand aside.[55]

The mob action proved to be counterproductive. In an effort to protect its prerogatives, the company responded by announcing that it would employ more Chinese.[56] In a lengthy editorial, "Driving Off Chinamen," the *Weekly Central City Register* also expressed its disapproval of the incident: "Our own opinion is that the men engaged in this affair, have not only acted unlawfully, but very foolishly. We believe that one month's trial of Chinese cheap labor about a mine or mill, would have settled the question forever, and that the company would be glad at the end of that time to replace them with men of any other nationality. By resisting the company in this move, they have admitted that the [Chinese] were nearly if not quite their equals, and that they were afraid of their competition."[57] Apparently, what the white miners feared was that Chinese workers might prove to be more than mere drudges. Some towns, such as Leadville, reputed to be the most brutal place in the state, were unwilling to wait to find out. They banned Chinese outright.

The *Denver Daily Tribune* of May 8, 1879, referred to the city's banning of Chinese as the "Leadville craze," noting that "Leadville has now written on her banners which are on the outer walls not [the familiar slogan] 'The Chinese must go,' but 'The Chinese must not come.'"[58] In fact, Leadville citizens were more blunt than this. The sign they posted read, "All Chinamen Will Be Shot."[59]

Oddly, long after the Chinese were banned from Leadville, they continued to be blamed for suppressing the wages of Leadville's mainly Irish mine workers. Dislike of the Chinese persisted for decades. As late as 1936, in a nostalgic piece published in the local paper *Holy Cross Trail* (Red Cliff) about Leadville's pioneer days, the editor O. W. Daggett recalled that sixty-five years earlier, after one Chinese had ignored the miners' ban in the district's Ora City camp, "Judge Lynch took the case and court was held under a tree." Daggett observed with satisfaction, "Even to this day a Chinaman going thru Leadville on a railroad train will not even look out of a window, and there will not be another Chinaman in Leadville in the next thousand years."[60]

In the late nineteenth century, Leadville's anti-Chinese policy resonated throughout Colorado. As the *Daily Register-Call* declared in 1880, "The mountains and mining camps of Colorado seem to be no abiding place for the Mongolian. Leadville's example is being imitated all over the state."[61] Cripple Creek, Balfour, Aspen, and Creede also proscribed Chinese. When two Chinese from Buena Vista came to work in Alpine, the townspeople decided that they should be disinvited at once; as a reporter noted, this was probably "the last, as well as the first, attempt of the Mongolian race to colonize Alpine."[62] Miners in Breckenridge decided the same for another group of Chinese, who had entered the city looking for work. The miners held a meeting and resolved, "The heathen must go."[63]

This sentiment was echoed in Como, Park County, which served as an important railroad depot for the Denver, South Park and Pacific Railroad, which transported people to the silver-mining areas during the Colorado Silver Boom (1879–93). Unlike the other local incidents, this one attracted national attention and raised the issue of racism in America. The Chinese-Italian War, as the RMN called it, is also important because it served as the main catalyst for the Denver race riot several months later. In Park County, Italian coal miners felt threatened by the Chinese, even though there were comparatively few of them. In 1880, there were 124 Chinese in the county, 81 percent of whom were coal miners. For the most part, the rest lived in the nearby mining communities of Fairplay and Hamilton. Fairplay was a gold-mining settlement founded in 1859, during the Pike's Peak gold rush. The name "Fairplay" was reputedly chosen as a rebuff to nearby Tarryall, which had earned the nickname "Grab-All" for the greed of its inhabitants. In contrast, Fairplay promised equal treatment for all of its residents. Those who had been driven out of Tarryall had founded the other town, Hamilton. Hamilton residents included some two hundred Chinese who worked in Como or engaged in placer mining. Altogether, Chinese constituted only 3 percent of the county's population, but 12 percent of its foreign population. Because of their sparse numbers, the Chinese were relatively inconspicuous except in the coal mines, where they came into conflict with the Italian miners.

Italians were a significant group in the predominately immigrant workforce in Colorado mines. Though Italians were among the Fifty-Niners and other early settlers in the Pikes Peak area, most came during the great railroad construction period from 1880 to 1895, lured to Colorado by publicity designed to attract cheap labor for mines, smelters, and railroad construction gangs.[64] In 1880, there were approximately 816 Italians in the state. By 1890, there were 3,882, most working in the industrial centers and coal-mining camps.[65] The Italians experienced labor discrimination, exploitation, and hostility. They were regarded as simple-minded people.[66]

Though the Italians were treated badly, they had one decisive advantage over the Chinese—they were Europeans. As American Studies scholar Thomas A. Guglielmo notes, "Italians' many perceived racial inadequacies aside, they were still largely accepted as whites by the widest variety of people and institutions."[67] In their dispute with the Chinese, the Italians affirmed not only their white identity but also their national identity as Americans. This proved an advantage in the Chinese-Italian War as it gained the Italians the support of pro-labor proponents like William A. H.

Loveland, the new owner of the RMN. Loveland placed the Chinese on the opposite side of the color line and his newspaper reflected this bias.

In June 1879, the Denver, South Park and Pacific Railroad Company founded the South Park Coal Company to exploit the Como coal mines in Park County. Italian miners were among the first brought in to work these mines. Later, the company hired Edward L. Thayer to recruit less-expensive Chinese miners from nearby Fairplay, Hamilton, and other parts of the state. Believing that ethnic homogeneity would result in greater productivity, the company segregated the two groups, with the Italians working in the upper shaft and the Chinese in the lower shaft. This practice proved to be a double-edged sword, for ethnic solidarity could also serve as the basis for interethnic rivalry. Indeed, by the fall of 1879, the Italian miners began to fear for their jobs, as more and more Chinese were brought in to work in the mines. On November 9, 1879, the Italians took matters into their own hands. They accosted the Chinese and demanded that they depart. However, the Chinese managed to persuade the Italians to wait for Thayer, who would provide them with transportation out of the area. The *Fairplay Flume* gave a matter-of-fact account of what ensued after Thayer arrived:

> One of the Dagos nearest [Thayer] knocked him down. He was thereafter kicked and beaten with rifle butts, and one man placed a gun to his head, but just as the trigger was pulled, another kicked his head, causing the bullet to graze his scalp. . . . Thayer's Chinks had witnessed the mob's action from the cracks in a nearby shanty where they had taken refuge. After the Dagos had thus handled the Contractor, they next moved upon the Chinese stronghold. Some of the Chinks were armed. These were quickly disarmed and the whole band was marched ahead of the angry, shouting Italians into Como where they were roughly handled, and after strong directions run out of town.[68]

After the Chinese were expelled, the Italians posted a warning in pidgin English that read, "Chinamen come again, Italians kill right away."[69]

Needless to say, the *Fairplay Flume*'s account of the episode is far from neutral. This is shown, for example, in the use of the pejoratives "Dagos" and "Chinks," the casual manner in which the brutality of the Italians and the cowardice of the Chinese onlookers are depicted (the Chinese hide in a nearby shanty rather than coming to Thayer's rescue, even though some are armed), and also in the description of the contractor as a hapless victim caught in a brawl between two minority groups. Here, the local newspaper reveals its perspective on race and ethnicity in what was ostensibly a labor issue. None of the participants in this story comes off very well.[70]

The response of the South Park Coal Company was similar to that of the Nederland Mining Company in the Caribou Mine affair (1874) described above. So far as the South Park Coal Company was concerned, the issue was about preserving its prerogative to hire the workers it wanted, so it insisted on retaining its Chinese laborers.[71] It hired Sheriff David J. Cook, president of the Rocky Mountain Detective Association, to do so. With a squad of twenty men, Cook recovered control of the mines, evicted the Italians, and protected the Chinese, who returned to work in the mines, thus ending the so-called Chinese-Italian War.

Though the conflict ended, prejudice against the Chinese persisted in the area, flaring up some two decades later on August 1, 1893, when a white mob in Como attacked the ethnic community, which consisted of some forty Chinese who were mining for gold at the nearby Peabody's placer.[72] The Chinese miners' cabins were set on fire. After the original fire had been put out by the local fire department, the enraged mob burned the cabins to the ground and robbed two laundrymen who served as the Chinese community's bankers.

One of the factors that kept the issue alive was the constant drumbeat of fear from the Colorado press. The RMN portrayed the inglorious conclusion of the "Chinese-Italian War" as the beginning of a Chinese invasion: "The Chinese triumph over white workmen in the Como mines is a cloud no bigger than a man's hand, but it is full of evil omen. It is the formal opening in Colorado of the struggle that has so long convulsed California... there is nothing but our superior fighting qualities to prevent them from eventually owning the whole country and reducing our grandchildren to be their servants... converting a land of plenty into a hive of mongrel paupers."[73] Another commentator warned that, unless the imagined invasion were stopped, the Chinese would move inexorably from coal mining into other occupations at the expense of Italians and other European workers. He cautioned: "When a Chinaman once gets a footing in a place, who ever knew of them throwing it up until he accumulated sufficient to branch into some other occupations more remunerative. Are the Chinamen going to confine themselves exclusively to coal mining? By no means."[74]

After the Como mine dispute had ended, its meaning was debated in the public press between former governor John Evans (Republican), owner of the railroad and mining companies, and William A. H. Loveland, owner of the RMN. Their discussion mirrored the larger debate on the "Chinese Question" that was taking place across the nation, which will be discussed in more detail below. Essentially, Evans made an economic argument for accepting the Chinese, while Loveland made a racial and class argument for rejecting them. In a letter to the RMN, Evans refuted the idea that the employment of the Chinese in Como presaged the arrival of an Asian flood.[75] The Chinese were hired because the Italians were unable to mine enough coal to supply the needs of the railroad. Moreover, the actions of the Italians were disruptive. When the Italians clashed with the Chinese, they delayed the supply of coal needed to run the trains and heat the homes in Denver, and to carry passengers and freight, an estimated hundred carloads' worth.

A few days later, in an editorial in the RMN, Loveland criticized Evans for supplanting white laborers on the pretext of public urgency.[76] The Italians may have been inefficient, but the South Park Company made no effort to hire other white laborers. Loveland insinuated that Evans preferred Chinese to his own people because they cost less.[77] By putting profit above everything else, Evans was endangering American civilization while furthering the interest of the emperor of China. Loveland concludes that the "logic of Governor Evans' action would eventuate . . . in expelling every white laborer from the United States through sheer starvation, brought on by Chinese competition."[78] In another editorial a few days later, Loveland continued to make a racial argument by comparing white laborers in Colorado to those in the northern states who were degraded by black slavery prior to the Civil War: "The poor white men of the north fought slavery because it degraded labor by putting them on a level with the negro [sic] race, which they despised. For the same reason they detest the capitalists who are again degrading white labor with the Chinese system, which is fully as odious as slavery."[79] In so doing, Loveland voiced a common comparison made by Sinophobes between Chinese labor and black slavery, capitalizing on antislavery sentiment in the United States following the Civil War. This was an argument calculated to appeal to fair-minded Americans, who could be expected to oppose the importation of Chinese labor on moral grounds—it was a labor practice that was bad not only for whites but also for Chinese, although the latter did not seem to know this.

The Chinese-Italian War in the Como coal mines is in many ways a classic case of what sociologist Edna Bonacich has identified as ethnic antagonism resulting from economic competition.[80] As her theory specifies, such a conflict emerges when a labor market is split along ethnic lines—in this case, with the Chinese being paid less even though they did essentially the same work. As the higher-paid workforce, the Italians feared they that would be displaced or that their pay would be lowered. However, contrary to the main tenets of Bonacich's theory, the Italians were ultimately unsuccessful in driving out the Chinese. Although better paid, the Italians were too weak politically to counter the determination of the South Park Company to restore order to its labor force. Among European groups in Colorado, the Italians had the lowest social status and least political power.[81] At one point, the company proclaimed that henceforth only Chinese would operate the mines, though that did not come to pass.[82] Instead, the majority of the workers were either Americans or Europeans. Perhaps in a calculated move to prevent further labor unrest, the company paid the Chinese the same wages as the Italians.

Of course, other ethnic groups besides the Chinese experienced ethnic enmity as a result of the split labor market. In Gilpin County, for instance, Cornish, Irish, Italian, and Austrians competed with one another.[83] The earliest to arrive were the Cornishmen, who engaged in lode mining. Mine operators welcomed them because many were experienced in sinking shafts and tracing veins. Like the Italians in the Como labor struggle, the Cornishmen felt that the ethnic groups that came after them were jeopardizing their jobs or wages. The antagonism of the Cornish toward the Irish may have been based on cultural and religious differences as well—hence the observation that "it did not take many drinks to precipitate a fight between members of the two groups."[84] However, in the case of the Italians and Austrians (usually referred to jointly as Tyrolese), ethnic antipathy really was a matter of economic competition; the Tyrolese were willing to work for lower wages than the Cornishmen, a situation that was exacerbated by a mining slump that lasted from 1886 to 1892. The mine owners were allegedly paying the Tyrolese twenty-five to fifty cents a day less than the Cornishmen. Reminiscent of (and perhaps influenced by) the Sinophobic movement were slogans such as the "Dago Must Go!" Eventually, these European miners were able to live in relative harmony with one another. As historian Ralph Mann has shown, European miners, specifically the Cornish and Irish, found common ground in their opposition to the threat of Chinese labor, which they identified with big capital.[85]

There were significant differences between the dissensions among European ethnic groups and those that pitted Europeans against Chinese. While European victims of ethnic hostility were invariably faulted for belonging to an alien culture, exhibiting exotic customs, and having a low standard of living, the Chinese were thus characterized because of their race. With the passage of time, most European ethnic groups could and did subsume their ethnic identity under the broader national identity of being American. In contrast, because of naturalizations laws that designated them, along with other Asians, as people ineligible for citizenship, the Chinese were excluded from the national polity. Many states enacted discriminatory local laws such as miscegenation statutes that forbade Asians from marrying white persons (though they could and did marry people of color), limiting their ability to establish families and nurture a succeeding generation.

Colorado has the distinction of being one of the few states that never included Asians in its miscegenation statutes against people of color. This may have been because there were simply too few of them to warrant it or because there was a lax attitude toward miscegenation. The issue of race, however, was important to Coloradans in other respects. One clue to its centrality is the fact that while interethnic struggles in Colorado remained largely local issues, anti-Chinese sentiment was part of broader regional and national social movements. Indeed, ever since the signing in 1868 of the Burlingame Treaty, which sanctioned the immigration of Chinese laborers, the "Chinese Question" had been a major national political issue.

The Chinese Question centered on whether Chinese immigration should be curbed. At the June 1879 commencement exercises of Boulder University, the featured debate was on this very issue, "Should Chinese immigration be restricted by law?" Speaking for the affirmative, R. H. Whiteley Jr. advanced common nativist arguments espoused elsewhere, particularly on the West Coast. He began by describing "the squalid habits of the Chinese, [who were] accustomed to live in filth and depravity, on a mere pittance, crowded together in masses and barely existing in vice and misery" as the products of an aberrant culture.[86] In essence, Whiteley argued that the Chinese were unassimilable, implying there would never be a place for them in America.

Whiteley's views were typical for his time. While Chinese culture was certainly different from American culture, it was only in the nine-

FIG. 2.7. "The Chinese Question, Columbia—'Hands off, gentlemen! America means fair play for all men,'" by Thomas Nast, *Harper's Weekly*, February 18, 1871. Nast's political cartoon captures the essence of the "Chinese question." At the center is the goddess Columbia, personifying America and speaking for its cardinal value of "equality for all." She stands between the Chinese man at her feet and the white mob that would harm him. Behind her is a wall with posters expressing the public's perception of the Chinese. Denver Public Library, Western History Collection, Z-3811.

teenth century that it began to be treated with contempt. In the eighteenth century, Chinese culture was viewed with curiosity tinged with respect, and Enlightenment thinkers held it up as a potential mirror to European civilization, in some ways even superior to it. But that perception had changed dramatically over the course of the nineteenth century, as China was found wanting economically and militarily. By the mid-nineteenth century, most Westerners were consequently prepared to see China, and, by extension, its people, as culturally inferior.

The most serious argument that Whiteley presented for restricting Chinese immigration was that Chinese workers constituted unfair competition for white workers. This was because the Chinese standard of living was so low that no white worker could possibly compete with them. He further claimed that the Chinese were predisposed to working for less money and under poorer conditions because of their inherent servility; this was an essentially racist contention that was widely accepted at the time.

To clinch his argument that restricting Chinese immigration was simply a matter of self-preservation, Whiteley drew on Social Darwinist ideology, which was becoming increasingly popular in the United States at the time. Social Darwinists embraced Charles R. Darwin's theory that, through the course of evolution, mankind had diverged into races with different attributes, including differing levels of mental ability. From this theory, the Social Darwinists developed an immutable hierarchy of races in which the white race—meaning the Anglo-Saxon descendants of Great Britain, Scandinavia, and Germany—was ranked at the top, while others followed in descending order. The theory provided pseudo-scientific support for a variety of traditional prejudices and contemporary political, social, and economic practices.

Speaking for the negative side of the debate proposition, J. J. McFarland rejected the idea that Chinese immigration should be restricted on the basis of America's democratic ideals, its tradition of free immigration, and economic necessity. He pointed out the inherent unfairness of the proposed restriction, which held that "all other nations are admitted, but the Chinaman alone is to be excluded, because his habits and religion do not agree with ours."[87] McFarland argued that such a restriction was unnecessary, in any case, because there were comparatively few Chinese in America.

Notably, McFarland sidestepped judgments about the relative inferiority of the Chinese. Instead, he made their treatment a test of commitment to American values and Christian duty. Failure to treat Chinese fairly was a threat to American identity, he suggested. In contrast to Whiteley, McFarland made American virtue rather than Chinese vice the focus of his argument.

However, both Whiteley and McFarland agreed that Chinese had certain cultural deficiencies. Both disapproved of Chinese idolatry, though McFarland saw this as an opportunity for the Chinese to be redeemed, while Whitely took it as evidence that they were beyond redemption. Both agreed that, as heathens, the Chinese would have difficulty integrating into American society, given its predominant Protestant religion and social standards. For many at this time, Christian beliefs were fundamental to an American identity and the basis for social unity. After all, the United States was founded, in part, for religious reasons. It viewed itself as a redeemer nation, with the duty to extend its evangelical empire. Hence, in the nineteenth century, enthusiastic American Protestant missionaries went to China to convert the Chinese to Christianity, and Protestant churches attempted to convert those in America. In retrospect, McFarland's hopes for the integration of Chinese Christians in Colorado proved overly optimistic. Although a number of Chinese embraced Christianity, this did not necessarily make them more acceptable to mainstream society, nor did it protect them from persecution, because when whites looked at them, they saw only their Chineseness.

Limited numbers of Chinese migrated to Colorado prior to the Exclusion Act in 1882. Though there were comparatively few of them in the state, and their work was too specialized to constitute competition, Chinese were still seen as an economic risk. European workers agitated against the Chinese, perceiving them as a threat to their livelihood and as willing puppets of company owners and managers. Also, Europeans managed to deflect anti-foreign prejudice away from themselves through their opposition to the Chinese, affirming their Americanness in the process.

Chinese Coloradans who had the temerity to remain in the territory despite the discrimination they faced often sought solace in Denver's Chinatown. Chinatown provided them with a community that they could belong to. It fostered an ethnic identity in America that transcended the village identity they once had in China.

THREE

EXOTIC OASIS IN THE QUEEN CITY OF THE WEST

ODAY, THERE IS NO EVIDENCE THAT CHINATOWN EVER EXISTED in what is now Denver's Lower Downtown Historic District (LoDo), apart from a small plaque on the side of a building at Twentieth Street between Market and Blake Streets. Indeed, it is difficult to imagine that LoDo, with its high-priced condominiums, upscale boutiques, and gentrified neighborhoods, once housed a thriving Chinese American community. Historically, there was only one Denver Chinatown. In memory, however, there were always two, though they occupied the same space.

First and foremost was Hop Alley, as whites called it. Hop Alley was perceived as an alien place, inhabited by people whose racial and cultural characteristics set them apart. This Chinatown, a mysterious place that captured the imagination, was more an idea than anything else, one that allowed whites to play out their fantasies about Chinese. To the extent that Chinatown is remembered at all, it is likely to be the white construction, Hop Alley.

Second, and nearly forgotten, was the ethnic enclave where Chinese found refuge in the hostile milieu that was Colorado. As with other ghettos, it was a ramshackle affair, as unwholesome as any of those that had emerged in the cities of mid-nineteenth century industrial America. But it was a place the Chinese could call their own, a community that provided them consolation. There, they could maintain their cultural identity, modifying the traditional Chinese social structure to fit the state's frontier society.

IMAGINARY COMMUNITY

Hop Alley gave rise to a number of urban legends about itself and the Chinese who lived there. Its name was suggestive: "Hop" referred to opium, which had become identified with Chinese life, and "Alley" referred to the locations of entrances to the buildings where Chinese lived. These entrances were probably situated in the back of the buildings for security. It was assumed that tunnels and secret rooms accessible only by trapdoors connected the buildings.

By and large, Denver's white population viewed Hop Alley with suspicion as well as a degree of fascination. Its inhabitants were "Heathen Chinee." These non-Christians were thought to indulge in immoral behavior, including opium smoking, high-stakes gambling, illicit sex, and presumably a few other vices unknown to the general public. The local press carried sensational stories about them as a social menace who exerted a corrupting influence on innocent Denverites, especially boys like William McClellan, one of the many whom they had allegedly turned into "hop fiends."[1] In common discourse, the Chinese were compared to a disease or contagion with the power to inflict harm entirely disproportionate to their modest numbers. "Like a festering canker," they were said to "gnaw at the vitals of the Anglo-Saxon backbone, undermining the health and morality of all who come in contact with them."[2]

To many, Chinese were dangerous, every one of them a potential thug, a *boo how doy*—a "hatchet man" or "highbinder."[3] Collectively, Chinese were suspected of being gangsters who protected the criminal activities of the *tongs* that were rumored to run Hop Alley and to engage in internecine turf wars (*tong* was the popular name for Chinese community organizations that were established to provide their members various services and to maintain public order). It was said that the rivalry between two Denver *tongs* was settled in the "good old Chinese way, by putting out highbinder committees, cutting each other up, and generally contributing to the usefulness of the police department."[4] The Chinese served as a convenient bogeyman to frighten Denverites. An 1896 *Visitor's Pocket Guide* to Denver recommended protection for any whites venturing into Chinatown: "Chinese quarters—Wazee, between Sixteenth and Seventeenth; Market, between Twentieth and Twenty-first. Visitors apply at Central Police Station for guides."[5]

Hop Alley was regarded as a notorious place, replete with brothels serviced by exotic women, gambling parlors frequented by glamorous people, and opium emporiums that catered to the drug cognoscenti. During Prohibition (1920–33), it acquired an additional reputation for rampant bootlegging.[6] Its unsavory reputation was perpetuated by yellow journalism, which circulated lurid stories ascribing an array of demeaning attributes to the Chinese residents. Sensational stories fed readers' apparently insatiable appetite for information about the Chinese community. Typical is S. A. Meyer's December 1909 article in the *Denver Times* depicting Chinatown as a "dark, narrow alley, a series of dingy entrances, cubbyholes, underground passages, dismal, all-smelling places . . . the much-discussed, much-feared rendezvous of the tongs."[7] As if Chinese dwellers were some sort of nocturnal creatures (vampires come to mind), Meyer goes on to say: "It is only at night that you can see the Mongol quarter of Denver awaken into exotic life. Its people come into being with the dark and disappear with the dawn. Its acrid odors sting the nostrils. Fiery, contemptuous, bland, serene, foul smelling, your Oriental maintains that indefinable barrier that has kept the East and West apart since the centuries began."

What Meyer describes is a nightmarish vision of hell on earth—a dark realm of the damned. It is a shadow world where only bad things happen to those foolish enough to go there. Ironically, Meyer blames the Chinese for maintaining a wall between themselves and the civilized world of the West, ignoring the legal restrictions and social anxieties that resulted in their segregation, which his description serves to confirm. Like many others of his time, Meyer refers to the Chinese as Mongols, even though they belong to a different ethnic group. By identifying them as one and the same, Meyer evokes the "barbarous" nature of the Chinese by implying that they are descendants of the Mongol horde that devastated Europe in the fourteenth century, the would-be destroyers of Western culture. He ends the passage with an allusion to the well-known refrain from Rudyard Kipling's "The Ballad of East and West," "OH, East is East and West is West, and never the twain shall meet," which reflects not only Kipling's attitude toward race but Meyer's as well.

In more recent times, popular films have perpetuated distorted depictions of Chinatown. In general, they were perceived as depraved places in the nineteenth and twentieth centuries. In his 1974 film of the same title, Roman Polanski uses Chinatown as a metaphor for corruption. Critic Murray Sperber, in his review of the film, observed that Polanski turned "Chinatown—the place as well as the idea—into a symbol of human corruption, chaos, and immorality unimaginable to most straight Westerners. It is possibly even a symbol of early sexual mysteries, primal scenes, about which, he suggests, it is best not to inquire. . . . And those people who see the world as inevitably corrupt and controlled by alien and dark forces will chant the movie's final line like a mantra, 'Forget it, Jake, it's Chinatown.'"[8]

Chinatown is also presented in the popular television series *Deadwood* (2004–2006), a Western set in 1870s Deadwood, Dakota Territory.[9] This Chinatown is portrayed as a slum inhabited by "Celestials," a term of ridicule in common use at the time. It was probably derived from the Qing dynasty's self-designation as the Celestial Court (*tian chao*). In the series, the Chinese are seen but never heard. The exception is Wu, their ruthless leader. His character embodies the well-worn depiction of Asian men as "villains or comic figures or subservient like Hop Sing, the Cartwright family's cook on 'Bonanza,'" as playwright David Henry Hwang observes.[10] The actual inhabitants of Chinatowns were, of course, different from the way they are represented in movies. This was certainly true of Denver's Chinatown.

CHINESE GHETTO

Besides Hop Alley, there was the *other* Chinatown, an ethnic enclave where Chinese gathered for mutual support in an unfriendly environment. As described in chapter 2, almost from the moment the Chinese arrived in Colorado, Sinophobic incidents occurred throughout the state and in the region, forcing them to flee to Chinatown, where they were essentially confined until World War II, with almost no possibility of moving into mainstream society.

Denver's Chinatown was similar to other ethnic enclaves established in the United States. It was based on an ethnic economy that served mainly the Chinese community. It was a place where Chinese could live among countrymen who could help them find an abode and a job. It was there that they could find goods and services denied them elsewhere. And, perhaps most important, it was there that they found a refuge, a place where they could socialize and practice time-honored customs. Like the larger city of which it was a part, Chinatown served as a base of operations for those working in the Rocky Mountain region, bringing together merchants, labor contractors, and workers into a pioneer community. Chinatown served as a transit center for those taking on supplies before heading off to the mines and construction projects, and as an entertainment center for those seeking rest and recreation.

The original Chinese community, called Chinaman's Row, was established around 1870 on Wazee Street between Fifteenth and Seventeenth Streets. It was next to the old red-light district on Holliday Street (which was later renamed Market Street). "Wazee" itself is probably a Chinese name that means "Street of the Chinese" in Cantonese.[11] From Wazee Street, Chinese residents eventually spread out to nearby neighborhoods.

The Chinese lived in Denver's skid row. Like its namesake in other urban areas, this was one of the poorest and most diverse neighborhoods in Denver, and as such there were few restrictions on the sale or lease of property to Chinese and other people of color. They lived near other ethnic enclaves where Europeans had settled. Italians, for instance, lived in a place known as "The Bottoms," which was located along the South Platte River sandwiched between downtown Denver and Highland, near the hills to the west. Like the Chinese, the Italians were forced to live in hovels, bearable only because of "the strength of their old-country heritage and their religion, " as Western historian Robert Athearn suggests.[12]

After the Denver race riot on October 31, 1880 (see chapter 5), devastated Chinatown, various community factions moved to different locations, though all were within the downtown district. The public identified these factions as *tongs*, but there was much uncertainty about what they were. The general muddle is reflected in a 1902 description of Denver's Chinatown in the *Rocky Mountain News* (RMN), which begins by tripping over the definition: "Once there were two 'tongs,' or cliques, or societies, or companies. Opinions differ as to the real nature of a tong."[13] In popular usage, any Chinese group could be called a *tong*, but especially those in publicly contested relationships.

During the latter decades of the nineteenth century, two such rival groups were at odds with each other—the Chin Poo and John Taylor factions. The Chin Poo faction was a comparatively small group. It was led by one of the most colorful figures in Chinatown history, Chin Poo (Chen Liangpu), who rose from the laundry business to become a powerful and wealthy Chinatown boss. At the end of this struggle, he emerged as the "King of the Oriental Colony," was nominated as Chinese consul for Denver, and was secure enough to bring an indictment against the ex-Denver police chief Henry Brady for soliciting a bribe of three hundred dollars from him to run a gambling house.[14] Chin Poo's group was probably associated with the Hip Sing Tong, one of the two largest *tongs* in Chinatown. John Taylor's faction (led by a Chinese who had adopted an English name) was considered less trustworthy than Chin Poo's.[15] This faction was probably associated with the Bing Kong Tong, the other major *tong* in China-town; it managed the local temple and gambling parlors.[16]

Chin Poo and John Taylor accused each other of being controlled by gangsters who were said to be as numerous as the fan-tan gambling games that Chinese played.[17] There were unconfirmed stories in the press about the two factions' ongoing rivalry. One sensational story involved Little Ho Juoy, a Chinese prostitute at the center of a complex plot to assassinate Chin Poo and his associate O. H. Fang.[18] It was alleged that John Taylor had hired Mucke Hoy, a Cantonese from San Francisco, as the assassin. In a previous episode in their long feud, Chin Poo had informed the authori-ties of John Taylor's illicit gambling activities.[19]

To end the rivalry between the Chin Poo and John Taylor factions, it was reported that Mayor Wolfe Londoner (1889–1901) persuaded them to relocate. The goal was to keep them physically apart as well as to give them each a piece of territory they could call their own, even within the limited geography of Denver's Chinatown. Though it was said that Mayor Lon-doner threatened to chase them out with clubs if they did not leave the old quarter voluntarily, the move was actually engineered by enterprising members of Chinatown, who used their understanding of Denver politics to improve the condition and reputation of the community.[20] Chin Poo agreed to go across the bridge to Blake and Thirteenth, where he reportedly "settled, and gathered sympathizers, and was happy for a short time."[21] O. H. Fang, Yale University graduate and an attorney for the Chinese Mutual Protective Association of Denver, worked with city officials to facilitate the transition to the new neighborhood. Meanwhile, John Taylor went to an area called Kennedy's Row on Holliday Street, between Twentieth and Twenty-First Streets, and eventually spread along Market Street to Twenty-Second Street.

Much to the chagrin of both Chin Poo and John Taylor, an outsider then tried to revitalize the original Chinatown on Wazee Street.[22] In the sum-mer of 1892, Ling Choo, a well-educated Chinese from Greeley, Colorado, who had made his money in Black Hawk mines, took out a ten-year lease on a large piece of property between Sixteenth and Seventeenth Streets. His plan was to construct a two-story terraced building there to accommo-date new residences and shops for Chinese, and also a temple—reportedly the central image would be imported from Beijing and make the religious images installed in the other Chinatowns pale in significance.[23] Predict-ably, Ling Choo was alleged to be a gangster associated with San Francisco's Sue On Tong. It was said that he had recruited former employees from the Black Hawk, Como, and Fairplay mining districts to live in this new Chinatown, and planned to augment their ranks with Chinese from San Francisco. Fearing that this newcomer with outside backing would prove too strong a competitor, both Chin Poo and John Taylor opposed him.

After moving, Chin Poo tried to create a Chinese community that was more acceptable to mainstream society. He rented a row of houses across the bridge on Blake Street from Joe Furraca, an Italian businessman who had been indicted earlier that year for running brothels, and renovated the buildings to accommodate the more respected members of the Chinese community.[24] This block came to house the Denver Mutual Protective Association and mercantile establishments, such as the Chinese Grocery Company and Chinese laundries.

Besides cleaning up his businesses, Chin Poo worked to develop better relations with mainstream society. He made efforts to project a new image of Chinese prosperity and cultural confidence by hosting lavish New Year's celebrations and involving Chinatown in the annual Festival of Mountain and Plain, a three-day celebration of the state's frontier traditions. However, he met with failure when he sought to protect the Chinese community from defamation by threatening to organize a boycott of *San Toy, or The Emperor's Own*, a popular musical comedy set in Beijing that had been the toast of London and New York and was now coming to Denver. Chin Poo thought it denigrated Chinese. He declared that it was "constructed and perpetrated upon the American public for the express purpose of holding up to ridicule the Chinese race [and] that it was a gross and entirely inexcusable caricature."[25] Chin Poo's proposed boycott (followed by the anonymous defacing of posters advertising *San Toy*) succeeded in alarming the production's advance agent, Harry Sloane. In a moment of panic, Sloane advised canceling the play, fearing that the Denver production would lead to a worse furor than the city's 1880 race riot. But in the end, the Chinese protest was disregarded. The play opened on schedule, sold a huge number of tickets, and enjoyed a long run in Denver, showing how little real influence Chin Poo had on the public outside of Chinatown.

BARRIER TO REDEVELOPMENT

The relocation of Chinese from the original Sixteenth and Wazee Street area served an additional purpose. Besides separating rival factions to avoid possible fighting in the community, it was part of an effort to uproot the original Chinatown that stood in the way of the redevelopment of the downtown district. As early as March 16, 1871, a group of white residents living in the Wazee area presented a petition to the Chamber of Commerce requesting the removal of the Chinese. On September 11, 1882, a group of nearby property owners presented the City Council with a petition to have the Chinese expelled from Wazee Street, claiming that their presence was not only injurious to business but also depreciated property values.[26]

As time went on, efforts to mobilize public opinion to oust the Chinese from this location focused on the public health threat they posed. The reason for this may not be immediately apparent. Chinatown was probably as filthy and as congested an area as the city's other ethnic enclaves, like those where the Italians and Irish gathered, and the rest of the city was not much better. As Denver City physician Dr. Frederick J. Bancroft (1872–78) noted, the city was one of the dirtiest in the country.[27] Its streets were littered with the carcasses of dead rats and cats, open sewers were common, refuse was simply dumped into the Platte River downtown, and, in keeping with the city's image as a "cowtown," livestock including pigs and cows were allowed to run loose on city streets.

The more important reason for wanting to rid the area of Chinese was that by the mid-1870s demographic changes in Denver acted to bring health concerns to the fore. With the completion of the transcontinental railroad link through Denver, the city grew rapidly. Among the new arrivals were many tuberculosis sufferers who had come for the only cure available—exposure to a dry, sunny climate and high altitude.[28] As the gateway to "the sanatorium of the world," as Colorado came to be known, Denver had a reputation to protect.

In 1876, concerns mounted when seven deaths were reported from tuberculosis contracted in Denver. Previously, deaths from tuberculosis had all been linked to cases from outside the state. By the 1880s, it was estimated that as many as one-third of the city's population—10,000 people—had come down with the disease.[29] Though there was no evidence to prove that tuberculosis was more prevalent among the Chinese than other city residents, the Denver Medical Association issued dire warnings that precautions were needed to prevent the outbreak of epidemics, citing downtown Denver, where Chinatown was located, as a place of particular concern. After the typhoid epidemic of 1879–80, the Denver City Council was galvanized into action, creating a Board of Health, authorizing planning for the city's first sewage system, and passing health ordinances that began to be enforced in 1881.

It was in this context that Denver's Chinatown was singled out as a warren of disease that needed to be eradicated. The area was vulnerable because the reputation of Chinatowns as centers of contagion was by this time a part of Western folklore. Coloradans who had never set foot in Denver's Chinatown were familiar with the images of squalor, filth, and disease consistently evoked in descriptions of Chinatowns in San Francisco, Portland, Seattle, and New York. This made it easy for Denverites to accept such a view.

In 1883, acting on complaints by the Health Committee of the Denver City Council, police raided Chinatown and arrested fifteen residents, fourteen of whom were subsequently convicted of maintaining a public health nuisance at Sixteenth and Wazee Street, fined five dollars each, and ordered by the judge to keep their houses clean, like the white men in their vicinity.[30] In keeping with the now-familiar image of Chinatown as a health hazard, the RMN in 1889 depicted Wazee Street as an unwholesome place:

> The houses and yards were crowded with the almond-eyed citizens [and] a foul sickening stench come[s] from their houses which is disgusting in the extreme . . . most of the property is owned by a Chinaman named Ah Fee, and a reporter approached him for the purpose of finding out what he intended to do about the petition against his tenants. After [he] thoroughly understood the nature of the document he exclaimed: "Melican man alle go to helle. Ah Fee no leave his house. Me stay here and Chinamen alle stay here too."[31]

Although the indignant landlord Ah Fee is a comical figure, with his blunt response in pidgin English cutting through the niceties of the reporter's approach and the legalisms of the eviction petition, he also reveals a determination to remain in his home, just like any other resident of the city threatened with displacement.

In early 1889, the RMN led the crusade to eliminate the evils of Chinatown and relocate its "500 loathsome Chinese."[32] Describing Chinatown as a noisome hive that constituted a health and fire danger to the downtown business district, the newspaper advocated its destruction and replacement with more reputable establishments. The Board of Health supported the call for cleaning up Chinatown. Even though there had not been an outbreak of disease, it was perceived as a potential "breeding ground [for all] kind[s] of . . . diseases from mumps to yellow fever."[33]

Condemnation of Denver's Chinatown as a health hazard reached its apex a year later, with the discovery of a case of the bubonic plague in San Francisco's Chinatown on March 6, 1900. As the outbreak spread, in May 1900, Walter Wyman, supervising surgeon general of the US Marine Hospital Service, ordered the inoculation of all Chinese and Japanese in San Francisco with an experimental vaccine (Haffkine prophylactic), even though it was known to have serious side effects and could sometimes be fatal. At the same time, Colorado governor Charles S. Thomas (Democrat) simultaneously closed the state's border to Chinese and Japanese, seeing them all as potential disease carriers.[34] In a letter to Secretary of State John Hay, Thomas argued that his action was not racially motivated, even though it was confined to Chinese and Japanese. In any case, such actions contributed to an image of Asians as a "contagious yellow peril."[35]

CHINESE DENVERITES

The Chinese who originally moved to Denver did so just as the city was expanding in size and population. Their increase in numbers paralleled the city's growth: in 1870, there were only four Chinese in a city of 4,759; in 1880, only 238 of 35,629.[36] After the 1880 race riot, one might have expected the Chinese to abandon Denver altogether. Instead, they chose to remain. In 1885, five years later, the Chinese population had actually grown to 461, mirroring the growth of the city's general population, which had increased to 61,491. In both cases, the populations had nearly doubled in size. By 1890, the population of Chinatown had reached its apex of 980.

A growing population brought a greater demand for and diversification of services and shops within Chinatown. According to sociologist Xi Wang, in 1885, most of the 461 (largely male) residents worked as laundrymen, but some engaged in other occupations. There were also three servants, six cooks, two porters, nine shopkeepers, two doctors, three clerks, seventeen cigar makers, four grocers, a butcher, three barbers, and a restaurant worker.[37]

Most of the businesses provided ethnic-related goods and services, allowing the Chinese to live in a more self-sufficient community. The shopkeepers carried goods imported directly from China. For their customers, the stores reportedly offered merchandise such as "herbs, lichee nuts, Chinese ginger, tea, canned fruits, sugar cane, pickled bamboo shoots, birds' nests, various kinds of sauces and relishes, incense sticks, jewelry, silks, and clothing."[38] They also served a white clientele who were attracted to luxury goods, especially silks.

Chinese medicine was among the services that could be found. Though legally prohibited from practicing medicine, Chinese doctors dispensed traditional herbal remedies to local residents. Some developed busy practices and even competed for patients by advertising their qualifications and specialties in English newspapers. One of the most prominent was Dr. Young Bong, who owned a store on Sixteenth Street. He was well known in Denver society. According to a laudatory description, he was "a finely educated gentleman, speaking and writing English quite as well as the best educated citizen in Colorado."[39] According to other biographical details, he had arrived in the country only eight years earlier, spending the last six in Colorado working as a common laborer, mostly in the Central City area, where he learned English without the aid of an instructor.

The early Denver Chinese had limited employment prospects. They were automatically excluded from those occupations that placed them in direct competition with whites. Nevertheless, they were able find work in service occupations that white men usually avoided, notably as laundrymen. Seeing the demand for laundry services, enterprising Chinese began opening hand laundries in the 1870s, following the example of Chinese in California, who had monopolized the business. Starting a hand laundry was comparatively easy, requiring no more than a scrub board, an iron and ironing board, and a small place in which to work. The laundrymen, or "washee" men as they were commonly called, cleaned clothes in the back of their laundries but ironed them in the front to attract customers.

A hand laundry was easy to operate since it required little skill and little knowledge of the English language. Customers were given tickets as claim checks for their laundry written in Chinese. These tickets had to be handed back when the laundry was claimed. As Denverites were informed in 1880, "When John receives a man's 'washee,' he gives a ticket, with queer-looking hieroglyphs spread over the brown piece of paper. The man must present this ticket, or else he wears a dirty shirt for another week. Sometimes a policeman comes and vouches for the customer. This is done by showing his star; otherwise, John would demand: 'No ticket, no washee!'"[40]

That concluding phrase, "No Ticket, No Washee," is one of the earliest versions of the familiar phrase "No Tickee, No Washee," which came to be indelibly linked with the Chinese and has since entered the common vernacular. While the phrase makes fun of the Chinese, it also shows that they have some power over their white patrons—without the ticket, there is no getting back the shirt unless the police are called in.[41] As a business that required few resources, laundry work allowed a common laborer to gain some control over his economic destiny by enabling him to become an independent businessman. Back in China, being a laundryman counted as a legitimate occupation and gave a worker a modicum of status, even though in America it was a low-prestige occupation, regarded as women's work.

Eventually, most Chinese Denverites made their living as laundrymen. In 1870, Chinese ran only three of the forty-five laundries in Denver. But by the end of the decade, the Chinese may have operated as many as 130 of the city's 262 laundries. According to the 1889–90 report by the Colorado Bureau of Labor Statistics, by 1890, there were three hundred Chinese laundrymen working in the city; in its 1891–92 report, of the 589 Chinese men listed, 405 worked as laundrymen. The growing Chinese dominance over the Denver laundry business seems to have been a source of irritation to the compilers of the reports. This is shown in annotations complaining that Chinese laundrymen were depriving a large number of whites from earning a decent living, a common charge against Chinese, as we have seen.[42] For example, one report notes that "no less than 1,200 more white persons would find employment at washing in the city . . . were there no Chinamen here."[43] Given the numbers provided, that would mean each Chinese did the work of three white persons, a striking tribute to imagined Chinese productivity.

Since they were unable to outwork the Chinese, white laundrymen sought to curtail their business hours by asking the city council to pass an ordinance that forbade the Chinese from opening their laundries on Sundays. As usual, whites considered the Chinese to be unfair competitors, complaining that their competitiveness was "a species of rivalry that smacks of convict labor."[44] At the same time, they noted that an ordinance might prove pointless, since keeping Chinese laundries from opening on Sundays did not prevent Chinese from working behind closed doors.

The Chinese hand laundry became a common sight in other Colorado cities as well, attracting the same criticisms everywhere. By 1881 in Pueblo, there were ten laundries employing forty-five Chinese workers, each of whom earned twenty dollars a week.[45] The *South Pueblo Banner* claimed they were depriving whites, particularly white women, of remunerative wages. In 1898, the employment of only two Chinese laundrymen in the State Insane Asylum in Pueblo was enough to cause an uproar.[46] Until steam laundries displaced the hand laundries at the end of the nineteenth century, the Chinese had a virtual monopoly on the Denver laundry business. Around 1900, when the Chinese were forced out of laundry work through discriminatory practices and the development of steam laundries, they began opening restaurants. This was the origin of the now-ubiquitous Chinese restaurant that caters to the general population.

Nevertheless, not all Chinese were forced to engage in menial work to survive. A few did better than that. Among them, none was more prominent than Chin Lin Sou, Chinatown's first "mayor." But as his life story illustrates, even he found it impossible to lead a completely independent existence beyond Chinatown.

CHIN LIN SOU: "WHITE CHINAMAN"

Like most Chinese pioneers, Chin Lin Sou was from southern China.[47] He was born on September 29, 1836, in Canton (Guangzhou), Guangdong Province.[48] Chin was atypical for a Chinese in his appearance. He was tall (at least six feet two inches in height) and had blue-gray eyes, characteristics that suggest his family may have originated in northern China.

In 1859, Chin emigrated from Canton to San Francisco. After mining for gold in California for a few years, he went to work for the Transcontinental Railroad. Chin was the foreman of the first Chinese crew who helped build the Central Pacific portion. He was probably selected because of his commanding height as well as his command of English, which he worked assiduously to perfect. In 1877, the *Weekly Register-Call* remarked that Chin spoke "English fluently as anyone and [was] a man of great executive ability and intelligence."[49]

Chin's fluency in Cantonese and English made him the interface between the owners of the Central Pacific and its Chinese workers. Under his leadership, the Chinese workers surmounted the formidable Donner Pass, blasting through the mountains and laying track through snow to get the job done. On April 20, 1869 (thereafter known as Victory Day), between sunrise and sunset, they laid an extraordinary ten miles of track across the Utah desert, bringing the Central Pacific within ten miles of the Union Pacific.

FIG. 3.1. Chin Lin Sou,
c. 1880s. History Colorado,
Stephen H. Hart Library and
Research Center, 10028088.

Twenty days later, on May 10, 1869, the Central Pacific and Union Pacific Railroads were joined at Promontory Summit, Utah, and the Transcontinental Railroad was completed, an achievement that is widely regarded as the greatest technological feat of the nineteenth century.

After being discharged from the Central Pacific, its rival, the Union Pacific, employed Chin and some of the other Chinese workers to redo its tracks so that they met government standards. Later, he was hired to construct secondary railroad lines connecting what would eventually be the states of Utah, Wyoming, and Colorado. He recruited and supervised Chinese workers to construct the Denver Pacific Railroad, connecting Denver to the Transcontinental Railroad. With this vital connection, Denver had access to national markets; without it, the city would have remained a backwater, or might even have become a ghost town, rather than becoming the "Queen City of the West." Once these offshoots of the Transcontinental Railroad were completed, Chin found himself in the Colorado Territory, where he became involved in mining activities.

In 1871, Chin moved to Black Hawk, Colorado, where he was employed by Warren Thomas to supervise three hundred Chinese miners. Over a decade earlier, in 1859, gold was discovered in Gregory Gulch, bringing a pack of prospectors into the area. As discussed in chapter 2, until the mid-1860s, white miners engaged in hard-rock mining, extracting the gold from the surface veins. Having exhausted the mines, they left them to later miners like the Chinese, who were willing to engage in the arduous work of placer mining to extract the residual gold deposits.

In 1873, Chin was employed by the Cameron brothers to oversee forty-five Chinese laborers at their placer-mining site near Central City, Colorado. While working for them, Chin also worked some mines of his own. Unlike most miners, Chinese or otherwise, he actually hit pay dirt. He sold two of his mines and became a wealthy man. It is said that Chin was able to make an initial deposit at the National Bank in Central City of sixty thousand dollars, an extraordinary sum of money at the time. Reportedly, upon seeing this sum, "the eyes of the clerks bulged out."[50]

In addition to working as a labor contractor, Chin was an entrepreneur who later owned and leased land, mainly abandoned mines no longer considered profitable. In association with the Six Companies of San Francisco, he owned a successful trading company that imported food, clothing, and furniture from China to the United States. He was the only Chinese to be listed in the Gilpin County tax records for the year 1874.[51] However, when he undertook a business venture, he found it prudent, if not absolutely necessary, to do so in partnership with a white friend or associate. For example, he owned stores in Nevadaville and Smith's Hill, Colorado, in partnership with Edward L. Thayer, the contractor who supplied Chinese miners to Como (see chapter 2).

Chin was finally able to settle down and bring his wife to the United States after a ten-year separation. The couple moved to Fairplay, then Como, and finally Denver's Chinatown. They had six children, all of whom were born and raised in the United States, making the Chins the first Chinese American family raised in Colorado. His daughter Lily was referred to as the richest Chinese woman in America and known as the "Queen of Chinatown." In keeping with the ostentatious style of the Gilded Age, she wore an imported wedding dress costing one thousand dollars and was festooned with five-dollar gold pieces during her three-day wedding celebration. In an age when most Chinese were relegated to Oriental schools, Chin's son Willie graduated from Denver's public primary

FIG. 3.2. Chin Lin Sou's family, c. 1914. From left to right: William Chin, Mamie Chin, May Gold Chin, Ruth Chin, Daisy Chin, Frances Chin, James Chin Jr., Wawa Chin, Lily Look (Lily Ling Sou), James Lin Chin, and Esther Chin. History Colorado, Stephen H. Hart Library and Research Center, 10044087.

and high schools. Later, Willie sent his own children to college. Chin's granddaughters owned the Lotus Room and the New China Restaurants, two popular Denver Chinese restaurants. His great-granddaughter became the first Chinese woman in the Denver police force, and his fifth-generation descendants still live in the Denver metropolitan area.

Besides being able to establish a family in Colorado, Chin had the additional distinction of becoming an American citizen. At the time, the 1790 Naturalization Law stipulated that only free white persons were eligible for citizenship. However, the rule was not applied uniformly across the nation. During the 1870s, petitions for naturalization were reviewed by local courts, allowing Chin to apply for and obtain citizenship.[52] Chin became a leader in the Chinese community. He made his home in Denver's Chinatown and in 1870 was considered its first mayor—that is, the spokesman for the community.[53] He was a prominent member of the local branch of the Chee Kong Tong (also romanized as Chih-kung t'ang and Zhigongtang), a benevolent organization and a political party. The Chee Kong Tong backed Dr. Sun Yat-sen, the so-called George Washington of China. Chinese Coloradans responded to Sun's appeal for financial assistance to support the overthrow of the Qing dynasty and replace it with a republic. Sun's vision of a strong China would mitigate the mistreatment of Chinese in America. As the eminent sociologist Rose Hum Lee observes, "The emigrants believed that their return to rejoin their families and show economic attainment could only be realized through supporting Dr. Sun's revolutionary movement and a change of government."[54] When the Wuchang Uprising broke out on October 10, 1911, precipitating the Xinhai Revolution that overthrew the Qing dynasty, Sun was in Denver raising money. At the old theater on Twentieth and Market Streets, he raised five hundred dollars before returning to China, where he was elected the provisional president of the Republic of China.

Because of Chin's reputation as an honest man, he was offered the office of Central City marshal. He turned down the offer, claiming that being Chinese gave him enough problems to manage. Such was the case on May 21, 1874, when Chinese were blamed for accidentally setting Central City afire while allegedly performing "a religious ceremony which required the burning of joss sticks and the sprinkling of myrrh and incense on live coals."[55] The townspeople were so angry that they wanted to lynch the Chinese responsible for the conflagration. Fortunately for the Chinese, they were spirited away before the enraged townspeople could harm them.

Chin felt compelled to defend his countrymen and set the record straight. On May 25, 1874, the *Daily Central City Daily Register* reported his comments:

> Chinese are too frequently made the victims of circumstances which any
> other nationality would escape without censure, and they desire to have their
> side of the case represented as it is. [Chin] asserts in the most positive manner
> that the . . . occupants of the house . . . were not engaged in any religious
> or funeral rites or ceremonies; were not celebrating a holiday as has been
> asserted. . . . [The Chinese] believe the accident was caused by a defective flue,
> or in an undiscovered parting of the pipe communicating with the chimney.[56]

Because of the high regard in which Chin was held, the newspaper concluded, "We are bound to accept [Chin's] story as much more truthful than any which have been previously reported."[57]

After a protracted illness, Chin Lin Sou died on August 10, 1894, and was buried in Denver's Riverside Cemetery. At the funeral, leaders of Denver's Chinese and white communities both expressed their admiration for Chin. Reverend George F. Seiver began his eulogy with the words "The mayor of Chinatown is dead." He went on to say that Chin was more "American than many of us gathered here today who were born in the United States. He lived Americanism."[58] E. L. Harris, one of Chin's business friends, said he was a man of "fine personality, strictly honest in business, and respected by all who knew him."[59] Later, the McFarlane and Kruse families, leading patrons of the famous Central City Opera House, honored Chin by dedicating a hickory chair to him there.[60] Intending to offer a compliment, the RMN obituary referred to Chin as the "White Chinaman" who had many white friends.[61]

In the decades that followed, Chin's image became even "whiter," and he was praised for possessing traits other Chinese lacked. A 1919 article on frontiersmen in *Farm and Field* described him as "more progressive than most of his sleepy race, " "as strong as a crowbar and as brave as a lion when it came to tackling the affairs of life," and "full of the unconquerable ambition to succeed where the Yankee spirit had laid down."[62] However, admired though he was, Chin was never able to advance beyond the Chinese community. In spite of his acknowledged intelligence and long years of experience, it is telling that he never managed white employees or occupied a leadership position outside of the Chinese community. He and his family resided in Chinatown rather than in the general Denver community, probably for the same reasons other Chinese did—it was safer.

On February 18, 1977, as part of the Colorado Centennial-Bicentennial observance, Chin Lin Sou was commemorated with a stained-glass portrait installed in one of the four "heritage windows" in the old Supreme Court room in the State Capitol, which were created for the event to recognize the contributions of representatives of the state's major ethnic groups (Latinos, Native Americans, blacks, and Asians). Unlike the other three windows, which are each devoted to a single individual, the Asian window is split. Chin's portrait occupies the upper half of the window, while a portrait of Naoichi "Harry" Hokazono, a Japanese labor contractor, occupies the bottom half of the window (see chapter 6 for an

FIG. 3.3. Stained glass windows honoring Chin Lin Sou and Naoichi "Harry" Hokazono in the old Supreme Court room in the State Capitol, Denver, Colorado. Photo by Jim Steinhart of TravelPhotoBase.com.

account of Hokazono's life).[63] The continuing distortion of images of Chinese Coloradans in the contemporary view is illustrated by a peculiarity in Chin's portrait. In the stained-glass window, Chin is shown dressed in a red Mandarin-collar jacket, but in the original photograph on which the portrait is based, he is wearing a Victorian coat and shirt with collar and cravat. As Chin's great-great-granddaughter Linda Jew observes, this is a significant alteration.[64] Perhaps the purpose was to make Chin adhere to a stereotype of what a Chinese should look like, though his life was a demonstration that such images were inaccurate. It is ironic that while seeking to honor Chin as a Colorado pioneer, the artist has converted him into a public representation of John Chinaman.

A STRANGE NEIGHBORHOOD

As with other Chinatowns, then and now, Denver's served as a tourist destination, attracting visitors in search of exotic sights and sounds, not the least of which were the Chinese inhabitants themselves. Besides their physical differences, other aspects of their lives and customs were intriguing to white society, such as the predominance of men over women. Like other Chinese communities in America, Denver's Chinatown was primarily a bachelor society that had been established by necessity rather than choice. It provided few opportunities for family life. Although a little over half of the men who lived in Chinatown were married, most had left their wives and children in China. The majority had gotten married and had a child before leaving for America, giving them extra incentive to find work to provide for their own families as well as their parents. Whenever possible, they returned home for a while and fathered more children. Later, when their sons were of age, they often joined their fathers in America to work. Occasionally, wives came over, but only after the husbands had established themselves and could maintain the family. Merchants rather than laborers were usually the ones who could afford to do so. On the whole, Chinese bachelors lived lonely lives. Except for work, they had little to occupy their leisure time. They sought diversion by playing *xiangqi* ("elephant chess") or *weiqi* (popularly known as "Go"), reading Chinese newspapers, drinking tea, and sharing stories of home in China. And like other men in Western frontier communities, they indulged in gambling and drinking, frequented brothels, and smoked opium.

Americans found Chinatowns populated mainly by men to be peculiar communities where the males made a living by engaging in so-called women's work, cleaning clothes and cooking food. This led to the mistaken belief that somehow Chinese were sexually different. Political cartoons from the period implied that Chinatowns were congregations of impenitent sinners, living in a Sodom and Gomorrah where homosexuality was rampant. By way of explanation, East Asian studies scholar Jean Pfaelzer suggests that "these hostile caricatures may have derived from homophobic fears surrounding crowded all-male mining communities, small-town boardinghouses, and tent camps where men cooked and sewed for themselves."[65] These fears were expressed through public anxiety, hostility, and mockery of Chinatown inhabitants.

Accentuating the abnormality of Chinatown's skewed gender distribution were the sartorial differences that set Chinese apart. Except on special occasions, Chinese men tended to wear shapeless black cotton pants and blouses and umbrella-shaped hats made of split bamboo or grass. Perhaps their most distinguishing feature was their hairstyle, which consisted of a shaven pate and a queue. For the Han Chinese, the predominant ethnic group in China, this was not their natural hairstyle but rather one forced on them. In 1644, the Shunzhi emperor of the newly established Qing dynasty required all Han Chinese males to shave their foreheads and wear a queue in the Manchu style as a symbol of their submission to the Qing. This decree placed Chinese in an awkward situation, to say the least. On the one hand, obeying the decree to shave their hair violated the Confucian belief stated in the *Classic of Filial Piety* that "one's body, hair and skin are inherited from one's parents, so one should not dare to mutilate them."[66] On the other hand, disobeying the decree meant arrest and execution. Their dilemma was captured in the popular saying "Lose your hair and keep your head, or keep your hair and lose your head" (*liutou bu liufa, liufa bu liutou*). Chinese queues attracted much ridicule from mainstream Americans, who derided them as women's "pigtails," but cutting them off was not an option for most. If a Chinese man ever wanted to see his family in China again, he needed to have his queue intact. For him, the queue constituted a physical passport.

Although whites found the ways of the Chinese strange, they appreciated the custom of the Chinese New Year celebration, with the posting of colorful red paper banners conveying good wishes and invoking good luck for the coming year, a dragon parade, and, of course, fireworks. Chinese New Year (also known as the Lunar New Year in other parts of Asia) is the most important Chinese holiday. In China, the comparatively long celebration begins on the first day of the first month of the lunar calendar and ends on the fifteenth day, with the Lantern Festival. In America, a much-abbreviated version was celebrated, lasting no more than a few days. Chinese as well as their non-Chinese friends visited one another to deliver New Year's greetings, partake of delicacies, and exchange gifts. It provided an opportunity for people to set aside differences and extend their hospitality to one another. Since the observance dovetailed with the American winter holidays, Chinese also celebrated Christmas. Joseph Emerson Smith, doyen of newspapermen in Denver, recalled the occasion fondly:

> We youngsters of Denver were all for our yellow friends. My very first recollection of Christmas day is associated with our Chinese laundryman. . . . Early Christmas morning our Chinese laundryman appeared grinning as mother opened the door to his knock. "Melly Clismas!" he said. "Clismas gif!" He handed mother a beautiful gold encrusted vase, a blooming Chinese lily . . . in an exquisite blue and white bowl. . . . He gave my little sister and myself packages of assorted firecrackers and bags of candy and those delicious round thin-shell nuts containing a fruity meat tasting like sugared honey and spices. And on each he bestowed with his wide grin and jerky bows a big tin of Chinese ginger.[67]

What comes through clearly in this nostalgic remembrance is the way in which the nameless laundryman uses Christmas as an occasion to show his respect and appreciation for each member of Smith's family, through his carefully chosen gifts. But this is not an exchange between equals. Implicit in the description is Smith's matter-of-fact acceptance of the laundryman's deference to his family because of their superior social status, which he enjoys even as a boy, and his view of the older Chinese man as a comical figure, with his "wide grin" and "jerky bows."

The Chinese New Year celebration became a popular event in Denver, attracting tourists to Chinatown. On one night in 1910, it was estimated that three thousand visitors came to Chinatown to participate in the festivities. Elements of the celebration were incorporated into local events. From 1895 to 1902, the Chinese participated in the Festival of Mountain and Plain, an annual celebration of pioneer days in the Old West held in early October in Denver. In the parade, they carried a long Chinese dragon made of phosphorescent silver cloth, which was later renamed the Silver Serpent in honor of Colorado's silver mines. In 1897, the year that Chin

FIG. 3.4. Chinese dragon in the Festival of Mountain and Plain, by James B. Brown, c. 1900. Chinese men carry a long, flexible figure of a dragon, which is believed to possess awesome powers that include wisdom and auspiciousness. Denver Public Library, Western History Collection, X-18242.

Poo headed the Chinese committee for the parade, the Chinese spent over twenty thousand dollars on their floats and on gorgeous costumes for their three hundred participants. They even fielded a Chinese band.[68] Their active involvement in the festival was a statement of their commitment to Colorado. It was also an expression of pride in their Chinese origins as well as a desire to have their cultural heritage recognized by the public at large. As such, the festival was an opportunity to express cultural affinity with rather than political loyalty to China.

If whites found Chinese New Year acceptable, they found Chinese religions—Confucianism (which whites considered a religion rather than a philosophy), Daoism, Buddhism, and local folk religions—less so. Chinese religions were family focused and pluralistic. Like all religions, they provided spiritual solace and a moral compass for everyday life. Unlike Western religions, however, Chinese religions did not require their members to adhere to any one of them exclusively. Western missionaries found this to be at the very least illogical, since the major tenets of these various Chinese religions seemed to be mutually exclusive. According to the influential missionary Arthur H. Smith, by practicing plurality in religion, the Chinese had committed a grave error in "carry[ing] intellectual hospitality to the point of logical suicide."[69] Because of their lack of familiarity with Chinese religions, Americans tended to conflate them and condemned them all as idolatrous.

"Heathen Chinee" was, in fact, among the commonest epithets used for Chinese, suggesting the importance of linking them with paganism in the formation of Western notions of their identity. The phrase itself, with its faux pidgin coinage "Chinee," never lost its currency after it was first popularized in 1870 in a widely circulated poem by Bret Harte about a hapless Chinese cardsharp (which had nothing to do with religion).[70] However, the phrase took on a life of its own, perhaps because it perfectly summed up the difficulty of what to think about the Chinese. On the one hand, Chinese were souls in need of salvation, potential converts deserving of compassion, the focus of American missionary work; on the other hand, they were suspected of being confirmed pagans who rejected Christianity and, by extension, Western values.

Wherever they went, Denver included, Chinese established temples where they could pray, meditate, and hold meetings. These temples were called "Joss houses" ("Joss" is supposedly derived from the Portuguese *deus*, meaning "God.") According to one description, the Denver Chinatown's Joss house consisted of a small room painted in red and gold, with other bright colors. At one end was a table, which served an altar on which were placed candles and other ritual objects. Behind the altar was a large picture of three deities.[71] In 1889, the Joss house was attacked and pillaged by a detachment of Salvation Army soldiers from the Curtis Street headquarters who carried away images and other sacred relics.[72] In 1890, the Joss house became the center of contention within the Chinese community as an important token of legitimacy, as the rival Chin Poo and John Taylor factions each sought to relocate it to their new Chinatown centers, on West Blake and Market Streets, respectively.[73] In 1892, as mentioned earlier, the outsider Ling Choo challenged Chin Poo and John Taylor both by threatening to establish a grander temple on Wazee Street.[74] The rivalry reached a climax when plans were made in 1896 to import furnishings for a large and commodious new Joss house from China, including "twelve great bass idols, weighing tons," to be built on Market Street between Twenty-Second and Twenty-Third Streets.[75]

Coloradans were fascinated by reports of the practice of Chinese idolatry, as shown by the detailed and often fanciful descriptions of worship in the Joss houses. Of particular interest were descriptions of idols. Chinese deities were typically described as comical or grotesque: "an obese, pleasant-looking Mongolian" made a ridiculous warrior god; there was also the "bow-legged, cross-eyed caricature," the "monster," the "God of Chop Sticks" who was a "grub-god or idol of supplies," and the like.[76] But Chinese deities were also consistently represented as sinister. There were repeated reports that Chinese worshipped images of "Satan Himself" on their main altars and conducted Devil worship to bring good luck and to destroy their enemies, like the Japanese during the first Sino-Japanese War.[77] Such paradoxical portrayals of Chinese deities reflect the ambiguous role assigned to Chinese as both objects of ridicule and a threat to Western civilization, which played out in representations of them.

Whites also found some customs associated with Chinese religions peculiar, none more so than reverence for the dead. Chinese culture attaches great importance to the proper observance of funerary rites; it has been said that the entire Chinese ethical system grows out of them. Funerary rites are also closely linked to ancestor worship, which is an expression of Confucian filial piety, a deeply rooted civic value in Chinese society according to which a child remains loyal to parents even after they have passed away. Not even death can break these family bonds. The observance of funerary rites and other Chinese traditional customs contributed to community cohesion, which was particularly important in the inhospitable American West.

Chinese funerals were very different from the solemn Christian funerals of the time, where mourners dressed in black. They were raucous affairs, and mourners wore white. A Chinese funeral procession usually included a brass band playing loud music (similar to the jazz funerals of New Orleans). Mourners offered food, drink, and clothing to the deceased and "spirit money" was burned to make the individual's life in the next world as comfortable as possible. Whenever possible, the bones of the deceased were transported back to China to be buried with those of their ancestors. The repatriation of remains to China was one of the most important services provided by the Six Companies to the Chinese laborers they recruited.[78]

Chinese funeral processions attracted curious onlookers as well as the disrespectful who came to deride the ceremonies. In 1882, one such funeral procession drew a thousand people, only two hundred of whom were Chinese.[79] The crowd caused such a disturbance that the ceremony had to be postponed. As a precaution, during large funerals the police were called in to maintain order, though this was a temporary measure. In 1894, when a white mob disrupted the burial of Sun Wah, there were no police to protect the fifteen hundred Chinese attending the funeral service. In a rare public protest, the community leader John Taylor, who was presiding over the funeral, called for an end to such humiliations:

> If an American was buried in China and our people acted as disgracefully as did the Americans yesterday, there would be satisfaction demanded of our government. We have a right to be treated with respect. We obey your laws and pay our way. We don't ask any favors, but we expect to be left alone. The Chinese in Denver are well behaved, intellectual boys. They are willing to learn American ways and do as the Americans say; but when we bury our dead we want their bodies and their graves respected, as are the graves of the Americans. No Chinaman would treat an American like that.[80]

CHINESE CHRISTIANS

Devout Christians attempted to sever Chinese from paganism through religious conversion. This was an extension of the evangelical effort in China, where missionaries proselytized and encouraged the adoption of Western culture. Besides their evangelistic activities, the missionaries engaged in important philanthropic work, providing education or offering health care and other assistance, often combining the two as a matter of course. The missionaries who worked among the Chinese in America seem to have had more success than those in China. As of 1881, there were as many as sixty identifiable Chinese Christians in Denver affiliated with different Protestant churches.

Perhaps to separate themselves from the more unsavory elements of the Chinese community, a group of Chinese Christians moved further uptown, with homes on Lawrence Street at Seventeenth and Twentieth Streets. This area had the added distinction of having the first Chinese hotel in Denver. In 1901, the Central Theatre was remodeled and converted into a hotel with a store in front. This was reputed to be the only Chinese hotel between the West and East Coasts.[81] But the whiff of Chinatown followed the converts. The surrounding Christian neighborhood notwithstanding, the hotel was soon accused of having an opium parlor.

Edward D. Stoddard and his wife, Mary C. Cowdrey, were two of the most influential evangelists to work with Denver's Chinese. They were independent missionaries in China who continued proselytizing after moving to Denver.[82] As early as 1874, the Stoddards and other members of the Central Presbyterian Church established a Chinese Mission school on Fifteenth Street between Curtis and Champa Streets. They taught Chinese men English, both so they could read the Bible but also to help them function in society. Church documents record that as many as two hundred Chinese attended the school between 1901 and 1920. In 1905, the name of the school was changed to the Oriental Mission School to accommodate its Japanese, Korean, and Filipino students.[83]

Following the example of the Presbyterians, other churches established schools for local Chinese. In 1884, the various Protestant churches unified their educational efforts through the establishment of the Union Chinese Sunday School. It was situated in the Metropolitan Hotel on the corner of Sixteenth and Holladay Streets. As part of the conversion process, the evangelists gave the Chinese students bibles, gospel hymns written in Chinese, and English-Chinese dictionaries. Since Chinese were forbidden to attend public schools, these church-sponsored schools were important to the Chinese community because they offered one of the few opportunities to learn English. Learning English and, if possible, acquiring an education were important ways for the Chinese to empower themselves. Besides sponsoring schools to teach English-language classes, the churches engaged in other social service activities for their Chinese members. Sometimes that meant taking a stand on their behalf in times of crisis.

One such moment came during the Denver race riot on Sunday, October 31, 1880. As the riot raged, Reverend Dr. Henry C. Westwood offered a prayer for Chinese victims from his pulpit in the Central Presbyterian Church; he then delivered a sermon condemning the rioters and defending the right of the Chinese to be in the United States, during which he declared: "I claim to stand up for the rights of the Chinese, as well as of any other foreigners who may come to our shores. . . . I make these remarks as a Christian minister and an American citizen, a native of the 'Land of the Free and the Home of the Braves [sic],' of the country which has been believed to be the asylum of the oppressed of all nations. God pity the man who, claiming to be an American citizen, will not join me in denouncing the great wrong."[84] This was not mere rhetoric, for Westwood, along with other members of the congregation, then left the church and went into the streets to rescue as many Chinese as they could from the mob and escorted them to the police for protection. They were joined by other Denverites who placed themselves in harm's way to defend the Chinese simply because it was the decent thing to do.

While some Christians stood by the Chinese in their time of need, other whites were suspicious of them. Sinophobes thought that many Chinese conversions were insincere. They considered the converts frauds who had embraced their new faith for the sole purpose of attending Sunday school so they could learn English or "enjoy the misplaced kindness of the women teachers."[85] Worse yet, they suspected that some Chinese had converted to facilitate their criminal activities in smuggling Chinese into the country.[86] The motives for Chinese conversion to Christianity are difficult to ascertain, but they were as varied as the individuals themselves and probably reflected a combination of reasons. Certainly, among the converts there were true spiritual seekers who were drawn to the Christian faith, but there were also "Rice Christians" who converted for the material benefits that they could derive. Others may have done so as a step toward assimilation and acceptance by American society.

In the final analysis, being Christian often made little difference to most Americans, who continued to consider Chinese heathens because of their race. A case in point was the treatment of one Ah Sin, who was subpoenaed to testify at the trial for Look Young's murder, which occurred during the race riot. Though Ah Sin was a member of the Presbyterian Church, the defense attorney objected to his being sworn in using the usual oath-taking ceremony, in which a witness is asked, "Do you swear to tell the truth, the whole truth, and nothing but the truth, so help you God?" Because it was widely believed that Chinese were inveterate liars who cared little for religious oaths administered by authorities in the United States, the defense attorney insisted that Ah Sin perform another ceremony, involving the blowing out of a candle, after taking the oath.[87] Presumably, if Ah Sin failed to tell the truth, his life would be snuffed out like the extinguished candle. This ceremony made a mockery of Ah Sin's participation in the legal proceedings. So far as the general public was concerned, Ah Sin would always be a heathen incapable of fully acculturating into American society.

PATHOLOGICAL TRAITS

When they could afford it, Chinese indulged in the usual vices available to men on the American frontier. But what whites considered ordinary entertainment for themselves, they considered deviant behavior for Chinese men. More consequentially, whites constructed a Chinese identity around vices such as gambling, opium smoking, and illicit sex, framing the way in which Chinese were consistently viewed.

Much was made of Chinese prostitutes, for example, far more than their small number warranted. They were considered more morally degenerate and sexually perverse than their white counterparts. Their depravity was presumably due to their peculiar physiognomy. The Chinese women were accused of being the bearers of a particularly loathsome venereal disease, making them a physical as well as a moral threat to their white clients and, by extension, their families. If white men were unprotected from them, it was thought that Chinese women could conceivably contaminate not only individual bodies but the body politic itself. The next chapter will explore the world of Denver's Chinese prostitutes and consider their significance in the American West.

Receiving equal attention was the Chinese enjoyment of gambling. For Chinese workers, gambling was one of the few recreational outlets available to them. It offered the irresistible lure of striking it rich and then taking their immediate wealth and returning to China as prosperous men. The Chinese were legendary in the American West for their games of chance, such as the card games fan-tan and pi-gow (aka cowpie poker), and their willingness to risk their money on them. And Denver's Chinatown was *the* place to go find a game of chance—the "Mecca for Celestial Sports," the place where Chinese from all over the state came to gamble.[88] It was said that Chinese saved for an entire year for the opportunity to try their luck in one of Chinatown's many gaming establishments, often only to lose their hard-earned money.

According to a 1963 article in the *Denver Post* describing Chinatown's past, "Somewhere in 'Hop Alley' there [were] a number of gambling games in operation, but the police . . . found it almost impossible to search out these places and arrest the players."[89] This account, of course, emphasized the mysteriousness of the Chinese community. It was also disingenuous, since the locations of Chinese gambling houses were well known at the time not only to the Chinese but also to the larger gaming crowd in the city, including white patrons who visited them to indulge in their favorite games of chance, which later included faro and roulette.

In 1921, gambling games that had previously been held in secret were now held in public. On both sides of one street in Chinatown, Chinese lotteries and faro wheels were being operated in full view of the public. That year, a reform-minded municipal government acted on public complaints to mount police raids against the city's gaming establishments, resulting in the temporary closing of Chinatown's gambling parlors along with fourteen white ones. Within two months, they reopened, attracting gambling enthusiasts that included Mexican railroad laborers and Japanese and Russian farm workers. Despite periodic raids on Chinese gambling houses, the problem persisted. By the end of Chinatown's existence after World War II, however, gambling had become little more than a small-stakes social event.

The vice most closely identified with the Chinese was opium smoking.[90] "The Heathen Chinee and the narcotic of death" arrived in Denver together in the 1870s, so far as the public was concerned.[91] A Denver revenue officer spoke for many when he said, "The opium habit is the very worst thing the Chinese have brought to this country and we should have laws for its suppression and then enforce them."[92] In 1880, the city had seventeen opium dens, twelve of them in Chinatown.[93] Citizens thought that most Chinese were opium fiends. One of history's cruel ironies is that while opium was legal in nineteenth-century Denver, it was illegal in China. The Qing dynasty condemned its sale and consumption, calling it "foreign mud" because Westerners, including Americans, smuggled it into the country. In the course of trying to suppress drug traffic, the Qing dynasty fought the Opium War (1839–42) against Britain, the British being the principal smugglers of the narcotic into China. Having lost the conflict, opium traffic continued in China for another century, while it was eventually condemned in the United States and elsewhere.

Certainly there were Chinese who smoked opium, but they were mostly social smokers. Included among them was Denver's first Chinese policeman, Louis Johnson (Kan Yun Yu), who, while explaining the operations of the city's opium dens to a white reporter in 1881, casually admitted that he "hit the pipe occasionally when [he had] a headache."[94] By 1894, high-quality opium was also being produced in Denver's Chinatown; it was seized by federal customs and revenue agents not because it was illegal to manufacture opium, but because the producers had not paid the required internal revenue tax on it.[95] In fact, opium dens flourished in Chinatown because of the large number of white patrons.[96] Before World War I, according to retired police captain Tom Russell, 60 percent of the dens' customers were addicts from uptown Denver.[97] While opium smoking was socially frowned upon, there was no law against it until the Harrison Narcotics Act of 1914. By 1915, the RMN was optimistically reporting that, because of the Harrison Act, the "darkened dens" of Chinatown had disappeared and in their place were "300 respectable hardworking Chinamen who are anxious to follow the customs of their white brethren."[98]

Given that most Chinese in America did not use drugs, why were they portrayed as addicts? The late *Denver Post* columnist Ed Quillen's explanation is that this past portrayal was part of the process of getting rid of Chinese who were considered surplus labor since they were no longer needed to work on the transcontinental railroad.[99] Identifying the Chinese with opium was one way their opponents tried to discredit them. As Quillen wrote in his 1997 review of Henry O. Whiteside's *Menace in the West*:

> During the formative years of Colorado Territory, the menace was opium. It or its derivatives were common ingredients in patent medicines then used by all classes of society, but the smoking of opium was portrayed as the peculiar vice of Chinese laborers, who were despised anyway because they worked hard and cheaply. . . . Exposés of the opium dens or "hop joints" of Denver's Chinatown on lower Wazee Street were a periodic feature of the local press. Newspaper accounts worked the association of opium smoking with the Chinese to the mutual discredit of both. . . . Then came published fears that white people were acquiring the vile habit."[100]

Quillen notes that Whiteside's work shows that the identification of Chinese with opium consumption was a part of a discernible pattern in the maligning of minority groups in general: "First create press hysteria over some substance. Tie that substance to a minority group, and fabricate fears that the plague is spreading into the majority population."[101] Three years later, Quillen revisits this issue in his column "Of course the Drug War is bigotry in action. What else is new?" He cites the Western historian Richard Wright, who points out that "associat[ing] immoral activities with particular ethnic and racial groups" is the key step. Thus, "attacks on drugs and prostitution became attacks on Chinese, who were supposedly drug addicts. . . . Such efforts were far more successful at punishing or driving off minority groups than in eradicating the evils under attack."[102]

The construction of Chinese identity around images of vice continued into the early twentieth century. Irresponsible journalistic accounts were supported by biased government reports. One example is the Colorado Bureau of Labor Statistics' biennial report for 1901–1902, with its dramatic findings on Chinatown's opium dens and gambling parlors: "If the secrets of Chinatown were published, while the exposure would no doubt involve many who occupy good positions in society, it would expose to the public gaze a condition of immorality, vice, crime, and indecency that would cause the masses of the people to rise up in righteous indignation and remove this plague spot from their midst."[103] Actually, "the secrets of Chinatown" never needed to be published because the insinuations were repeated so often that they were already believed. To the public at large, the Chinese *were* the conveyors of social disease.

DECLINE OF CHINATOWN

Though the repeated efforts to evict Denver's Chinese community because of its various social ills all failed, the 1880 race riot came close to doing so. In spite of this horrific event, most Chinese chose to rebuild their community. It was their home, after all. In doing so, they declared that their future lay in the United States; just as countless other immigrants have done before and after them. In the aftermath of the riot, they tried to improve relations with the white population through the establishment of the Chinese Mutual Protective Association, a service organization that sought to safeguard and represent the interests of the Chinese in its interactions with mainstream society. But there were larger national and international forces at work against which the Chinese had no recourse.

What sounded the Chinatown community's death knell were the exclusion laws beginning in 1882 that prohibited the entry of emigrants from China. For Sinophobes, these laws were the final solution to the Chinese problem. Such strictures ensured that the Chinese population would remain small in size. With so few Chinese women, there was no significant increase in population to replace those who passed away. The few young people who grew up in Chinatown tended to leave in search of opportunities denied them in Colorado. Those who remained in Denver tried to survive the best they could, finding work mainly in local Chinese restaurants.

With the passage of time, it could be reasonably anticipated that the Chinese population would diminish in size and eventually disappear altogether.[104] From about 1880 to 1930, the Chinese population in the United States declined nearly 30 percent, from 105,465 to 74,954. The Chinese population in Colorado likewise decreased, though paradoxically it went through an initial growth spurt, growing from 612 to 1,398 in the 1880s. Attacks on Chinese in the American West caused many to gravitate toward Colorado even though it, too, experienced a paroxysm of violence. They fled to Chinatown, which enjoyed a brief renaissance. After reaching its peak in 1890, Denver's Chinese population began to decline. By the end of the century the state's Chinese population had steadily dwindled: from 599 in 1900, to 373 in 1910, to 291 in 1920, and to 233 in 1930. During the same half century, some twenty-eight million whites emigrated from Europe to the United States.

By 1940, the Denver Chinese population had fallen to a mere 110.[105] The residents consisted of three Chinese families—the Fongs, Looks, and Chins (lineal descendants of the previously discussed Chin Lin Sou)—and a group of elderly Chinese men. They lived in an area of abandoned, decaying buildings near other people of color who could not afford to live elsewhere. According to a report on Chinese women written at the time, "The living conditions are bad. There is no place for the children to play except on the street in a miserable neighborhood. Mexicans and Negroes with low ideals of life abound in this section of the city and make a bad situation worse."[106] During the post–World War II period, the neighborhood was considered a blighted area, subjected to urban renewal, and replaced by warehouses and small factories.[107] Denver's Chinatown was no more.

FOUR

IMPORTING CHINESE PROSTITUTES, EXCLUDING CHINESE WIVES

THE MOST VULNERABLE AND LEAST KNOWN CHINESE COLORA-
dans were the prostitutes who plied their trade in mining camps and
Denver's Chinatown. Chinese prostitutes joined the community early
on, the first group arriving in Denver in 1870.[1] Though powerless, they
played a significant role in Chinese American history. Besides their importance to the mostly male Chinese community, they became a symbol of all
that whites found abhorrent about Chinese. Moreover, Chinese prostitution became the pretext for the de facto exclusion of Chinese women from
the United States in 1875, which in turn set a precedent for the later exclusion of Chinese laborers in 1882.

The fate of Chinese prostitutes was markedly different from that of
Chinese laborers. Both were exploited, but the men hoped to return to
China someday if they could save enough money; if they died, at least their
bones would be repatriated. In contrast, indentured Chinese prostitutes
had no prospect of returning home in any form and little chance of
working off the debt they had incurred for their passage to America. The
women signed contracts promising to prostitute themselves for a certain
number of years. According to sociologist Lucie Cheng, the typical
contractual term was about four and a half years.[2] In actual practice, it was
usually longer because of penalties. The contract of one California brothel
specified that the penalty for working fewer than 320 days a year would
be one additional year of service. Another contract restricted women to
one month's rest leave per year for "menstruation disorders," after which
penalties would be assessed; one additional month was added if a woman
took more than fifteen sick days a year, one additional year for a pregnancy,
and, if the woman ran away, she had to reimburse the expenses incurred

for her return.[3] These might include bounties the brothel owner had paid to police to arrest her.

While Chinese men had supporters among those who wanted their labor (for example, the capitalists who collaborated with the Six Companies to recruit them), Chinese prostitutes had no advocates except for those who wanted to save them from "a life of sin." Although a few Chinese prostitutes became known publicly, most lived in the shadows, occupying the lowest rung in the demimonde social hierarchy, below white prostitutes, who had greater opportunities to integrate themselves into mainstream society.[4]

A CHINESE ROMANCE

The experience of the King sisters in Denver was exceptional in this context. Condemned to a grim existence in a Chinatown brothel from which there was little chance of escape, they found a way out through marriage. A summary of their improbable story sounds like fiction: "Chinese sex slaves flee cruel bondage to marry their childhood sweethearts and live happily ever after in Fairplay, Colorado." That is the gist of "A Chinese Romance," an article on the King sisters published in the *Daily Denver Tribune* on June 1, 1874.[5] The article is a more detailed version of one published in the *Rocky Mountain News* the previous day, entitled "Chow Chow."[6] Both seem to have been written by the same person, prominent writer and newspaperman J. P. C. Poulton, who identifies himself in his private papers as the reporter who witnessed the events.[7] This account is atypical of coverage of Chinatown in its focus on women. It offers a rare glimpse into the lives of those caught up in the commercial sex trade as well as insight into how the public perceived them.

According to "A Chinese Romance," King Yow and King Yok were two orphaned sisters. They were sold to the Hok Yop Tea and Coolie Importing Company of San Francisco to serve as prostitutes in Denver's Chinatown. An intermediary, one So Frane, "a worthless loafer in Canton" whose relationship to the girls was unknown, arranged their contract. Ah Fee and his brother Wah Kee, the owners of a gambling den and brothel on Wazee Street that was under the protection of the Hok Yop Tong, bought the sisters. At the Wazee Street brothel, the King sisters, along with fifteen other Chinese prostitutes, were put to work to pay off their passage fee, which was set at eight hundred dollars each. Their original term of service was two years, but when the contract expired Ah Fee refused to release them.

Women like the King sisters who were forced into the China-US sex trade began their ordeal in a Chinese treaty port such as Canton or Hong Kong, where they boarded a ship bound for San Francisco. Upon their arrival, they were sold to buyers like blacks at slave auctions in the antebellum South. Their degradation included being stripped and paraded in front of prospective customers. According to an 1881 report by Denver's first Chinese policeman, Louis Johnson, the women were bought in China for $250 to $350 each but sold in San Francisco for $300 to $800, with young girls fetching the highest prices.[8] Research suggests that most of the prostitutes were sixteen to thirty years old, although some were younger and a few were as old as fifty.[9] Some of the women were kidnapped, but many young women came voluntarily, lured by glowing descriptions of life in America. Their families, who falsely believed that they would be treated well, had sold most of the young girls outright. None of the women could have known the grim reality that awaited them.

Chinese American merchants purchased some of the women to serve as secondary wives, concubines, or domestics. They were the fortunate ones. As secondary wives or concubines, they would be inferior in status to the first wife, who was the matriarch, but they would at least be household members. If they gave birth, their offspring would be considered legitimate according to Chinese law and custom.

However, most of the women were sent to work in brothels in frontier towns or mining camps, where they became "wife to a hundred men" (in Cantonese, a *baak haak chai*). In town bordellos, they probably served as many as ten men daily and were subjected to abusive treatment, including beatings. Still, life there was preferable to that in the mining camps, where living conditions were worse and brutality commonplace. For sex workers, life was Hobbesian—nasty, brutish, and short. The average life of a prostitute was brief, lasting about four to five years before venereal disease or illness ended it. Which of them would not have been grateful to change their fate as the King sisters did?

According to the *Tribune* writer, the King sisters' would-be husbands, Loo Quong and Fong Lea, had known the girls in Canton when they were all children. After their old affection was rekindled in Denver, Loo and Fong decided to marry the sisters, but Ah Fee refused to free them. Loo and Fong retaliated by burning down two of Ah Fee's houses, but to no effect. Finally, Loo and Fong, with the assistance of men from the Sam Sing Tong, made a surprise raid on Ah Fee's "vile den" and succeeded in rescuing the King sisters.

From this point on, events in "A Chinese Romance" are determined by the intervention of whites, who represent the forces of law and order. In the presence of the *Tribune* reporter, the King sisters were married to their rescuers in a civil ceremony presided over by Judge Sayer and attended by some forty people, including members of the Sam Sing Tong and "washee-house men, town-swells, Tartar-courtesans and a few ordinary people who happened to wander into the court room when the ceremonies were about to take place."[10] Judge Sayer is described as "generously [declining] to enact his legal perquisites of the first kisses upon the brides; both of whom stood patiently waiting and blushing." Foreshadowing problems to come, the couples were photographed before they left the courthouse in case they were kidnapped later on by the Hok Yop Tong.

In addition to Judge Sayer, City Attorney Patterson also played an important role in determining the sisters' fate. He served as the sponsor for their marriage and then defended them as their lawyer when Ah Fee sought revenge later that day. After Ah Fee discovered that the sisters had escaped, he tried to prevent them from leaving town by accusing the older sister, King Yow, of stealing four hundred dollars from his pillow the previous night. She was arrested and jailed. Patterson contended that Ah Fee was lying. Without supporting evidence, the prosecution failed to prove larceny and the sister was set free.[11]

Meanwhile, Ah Fee sent at least twenty Hok Yop men, reportedly armed with pistols, to harass the Sam Sing bridal party once they left the courthouse. A detachment of police was called in to quell the confrontation and restore order once more. With their problems resolved, the two couples left Denver for Fairplay accompanied by forty Sam Sing men, who worked there as miners.

While the "Chinese Romance" appeared to head toward a happy ending—the prostitutes were redeemed from a life of sin through marriage—the author concludes with a prediction of future fighting in Fairplay involving Chinese hatchet men who work for the *tongs*: "There will be some Celestial blood spilled here before long, as the Sam Sing men threaten to marry all of the Hok Yop women." In keeping with the light-hearted depiction of violence in the article, the tone is droll but the reference to the *tongs* serves to remind readers that it is they who control Chinese prostitution and who will ultimately determine the women's fate. A more pessimistic reading has the King sisters continuing to serve as sex workers, though for the Sam Sing men. As Western historian Jan McKell notes, whites believed that even if Chinese prostitutes got married their husbands usually ended up pimping them.[12] The fact of the matter is that no one knows the fate of the King sisters since with their departure for Fairplay they disappeared from the historical record.

ORIENTALISM IN THE OLD WEST

The "Chinese Romance" narrative is a comic piece. Although the article's sympathies are clearly with the King Sisters rather than Ah Fee, its purpose seems less to inform the public about their plight than to entertain the public at their expense. However, it does provide some insight into white perspectives on Chinese sexuality.

The white readers of such stories saw Chinese people through an ideological lens that literary critic Edward Said has termed "Orientalism." As historian Henry Yu says in his analysis of Said's theory, Orientalism not only points to an underlying pattern in Western constructions of the East as separate, different, and inferior; it also explains the role of writing as the instrument for achieving colonial and racial domination. As Yu says, "Orientalism was not just a set of ideas that made an exotic object called 'Orient,' it was a set of relations of power, a form of knowledge that inscribed upon people all kinds of meanings about ignorance, inferiority, [and] sexuality; and most importantly, it embodied the desire for one set of people to dominate and control another."[13] However, Said is mistaken when he says that prior to World War II, Americans had neither a deeply invested tradition of Orientalism nor an imaginative investment in it because their frontier was the American West rather than the Orient.[14] On the contrary, it was precisely because America's frontier was the West that Americans were invested in Orientalism. In this context, Said's theory is useful in exposing the darker side of writings like "A Chinese Romance," with its playful but nonetheless effective degradation of the Chinese depicted therein.

The Wild West gave whites license to fantasize about the Chinese men and women they encountered there. To whites, Chinese appeared to be a different species with a constellation of defects. When filtered through an Orientalist mentality, Chinese and other Asians typically appear irrational, aberrant, backward, crude, inferior, deceptive, passive, feminine, and sexually corrupt. Asians in the American West were especially identified with licentious sex. Enterprising madams installed "Mikado parlors" in their bordellos to stimulate sexual fantasies.[15] These lavishly decorated rooms were meant to convey a sense of the luxurious but decadent Orient, where every whim of the imagination could be satisfied. Even young white boys would pay for a ten-cent "lookee" to see whether Chinese women had slanted vaginas.[16]

The world of "A Chinese Romance" is another Orientalist construct in which white fantasies about Chinese are acted out. Here, Chinese sexuality erupts but white men can be counted on to constrain it. The events in the first half of the story take place in a Chinatown brothel, a place of illicit sexuality, abasement of women, sadism, and confusion. The events in the second part of the story are set in a contrasting location, the city courthouse, where whites take charge, law and order reign, the weak are protected, women are treated with chivalry, and Chinese sexuality is normalized by Western marriage. The role of whites is to dominate Chinese for their own good, and readers can take pleasure in the story partly because it enacts this. The story arc suggests that maintaining order may be a continuing challenge since Chinese will always need controlling by whites. Violence and chaos to seem follow the Chinese wherever they go. This is evident as soon as the couples leave the courthouse. Hop Yok men threaten them, and once more, whites must intervene to instill order. But the prospect of more violence looms on the horizon when the Sam Sing men return to Fairplay with the Hok Yop women.

Readers are constantly reminded of the distance between themselves and the Chinese through references to the latter group's physical features, exotic customs, and strange-sounding names.[17] Loo and Fong are described as unappealing "tallow faced shaved headed lovers," emphasizing their peculiar appearance. They are also portrayed as childish—naïve in asking Ah Fee to give them the women, impulsive and violent in retaliating against him and then seeking to run away, and needing to be extricated by whites from the mess they have created. Except for their initial resistance to continued bondage, the King sisters are also characterized as passive victims whose destinies are determined by men, including their would-be saviors.

The tone of the narrative further encourages readers to distance themselves by emphasizing Chinese behavior as both cruel and ridiculous. The writer instills this image at the beginning of the article by describing what Ah Fee does to the older King sister when she demands her freedom. He "tied a cat to the girl's leg, and beat the girl about the room, causing the cat to scratch and bite the girl's legs in a manner most fearful." This curious scene deserves a closer look. Ah Fee's behavior fits the image of sadistic Chinese torturers who are able to transform the most innocuous objects into instruments of pain—in this case, a frightened cat. The use of the cat is suggestive because cats, with their distinctive eyes, are often used to symbolize Chinese, who are characterized as having sly, feline qualities.

The reporter's account of the farcical rescue of the King sisters resembles a scene out of the Keystone Kops. At least "twenty yelling and shrieking Chinese men and women" try to prevent the escape of the two girls, who improbably "[turn] complete summersaults over the carriage doors landing flat upon their backs in the arms of their . . . lovers." The carriage drives off "in a babel of confusion," with the Hok Yop men in hot pursuit. The seriousness of the situation is overshadowed by the circus-like antics of all involved.

By turning the King sisters' experience into comic melodrama, the writer preempts any serious concern about the welfare of the Chinese characters portrayed. Although the "Chow Chow" version concludes with a perfunctory condemnation ("It is a disgrace that a foreign company can, through their venal agents, hold women as slaves in free America"), the style communicates the message that these events are presented for the amusement of white readers rather than as a call for moral action. The incongruity between the pathos of the situation and the tone in which it is conveyed is emblematic of the greater disconnect between normative society and Chinatown, at least in the minds of whites. As for the author himself, Poulton's true feelings about his subject are disclosed in his memoirs recalling the event, in which he vents his disgust with all Chinese, concluding, "The Chinese are of no possible benefit to the country. On the contrary, they are a positive injury."[18] These remarks disclose a deep antipathy masked by the humorous tone, suggesting an underlying desire to degrade the subjects he portrayed.

The persistence of Orientalism in constructions of Chinese identity through the twentieth century is shown by their portrayals in Western narratives perpetuating familiar nineteenth-century stereotypes. In Westerns, Chinese female characters are limited to two main roles: depraved prostitutes ("Chinese Mary" characters) or sensual villainesses with designs on the white male protagonists. In both cases, they are invariably subordinate to male characters, both white and Chinese.

Director Robert Altman's *McCabe and Mrs. Miller* (1971) provides an example of how Chinese are constructed through white eyes. Although Altman's film is regarded as an anti-Western for its gritty portrayal of frontier life, it is quite conventional in the way it presents Chinese characters. The film is set in Presbyterian Church, a town located somewhere in the Pacific Northwest, though it could just as well be any small mining community on Colorado's Western Slope. *New York Times* film critic Vincent Canby describes the town as a "scenic mess of squalid shacks, bordered by an even more squalid ghetto for Chinese laborers," which is referred to by the white characters as "Chinkyville."[19] Altman's Chinese have no identity beyond what white characters project onto them. Throughout the film, white characters make derogatory remarks about Chinese people, revealing their own racism and ignorance. The Chinese are held in such low regard that, upon their arrival in town, one of Mrs. Miller's white prostitutes tells her companions that she will not fornicate with them, an attitude that helps to explain the importation of Chinese prostitutes. The character who is most clearly a white invention is the Chinese prostitute Masie, who never utters a word during the entire film. It is precisely Masie's silence that identifies her as an exemplar of the voiceless, objectified Oriental woman that Edward Said describes.[20] White men in the film pay to have sex with Masie because they think her vagina is slanted like her eyes and that she is adept at deviant sexual practices. She functions simply as an exotic. Her real anatomy as well as her culture is irrelevant because she is not part of the white world that Altman explores. She is a stereotype, pure and simple.

Altman's preference for using stereotypes in his otherwise realistic presentation of life on the frontier is evident in the film's final scene, during which Mrs. Miller drifts off into a drug-induced haze in a Chinese opium den. Even though Mrs. Miller possesses her own paraphernalia and could just as easily smoke opium in her own room, the setting implicitly reminds viewers that the drug is intimately associated with Chinese, and by extension, with moral degeneracy.

A MENACE TO AMERICAN MANHOOD

During the latter half of the nineteenth century, a serious disparity developed in the ratio of Chinese women to Chinese men in the United States, one that endured for more than a century. According to the conventional view, the reason so few Chinese women immigrated to the United States was that Chinese culture was patriarchal. Custom dictated that a married woman remain in China to care for her husband's parents and perform the mourning rites should her in-laws pass away, so keeping the wives at home guaranteed that the husbands would send remittances to sustain their families. Husbands were expected to eventually return home to fulfill their filial obligations. Until they did, maintaining their families in China was far more economical than attempting to do so in America. Only a wealthy merchant or well-off tradesman (or successful gambler) had the financial wherewithal to maintain a family in the United States. In some cases, of course, wives who were tired of caring for their in-laws or waiting for their husbands to return tried to join them. Another widely accepted explanation for the absence of wives was that Chinese immigrants had a sojourner's mentality. They were unwilling to bring their wives or send for them because they themselves did not plan to stay. However, historian George Anthony Peffer concludes from his study of Chinese female immigration to the United States that the central barrier to the entry of Chinese women was actually racial antipathy; the other reasons were secondary.[21]

This imbalance in the sex ratio of the Chinese in America gave rise to bachelor societies and the procurement of prostitutes to provide the men with sexual services. According to the 1880 national census, there were only 4,779 Chinese women in the United States, while there were as many as 100,686 Chinese men, a ratio of 4.5 percent women to 95.5 percent men. The gender ratio in Denver's Chinatown was somewhat better. There were at least 29 Chinese women among the 238 Chinese in Denver, or 12 percent women to 88 percent men. Actually, it is difficult to ascertain how many of these women were prostitutes since the statistics on them are unreliable. In her study of prostitutes in the American West, historian Anne E. Butler identified only three Chinese women among the 360 prostitutes of all nationalities plying their trade in Denver in 1870 to 1888, the great majority of whom were white.[22] This is almost definitely an undercount, since a local newspaper had reported the arrival of a shipment of Chinese women to Denver in June 1870.[23] Poulton refers to seventeen women in one Wazee street brothel in 1874 and William E. Roberts, a local fireman, reports that as many as forty prostitutes left the city after the 1880 race riot.[24]

Chinese prostitutes were worse off than their non-Chinese counterparts who worked in the Market Street red-light district adjacent to Chinatown. According to local historian Jan MacKell's study of prostitution in Colorado, white prostitutes were, more often than not, free agents who hoped—though mostly in vain—to "make money fast, marry well, and become socially acceptable."[25] By contrast, sociologist Lucie Cheng concludes that, after a brief "period of free competition" during which select Chinese prostitutes could exercise individual initiative and enterprise to make money and leave the trade (circa 1849–54), most of them fell into the net of organized trafficking monopolized by the *tongs*. Because of their race, they were abused in ways that their white counterparts never were.[26] White men took advantage of Chinese prostitutes' powerlessness to fulfill their sexual fantasies, forcing them to perform deviant sexual acts in pursuit of unconventional erotic gratification.

The main moral complaint against the Chinese was the existence of Chinese prostitutes. Whites perceived their sexuality as a peril to the purity of white America and blamed Chinese prostitutes for the country's opium problem, castigating them as both users and purveyors.[27] As far as whites were concerned, opium and prostitution went hand-in-hand since opiates were believed to be aphrodisiacs that caused users to experience uncontrollable sexual desire leading to promiscuity. From a review of testimonies at state and congressional committees that investigated Chinese immigration in 1876, Asian American studies scholar Sucheng Chan concludes, "Chinese prostitutes were seen as potent instruments for the debasement of white manhood, health, morality, and family life. Thus, their continued presence was deemed a threat to white civilization."[28]

EXCLUSION OF CHINESE WOMEN FIRST

To rid the country of Chinese completely, Sinophobic groups in the nineteenth century were able to obtain the passage of immigration laws preventing Chinese from entering the country and miscegenation laws prohibiting them from intermarrying with whites. Miscegenation laws were initially written to forbid black-white marriages but were later amended to include Asians.[29] They were efforts to criminalize Chinese men, who were characterized as sexually deviant bachelors who preyed on innocent white women. With the passage of these two types of laws, the proponents believed that they had successfully ended the economic rivalry as well as the sexual danger that Chinese men posed. Chinese men would no longer compete with workers for jobs, no longer endanger the purity of the race through intermarriage, and no longer create corrupt communities since they were denied the right to have families. All of this could be justified in the name of preventing national decline, a particular fear of American nativists.

Concerns focused on Chinese women, who were central to the life of the Chinese community and its perpetuation. Women stand "with one hand grasping the generations that have gone before and with the other the generations to come," as one elderly Chinese woman explained in social worker Ida Pruitt's classic study of a Chinese working woman.[30] Excluding Chinese women from the country meant breaking the link between generations, leading to the eventual extinction of Chinese American communities.

Anti-Chinese partisans sought to attain this goal through the passage of the Page Act (March 3, 1875), named after its sponsor, California congressman Horace F. Page (Republican). The Page Act forbade the entry of "undesirables," specifically the involuntary immigration of Asian laborers and the importation of Asian women for the purpose of prostitution.[31] Though the Page Act appeared to protect Chinese men and women from servitude as coolies or prostitutes (when introducing the bill, Page claimed that 90 percent of Chinese women in America were prostitutes), its actual intent was to safeguard the United States as a homogeneous nation—that is, a nation for, and of, white people.[32] Hence, the Page Act reaffirmed that Chinese were ineligible for naturalization to ensure that they remained aliens in America. The fear was that the coming of Chinese wives would result in the creation of a permanent Chinese American community, whose descendants would be even more problematic. Though US citizens under the Fourteenth Amendment, these unwelcome Americans would be unassimilable because they could be expected to adhere to alien customs such as concubinage (considered as bad as Mormon polygamy), which would undermine the institution of monogamous marriage and change the United States for the worse.[33]

To keep Chinese from reproducing was the law's actual intent, as Chief Justice Lorenzo Sawyer of the California Supreme Court discloses in his discussion of the Chinese Question in 1886: "If [the Chinese] would never bring their women here and never multiply and we would never have more than we can make useful, their presence would always be an advantage to the State . . . so long as the Chinese don't come here to stay. . . . When the

Chinaman comes here and don't bring his wife here, sooner or later he dies like a worn out steam engine; he is simply a machine, and don't leave two or three or a half dozen children to fill his place."[34]

Even though the Page Act was a restrictive immigration law that violated the Burlingame Treaty of 1868, Congress passed it anyway. It did so because the Page Act was considered an extension of the struggle to abolish slavery, which had ended a decade earlier, and because the Chinese were judged to be a people who could never integrate into American society. Many whites probably agreed with Judge Sawyer's flat judgment: "The Chinese are vastly superior to the negro [sic], but they are a race entirely different from ours and never can assimilate and I don't think it desirable that they should."[35]

The unprecedented Page Act was supposed to strengthen the prohibition on coolies by imposing a heavy fine and term of incarceration on anyone bringing them into the United States. Of course, as noted earlier, Chinese workers were not coolies but had voluntarily immigrated to America, usually borrowing the money from a broker and incurring the responsibility to repay it with interest. For that reason, the Page Law was ineffective and proponents remained unsatisfied. Since the Page Law failed to end the danger of cheap Chinese labor, further actions were taken. These actions included more assaults and more draconian laws against Chinese people, notably the Chinese Exclusion Act of 1882, which banned them solely because of their ethnicity.

The Page Law, however, proved to be quite effective in preventing the entry of Chinese women because of its intensive enforcement. According to George Peffer, from 1876 to 1882, the number of Chinese women entering the country declined 68 percent from the previous seven-year period.[36] Though Chinese women in America actually included wives and daughters, students, workers, and others, the popular press branded them all as prostitutes, making it nearly impossible for all but the wives of merchants to avoid being treated as such. Not surprisingly, immigration officials enforced the Page Law zealously because they believed they were protecting American society from a serious physical and social threat that was understood in racial terms.

During the prudish Victorian period, immigration officials became the guardians of middle-class morality. Besides viewing Chinese prostitutes as disease transmitters, immigration officials believed that their sexuality promoted immorality in American men. They also assumed that Chinese men would continue their indigenous practice of polygamy and mistreatment of women, making them ill suited for life in America.

In their efforts to keep Chinese women out, immigration officials were abetted by the American Medical Association. The AMA erroneously declared that Chinese carried unique strains of diseases that were fatal to whites and most easily transmitted through intercourse with Chinese prostitutes.[37] In 1876, in his presidential address at the centennial jubilee of the American Medical Association, internationally renowned gynecologist Dr. J. Marion Sims sounded the alarm about the virulence of "Chinese syphilis tocsin."[38] Eventually, medical research determined that there was no Chinese syphilis, but the damage had already been done. Chinese prostitutes were stigmatized as carriers of a loathsome venereal disease. In actuality, they were no more diseased than their non-Chinese counterparts, and given their fewer numbers and mainly Chinese clientele, they were probably less of a health threat to general society.

For a Chinese woman to enter America, she had to overcome major hurdles that began in Hong Kong (the port of embarkation) with a thoroughgoing screening process and repeated interrogations that continued in San Francisco (the port of disembarkation). The interviews were intended to determine whether the woman was from a respectable family and whether her husband would be able to support her when she was in the United States. Assuming that all Chinese were fundamentally deceitful, American and British officials asked a battery of obnoxious questions to ascertain the woman's true character. Among them were: Do you go to the United States for the purposes of prostitution? Have you lived in a house of prostitution in Hong Kong, Macau, or China? Since it was virtually impossible to differentiate between wives and prostitutes, the officials erred on the side of caution, excluding practically all women from emigrating. The fact that wives were willing to submit to such a humiliating ordeal to join their husbands in America was a testament to the strength of family bonds.

In preventing Chinese women from immigrating to the United States, the Page Act curbed the creation of normal Chinese American families while producing three paradoxical effects. First, the law gave rise to an abnormal community, the Chinese bachelor society, which Sinophobes then condemned. Secondly, by keeping the ratio of Chinese women to men low, the law had the unintended consequence of encouraging prostitution rather than discouraging it. And third, the law inadvertently encouraged intermarriage. Indeed, intermarriage was considered worse than the other effects because it blurred racial boundaries and subverted the effort to maintain a pure white race.

Sinophobes enacted miscegenation laws to prevent Chinese men and women from intermarrying with whites, or they added such provisions to existing miscegenation laws, as noted earlier. These laws were usually broadly construed to encompass anyone identified as Mongolian. They were meant to prevent racial contamination and maintain white supremacy, especially in the post–Civil War period, when other race-based institutions were under attack.

There is little information about Chinese-white marriages. It is estimated that between 1882 and 1952, there were fewer than fifty such marriages in the American West.[39] Given the greater number of Chinese on the East and West Coasts, most of these intermarriages probably occurred there. Usually Chinese men married white women. In a sympathetic article, the *New York Herald* observed that the absence of Chinese women had compelled them to marry whites.[40] It noted that in New York City, nearly three hundred Chinese men had white wives, mainly Spanish and Irish women, the latter preferred because of their domestic skills. Moreover, marriage between Chinese men and Irish women were giving rise to a generation of "Chino-Celtic" offspring who would serve an important role in strengthening relations between Americans and Chinese.

White women who married Chinese men were considered suspect. They were judged neurotic or romantic. In the aftermath of a police raid on New York's Chinatown, during which all the white wives were arrested and held until they could produce their marriage certificates, a newspaper reporter observes that, while there was "no evidence to prove that they were disorderly characters in the legal sense . . . morally there was no question about it."[41] Among other things, the white wives were believed to be drug addicts because all Chinese smoked opium, and this was required for acceptance in the Chinese community. Thus, the reporter states, "as soon as one of these women devotes herself to the opium habit she becomes as Chinese as the pig-tailed laundrymen themselves."[42]

In the nineteenth century, a few states permitted intermarriage between Chinese and whites. One of them was Colorado, which did not include marriage to Chinese, Japanese, or the more inclusive term, Mongolians, in its miscegenation law. Some Chinese-white marriages were noted in the public press. One example was the Chinese policeman Louis Johnson.

FIG. 4.1. "Pacific Railroad Complete," *Harper's Weekly*, June 12, 1869. This political cartoon, published about a month after the completion of the Transcontinental Railroad, shows an interracial couple leaving the "Church of St. Confucius." It represents popular fears about miscegenation between discharged Chinese railroad workers and white women. To accentuate the "mismatch," it draws the Chinese man in a stereotypical fashion, with traditional clothing, skullcap, and queue. Denver Public Library, Western History Collection.

Before moving to Denver, in 1873, he had married a Miss Burt, a woman of German descent, in Louisville, Kentucky. A Christian minister married them since they were both Methodists. In an interview, Johnson proudly says that he had courted her for a year in the parlor, just like any other young American, and he is at pains to point out that even though his wife is employed outside the home, she is markedly different from the "usual kind of cast off American women selected as wives by Chinese, but a lady in all senses of the term."[43] The "cast off American women" whom Johnson contemptuously refers to were the ill-bred, lower-class white women, perhaps even white prostitutes, whom most Americans assumed were the type to marry Chinese men.

Johnson's story is exceptional in other respects. Besides being Denver's *and* the country's first Chinese police officer, Johnson was a naturalized American who had obtained his citizenship papers in Evansville, Colorado. He was determined to live the life of a respectable American citizen, even taking pride in the fact that he was the only Chinese in Denver who was capable of voting for Robert Morris for mayor. What he meant by this is unclear. Perhaps he was simply saying that he was proud to have the right to vote, though other naturalized Chinese could do so as well. Or he may have been declaring himself open-minded enough to vote for an Irishman, when the Irish were known for their enmity toward the Chinese.

It is evident that Johnson had consciously separated himself from the Chinese community and tried to integrate into American society, adopting an Anglo name and accepting Western values and customs. He even embraced some American prejudices toward Chinese. Speaking with the white reporter, he pronounces other Chinese uncivilized, immoral, envious, and underhanded, observing bitterly, "When [other Chinese] see a Chinaman has a good thing they try to get it away from him by underbidding him."[44] It was a personal observation probably based on his many years of experience as a tea merchant.

A contrasting example that provides a virtual inventory of the kind of problems that Chinese and white couples might face on the path to marriage is the experience of Leo Latt Sing and Nellie Mershon. Sing and Mershon were coworkers at the Beebe Hotel in Idaho Springs, Colorado, when they decided to get married in 1902. They encountered many difficulties.[45] Upon learning of their intentions, the *Denver Times* made a laughingstock of Sing, depicting him as a grotesque-featured Mongolian, a greasy-looking Chinaman who was anything but handsome. His large nose and glassy eyes were said to make him look like "a god in the Chinese joss house." Mershon, by contrast, was described as a rather "good-looking white woman, with blue eyes and light hair . . . plump and prepossessing." The effect was to emphasize the mismatch. But this public embarrassment was just the beginning of their trials.

Fearing racial mongrelization, some of the locals tried to prevent their marriage by hanging Sing from a telephone pole until he nearly died. They then ordered him to leave town.[46] The couple eloped to Denver, only to have Mershon's brother-in-law, Charles Thorpe, obtain a warrant for their arrest for violating the state's miscegenation law. As Mershon complained, "[Thorpe] says he thought there was a law preventing my marriage to Leo Sing, and he got the police officers to act first and find out afterward. There is no such law—nor does there seem to be one that might have protected me in the case. I have been a byword on the streets, and my personal affairs have been talked about all over the country."[47] As Mershon indicates, the scandal value of Chinese-white marriage was sufficient to warrant national attention.

Charles Thorpe also claimed that Sing had seduced Mershon by giving her opium, a charge that Mershon firmly denied, saying, "It is not true that he gave me dope. He does not use it." Mershon explained that she fell in love with Sing because he was kind to her and was "one of the truest gentlemen I ever saw, and much nicer than the majority of white men." Mershon may be forgiven if she exaggerated her fiancé's personal qualities; he probably did compare favorably with her first husband, whom she had had to support for five years while he languished in a madhouse.[48] Given the racial climate of the era, her rebuke probably outraged white men near and far.

After being discharged from jail, Sing and Mershon searched for a judge to marry them. The second judge they tried, Justice Hynes, refused to even see the couple, let alone marry them. Having studied the state statutes beforehand, Justice Hynes reportedly concluded that the "legislature never intended that people of the character of Chinese coolies should become assimilated into the American nation." Finally, Sing and Mershon found a sympathetic party in Justice William T. Printz. Justice Printz saw no reason to disregard the marriage license that had been duly made out and presented to him, so he married the couple without further delay. Afterward, a reporter paid Sing a backhanded compliment, saying: "No Chinaman has ever been known to abuse the white woman he takes to wife. . . . An Irishman, an Italian, a German—men of almost any nationality figure in the police courts for brutality to the woman they made a drudge and buffet of, but never the Chinaman. John [Chinaman] isn't lovely, but he is known to be devotion itself—if one cares for the devotion."[49] Hopefully, Leo Latt Sing and Nellie Mershon were able to live out their lives together in relative peace. But if the experience of other Asian and white couples is any indica-tion, they probably faced continued challenges.[50]

More than a half century after Sing and Mershon were married, the issue of intermarriage between Chinese and whites was taken up as a theme in two Western films, James Clavell's offbeat *Walk Like a Dragon* (1960) and Maggie Greenwald's provocative *The Ballad of Little Jo* (1993). These films reveal the complexity of intermarriage between Chinese and whites in the American West.

James Clavell's film focuses on the predicament of Kim Sung, played by the late Japanese Canadian actress Nobu McCarthy. Like the King sisters of "A Chinese Romance," Kim is an orphan who has been sold into prosti-tution. Lincoln (Linc) Bartlett, the film's protagonist, sees Kim being auc-tioned off as a sex slave. As a former Civil War soldier who fought to end slavery, he cannot abide the idea and buys Kim to set her free. One of the unintended consequences of his noble act is that he finds himself responsi-ble for Kim, since she is a stranger with no place to go. Reluctantly, he takes her back home to Jericho, a rowdy mining town somewhere in California. Kim is a beautiful, intelligent young woman who acts as a servant to Linc and his mother, whom she calls "Master" and "Mistress," respectively. She walks behind them to show her submissiveness. She is also prepared to do this for Cheng-lu, played by the late Japanese American actor James Shigeta. Cheng-lu is a missionary-educated young Chinese laundryman who becomes Linc's rival for Kim's affections.

Walk Like a Dragon is an unusual Western because of its exploration of racism in the American West. As more than one character notes in the film, there is a tacit color line preventing any "romantic" relationships between whites and Chinese. Though Linc is the macho cowboy hero of the movie whose code of honor requires him to stand up for what he believes and to save Kim from slavery, he is also a man of his era, with decidedly Sinopho-bic sentiments. This is reflected in his unwillingness to shake Cheng-lu's hand, even though Linc offers to give Cheng-lu a ride to Jericho, where he will work in his uncle's hand laundry in Chinatown. Linc's ambivalence is also reflected in his mixed feelings toward Kim. Hovering in the back-ground are the questions: Will Linc cross the color line because of his love for Kim? Will he marry Kim? If Linc does so, will it be in opposition to the rest of his community?

In the nineteenth century, it was Western culture's contention that Christianity would save the Chinese, especially women, from the degrading customs of their own civilization. Clavell exposes the hypocrisy of Christianity when he shows that, while the folks of Jericho condemn Kim and the other Chinese as heathens, they actually despise them because of their racial difference and find the idea of intermarriage with Chinese revolting. The subtext is that intermarriage between whites and Chinese results in genetic contamination and the creation of inferior biracial off-spring, thus weakening the white race through the inheritance of Chinese deficiencies. Cheng-lu and his uncle are also appalled by the idea that Kim might marry Linc, and they think that Kim should marry one of her own people. They, too, believe in the immutable separateness of the races. Given Cheng-lu's remarks about how badly whites have treated Chinese, his opposition may also be a reaction to his own personal experience.

Clavell's film also breaks with tradition in another sense. In Westerns, Chinese characters usually play stereotypical roles as servants and laundrymen. In Clavell's film, they are portrayed as individuals with inner lives. Cheng-lu is ambivalent about America, though he sees it as a land of free men. In America, Kim Sung feels for the first time that she belongs, at least as a member of Linc Bartlett's family. In the course of the film, both Cheng-lu and Kim are transformed into Chinese Americans, though this is never stated outright. Cheng-lu adapts to the Wild West and becomes a gunfighter, allowing him to "walk tall like a dragon." Kim realizes that she is now a free woman and is able to choose, rightly or wrongly, whom she wants to be with. The question of which man Kim will end up with—Linc or Cheng-lu—is the driver of the plot. The answer is likely Cheng-lu, because it's much too soon for integration, as Bosley Crowther, *New York Times* film critic, observes.[51] What Crowther means is that, because of opposition to miscegenation, the Chinese protagonist must end up with the girl. Within a few years after Clavell's 1960 film was made, the controversy over discrimination and miscegenation reached a boiling point in the United States, a subject that I discuss in the epilogue to this book.

In Maggie Greenwald's film *The Ballad of Little Jo* (1993), the Chinese protagonist also ends up with the girl. It is one of the rare films that deals with the taboo topic of sex between Asians and whites, particularly Asian men and white women. Tinman, the film's Chinese character, has a de facto marital relationship with the central character, Little Jo Monaghan. They transgress the social prohibitions of the nineteenth century to become lovers and soul mates.

As the critic Roger Ebert perceptively observes, the film is about the "role-playing that allowed women and minorities to survive in the macho, racist West."[52]

The film opens with the prologue, "In the Wild West, a woman had only two choices: she could be a wife, or a whore. . . . Josephine Monaghan chose to be a man." Masquerading as a man on the American frontier, Little Jo Monaghan rescues a Chinese man from a lynching. Tinman (Wang Tianma), a former railroad laborer looking for work, has wandered into the mining town of Ruby City, where he is immediately set upon for no other reason than his being Chinese. The white men who are about to hang Tinman claim that he is trying to steal a job that rightfully belongs to some other white man; besides, he must be up to no good because, as Little Jo's closest friend in town, Frank Badger, says, it is a well-known fact that Chinese are all ravishers and opium smokers. But as the film progresses, it is clear that Tinman is the better man. His gentle manner stands in marked contrast to the boorishness of the main white male characters, who are depicted as hard-drinking, rapacious Westerners prone to violence.

Even this feminist interpretation of the Old West cannot resist the temptation to traffic in clichés about Chinese vice and the sexual ambiguity of Asian males. Tinman, played by Korean American actor David Chung, is portrayed as a recreational opium smoker who introduces the practice to Little Jo as a postcoital activity; affectionately, she repeats Frank Badger's earlier remark that Chinese are ravishers and opium smokers. Although Tinman is Little Jo's lover, Greenwald mutes Tinman's virility, associating him with the familiar image of the emasculated or feminized Oriental by partnering him with a white woman who transgressively pretends to be a man. While the change in Jo's gender role allows her to express her independent spirit and ultimately alters her personality, it also prevents Tinman from claiming his identity as a Chinese male. Tinman remains in a subordinate position throughout the film: he is Jo's cook and servant, her kept man—in a sense, her Chinese prostitute. Since there are no Chinese women in the area, Tinman's prospects of ever having a family, raising a child, and doing the other things expected of Chinese men are nil. In the eyes of society, he remains sexless.

Even when Little Jo tires of pretending to be a man and tries to revert to a feminine role by wearing a dress and baking a pie, it becomes painfully evident to them both that she can never be Tinman's wife and he can never be her husband. They must remain in an interracial liaison without the benefit of even common-law marriage status. As a matter of necessity, both

Little Jo and Tinman are outsiders. In the hostile milieu of the American West, they must maintain their roles as white master and Chinese servant rather than normalize their relationship through marriage. The failure to maintain this charade could result in their deaths.

CHINESE PROSTITUTES AND PRESIDENTIAL POLITICS

Like other prostitutes, Chinese prostitutes usually lived anonymous and oppressive lives of sexual abuse. In nineteenth-century Colorado, they were also exploited for political advantage as part of the larger anti-Chinese movement, and as such, their fate became intertwined with national and local politics. During the 1880 presidential campaign between Winfield S. Hancock and James A. Garfield, Hancock supporters vilified Garfield for failing to restrict Chinese immigration. In McCune's paint shop at Larimer and Fourteenth Street in Denver, there was a sign depicting Garfield in the embrace of a Chinese woman, which in the public eye meant a Chinese prostitute.[53] Such inflammatory displays aroused anti-Chinese feelings, setting the stage for the Denver race riot on October 31, 1880, when mobs destroyed Chinatown.

Among those who suffered some of the worse barbarity at the hands of the rioters were Chinese women. William E. Roberts, a city fireman, witnessed the following outrage at Sixteenth Street and Wazee:

> There were about two hundred degenerates, about to outrage and ravish the poor unfortunate occupants of that block of Chinese. . . . A half dozen white bums had torn all the clothes from those little Chinese girls. Had ravished and beaten them. . . . The next dive we entered, there were four little girls . . . beaten and ravished. One little girl not over fourteen, fell on her knees and pleaded. Please don't hurt me any more. They have nearly killed me already. I didn't think white men could be so cruel.[54]

Among the few defenders of the Chinese during the race riot were the city's prostitutes. According to Roberts, the "Denizens of Holladay Street, the center of the red-light district, waded into the mobs to rescue thirty-four Chinese, one of whom had an eye-gouged out and another his tongue torn out."[55] Perhaps the most notable was Lizzie Preston, "Queen of the Demimonde," who stood between the Chinese and the mob, wielding an unloaded double-barreled shotgun and threatening to shoot the first man who dared to go after those she was protecting. In this, Preston was backed up by "ten Amazonian beauties, armed with champagne bottles, stove pokers, [and] high heeled shoes, wicked weapons when used by experts."[56] After the race riot, Preston performed another act of kindness toward the Chinese prostitutes. She asked the other madams of the red-light district to contribute money to help them depart for San Francisco, which had the largest Chinatown in the region. Preston collected an estimated $1,250, including $200 of her own money, for this purpose.[57] She pleaded with a Union Pacific official to furnish forty half-priced tickets for the Chinese prostitutes to get them to the West Coast and she also provided each with money for provisions during the trip.

Why Preston and the other prostitutes, at personal risk to themselves, helped the Chinese is unknown. It may have been because they were neighbors living in the same seamy part of Denver. But so too were many of those who committed the acts of brutality against the Chinese. It may have been because these women identified with the Chinese as social pariahs, standing against the rioters representing the dominant society, with its prejudices against the Chinese. Perhaps it was simply to assist their sisters in the world's oldest profession.

Only a small number of Chinese women lived in Colorado and most of them were prostitutes. Given their scarcity, they should have been perceived as a precious commodity. But that was the problem: they were regarded as a commodity. As professors Ian Buruma and Avishai Margalit observe, "The most symbolic figure of commodified human relations . . . is the prostitute."[58] Like the mineral resources of Colorado, Chinese prostitutes were fought over and ruthlessly exploited.

In different ways and in different places, the experience of the King sisters was repeated throughout the country. Chinese prostitutes opposed their oppression however they could and fled from sexual slavery whenever they could. Runaway prostitutes divided Chinatowns between those who wanted them returned to the brothel owners and those who did not, causing turmoil in the Chinese community as others decided their fate. These women faced the threat of being kidnapped, and they looked to the American legal system to secure their freedom. Those who did attain their freedom were able to found families and contribute to the Chinese community as wives, mothers, and workers in a variety of so-called women's occupations available to them in the American West, such as laundrywomen, seamstresses, cooks, and domestics. However, most Chinese prostitutes who fled were eventually captured and returned to their owners, who forced them to continue working as sex slaves. Though slavery had been abolished in the United States, it continued in the Chinese communities.

Besides being victimized sexually, Chinese prostitutes were victimized politically. Sinophobic agitators and propagandists singled them out as a symbol of all that they found objectionable about the Chinese people. They used Chinese prostitutes to justify the expulsion of every Chinese from Colorado. Chinese prostitutes were condemned as morally degenerate and disease-ridden, and considered a danger to white men and, by extension, to all of white society. Opponents realized that the most effective way to eliminate the ethnic community was to remove its women. For that reason, Sinophobic elements worked to pass the Page Act, which ostensibly prohibited the entry of Chinese prostitutes to the United States but effectively kept most Chinese women out of the country, thus encouraging Chinese men to return to China. In the guise of protecting the moral integrity of American society, the Page Act distorted the development of the Chinese community in Colorado and elsewhere in the country. It was a preemptive measure against the threat of overwhelming numbers of Chinese invading and eventually dominating the country. Meanwhile, to cleanse the country of those who were already here, whites resorted to acts of savagery such as the Denver race riot.

FIVE

THE DENVER RACE RIOT AND ITS AFTERMATH

WHILE THE DENVER RACE RIOT OF 1880 WAS ONLY ONE OF about two hundred anti-Chinese incidents in the American West during the latter half of the nineteenth century, it was one of the worst.[1] The scale of the riot dwarfed earlier Sinophobic attacks in the state. Chinatown was nearly destroyed as a result. Local approval of the riot was evident in the way in which the *Rocky Mountain News* (RMN) summed up the wreckage the day after: "Washee washee is all cleaned out in Denver."[2] The headline makes a mocking reference to the destruction of the laundry business that symbolized the Chinese community, while the choice of language suggests that it was more a lark than a tragedy.

The race riot had its roots in animosity toward Chinese that had been building during the preceding decade. As discussed in previous chapters, Chinese were viewed variously as mysterious and unassimilable aliens, unfair competitors for jobs in the state's unstable economy, or bad elements who constituted a social menace to whites for trafficking in vices such as gambling, opium, and prostitution. Initially, the Chinese were represented and mocked as strange-looking pagans ("Heathen Chinee"). But gradually they came to be seen as bearers of disease—moral, social, and physical. A popular image was created of Chinese as disease-ridden lepers who existed in squalid colonies that could spread contagion far beyond their boundaries. Along with the change in emphasis from heathen to health hazard, there came a call to eradicate Chinese people as one would any other disease. Since every Chinese was a potential plague carrier, capable of transmitting an illness or a moral corruption that could infect Western civilization, none could be tolerated. Following such logic, it is little wonder that Coloradans felt empowered to eliminate the entire ethnic community. This mentality also explains why Coloradans' actions seem strikingly disproportionate to the small number of Chinese among them.

The race riot is significant in that it offers a clear case of how antagonism toward the Chinese could intersect with partisan politics, creating the conditions for violent attacks. The riot was incited by political propaganda and was understood as such at the time, at least by some. Because it occurred in the context of a bitterly contested presidential campaign, it was widely publicized. As an example of the destabilizing effect of Chinese on the public order, it was a factor contributing to the passage of the federal Chinese Exclusion Act in 1882, which was enacted to prevent similar civil disruptions.

The fate of Chinatown's residents was decided when the "Chinese Question" became a flash point in the 1880 presidential election battle between Republican James A. Garfield and Democrat Winfield S. Hancock. For some years, Democrats had been accusing Republicans of trying to increase their electoral strength by making voters out of "base, degraded, miserable Chinamen."[3] In Colorado, the charge was renewed in 1880 with reports of Republicans naturalizing some Chinese in Central City while urging the entire Chinese population to become naturalized citizens and vote. Democrats warned that once word got out that Colorado's Chinese were able to vote with Republican support, "the lepers will flock to this state in swarms."[4] Democrats also accused the Republicans of buying votes, citing a report that a Chinese mine owner in Gilpin County, Ah Moon, planned to deliver fifty Chinese pro-Republican votes on Election Day for about ten dollars a head. Republicans denied the claims and shot back that the Democratic Party, not the Republican, was naturalizing Chinese in California to grab votes.[5] While the allegations on both sides warrant discussion, it is inarguable that Chinese Coloradans (whether citizen or immigrants) hardly counted as a voting bloc given their modest numbers. As a campaign issue, however, they mattered a lot because the Chinese Question was, to use the RMN's term, a "red-hot" focus of contention.

In actuality, there was little difference between the Republican and Democratic Parties on most issues in the 1880 election. Both parties advocated immigration restriction and support for the American workingman. But they had an important disagreement on tariffs. Garfield and the Republicans supported a high protective tariff to shield American industrial workers. By contrast, Hancock and the Democrats endorsed a tariff for revenue only, that is, a lower levy on imported goods that was intended to do no more than cover government costs. The Garfield campaign seized on the issue to paint Hancock as unsympathetic to the plight of American workers, undermining Democratic support in the industrialized Northern states, which were considered essential to win the election. The Democrats needed something to counter this vulnerability, something that showed Garfield was no friend of the workingman. So they prepared an October surprise.

The Democrats sought to prove that Garfield secretly planned to betray American workingmen by producing the "Morey letter," a missive from Garfield to one H. L. Morey, a member of the Employers Union in Lynn, Massachusetts, revealing that Garfield intended to abandon American workers after the election and to support the importation of "coolies" to promote manufacturing interests. The letter was dated January 23, 1880, but it surfaced dramatically on October 20, two weeks before the election. Copies immediately flooded the country. The letter was widely reprinted in pro–Democratic Party newspapers such as the RMN.[6] The bombshell was intended to win the support of Western states, where the Chinese Question was a matter of great importance.

Garfield denied writing the Morey letter and it was later proven to be a forgery.[7] Nonetheless, as a desperate last-minute attempt to derail his candidacy for the presidency, it nearly succeeded. In terms of the popular vote, Garfield beat Hancock by less than two thousand votes, the smallest margin for a popular vote victory in American history; he won by gaining 58 percent of the electoral votes (214 out of 369), including Colorado's three electoral votes. While the fraudulent letter failed to capture the presidency for the Democrats, it did cost the Republican Party the US Senate as well as other legislative positions around the country.

The Morey letter and the heated campaigning around it elevated the Chinese Question to national prominence as the election loomed. The Chinese Question was no longer just an American West issue. It became a coast-to-coast crisis. Rumors abounded, with stories about greedy Eastern capitalists working in tandem with the powerful Six Companies to transport millions of coolies to the Interior West to compete with white workers there, just as they did on the West Coast. It was claimed that the Six Companies' operations reached every part of the state, from Gilpin to Como and from Denver to Park.[8] Newspapers began printing the speeches of Denis Kearney, a prominent Irish labor leader and charismatic demagogue, known for beginning and ending his speeches with the slogan "The Chinese Must Go!"[9] The specter of an impending invasion of coolies and the consequential impoverishment of white workers loomed large in the minds of worried Coloradans, who remembered the Chinese as the victors in the Chinese-Italian War in the Como coal mines a year earlier.

ROLE OF THE *ROCKY MOUNTAIN NEWS*

In the weeks leading up to the November 2, 1880, election, partisan newspapers trumpeted the merits of their chosen candidates and derided their opponents in an attempt to secure votes. Pro-Democratic newspapers vigorously engaged in negative campaigning, devoting numerous articles to attacking the Republicans and their standard-bearer Garfield and fewer articles to lauding the Democrats and Hancock. They railed against so-called Garfieldism, a pro-capitalist stance favoring the importation of coolies at the expense of white workers. In actuality, Garfield was opposed to the importation of Chinese since he regarded them as indentured laborers rather than authentic immigrants. In line with the Republican platform plank on the Chinese Question, Garfield endorsed immigration restrictions in his July 12 letter accepting his party's nomination.

Among the leaders of the anti-Chinese, anti-Garfield effort was the RMN. Under the ownership of prominent Democrat W. A. H. Loveland, who aspired to become governor of Colorado, the RMN made the Chinese Question a central campaign issue in the state. The 1880 presidential campaign become a continuation of the paper's ongoing crusade against the Chinese, providing a wealth of opportunities for even more inflammatory articles. On the day of the race riot, the newspaper devoted no fewer than eight of its twelve pages to major articles repeating shrill attacks against the Chinese and linking the Chinese to Garfield. Afterward, Republican leaders publicly accused the newspaper of being the primary instigator of the tragedy.[10] A modern historian of the newspaper sums up the paper's role in the anti-Chinese movement with regret: "In its Democratic affections for the workingman and his vote the *Rocky Mountain News* fanned the flames of public violence in these years with as dishonorable a result . . . as the bloodthirstiness with which it had promoted and justified the Sand Creek Massacre."[11]

The RMN's denunciations were cast in nativist terms, portraying Garfield and the Chinese as enemies of Hancock and American citizenry. In this contest for survival, the newspaper declared it stood with the white race and against the Chinese.[12] On October 23, 1880, just days before the riot, the newspaper ran a Sinophobic editorial under the headline "John Chinaman—The pest of the Pacific Coast . . . Workmen starving and women following prostitution through the competition of the wily heathen."[13] The contention was that Chinese had ruined the "pastoral paradise" that once was California, and that the despoliation of California and Nevada would soon be followed by that of Colorado.

To whip up fear, the RMN published subsequent articles conjuring up bleak images of life in Colorado after Garfield's Chinese had overrun it. The future Colorado bore a striking resemblance to China, except that the starving masses were white rather than Chinese. The newspaper solicited confirmation of this scenario from prominent citizens, including those tied to the mining industry, who presumably had the most to gain from cheap Chinese labor. For example, on October 30, the RMN published an interview on the subject with General H. B. Bearce, former representative of Arapahoe and Douglas Counties in the Territorial Legislature.[14] Bearce predicted that because Chinese laborers were so profitable, capitalists would be unable to resist the temptation to bring them into the state unless such actions were opposed by overwhelming public sentiment. He recalled his role in preventing the importation of five hundred Chinese scabs to work in the Erie coal mines near Boulder when he negotiated an end to a miners' strike four years earlier. He noted that, although he and other mine owners could profit immediately from the employment of Chinese workers, importing them would be "a curse to my children and grandchildren, who might be starved in competition with them." To safeguard America's future, it was necessary for Coloradans to keep them out. Bearce concluded that the "first and vital step to be taken in this direction [was] to pronounce in thunder tones against them by carrying Colorado for Hancock."

On the eve of the riot, Bearce made his political position known to all when he marched alongside Jerry Mahoney, secretary of the State Democratic Committee, at the head of the raucous pro–Democratic Party procession through downtown Denver, decrying Garfieldism and creating apprehension in the city's Chinese community. It was the biggest parade that Denver had ever seen.

The Democratic Party's anti-Chinese demonstration on the evening of October 30 set the stage for the Denver race riot.[15] Crowds of supporters lined the route to cheer on the demonstrators, while residences and businesses fronting the streets threw open their shutters and lit candles or hung lanterns to illuminate the way in a show of support. Demonstrators drove wagons carrying anti-Chinese displays, including one with representations of Chinese making bricks, which was greeted with jeers as it passed. Marchers carried signs bearing Sinophobic slogans such as one proclaiming, "Garfield may become a Mandarin but a President never," which implied that Garfield was more Chinese than American. In the windows of businesses they passed, participants could see sympathetic displays, including one exhibit in a shop window showing Garfield's future all-Chinese cabinet appointments.

An estimated three to four thousand torch-bearing marchers assembled to hear speeches at a rally in the public square. There, seven out of eight speeches condemned the Chinese. The Honorable S. S. Wallace, candidate for presidential elector, spoke first. He predicted that the various issues of the day—the Ute Question, the Silver Question, and the Chinese Question—ensured Hancock's victory in Colorado. John McGilvray, chairman of the Association of Trade Unions, offered the gathering a resolution to keep out the Chinese, who were "flocking to our young state and will not only take our work from us, but by manufacturing here articles we now buy from the east, will ruin this as a market for eastern manufacturers." Mr. Graves then told the audience that a Republican victory would mean the state would be inundated with Chinese. Following him, Mr. Benedict complimented the crowd for recognizing the evil of flooding the land with Chinese. Next, Mr. Stephenson, a former Garfield supporter, told the audience that he had switched sides. Though Stephenson liked Garfield personally, he was opposed to his support of Chinese and disagreed with Garfield's vote against restricting Chinese immigration.

With the crowd now fired up, the last speaker drove the point home. Former Colorado congressman Thomas M. Patterson, Jr., who had staked his personal reputation on the authenticity of the Morey letter, created a sensation when he related the story of a capitalist who had told him, "If Garfield is elected he will immediately bring one thousand Chinamen into

Colorado and knows where he can place them at a big profit."[16] Two nights earlier, at a political rally in Central City, Patterson had conveyed a similar message to an enthusiastic crowd of twenty-five hundred citizens, predicting that with Garfield's election, "It would only be a few years until our mines would be filled with pigtailed Chinamen."[17] He warned the audience that "the principal mines" in neighboring Lake County, where Leadville was located, were all owned by "California capitalists, men familiar with [the] cheap labor" that had "ruined California," and he advised the audience to "jealously guard their rights and liberties." Patterson said he was comforted by the knowledge that the miners of Gilpin County "would never vote for a man for president who favored servile labor." The success of Patterson's anti-Chinese speech in Central City may have encouraged him to repeat and embellish his charges ("one thousand Chinamen") in Denver.

In the midst of the Sinophobic speeches, loud and prolonged cheering erupted when Jerry Mahoney informed the crowd that the demonstration was already having the desired effect of ridding the state of Chinese. An RMN reporter had just told him that a few hours earlier he had witnessed a number of Chinese enter the Western Union office to send off telegrams to friends in California who had been planning to come to Colorado, warning them to stay put and announcing that they were leaving Denver themselves. One of the agitated Chinese had explained to the reporter that "Garfield men were good men and no want to kill Chinamen," implying that Hancock men were the opposite. If true, the report suggests that the political parade had succeeded in creating an atmosphere of intimidation. Imagined or not, Chinese fears were borne out in the ensuing rampage.

START OF THE RIOT

Various explanations have been offered about how the Denver race riot started. Contemporary accounts differ significantly but tend to place the onus on the Chinese for overreacting to provocations in a Chinatown saloon. According to Mark M. Pomeroy, a well-known businessman: "Several railroad toughs under a head of payday steam entered a saloon on Wazee Street near Sixteenth and found two Chinese there. They hit one of them over the head with a billiard cue. The other drew a pistol and took a badly aimed shot at his tormentors. Within a few minutes word had spread through town that a Chinaman had killed a white man. A mob formed and began to ransack Chinatown, seeking victims."[18] In the same vein, William E. Roberts, assistant fire chief, reports:

> A Chinaman passed through a pool hall, nearly opposite the old American House at 16th and Blake, and unfortunately, jostled a pool player who missed his shot. The white man struck the offender on the head, and the Chinaman retaliated by slashing his adversary in the arm with a butcher knife he had hidden in his capacious sleeve. And then, hell broke loose, —it seems that everyone in the room took a punch at the Celestial. They nearly beat him to death, then threw him out in the street. . . . A few minutes later, the dives in the vicinity, were emptied of their half drunken cargoes. And then wild cries of "Lets clean out the damned Chinks."[19]

The two reports differ in many details, but one point they both make is that the whites retaliate only after a Chinese resorts to deadly force (a gun or knife) in response to an injury, being struck on the head with a billiard cue. The sense that the Chinese were somehow responsible for the riot survives in the RMN's seventy-fifth anniversary edition (1934), which claimed that the riot had been caused by a Chinese laundryman who had demanded ten cents more for the wash than his white customer was willing to pay. The Chinese slashed the customer across the face with a knife and then fired a gun at the crowd who had been attracted by the dispute.[20]

John Asmussén, owner of the saloon where the altercation between the whites and the Chinese took place, gives what is probably the most reliable account of what actually happened. In sworn testimony, he reported that about 2:00 P.M. on October 31, 1880, several drunken whites entered his saloon, John's Place, which was located at 404½ Wazee Street, and interrupted two Chinese who were quietly playing pool with George E. Shallee. According to Asmussén:

> One of the Chinamen asked them to quit; the men then commenced abusing the Chinamen, and I remonstrated with them, and they said they were as good as Chinamen, and they came up to the bar and got some beer. While they were drinking I advised the Chinamen to go out of the house to prevent a row, and they went out at the back door. After a few minutes one of the white men went out at the back door and struck one of the Chinamen without provocation. Another one of the crowd called to one of the gang inside to "come on Charley, he has got him," and he picked up a piece of board and struck at the Chinese, which the Chinese defended against as

well as they could, and tried to get away. *This was the beginning of the riot.*
[Emphasis added][21]

In contrast to the other accounts, Asmussén's testimony identifies the whites as the sole instigators and perpetrators of the violence.

After the fighting started, a mob estimated to be between three and five thousand people, approximately 10 percent of Denver's forty thousand residents, went on a rampage in Chinatown, engaging in rape and pillage from the afternoon late into the night.[22] The rioters seemed bent on destroying the Chinese community and killing or expelling its estimated 450 residents, as Pomeroy implies in his vivid description of the behavior of the whites:

> At this time about 3,000 persons were assembled . . . about the houses occupied by Chinese on Blake street; the houses were entirely surrounded by a surging, infuriated mob of brutal cowards, with clubs, stones, &c. They were breaking in windows and doors, cursing, howling, and yelling "Kill the Chinese! Kill the damned heathens! Burn the buildings! Give them hell! Run them out! Shoot them; hang them!" &c. I saw doors broken, saw men enter the houses and with impromptu torches look for those who inside were hiding; saw clothes and other articles brought and thieves run away with them.[23]

As is usually the case with riots, the identity of the rioters was difficult to discern, but publicly, at least, immigrants and blacks were named as the culprits. The *Denver Times* said that the mob consisted of "illegal voters, Irishmen, and some Negroes."[24] Instead of accepting that whites shared any of the responsibility for instigating the riot, the RMN focused attention on the participation of blacks. As proof, it cited a conversation between a white Democrat and a "colored Republican" on the day of the riot, in which the Democrat tries but fails to persuade the Republican not to go out and attack the Chinese. The Republican rebuffs him, saying, "No sir. I'm a colored man and I want to kill one. You democrats shan't have this thing all to yourselves." The Republican explains that he wants to kill Chinese because they have robbed blacks of their laundry business: "Chinamen in this town are injuring my people the most. Every colored washerwoman could make money before they came. Now they can hardly make bread."[25] The conversation trades so closely on clichés that it was likely concocted. Besides, given that there were only about 465 blacks in Colorado, their role in the riot would have been quite limited. However, it

FIG. 5.1. "Colorado—Anti-Chinese Riot in Denver, on October 31st—From a Sketch by N. B. Wilkins," *Frank Leslie's Illustrated Newspaper*, November 20, 1880. Although the Denver race riot was the worst Sinophobic incident to occur in the Centennial State, most of the Chinese residents remained to rebuild their community. However, the Chinese exclusion laws ultimately sounded the death knell for the city's Chinatown. Denver Public Library, Western History Collection, Z-3820.

is said that the Democratic Party wanted to split the black vote by arguing that Garfield's election would mean the arrival of large numbers of Chinese in the state, which would adversely affect black workers the most. A belief that blacks therefore hated Chinese would make the *Denver Times'* story credible to readers.[26]

In sworn testimonies about what happened that day, witnesses variously referred to ringleaders who appeared to be Irishmen and to a mob that was "a democratic crew ... continually shouting for Hancock."[27] Since Denver's Chinatown was located in the middle of an area with a foreign population that exceeded 35 or even 40 percent, it is likely that many of the rioters were the impoverished Europeans who lived nearby.[28] Ironically, the Europeans had much in common with the Chinese, since they, too, were foreign and poor. But as much as alienated European immigrants may have blamed the capitalists for their poverty, the latter were out of reach. The Chinese were easy to get at.

RECONSTRUCTING THE RIOT

When the race riot broke out, all Chinese became potential victims. Any Chinese passersby caught in the area were swept into the melee. For example, seven Chinese miners from Black Hawk who had the misfortune of being in Denver during the riot were robbed of their life savings, which amounted to about seven hundred to one thousand dollars per person. Many Chinese tried to hide from the men who were hunting them down. A few managed to flee the city or sought refuge at farms and ranches within a dozen miles of Denver, away from the havoc. The extent to which individual outcomes depended on sheer fate is illustrated by the experience of Ching Lee, a laundryman who worked on Sixteenth Street near Wazee.[29] He managed to hide himself in a wagon belonging to a Mr. Goldsmith, a farmer living near Golden. When Goldsmith returned home, unbeknownst to him, Ching Lee went with him. As it happened, two brigands were waiting at Goldsmith's farm. After Goldsmith entered his house, Ching Lee, still hiding in the wagon, overheard their plans to rob and even kill Goldsmith. Disregarding his own safety, Ching Lee emerged and clubbed one of the robbers. Meanwhile, alerted by the noise outside his house, Goldsmith stepped outside to shoot the other robber. Out of gratitude, he invited Ching Lee to stay on his farm, where in a few years Ching reportedly became "one of the best farmers and fruit growers in the country."[30] The lives of both men were changed by the riot, but they were among the fortunate few.

Denver's civil authorities proved unable to prevent the rioters from ravaging the Chinese community, destroying businesses, looting homes, and hurting inhabitants. This was due to insufficient manpower and inadequate leadership. At the start of the riot, only eight police officers were on duty, clearly too few to deal with a mob that numbered in the thousands. Civil authorities had to deputize many men to assist them. None of the principal officials on the scene—Mayor Richard Sopris, Sheriff Michael Spangler, and General Dave Cook—took the actions necessary to suppress the riot. And in the case of Mayor Sopris (1878–81), his actions reportedly made matters worse.

Mayor Sopris tried to calm the mob with his words, but to no avail. He then ordered the fire department to turn a fire hose on the mob to disperse them, which only antagonized them further. According to Assistant Fire Chief Roberts, it was the hosing down that "transformed that curious crowd into a mob of hellions, bent on vengeance, incendiarism, destruction, and murder."[31] While the riot was attributable to a confluence of factors, not just the simple drenching of curious onlookers, the hosing hardly helped matters.

The civil authorities had other options, but they refused to take them. The police could have used their guns. According to Pomeroy, "Had there been a prompt meeting of the mob with lead instead of streams of water . . . the riot would have died a-borning."[32] While the result of such a scenario will never be known, it is at least apparent that in the recorded instances, when the threat of deadly force was employed to protect the Chinese, the mob backed down. Certainly, Chinese government officials agreed that Denver authorities had failed to meet the mob forcefully. Moreover, Chinese officials implied that the ineffectual response was due to the fact that the victims of the riot were Chinese rather than white. From an outsider's perspective, the reluctance of police to use guns to settle the matter seemed an atypical choice for Coloradans.

At the height of the rampage, Mayor Sopris acceded to a request by Governor Frederick W. Pitkin (1879–83) to appoint General Dave Cook as acting police chief and place him in charge of preserving the peace. Cook then appointed 125 special policemen who worked with Sheriff Spangler's newly appointed deputies to try to control the crowds, who were roaming the streets in packs of hundreds. Cook and Spangler could have augmented their forces by requesting the assistance of the Chaffee Light Artillery and the Governor's Guard, which had been called and were standing by. However, these militia units were not utilized, even though it was obvious that the forces of law and order were greatly outnumbered. The RMN attributed Pitkin's refusal to declare martial law to partisan politics, saying that he did not call out the militia to avoid alienating voters right before the election.[33] The newspaper dryly observed that Pitkin had been more than willing to declare martial law earlier in Leadville, during a miners' strike and for even less cause.

The civil authorities' lapse in judgment cost the Chinese dearly. With the meager forces at their disposal, Cook and Spangler could not stop the ongoing mayhem. Unable to keep the Chinese safe, they rounded up as many of them as they could find. Nearly four hundred Chinese were incarcerated in the county jail for their own safety. While they remained in protective custody for three days, the mob pillaged their unprotected property.

The worst thing that happened during the riot was the murder of Look Young, a twenty-eight-year-old employee of Sing Lee's laundry. He was at Sing Lee's laundry when the mob sacked it. Nicholas G. Kendall, a shoe store clerk, offered the following eyewitness testimony: "[The rioters] went straight to Sing Lee's house and commenced to breaking in the windows. A portion of the mob went into the house in the rear. They proceeded to break up everything and throw it out. There were about ten who went into the house. They caught one Chinaman [Look Young] and brought him out with a rope around his neck, and they were dragging him with the rope while he was on his back."[34] Other witnesses testified that the mob shouted, "Cut off his cue [sic]; cut off his nose." After cutting off his queue, perhaps for a trophy, the mob then proceeded to torture him before hanging him from a lamppost. They forced him to run a short distance, catching him and beating him severely, and then forced him to run again, catching him and beating him once more. Finally, he was pushed to his knees and held there while one person kicked him and another hit him repeatedly in the head.

Somehow, Dr. Cotton C. Bradbury was able to secure Look Young's release and brought his nearly lifeless body to the office of Dr. O. G. Cranston. Cranston found Look Young's injuries to be extensive:

> I found a cut on the left side of his head through the scalp clear to the
> skull. . . . He had a wound on his forehead, over the right eye, and the right

side of his face was swollen considerably. His teeth were mostly all loose and we took out some which were entirely broken out. He was bruised all over the body as though he had been kicked. . . . The indications were that he was hurt internally and probably some rupture of a blood vessel. . . . There were marks on his neck as though caused by strangulation, but don't think that was the cause of his death.[35]

In spite of Cranston's and two other physicians' best efforts to revive him, Look Young died of his wounds, specifically from the concussion to his head. Look Young had been born in Hock Sun, eighty miles from Canton, China.[36] He had been in the United States for four and a half years before coming to Denver, where he worked for six months. He had left behind a wife, father, and mother in China, who were dependent on him for support. Although he died gruesomely, Look Young was at least spared the horror of being lynched. Lynching was a type of extrajudicial punishment peculiar to the American West and South; often, victims were tortured before they were hung and afterward their bodies were mutilated through castration and decapitation.[37] The savagery of it was meant to terrorize and enforce subordination.[38]

Given the sheer size of the riot, it is surprising that only one person died. Though the mob only murdered one Chinese that day, it was not for lack of trying. Summing up the spirit of the day, one rioter declared, "He was going to take the town in and kill every damned son of a bitch of a Chinaman he could find."[39] Although the rioters may have been intent on murdering as many Chinese as possible, other Denverites intervened when the civil authorities lagged. As discussed in chapters 3 and 4, Reverend Dr. Henry C. Westwood and the parishioners of the Central Presbyterian Church went into the streets to rescue Chinese. At the other end of the social spectrum, Wazee Street madam Lizzie Preston and her ladies protected the Chinese who were being sheltered in their bordello from further harm.

Preventive action taken by courageous civilians and law enforcement officers made a significant difference. The civilians defended the Chinese simply because they felt it was the right thing to do. The officers did so because it was their duty to protect the innocent, though in some instances they went well beyond the call of duty. Their actions merit recounting since it is always worth remembering those who are willing to take a stand against injustice.

More loss of life would have occurred without the intervention of Denverites such as George C. Hickey, a printer, who helped to prevent Ah Chung (Wang Tan Chung) and Ah Sin from being lynched.[40] Police officer Timothy J. Ryan provided important assistance in this. Ryan, a "huge fighting Irishman, that feared neither man, nor the devil" was seen "busy knocking men down like tenpins" with his bare fists.[41] As stated in a report of his actions that day, Ryan went on to "single-handedly sav[e] fourteen other beaten and battered up Chinaman from different mobs, a record showing what one brave Irishman could do in a pinch. A great Policeman."Another Denverite who defended the Chinese that day was Jim Moon, a professional gambler and reputed killer. According to an account that reads like a scene straight out of a Louis L'Amour novel, Moon single-handedly held off a mob of at least three hundred. Standing in front of a Chinese laundry, Moon faced them and declared, "Folks[,] this Chink is my friend. My clothes, and my Wife's, are in this Laundry; and I am telling you, that the only way you can get this Chink, is over my dead Body."[42] When one of the rioters went to throw a brick at him, "Like lightning, [Moon] aimed his forty-five Colt Peacemaker at the brick thrower and said, 'One more move from you, and you will get it between the eyes.' That was enough for the cowardly mob." After that, most of the mob dispersed.

By about 10:00 P.M., the riot had run out of steam. The violence had gutted Chinatown. The rioters went home to sleep off their physical exertions while the Chinese languished in the county jail. In the days following, sporadic acts of brutality and looting were reported, but by and large, public order was restored.

In the aftermath, the Republicans lost no time making political hay over the riot. On the following evening, November 1, Republicans took to the Denver streets for a counter-demonstration, making a special appeal to law-abiding citizens. The torchlight parade comprised some twenty-eight hundred to three thousand participants, one thousand of them on horseback, and, reportedly, "a large number of business men, many of whom never marched with any political procession before," who were "indignant with the riot, and took the occasion to rebuke the mob."[43] Meanwhile, that night in Leadville, immense throngs of Republicans and Democrats rallied for the final parades of the presidential campaign. As described in the *Leadville Daily Herald*, the two groups presented a study in contrast in responses to the events in Denver of the previous day. Some seven hundred Democratic demonstrators reportedly celebrated the riot "with considerable rejoicing," while more than a thousand Republicans marched, then listened to speakers denouncing it. One speaker hoped that the spectacle of "democrats murdering Chinese" would bring a windfall of votes to the Republicans. As the speaker's comment suggests, the purpose of the rally was not to express support for Chinese but to rally support for the Republicans. As another Republican speaker put it, "He did not desire to see the Chinese in this country any more than the anti-Chinese did, but he was in favor of humanity. If the Chinese were obnoxious they should be removed in some other way" rather than be exterminated, as Democrats advocated.[44] The contrast between the Democratic and Republican responses indicates the immediate division in public opinion on rights and wrongs of the riot, but it does not reveal much sympathy for the victims by either side.

MISCARRIAGE OF JUSTICE

Rather than passively accept their victimization at the hands of the mob, Chinese Denverites appealed to the city government to compensate them for the property damage they suffered. For example, the prominent Dr. Young Bong urged the city to indemnify the Chinese residents.[45] He himself had lost twenty-six hundred dollars when the rioters robbed his store on Sixteenth Street. He also sent lengthy correspondences to the Chinese minister as well as to other government authorities in Washington, DC. However, the Denver City Council accepted no responsibility for the riot, rejecting all Chinese claims for reparations to the victims. In the absence of any government assistance, many Denverites took it on themselves to offer shelter and other forms of emergency help to the Chinese.

Although the municipal government was not interested in compensating the victims, local officials proved more responsive to making the rioters pay for their crimes, since they perceived this as a matter of civil order. The failure to properly reprimand the perpetrators would only encourage lawless behavior in the future.

The city government sought to bring the rioters to justice, particularly those responsible for the murder of Look Young. Soon after the race riot, the Second Judicial District Court of Colorado initiated the "riot" cases.[46] In Denver's Sinophobic climate, bringing the rioters to justice proved to be a daunting task, but eventually, the government indicted more than a dozen individuals for "unlawfully, riotously, tumultuously and maliciously [assembling and gathering] together to disturb the peace, the same being an unlawful act!"[47]

During the riot cases, the prosecution called in numerous witnesses to testify against the rioters. These included not only law enforcement agents but also Chinatown residents like John Taylor, a well-known Chinese community leader, and Ah Sin, a Chinese Christian. The prosecution faced an immense challenge in meeting the higher burden of proof required in criminal cases. While the eyewitness testimonies of prosecution witnesses were considered credible, they lacked the sort of specificity needed to prove beyond a reasonable doubt that the defendants were guilty of rioting. Meanwhile, the defense called even more witnesses, many of whom were willing to perjure themselves by providing the defendants with false alibis, usually concerning their whereabouts at the time of the alleged events. In doing so, the defense witnesses created enough doubt to allow the juries to find the defendants innocent. Most of the indicted rioters were given the benefit of the doubt and avoided punishment of any sort. Still, several individuals were found guilty of rioting and sentenced to a year in prison. Though the Chinese had their day in court, the punishments meted out to those found guilty of rioting were modest, given the extent of the injuries inflicted and the damage done.

Immediately after the riot, on November 1, 1880, Thomas Linton, the county coroner, convened an inquest into the death of Look Young.[48] After two weeks of deliberation, the grand jury of six indicted James Corrigan, Henry Miller, and Edward Troendell for murder. They were accused of "feloniously, willfully, and deliberately with premeditation and malice aforethought" placing a rope around Look Young's neck and beating him to death with their hands and feet and with a club.

Denverites considered the murder trial a cause célèbre and followed the proceedings avidly. The three-day trial began on February 16, 1881, and a jury of twelve, mostly working-class, men was impaneled to hear the evidence. The prosecution and defense subpoenaed a slew of witnesses. The prosecution witnesses placed the defendants at the scene but were unable to say conclusively who the actual assailants were. Among the witnesses was Ah Sin, who was present during the attack and had narrowly escaped being lynched by the mob. But he, too, was unable to identify those who had bludgeoned his friend Look Young.[49] The main witness for the prosecution was Dr. Cotton C. Bradbury, who himself had been hurt while rescuing Look Young from the mob. Bradbury testified that Corrigan and

Troendell were the leaders of the mob that killed Look Young.[50] Officer M. S. Gill corroborated Bradbury's testimony and testified that he heard Troendell say that he intended to finish off Look Young.[51] Another witness, E. L. Schumacker, testified that it was Miller who struck Look Young with a five-foot piece of lumber. Graham and Cranston, the physicians who attended to Look Young's wounds, testified that he had died of a brain injury. Meanwhile, the defense witnesses, mainly friends and coworkers, testified that the defendants were elsewhere when Look Young was murdered. They claimed that Troendell was at home and that Corrigan was at dinner when the crime was committed. Miller was also provided with an alibi.

After several hours of deliberation, Francis V. Kirk, foreman of the jury, announced a verdict of not guilty on the murder charge.[52] While Corrigan, Troendell, and Miller were found innocent of murdering Look Young, they pleaded guilty to the charge of participating in the riot, contradicting the witnesses at their trial who testified that they were elsewhere, and were sentenced to a year's imprisonment. The three men got away with murder, receiving only the punishment meted out to rioters. This miscarriage of justice was not the end of the story, however, since the Denver race riot became a diplomatic dispute between China and the United States.

DIPLOMATIC DANCE

Upon learning of the Denver race riot, Chen Lanbin, Chinese minister to the United States, Peru, and Spain, promptly requested a meeting with Secretary of State William M. Evarts to demand an investigation. In 1875, at the repeated requests of the Chinese Six Companies, the Qing government had sent Chen to protect the interests of the Chinese in America. In many respects, he was an ideal choice. Besides having the scholarly credentials required of government officials, he had foreign experience. He had served abroad as a member of the Chinese Education Mission, and in 1875 became its commissioner.

In 1878, Chen assumed his ambassadorial post in Washington, DC. One of the first things he did as minister was to apprise himself of the situation facing the Chinese in America, especially the causes for their persecution. To assist the Chinese, Chen opened a consulate general in San Francisco. He appointed his assistant, Chen Shutang, as consul general, and Frederick A. Bee, an entrepreneur and attorney, as vice consul. Appointing an

American to this position was an unusual step. Chen did so because of Bee's long-standing association with the Chinese American community. As early as 1855, he had defended Chinese miners who were being harassed in El Dorado County, California. In 1876, he served as the attorney for the Six Companies in San Francisco when Congress was studying the issue of Chinese immigration. Later, the Qing dynasty government awarded Bee a medal for his contributions to China.

Chen realized that, although he could not stop the anti-Chinese movement that had engulfed the American West and was spreading beyond it, he could at least try to provide his countrymen with some protection by appealing to America's commitment to the rule of law. His first real opportunity to do so was after the Denver race riot. On November 10, 1880, Chen sent Secretary Evarts a letter demanding that those responsible for the riot be punished and the victims compensated. In his December 30, 1880, reply, Evarts smoothly dismissed Chen's requests. Evarts began by expressing his and President Hayes's personal indignation and regret over the tragedy, but he ultimately rejected Chen's claims on jurisdictional grounds, saying that such matters were the responsibility of Colorado and Denver rather than the federal government.[53] Evarts reminded Chen that the federal government could directly intervene in local matters only under circumstances expressly provided for by the US Constitution. But he wanted to assure Chen that the federal government would protect Chinese residents in the same manner and to the same extent as it did its own citizens.[54] In the context of the many anti-Chinese episodes in Colorado and in the American West during the preceding decade, and given the federal government's failure to punish most of the perpetrators, Evarts's pledge was laughable.

Evarts also defended the way in which Denver authorities had handled the race riot, offering the fiction that local authorities had in fact moved briskly to restore order in twenty-four hours and had arrested "many of the ringleaders."[55] Other federal officials later echoed this revised history of the riot. To signal to Chen that no indemnifications or other actions would be forthcoming, Evarts stated that he had done all that "the principles of international law and the usages of national comity demand."[56]

The West Coast anti-Chinese lobby may have influenced Evarts's response. Yielding to pressures from them, in the summer of 1880, Evarts had sent James B. Angell, US minister to China, to negotiate changes to the 1868 Burlingame Treaty authorizing Chinese immigration. The resulting Angell Treaty, which was signed on November 17, 1880, a month and half after the Denver race riot, allowed the US government to regulate and limit the immigration of Chinese laborers, though not to prohibit it outright. Outright prohibition would come two years later, with the passage of the Chinese Exclusion Act.

Given Evarts's efforts to keep Chinese out of the country, the prospects for a meaningful resolution to the riot were rather bleak. Chen persevered nevertheless. He sent Vice Consul Frederick A. Bee to Denver on a fact-finding mission. Bee's investigation of the riot would be his first, but not his last, inquiry into mass violence against the Chinese. He would be sent on a similar assignment to investigate the Rock Springs massacre in nearby Wyoming five years later.

After arriving in Denver on November 27, Bee carried out a thorough study of the riot based on extensive interviews with Chinese residents and prominent Denverites. His reports reckoned that the Chinese community had sustained at least $53,655 in property losses.[57] In addition, he concluded that the efforts of the civil authorities to suppress the riot were weak and ineffectual. To support this contention, Bee cited the coroner's inquest:

> The evidence shows that the said mob could have been suppressed by
> the regular force had they fearlessly arrested the ringleaders; but which,
> owing to the disorganized condition of the police force of the city and the
> incompetency and inefficiency of its government by the proper authority
> and the failure of the county authorities to render the necessary aid and
> assistance required in such emergencies, the mob assumed such proportions
> as culminated in the destruction of human life and the disgrace of the city in
> not affording protection to life and property.[58]

So confident was Bee that the evidence marshaled in his investigation would speak for itself that he told a *Denver Tribune* reporter that the federal government would settle the claims of the Chinese. Speaking as a lawyer, he noted that China's treaty was with the United States and not with Colorado, and besides, there were no state or city laws that provided redress in a case of this sort. As it turned out, Bee's optimism was unwarranted.

Citing the results of Bee's investigation and invoking treaties between the United States and China, Chen tried again to persuade Evarts that the federal government was in fact required to act. He argued that since the American government had failed to protect the Chinese as called for by Sino-American treaties, it was responsible for compensating the Chinese for their losses. But Evarts did not budge. What Chen failed to appreciate was that the Chinese were being treated less like citizens of another country than like other people of color in the United States, and the federal government had a dismal record of fulfilling its obligations to its people of color. For contemporary examples, Chen had only to consider the government's broken treaties with Native Americans and its failure to protect blacks during the Reconstruction Era.

Still, Chen persisted. After James G. Blaine, the Republican senator from Maine, replaced Evarts, Chen resubmitted his claims. Blaine, however, was the wrong man to appeal to. An ardent advocate of banning the Chinese from the United States, Blaine had previously argued in the Senate for the abrogation of the Burlingame Treaty as a necessary step to achieve this. In what was likely an effort to garner political points for his presidential candidacy, Blaine had done his best to drive a stake through the heart of efforts to treat Asians like other immigrant groups. He argued on the Senate floor that, no matter how long the Chinese stayed, they would never "make a homogenous element" with American society because they lacked family values, an idea that seems to betray a complete ignorance of the family-oriented Chinese culture. Blaine insisted that there was no logic in "comparing European immigration with an immigration that has no regard to family, that does not recognize the relation of husband and wife, that does not observe the tie of parent and child, that does not have in the slightest degree the ennobling and civilizing influences of the hearthstone and fireside."[59] Given Blaine's mentality, it is hardly surprising that he refused to do anything in response to Chen's pleas and merely referred Chen to Evarts's earlier arguments. Like Evarts, Blaine tried to deflect the government's responsibility by lauding the local authorities' actions to end the riot, "efforts that happily proved successful with only the loss of one life, although the mob numbered thousands."[60]

It is apparent that Chinese and American governments were engaged in a diplomatic pas de deux, with the United States leading and China forced to follow. The American government's refusal to intervene in the settlement of the Denver race riot was less a matter of conforming to the requirements of the US Constitution and international law, and more a matter of power politics. At the time, China was politically too weak and its international status too low to wrest any concessions from the US government. The reverse was not the case, for the Chinese government had to indemnify American victims who suffered violence at the hands of mobs in China. When it came to the rights of Chinese, there was obviously a double standard at work. Though the Chinese had the right to residence and protection under Sino-American treaties, this right was not automatically guaranteed.

EXCLUSION AND ITS AFTERMATH

The Denver race riot and other instances of racially motivated assaults on Chinese served as an implicit rationale for prohibiting them from entering the country. Since the United States did not want the Chinese to be permanent residents and would not protect those who were in the country, Congress enacted legislation to keep them out of the country. On May 6, 1882, President Chester A. Arthur signed the Chinese Exclusion Act, banning the immigration of Chinese laborers for ten years as a way to ensure social order. Adding insult to injury, the Exclusion Act blamed the Chinese for local disturbances. The act's preamble says, "In the opinion of the Government of the United States the coming of Chinese laborers to this country endangers the good order of certain localities within the territory," holding the Chinese accountable for the very brutality that had been visited on them.[61]

The Chinese Exclusion Act was a discriminatory piece of legislation. Massachusetts senator George Frisbie Hoar (Republican), a well-known opponent of slavery and imperialism, aptly described it as nothing less than the legalization of discrimination.[62] This was the first time in American history that the government had singled out a specific ethnic group for exclusion from the country. Indeed, the Chinese have the unfortunate distinction of being the only national group to be identified in federal legislation as undesirable immigrants. The legislation had consequences for the United States far beyond the Chinese. The act ended the country's cherished tradition of free immigration, replacing it with a policy of selective immigration. With the exclusion of the Chinese came the beginnings of an elaborate bureaucracy dedicated to carrying out restrictive immigration laws that required policing the borders and documenting the aliens who crossed them.[63] It took more than a century before the US Congress agreed with Frisbie and expressed regret for having enacted an ugly law now recognized as un-American. In 2011, the US Congress passed a joint resolution apologizing for the Chinese Exclusion Act and other laws that victimized Chinese immigrants.[64]

The exclusion law did little to diffuse Sinophobic sentiment, which

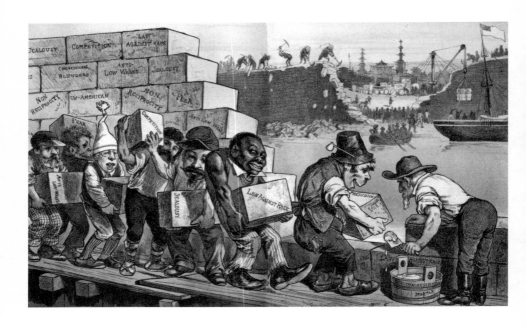

FIG. 5.2. "The anti-Chinese wall—The American wall goes up as the Chinese original goes down," by Friedrich Graetz, *Puck* (March 29, 1882). This political cartoon shows laborers—Irishmen, an African American, a Civil War veteran, an Italian, a Frenchman, and a Jew—building a wall against the Chinese. Across the sea, a ship flying the American flag enters China, as the Chinese knock down their own wall and permit trade of such goods as rice, tea, and silk. Denver Public Library, Western History Collection, Library of Congress Prints and Photographs Division, Illus. in AP101.P7 v. 11 Case X [P&P].

continued unabated throughout the West. In the short term, the legislation may in fact have intensified it. On the day that the act became law, in Rico, Colorado, a mob of fifty to sixty people attacked the town's Chinese residents, dragging them from their homes, assaulting them brutally, and plundering their possessions.[65] Increasingly, organized labor took the lead in agitating against Chinese, playing to racial resentment and using the all-too-familiar slogan of "The Chinese Must Go!" to recruit workers into the fledgling labor movement.[66] Three years after the passage of the exclusion act, the intersection of Sinophobic interests with the labor movement produced a volatile combination that led to the infamous Rock Springs massacre in Wyoming. On September 2, 1885, white miners killed twenty-eight Chinese, wounded an additional fifteen Chinese, and drove out six hundred of them, destroying their property.[67] Many sought refuge in Denver's Chinatown, arriving penniless and in need of a job.[68]

About two weeks after the massacre, the Denver branch of the Knights of Labor continued what the Rock Springs Knights had started and sent a letter to the Union Pacific Railroad Company demanding the expulsion of all Chinese from the mines they operated.[69] Perhaps as a move to exercise its newfound power or simply to sow discord between the Union Pacific Railroad Company and its employees, the Knights of Labor also ordered five hundred coal miners in Carbon, Wyoming, and two hundred in Louisville, Colorado, to go on strike to protest Union Pacific's retention of Chinese miners at Rock Springs.[70] A large number of the coal miners in Colorado, however, chose to ignore this order and continued to work for Union Pacific.[71] In all likelihood, this action, or rather non-action, was motivated by self-interest rather than a desire to show sympathy for the Chinese miners.

While the Chinese were now prevented from entering the country, there was still the problem of getting rid of those who were already here.[72] In the post-exclusion period, Sinophobic actions against local Chinese communities throughout Colorado spread.[73] By 1900, the *Denver Tribune* reported that "all the towns and cities of importance [had] fired [Chinese] by sheer force."[74] As in the case of the Rock Springs massacre, organized labor took the lead. Local labor unions considered it their particular responsibility to remain vigilant to keep Chinese workers from "invading the American field."[75] The Industrial Workers of the World, an international workers' union established in 1905, was the sole exception. From the very beginning, much to the union's credit, the Wobblies, as its members were known, openly opposed the ban on Chinese workers.[76]

In addition to union-led actions, many spontaneous anti-Chinese incidents also occurred in Colorado. For example, in 1895, an ad hoc committee of twenty-five white miners in Idaho Springs stopped eight Chinese who had been recruited by the Wallace mining company to put a tunnel through their property and prevented them from starting work. Prior to this, the white miners had been offered the job but turned it down. The white miners resented that the Chinese were willing to work for the low wage of $1.50 per day and reportedly "set up a terrible howl against Coolie labor."[77] In 1898, when the *Pueblo Courier* found out that two Chinese,

Fong Sing and Fong Jue, were working as laundrymen for the state insane asylum, the newspaper accused the institution's trustees of employing coolie labor. Pueblo labor organizations took up the issue and demanded to know why a state institution was employing aliens when there were "hundreds of able bodied Americans willing and anxious to wash and iron the dirty linen of the asylum."[78]

EXCLUSION EXTENDED

When the 1882 Chinese Exclusion Act expired, Sinophobic groups such as Denver's Anti-Chinese Club supported a bill that would keep the Chinese out of the United States *permanently*. National lobbying efforts fell short of achieving this goal, but anti-Chinese campaigns did result in renewing the Chinese Exclusion Act for another ten years with the passage of supplemental regulations in the Geary Act (1892). The Geary Act made it clear that the Chinese were perceived as a racial problem rather than an economic or public safety issue.[79] California congressman Thomas J. Geary (Democrat) sponsored the eponymous bill extending the prohibition of Chinese workers for another ten years while adding obnoxious provisions that included the requirement that *all* Chinese (including the exempt classes) currently living in the United States carry certificates of residence to prove that they were in the country legally. The certificates were required to bear a photograph of the individual because Chinese were considered to be virtually indistinguishable from one another.

The Geary Act placed the burden of proof on the Chinese, who had to keep these certificates on their person to be produced at will. Chinese were given a year to register with local authorities and apply for their certificate, a duplicate of which was kept in the Internal Revenue Service office. There were penalties for those possessing fraudulent certificates and for those without them. Chinese lacking certificates were considered illegal aliens. They were subject to arrest and liable to be sentenced to perform hard labor for a year before being deported back to China.

Many of Geary's congressional colleagues who voted against the bill objected to the certificate provision. For example, Illinois congressman Robert R. Hitt (Republican) declared it an abomination, saying: "Never before in a free country was there such a system of tagging a man, like a dog to be caught by the police and examined, and if his tag or collar is not all right, taken to the pound or drowned and shot. Never before was it applied by a free people to a human being, with the exception (which we can never refer to with pride) of the sad days of slavery."[80] Hitt's analogy caught on, and the Geary Act became known as the "Dog Tag Law." The association of Chinese with dogs calls to mind the apocryphal sign at the Public Garden in Shanghai, China, that supposedly said "No Dogs or Chinese Allowed."[81] Even as a myth, the sign remains a potent symbol of the humiliations the Chinese suffered in their own country during China's domination by Western and Japanese imperialists during the nineteenth and twentieth centuries.

The Geary Act was demeaning. It was clear to opponents that it was a piece of Sinophobic legislation designed to harass all Chinese residents as well as to extend the ban on Chinese workers. Until 1928, no members of any other group were required to possess documentation certifying that they were lawful residents. Beginning that year, all new immigrants were required to have identification cards.

In Denver, aggressive efforts were undertaken to enforce the Geary Act under the direction of Chief Inspector William P. O'Malley.[82] With the assistance of the local police department, he made a raid on Chinatown to find illegal aliens on January 7, 1897.[83] The police arrested dozens of men but found only two without certificates—Sung Ching and Sing Quong. The two men claimed that they had left their "chok chee" papers, as the certificates were known, in their homes in Boulder and Fairplay, respectively. Apparently, they were later able to produce them, thus avoiding deportation. Two of their brethren, Yee Hong and Wing Lee, were not so lucky.[84] In March 1897, they were sent back to China from Colorado for being illegal aliens.

On October 22, 1897, a day later referred to as Black Friday by the local Chinese, there was another major raid on Denver's Chinatown. With the help of the local police department and US marshals, W. H. Chamberlin, special agent of the Treasury Department from Saint Louis, Missouri, rounded up three hundred Chinese and compelled them to show their certificates.[85] Only nine were without them, but they claimed they had left them at home. Presumably, they either produced their certificates or suffered the same fate as the abovementioned Yee Hong and Wing Lee. These roundups proved to be difficult undertakings since they required the assistance of local law enforcement agents and the presence of an interpreter, who translated for both the court and the Chinese. They typically congested the courts but produced scanty results.

The Chinese made efforts to fight the Geary Act. Under the leadership of Chinese ambassador Wu Ting-fang, the Chinese in America tried to generate support against the Geary Act and lobbied Congress to repeal it, but they were unsuccessful.[86] The Chinese government also threatened to end diplomatic relations with the United States over the issue. Meanwhile, the Six Companies advocated that Chinese resist the law through noncompliance and contribute to a legal fund to challenge the law's constitutionality. Initially, the boycott appeared to be successful; by the April 1893 deadline, only 3,169 of the estimated 110,000 Chinese in the country had registered.

One of the resisters, Fong Yue Ting, who lived in New York City, appealed his deportation. His case eventually went to the US Supreme Court as a challenge to the constitutionality of the Geary Act. Implicit in his lawsuit were significant questions such as whether the Geary Act violated the Burlingame Treaty (1868) and various other constitutional amendments and safeguards in punishing violators with hard labor and deportation. In 1893, in the case of Fong Yue Ting v. United States, the High Court decided to defer to Congress in immigration matters. It ruled that the federal government could deport anyone it wanted to as a right of national sovereignty. Furthermore, the High Court asserted the pernicious judgment that the American government could consider the "presence of foreigners of a different race . . . to be dangerous to its peace and security."[87]

Chinese across the United States protested the exclusion laws. They tried to go through the courts to fight them, but they encountered insuperable obstacles. To begin with, the Chinese were a weak ethnic group, while their enemies had the power of the US Congress behind them. There were comparatively few Chinese, about 100,000 out of a general population of 76 million, and with the exclusion laws in place, their numbers were going to diminish even further. Equally important, they were denied American citizenship. Except for those born in the United States, the Chinese were disenfranchised and lacked a political voice to gain the attention of American authorities.

Under the circumstances, the Chinese had few alternatives but to go outside the United States and the regular channels of redress to seek assistance from their compatriots in China, if they were to have any chance of changing the exclusion laws. Chinese in America complained about their persecution to their countrymen in China, who sympathized and shared their sense of humiliation, frustration, and anger. The immediate challenge faced by Chinese on both sides of the Pacific was to find a way to end or moderate the exclusion laws as well as the repeated affronts to their ethnic group. Chinese in China considered alternatives to negotiation, including retaliation against the American interest in China, to achieve their aims.

FUTILE RESISTANCE

In 1902, a decade after the Geary Act, the Chinese Exclusion Act was extended again for another ten years. One of the influential figures in the passage of the bill was Samuel Gompers, leader of the American Federation of Labor. In 1901, Gompers and Hermann Gutstadt published "Some Reasons for Chinese Exclusion. Meat vs. Rice. American Manhood Against Asiatic Coolieism. Which Shall Survive?" This propagandistic pamphlet recycled the usual argument that Chinese lowered the standard of living of white workers and, for that reason, Congress should continue to ban them from the country.

With the renewal of the exclusion act for the second time in 1902, there was also a revival of anti-Chinese incidents in Colorado. That year, in Silverton, the Western Federation of Miners, the Cooks and Waiters Union, and the Federation of Labor of San Juan County organized a joint boycott of Chinese businesses and demanded that Chinese residents leave the area.[88] It was alleged that the Chinese were a long-standing problem because they had monopolized the restaurant business in the city.[89] They had attracted diners by offering less expensive fare, and this was considered unfair to white restaurant owners.

The problem was evidently more than simply an economic issue. After all, not all the Chinese in Silverton ran restaurants—some were employed in laundries and others worked as porters in saloons. Yet the unions demanded that "all of the race and the entire yellow population of the city, about seventy-five, [be] ordered to move on" under threat of violence.[90] The usual charges were made that Chinese operated opium dens and were a pernicious influence on society.

Secretary of State John Hay tried to intervene on behalf of Silverton's Chinese without success. Hay requested that Colorado governor James B. Orman (Democrat) take the necessary steps to protect the Chinese and their property since there had been reports of brutality, with some Chinese being badly beaten and their homes broken into and robbed. When two Chinese restaurant proprietors tried to resume business in Silverton, they were reportedly "roughly used, ropes being placed around their necks and . . . led out of town."[91] The New York Times characterized Hay's involvement as a ploy on the part of the Chinese: they were trying to provoke whites into taking illegal action against them in the hopes of coming under federal protection. This would ensure their continued presence in the Western mining country. The resistance of local Chinese in Silverton to being driven out was described as the "last stand" of Chinese in the mining camps of the West.[92]

Sinophobic sentiment in Colorado was not confined to Silverton. Other communities, such as those in Florence, Salida, and Ouray, reported union-instigated anti-Chinese disturbances.[93] Most Chinese left peacefully, usually for Denver's Chinatown. But the community they fled to for security was itself dying, with a declining population. With so few Chinese women, there were not enough families with children to replace those who passed away. The young people who grew up in Denver's Chinatown tended to leave in search of opportunities denied them in Colorado.

COMING OF THE JAPANESE

In 1904, Congress passed a resolution to extend the exclusion of Chinese from the country indefinitely. That is, Chinese were permanently prevented from entering the United States. While congressional legislation singled out the Chinese to be kept out of the country, it did not prohibit the immigration of other Asians to the United States, though the labor movement and other anti-Asian agitators wanted lawmakers to do so. In the wake of the banishment of the Chinese came the Japanese, who replaced the Chinese as workers and inherited the same antipathy despite the fact that there were even fewer of them. In 1890, two years before the passage of the Geary Act, the census had counted 107,488 Chinese and 2,039 Japanese in the country, including 1,398 Chinese and 10 Japanese in Colorado. Even though Asians made up just 0.17 percent of the total American population and 0.1 percent of the Colorado population, they were resented in any number.

Several years after the Geary Act (1892), the journalist George Hamline Fitch wrote a postmortem on the gradual disappearance of the Chinese

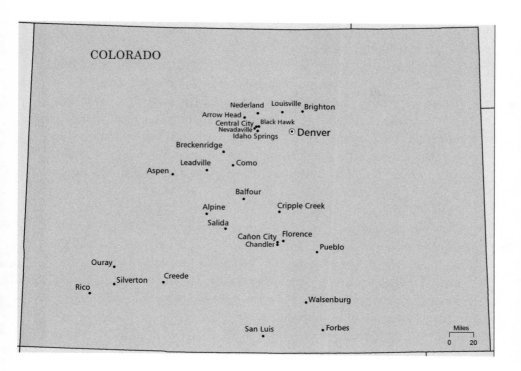

MAP 5.1. Locations of anti-Asian incidents in Colorado. Map by Thomas Dickinson, Institute of Behavioral Science, University of Colorado, Boulder.

in America.[94] Fitch extolled the Chinese for their business acumen and honesty and condemned them for their vices and failure to assimilate. He then sounded an alarm about the Japanese arriving to replace the disappearing Chinese. He observed that Japanese appeared to conform to Western civilization but warned that looks were deceptive. The Japanese constituted as great a menace to American institutions as the Chinese ever did.

Japanophobia replaced Sinophobia. Labor leaders continued to play the race card to advance their political agenda. Predictably, they complained that the Japanese would displace white workers, overrun the whole Trans-Missouri section of the country, if not the entire country, and reduce workingmen's pay to some abysmally low "Oriental" wage scale.[95] Leaders of the Western Federation of Miners (WFM) even thought that President William McKinley (1897–1901) was conspiring with capitalists against organized labor to invite other countries, including Japan, to flood the American labor market with workers.[96]

In Colorado, the WMF endeavored to prevent Japanese from working in the coal mines in the southern part of the state. The federation was alarmed by reports of corporations employing Japanese labor in Fremont and Huerfano Counties, where they would displace white labor. The federation's anti-Japanese campaign occurred at about the same time that the Chinese were being driven out of Silverton. The RMN succinctly expressed the unions' attitude toward both groups with the bold headline "UNION MINERS BANISH CHEAP ASIATIC LABOR," which was flanked by the words "Japs Run Out of Chandler" on the left and "Chinese Must Leave Silverton" on the right.[97] Not to be outdone, the *Denver Post* ran a similar set of stories with the headline "Asiatic horde driven out of Colorado mining camps and promise is given that no further importations will be made."[98] Following up on these incidents, the Colorado State Legislature passed a joint resolution to encourage the US Congress to take steps to exclude all Asiatic labor from the country.[99]

Within the span of about one generation, Colorado's attitude had gone from encouraging Chinese to immigrate to the state to supporting the exclusion of *all* Asians from the nation. As I discuss in the following chapters, the United States was transformed from the land of immigrants to the land of select white immigrants and no Asian immigrants. It was a policy that would take decades to undo.

SIX

JAPANESE IMMIGRANTS: FROM FEUDAL PEASANTS TO INDEPENDENT FARMERS

I T WAS AS *WATARIDORI*—BIRDS OF PASSAGE—THAT JAPANESE IMMI-grants began their journey to the Centennial State. In some ways, their experience was similar to that of the Chinese who preceded them. But it was also dissimilar due to the cultural differences between the two groups, the changing circumstances for immigrants in the late nineteenth and early twentieth centuries, and the effects of the earlier anti-Chinese movement. Both the similarities and dissimilarities significantly shaped how the American state and society treated the Japanese as well as how they responded to that treatment.[1]

DEPARTING FOR DISTANT SHORES

As was the case for Chinese immigration, the initial impetus for Japanese immigration to the United States came from Western imperialism and the push-pull factors resulting from it. Among the factors that led Japanese to leave their country, the most important was the new Meiji government's tax reforms, which dispossessed peasants of their land. During the 1880s, over 367,000 peasants were forced into tenancy or left their villages to become wage laborers in the cities.[2]

For many peasants, this was the beginning of an arduous two-stage trip that started with their departure from the countryside and then from Japan itself. They became part of the *dekasegi* tradition of leaving home temporarily to find work to supplement their family incomes. Having already left their villages to look for employment elsewhere, they found going abroad easier. For many overseas Japanese immigrants, or Nikkei, as they were called, the journey eventually led to Hawaii and then the American mainland.

Most Nikkei went to the United States between 1890 and 1924, with the largest number arriving between 1901 and 1908. According to the US census, in 1890, there were only 2,039 Japanese in the country. But by 1910, there were more than 72,000 of them, exceeding the number of Chinese. Altogether, about 150,000 Japanese immigrated to the United States, a miniscule portion (less than 1 percent) of the 16 million immigrants who reached American shores between 1890 and 1914.

Many Japanese went to the American mainland to seek higher wages and to escape the onerous conditions on the Hawaiian sugar plantations. Upon arrival on the West Coast, many found jobs in the agricultural areas surrounding their ports of entry; others moved inland along the railroad lines that had been built earlier by the Chinese and others. Colorado was the farthest east that most of them ventured.

Like the Chinese before them, the Japanese usually worked in unskilled, undesirable occupations that required hard physical labor. And like the Chinese, they also encountered enmity. Though Japanese experienced problems similar to those of Chinese in Colorado, the shared experience produced little unity between them. Instead of developing some degree of pan-Asian solidarity, which might have been useful in confronting enemies who clamored for the exclusion of *all* Asians from America, an inter-ethnic acrimony arose between the two groups. Homeland politics were largely responsible for their mutual aversion, which trumped any sense of common cause.

For a brief period, Americans initially looked favorably on the Japanese, romanticizing their culture and even their physiognomy. They thought Japanese society embodied the American virtues of industry, simple living, and social egalitarianism.[3] They imagined that the Japanese looked different from other Asians. In their mind's eye Japanese faces looked more like those of Europeans and therefore Japanese were closer to Europeans in mental attributes.[4] A *Denver Evening Post* writer even suggested that some Japanese leaders were so Western-looking that they could be mistaken for whites: Premier Ito, the great diplomat, could pass for a wealthy "Colorado silverite or a North Dakota speculator in town lots"; General Yamagata looked like the novelist Robert Louis Stevenson; Marshal Oyama bore a resemblance to Grover Cleveland; and Viscount Mutse made "a fine-looking white man."[5] Such comparisons were encouraged by the familiarity Americans felt in interacting with educated Japanese, who spoke English, dressed like Europeans, and were well versed in Western customs.

Realizing that Americans had a history of hostility toward Chinese, Japanese endeavored to be treated like whites and framed their identity in opposition to the Chinese. Japanese took umbrage whenever they were lumped together with the "dirty" Chinese. Some Japanese uncritically accepted the prevailing negative views of the Chinese community, as shown in one Japanese student's description of San Francisco's Chinatown as "a world of beasts in which, behind its outward façade, exists every imaginable depravity, crime, and vice known to the human world—assault, homicide, gambling, illicit business, prostitution, robbery, and drunken disorder," an idea informed by white fantasies.[6] In a similar vein, Kiyoshi Karl Kawakami, who served as director of the Pacific Press Bureau, was at pains to point out that the Japanese community in America was law abiding and "not plagued by so-called hatchet men whose deeds strike 'terror in the hearts of all [Chinatown] denizens.'"[7]

The Japanese faulted the Chinese for failing to adapt to American culture. They claimed that Japanese people were capable of assimilating while the Chinese were not. Indeed, they believed that historically the Japanese had shown a unique capacity to absorb foreign cultures.[8] Sidney L. Gulick, a former missionary and a peace activist during World War I, put it this way: "The Japanese go to the West in order to acquire all the West can give," while "the Chinaman goes steeled against its influences."[9]

Japanese emphasized this distinction by wearing modern apparel, a custom adopted during the *bunmei kaika* (civilization and enlightenment) movement in the early years of the Meiji era (1868–1912). Gulick, who spent much of his life trying to bridge Japanese and American cultures, saw such differences as reflecting a Japanese willingness to acculturate and a stubborn Chinese refusal to do so: "Contrast a Chinaman and a Japanese after each has been in America a year. The one to all appearances is an American; his hat, his clothing, his manner, seem so like those of an American that were it not for his small size, Mongolian type of face, and defective English, he could easily be mistaken for one. How different is it with the Chinaman! .... [Chinese] make no effort to conform to their surroundings. He seems to glory in his separateness."[10] For Gulick, the inherent difference between Japanese and Chinese people was shown by such externalities. But as Japanese discovered, their choice of sartorial style as well as other adaptations failed to shield them from suspicion. As one newspaper commented, "Cutting the hair and tucking in the shirt tail is not enough."[11] For Japanophobes, the adoption of American customs only made the Japanese more dangerous than their Chinese predecessors because it disguised who they really were.[12]

Despite the willingness of some to place Japanese in a category separate from Chinese, many Americans thought their shared racial character mattered more, and they based their treatment of both groups on this. Inasmuch as Asians looked alike physically, they were thought to be alike in other respects. For those harboring anti-Asian sentiments, the Japanese were equally detestable as the Chinese and for the same reasons. Writing in 1915, Dr. Harry A. Millis, an economist and member of the National Labor Relations Board, explained why the Japanese were lumped with the Chinese as an inferior people:

> [The Japanese] came from the same "quarter of the earth," were of related color, had a similar language, accepted the same economic rank as the Chinese, frequently occupied their bunkhouses, and underbid for work as did the Chinamen. What wonder, though they were vastly different peoples, that the Japanese should be set down as being in the same category as the Chinese? In men's minds they were assigned the same place to begin with. Moreover, it was assumed that they should continue to occupy it. Not to do so was to be regarded as undesirable.[13]

In sum, the Japanophobes were cut from the same cloth as Sinophobes. It was a simple matter for them to transfer their prejudices against the Chinese to the Japanese who had been recruited to develop Colorado's economy.

COMING TO COLORADO

It is difficult to determine with any precision the number of Japanese who migrated to Colorado or even when they arrived, though a few probably arrived in the mid-1890s. In 1900, twenty were known to have lived in downtown near the original Chinatown, around Blake and Market Streets. By the end of the decade, it was estimated that there were about 526 (489 men, 24 women, and 13 children) living in Japantown, an ethnic enclave located on Larimer Street between Eighteenth and Twenty-First Streets.[14] Augmenting the resident population were large numbers of transient workers, perhaps as many as fifteen hundred at any one time.

Japantown functioned as a service center for Japanese who traveled around the state performing seasonal labor. It also served other ethnic groups living nearby such as Slavs, German-Russians, Poles, and other Eastern European who had settled in the Globeville neighborhood in north Denver, where they worked for the Globe Smelting and Refining Company or the railroad and packing plant industries. By 1903, Japantown had a handful of small businesses; by 1909, the number of these businesses had increased to 67, employing 133 people.[15] These businesses offered inexpensive places for Japanese workers to live between jobs, along with laundries, bathhouses, and barbershops where they could refresh themselves. Perhaps most important, Japantown was where they could find restaurants serving Japanese cuisine, which more than anything else reminded them of their native land.

Because of Japantown's proximity to Chinatown, Japanese went next door for some of their recreational needs, especially to play games of chance. They were particularly partial to playing cards or, as they liked to put it, *hana wo hiku*—literally, "pulling out the flowers," that is, dealing flower-decorated Japanese playing cards.[16] Japanese community leaders thought that these gambling parlors had a corrosive effect on their countrymen and launched anti-gambling campaigns, to little effect. A survey of losses revealed that the Japanese were squandering an estimated three million dollars annually on gambling.[17] In his book *Asia at the Door*, the above-mentioned Kiyoshi Karl Kawakami wryly suggests that the Japanese indirectly financed Dr. Sun Yat-sen's 1911 revolution through their losses in Chinese gambling parlors.[18]

Given the state's racial climate, it is hardly surprising that Japanese encountered problems. In December 1897, the Cooks and Waiters Union launched a campaign to drive Japanese restaurants out of business on the pretext of stamping out the evil of "coolie labor."[19] Even though there were only three Japanese restaurants in the city at the time (the Oriental, Yokohama, and Tokio), the union argued that, unless checked, they would open the floodgates to Japanese who would overrun the city.

The campaign organizers rehearsed the same tired arguments against the Japanese that had been directed against the Chinese. In his speech to white workers at Denver's Coliseum Hall, Harvey E. Garman, president of the Trades Assembly, warned that the Japanese would worm their way into all branches of trade, affecting every business in the city just as they had done on the Pacific Coast.[20] Willis Hall, editor of the *Industrial Advocate*, expressed the widely held belief that Asian workers worked too hard for too little; thus, they constituted unfair competition.

What made this campaign different from the earlier Sinophobic movement in Colorado was its sophistication and its appeal to Americanism. There was no direct intimidation to speak of, although whites who patronized Japanese-owned restaurants were harassed and customers at the Oriental Restaurant on Larimer Street were twice forced to vacate the premises when stink bombs were released.[21] Instead of resorting to violence, opponents organized a boycott of the Japanese restaurants. Japanophobes claimed that these restaurants, as well as boardinghouses and other Japanese businesses, were hotbeds of vice where prostitutes could be found.[22] Such accusations prompted local authorities to consider the possibility that Japanese enterprises were fronts for human trafficking, part of an underground "white slave" operation that kidnapped white women and forced them into prostitution.[23]

The Cooks and Waiters Union asked customers to stay away and local businesses to stop supplying the Japanese restaurants with goods as an act of patriotism. White restaurant owners threatened to shun merchants who supplied their competitors.[24] Both the white restaurant owners and the union demanded that the Japanese restaurants take American dishes off the menu and make them noodle-only joints. The union also sent out messages to local patriotic organizations, such as the Grand Army of the Republic, Sons of Veterans, and the Patriotic Orders of Sons and Daughters of America, to inform them that these un-American institutions were being established in Denver and to urge their members to avoid them.[25] Nobody patronizing these restaurants could be considered a true American or a good citizen.

Japanese restaurant owners initially derided the boycott, predicting that the union would be unable to keep their customers away. If local suppliers refused to do business with them, they would go to Kansas City or Omaha, if necessary, to get meat and other supplies, and they would rely on local Japanese farmers for fresh vegetables.[26] But the boycott hurt their business as customers dwindled. In response, Japanese restaurant owners engaged attorneys to go to court to contest the action as a violation of the boycott law recently passed by the Colorado General Assembly. Though the union thought the law questionable, the Japanese restaurant owners had the law on their side and the federal court declared the boycott illegal.[27]

What the boycott taught the Japanese business community was the necessity of becoming organized to defend their common interest in a hostile milieu. Japanese business owners established American-style civic organizations to engage mainstream society on its own terms. To that end, they organized the Japanese Business Men's Association, the Japanese Restaurant Keepers' Association, and the Japanese Boarding and Lodging House Keepers' Association, among others.[28]

"HARRY" HOKAZONO: COLORADO ENTREPRENEUR

A diverse group of Japanese civic leaders governed Japantown. They served as intermediaries representing the community's interests to white society. They also worked with consular officials to ensure that Japanese immigrants behaved properly, both to avoid embarrassing Japan and to preserve their Japanese cultural identity while living and working in America. Of these community leaders, none was more influential than Hokazono Naoichi.[29]

In 1893, "Harry" Hokazono, as he was known, immigrated to the United States to acquire an education, later studying at Stanford University.[30] He became a pillar of the Japanese Coloradan community, serving as the fourth president of the Japanese Association of Colorado, organized in 1907 in response to the Japanese and Korean Exclusion League that had emerged two years earlier in San Francisco. The Japanese Association worked to counter the anti-Japanese activities of the local labor unions and the Exclusion League's Colorado chapter, which was established in 1908.[31]

In keeping with his responsibilities as a community leader, Hokazono made efforts to prepare his countrymen for life in Colorado. He published a pamphlet advising them on how to behave. His opening paragraph reveals much about the precarious circumstances under which Japanese lived: "At this time the White Union [that is, organized labor] has formed the Japanese Exclusion Association in order to expel us from Colorado, like our compatriots were in San Francisco and other regions. . . . Therefore, each and every one of us, as Japanese, should behave discreetly to avoid dishonoring the Yamato race, while striving to obtain the sympathy of honest and decent Americans."[32] Hokazono then provided a list of rules to guide Japanese workers' behavior—for example, they were to steer clear of gambling houses, brothels, and other immoral establishments, and to always carry a whistle to call for help. In retrospect, Hokazono's mainly negative injunctions on how to avoid alienating whites appear naïve. He failed to understand the underpinnings of white antagonism toward the Japanese. Even if Japanese workers had closely adhered to his guidelines, these accommodations would have had little if any impact on the deep-seated bias against them, and no effect at all on the Japanese and Korean Exclusion League's call to restrict Japanese immigration to America.

In the course of his eventful life, Hokazono became an affluent businessman in the Centennial State. It was said that he was so successful that he had a thousand horses and mules at his command for hauling earth-moving scoops. Hokazono made his fortune primarily as a labor contractor. To meet manpower needs in the state, he began recruiting Japanese for important infrastructure projects. As the well-known journalist and writer Bill Hosokawa reports, Hokazono organized a crew of more than five hundred to build irrigation systems, lay railroad tracks, and clear land for power lines.[33] He made major contributions to the Centennial State's development, working on structures that are landmarks today, such as the Moffat Tunnel and Trail Ridge Road.[34]

Hokazono supervised a workforce of over two thousand to build the massive six-mile long Moffat Tunnel, a railroad and water tunnel that cuts through the Continental Divide in north-central Colorado. The railroad tunnel provided Denver with a key western link across the Continental Divide, and the water tunnel supplied it with a portion of its water. Accompanying the tunnel was Moffat Road, which connected Denver to Steamboat Springs across the Continental Divide. Not surprisingly, the employment of Japanese in the state's construction projects sparked controversy. For example, in 1905, when Denver labor contractor George Easton employed fifteen Japanese workers to prepare ties for the railroad, the residents of Arrow Head, which was at the terminus of Moffat Road, demanded their departure. Easton's defense was that he needed men to work that winter and was unable to recruit white men who were willing to do the job.[35] Though the residents threatened to take matters into their own hands, the situation ended in a stalemate.

Hokazono's men navigated the Continental Divide again when they worked on Trail Ridge Road over Milner Pass, the popular roadway between Estes Park and Granby in what is now Rocky Mountain National Park. They also worked on the Barker Dam, near Nederland, for the Public Service Company. The dam provided water to a downstream hydroelectric power–generating facility, and its reservoir still provides water for nearby Boulder, Colorado.

Besides working as a labor contractor, Hokazono was an agriculturalist. The historian Iwata Masakazu credits him with laying the groundwork for Japanese American agriculture in Colorado.[36] After arriving in Denver in 1898, Hokazono became a Colorado booster, writing an article in the San Francisco *Shinsekai Shimbun* describing in glowing terms the agricultural prospects for Japanese in the state. As a result, several Japanese were motivated to move to southern Colorado, where they leased two hundred acres of land in Rocky Ford to grow sugar beets and cantaloupes. In 1903, Hokazono, who lived in the city of Brighton, in northern Colorado, recruited seventy of his countrymen to work on two thousand acres of sugar beet fields in nearby Greeley for the Great Western Sugar Company.[37]

As often happened in Colorado, where fortunes were quickly made and lost, Harry Hokazono was destitute when he died in 1920. His poverty notwithstanding, he has been honored as one of Colorado's pioneers and is memorialized in a stained-glass window along with Chin Lin Sou in the old Supreme Court room in the State Capitol building (see Fig. 3.3).

FROM MIGRANTS TO FARMERS

Because 70 percent of the Japanese immigrants came from farming backgrounds, it was natural for them to work in the agricultural sector. They were encouraged to come to Colorado to perform farm work in 1924 and 1925. According to rural sociologist Richard W. Roskelley, a group of promoters was interested in selling or renting tracts of land in the San Luis Valley to Japanese in order to cultivate the land and to increase the railroad business.[38] But San Luis residents were resistant to the arrival of the people whom they called "rice-eaters." The *Creede Candle* stirred up local hostility to having this "class of California outcast stuff in the valley."[39]

Japanese Coloradans played an important part in the harvesting and processing of sugar beets, which became a mainstay of the state's commercial agriculture and made the Centennial State one of the nation's leading sugar beet exporters.[40] Colorado's sugar beet industry became a way to attract settlers from nearby Nebraska and Iowa, and from as far away as Germany.[41] In the sugar beet industry, the recruitment of foreign workers proved to be less of an issue than in some other sectors of the economy. Terence Powderly, US commissioner general of labor, thought the recruitment of foreigners to work in the beet fields and factories did not violate existing contract labor laws, despite his previous opposition to immigration from China and Southern and Eastern Europe in his role as grand master workman of the Knights of Labor.[42] Nevertheless, when sugar beet companies began bringing foreign workers into the state, their arrival caused considerable consternation among existing workers, who feared that it would result in decreased wages.[43] The Sugar Beet Workers Union protested the importation of immigrants, demanding that foreign workers be paid wages comparable to those of union workers.

By 1909, 2,672 Japanese were employed in the production of sugar beets. Though they made up only about one-fifth of the fifteen-thousand-man workforce, by some accounts, they were the most productive part. Because of their greater industry and efficiency, they were considered better than German-Russian, Mexican, and other migrant workers.[44] As the US Immigration Commission noted in 1911, "The importance of the Japanese . . . is greater than their numbers indicate, as they do more work per individual than the laborers of any other race."[45]

Japanese Coloradans became a prominent part of the seasonal migratory workforce needed in the labor-intensive sugar beet industry. They engaged in the backbreaking work of bunching, thinning, hoeing, topping, and loading sugar beets. They were available in large numbers and were willing to follow the seasons. They lacked family ties and initially possessed little property to confine them to an area. Consequently, most white farmers welcomed them, at least until they bought or leased land of their own and became competitors. As Bill Hosokawa observes, "Like the Negroes of the South, the Japanese were accepted without rancor only so long as they remained in their place."[46]

Outside of the sugar beet industry, Japanese worked as farmhands and sharecroppers, growing other crops needed to feed the state's people. Many of them made the transition to full-fledged farmers in northern, southern, and western Colorado. According to Japanese records, in 1909, there were 500 Japanese farmers in the Centennial State; in 1933, the number had grown to 725, some of whom were second-generation Japanese Coloradans.[47] They established farms in the Arkansas River Valley, in Denver, and north of Denver in Weld County. By 1909, a total of 14,000 acres in northern Colorado was leased or rented by Japanese, and a total of 4,400 acres in southern Colorado. In the north, Japanese started the first vegetable farms in the South Platte watershed north from Denver toward Greeley to the state's northeast corner. In the south, they became the mainstay of the region's melon industry. As early as 1902, near Rocky Ford, they began growing the cantaloupes for which the region has since become famous. Besides Rocky Ford, they settled in Swink, Crowley, Ordway, La Junta, and other towns along the Arkansas River.

The trajectory of early Japanese agriculturalists in Colorado was remarkable. Within their lifetime, they went from being peasants engaged in subsistence wet rice agriculture in late nineteenth-century Japan to farmers who produced fruits and vegetables in Colorado for the American market during World War I. As historian Iwata Masakazu observes, Japanese "under[took] independent agricultural operations on a scale and with success they themselves had hardly envisioned when they left Japan. Farming in the old country meant cultivating at most several acres. In Colorado they were undertaking the tilling of hundreds of acres!"[48] On their farms, Japanese raised a variety of farm produce, which they marketed in the state and also in nearby Kansas and Nebraska. Their success was due to diligence as well as their ability to apply traditional Asian farming practices and modern American agricultural techniques as needed. Perhaps because most of them were relatively well-educated individuals, they were willing to experiment with innovative techniques, especially in irrigation, to raise crops adapted to Colorado's severe soil and climate conditions.

Equally important, Japanese Coloradans assisted one another as a matter of ethnic solidarity or a cultural propensity to engage in collective activities. Dick Momii, who was raised in an impoverished sharecropper's family in northern Colorado, recalls that "the Japanese American community had good relationships and there was little if any jealousy or animosity, and [they] were always willing to help each other if needed."[49] For Japanese farmers, this system of mutual support often took the form of agricultural cooperatives. In northern Colorado, 95 percent of the Japanese vegetable growers joined the Colorado Japanese Growers Cooperative Association in order to obtain better prices for their produce.[50] In southern Colorado, their counterparts organized San Luis Valley Vegetable Packers, Inc., to facilitate the packing and selling of their produce.

Because most Japanese came to America with little money, less than fifty dollars in many cases, they needed credit to operate their farms. Often this credit was extended to them from bankers, storekeepers, and landowners who had a financial interest in their success. These lenders thought them worth investing in, and Japanese Coloradans proved that they were indeed credit-worthy. Also assisting them were white friends who lent them a neighborly hand in times of need.

One example of a successful Japanese farmer is Nakamura Shingo.[51] Because of the scarcity of food in Japan following the Russo-Japanese War (1904–1905), he left Fukuoka Prefecture to work abroad. In 1906, he first went to work in the sugarcane fields of Buena Vista, Mexico; in 1908, he moved to the sugar beet fields of northeastern Colorado. In 1912, he and some friends pooled their resources and borrowed money from a bank to cultivate sixty acres of land in Logan County. Later, Nakamura and a friend rented a 180-acre farm near Iliff and then another 160 acres near Sterling.

Once Nakamura had achieved a modicum of stability, he decided to get married. In 1916, he returned to Japan to find a wife. Nothing is known about his bride, Kichi, except that she was willing to marry him and return to his farm on the Colorado prairie, where they raised eight children. By 1941, through unstinting labor, they had developed a 225-acre farm, growing sugar beets, wheat, corn, and vegetables. In addition, they had twenty-five head of cattle, five horses, three tractors, two trucks, and two cars for family use. The Nakamuras are a classic American success story. Japanese Coloradans like them contributed significantly to the agricultural sector, producing 33 percent of the vegetables, 70 percent of the cantaloupes, and 25 percent of the sugar beets grown in the state.[52]

Because Japanese farmers were dispersed throughout the countryside, they experienced few incidents. In rural Colorado, despite some concerns about the impact on local institutions, the prevailing attitude seems to have been to live and let live. For example, Dick Momii could remember only a few instances of Japanophobic sentiment in Wattenberg, Weld County: "The mayor of Brighton was very anti-Japanese, as was his daughter, who taught in the high school. On one occasion, she expressed her animosity for Japanese Americans, whereupon one of the valedictorian Japanese American students promptly challenged her racism." This having been said, Momii focuses on the relationships between Japanese and other ethnic groups in the area rather than on the behavior of specific individuals: "We got along well with most of the other nationalities, mainly German, Italian, and Hispanic. There were a few Italians and Hispanics who did not like the Japanese. . . . My friend Rose Tanaka Tanabe recalls that in the small rural town of Brighton, the Italians were quite racist, but the German community was very tolerant of the Japanese Americans."[53] Momii's comments indicate his belief that white attitudes toward Japanese were best understood in terms of differing ethnic identities, suggesting that, while Japanese were sensitive to perceived prejudice, they were just as prepared as everyone else to think along ethnic lines.

Generally speaking, there was relatively little interaction between Japanese farmers and white farmers as they spread out in small farming communities. Some of the white farmers thought the Japanese farmers were mysterious and secretive. In 1944, reviewing the data on Japanese in Colorado, Roskelley reported that the earlier appearance of Japanese in rural Coloradan communities during World War I "did not go unnoticed," but that some white residents believed that the Japanese had entered the community at night, unseen. Suddenly, the Japanese had moved in. There the Japanese remained, a puzzle to locals: "Individuals reported that it was hard to keep an account of them because 'they all look alike.' Farmers said that 'you never really knew whom you rented your land to because you couldn't tell them apart and like as not one person could never tell the difference until midseason because they helped each other so much you never knew who was on your farm.'"[54] Rural Japanese may have been generally invisible to other farmers, but their countrymen working for the railroad and mining companies were more visible and were less fortunate for it.

WORKING ON THE RAILROAD

In the Interior West, the first Japanese railroad workers were probably employed as section hands for the Union Pacific Railroad; later, they worked on construction crews. In 1900, there were an estimated four hundred Japanese railroad workers in Colorado. About one hundred of them constructed the railroad line over the Continental Divide to Steamboat Springs. They were hired primarily because of the decreasing supply of white laborers, many of whom had left for better-paying occupations in the expanding economy, and Chinese laborers who were no longer available because of the exclusion laws. The Japanese were also willing to work for lower wages than workers from Italy, Greece, and Eastern Europe. Finally, the Japanese were often preferred over their competitors because they were good workers, although this was rarely acknowledged publicly.

Japanese railroad workers attracted various complaints. Veteran railroad men grumbled that the limited English of Japanese workers made it difficult for them to understand instructions.[55] Boardinghouse owners groused that they could not make a profit because of Japanese frugality.

FIG. 6.1. One of the earliest jobs that Japanese immigrants had was as section hands to maintain railroad lines, c. 1900. Denver Public Library, Western History Collection, Z-190.

Japanese tended to save much of their wages and spent as little as possible. To the annoyance of local business owners, Japanese preferred to live in railroad cars for free and to prepare their own food.[56] But the railroad companies turned a deaf ear to these complaints and continued to hire Japanese workers.

When railroad companies began replacing section hands with Japanese workers, they received a flurry of petitions protesting such action. To diffuse the criticism, the Denver and Rio Grande Western Railroad Company explained that hiring Japanese to work in the desert was an experiment; it did not conflict with the interests of white workers because they were unwilling to work there. If past experience with Asian workers was borne out, the experiment would not be continued, as the company "had been in the habit of employing Chinese and other aliens in the past, but they do not give the best satisfaction, especially the Chinamen, being about as low as it is possible for a human being to get."[57] Still, the railroad companies continued to hire Japanese workers.

As usual, the *Rocky Mountain News* was alarmed by the prospect of increasing numbers of Asian workers and the threat they posed to American workers, warning that if companies began employing contractors to "bring the hordes of Japanese into the United States to replace American labor, we shall have a combination of contract labor and the 'yellow danger' in the most vicious form."[58] The newspaper reminded readers that the earlier Chinese Question had been settled only with the exclusion of Chinese laborers from the country, implying that the same might be necessary in the case of the Japanese.

Joining the call to exclude Japanese from the country, the labor movement was once again in the vanguard. As I discuss in the next chapter, the labor movement took up the fight to ban Japanese immigration as a patriotic crusade to prevent the so-called Yellow Peril from endangering national security and undermining the American way of life. The development of anti-Japanese sentiment among organized labor is considered here.

OPPOSITION BY ORGANIZED LABOR

At the time of the Denver race riot in 1880, only a mere handful of labor unions existed in Colorado. In 1884, there were 34 unions; by 1888, there were as many as 112.[59] This growth paralleled the national trend, as workers began to realize the advantage of collective bargaining to attain their demands for higher pay, better working conditions, and shorter working hours. During the Progressive Era (1890–1920), workers benefited from the growing acceptance of organized labor as a legitimate means to improve their lives and seek redress for grievances against management. Labor unions gained support as the public became increasingly concerned about the rise of big business, its influence on politics, and its role in economic unrest.

Ironically, even though unions were better organized and more powerful than ever at the beginning of the twentieth century, they continued to be fearful of competition from Japanese labor. In the intermountain states, the Western Federation of Miners (WFM) made opposition to Japanese workers and other Asians one of its principal goals.[60] As the WFM saw it, the coming of the "yellow man" was a growing threat. Before it grew any stronger, steps needed to be taken to eradicate the "pest." [61] As a first step, the "Miner Legislator" Max Morris (Democrat, Arapahoe County), a vice president of the WFM, authored and obtained passage of a House joint resolution in the Colorado Legislature (March 12, 1902) calling for the exclusion of Japanese from the country.[62]

Around this time, rank and file union members in Colorado were on alert, expecting a possible influx of Japanese workers. A month earlier, in February 1902, when it was reported that the Victor Fuel Company was thinking about employing Japanese workers, white union miners had organized a protest in Chandler, Fremont County.[63] Delos A. Chappell, the company's head, tried to allay the union's concerns by explaining to the assembled men that the company did not want to employ Japanese or Chinese any more than the white miners but had little choice because labor was scarce. From the company's perspective, it was simply a matter of getting workers or not.[64] But J. C. Sullivan, president of the State Federation of Labor, accused Chappell and Victor Fuel of "unpatriotic conduct for importing cheap foreign labor, namely, Japanese, Italians and negroes [sic]—who work for their bacon and beans."[65] In the face of union dissent, Chappell ultimately abandoned the plan.

Unionized mine workers were deeply suspicious of Chappell and the other Victor Fuel owners, whom they believed had a secret agenda. Thus, Chappell's claim that the company had been forced to recruit Japanese labor was met with derision by one WFM protester: "It is the known intention of the Colorado Fuel and Iron company [CFI, the company that owned the Victor Fuel Company] to cut down the wages of white miners when they have got enough foreign labor to weather them through the strike that would be sure to follow. They are, in a sly, underhand way, gradually putting Chinese and Japs in the mines everywhere and excluding in preference to them experienced American miners of which there are hundreds unemployed in this very state and the neighboring states." Such schemes were sure to fail, the protestor continued, because the miners had "spunk," they knew what the company was up to, and they had a strong union. If they took a stand and stuck with it, they could hope to eventually "bring about the exclusion of Asiatic labor in all the districts of the great trust"—that is, to ban Asian workers from CFI entirely.[66]

Organized labor's antipathy toward Asians limited the kind of work Japanese were permitted to do. Because of vehement objections from the WFM, Japanese found it difficult to find work in the hard-rock mining industry in the state.[67] They were, however, able to secure jobs in the smelting industry. In 1904, about five hundred of them were employed at the CFI steel mill in Pueblo.[68] According to one report, the Japanese did not fare well in smelting and refining; they were accused of being lazy (an unusual charge) and too weak for the heavy work of smelter laborers.[69] Still, the CFI was willing to add another five hundred the following year, an action that the Denver Trades and Labor Assembly considered proof that the Japanese were "inundating" the state.[70]

Because of the resistance of the United Mine Workers of America, Japanese were prevented from working in the northern coal mines, but they did find jobs in southern coalfields near Florence, Walsenburg, and Trinidad, where the labor movement was weaker. As a general rule, wherever union organizing was ineffective, it was easier for Japanese to find employment. In the southern coalfields, they held down comparatively high-paying jobs (earning up to fifteen dollars a week) that were open to anyone willing to do them.[71] Perhaps just as important, the coal companies were willing to pay them the same wages they paid whites. After winning the Colorado Labor Wars (1903–1904), a bloody struggle between the WFM and mine operators, coal mine owners began recruiting foreign miners—Mexicans, Southern and Eastern European workers, and a small number of Japanese workers—as nonunion miners.[72]

Though Japanese worked alongside the other nonunion miners, this did not mean they were welcomed or got along. On the contrary, according to journalist Barron B. Beshoar: "Hatred and despair gripped the polyglot peoples of the Colorado coal district. . . . The newcomers . . . despised each other, according to race. The Italians looked down on the Greeks, and the Greeks scorned the Poles as social inferiors, and the latter had only contempt for the skinny-armed Mexicans. They were united only in their hatred for their employers and their belief that Japanese were scum of the worst sort."[73]

Building on efforts to renew the Chinese Exclusion Act in 1902, the labor movement orchestrated a comparatively complex campaign against the Japanese and also against Koreans, who had been incorporated into the Empire of Japan when Korea was made a Japanese protectorate in 1905 and annexed in 1910. Organized labor lobbied the US Congress to enlarge the scope of the exclusion law against the Chinese to include Japanese and other Asian workers, and to enforce the 1885 anti–contract labor law prohibiting the hiring of coolies.[74] They appealed to voters to stop the "flooding [of] the labor market with leather-colored Mongols and Japs."[75]

To achieve their aim of eliminating Asians from the United States, they organized a grand alliance of unions.

SEGREGATING ASIAN CHILDREN

On May 14, 1905, in San Francisco, sixty-seven labor unions founded the Japanese and Korean Exclusion League (later known as the Asiatic Exclusion League) to promote an anti-Asian agenda. The league was reported to have eighty thousand members and claimed the support of independent organizations with several million members. Its plan was to promote the growth of organized labor at the expense of Asians through a patently racist appeal to preserve America for white people, specifically those from Northern and Western European countries. The league was implicitly committed to the doctrine of Nordic superiority in its belief that American culture should be based exclusively on Anglo-Saxon and Teutonic cultures.

The league sought to achieve its aim of stopping Japanese and Koreans from entering the country through agitation and propaganda recycling the old canards about the Chinese. For example, at a 1908 league meeting in San Francisco, resolutions were adopted identifying Japanese and Koreans as unassimilable coolies who would "inevitably impair and degrade, if not effectually destroy our cherished institutions and our American life."[76] In a telling presentiment of the charges against the Japanese during World War II, Asians were characterized as an inherently subversive fifth-column element in American society. They arrived in the country "entirely ignorant of our sentiments of nativity and patriotism, and utterly unfit and incapable of discharging the duties of American citizenship."[77] They were America's enemies: "Asiatics, the greatest number of whom are armed, loyal to their governments, entertaining feelings of distrust, if not of hostility, to our people, without any allegiance to our government or institutions, not sustaining American life in times of peace, and ever ready to respond to the cause of their own nations in times of war, [are] an appalling menace to the American Republic, the splendid achievements wrought by the strong arms and loyal hearts of *Caucasian toilers, patriots and heroes* in every walk of life" (emphasis added).[78] As the last phrase indicates, the problem with Asians is fundamentally racial and hence innate.

Ultimately, the league hoped to persuade Congress to pass legislation similar to the Chinese Exclusion Act. To that end, it recruited California's congressional delegation into the organization to craft the bill. It also endeavored to organize the Western states to exert political pressure on Congress to pass an immigration law that would ban the Japanese from entering the country. As mentioned previously, in 1908, the Colorado State Federation of Labor organized a state chapter of the Japanese and Korean Exclusion League.

In the meantime, the national Japanese and Korean Exclusion League had achieved a singular success that attracted international attention. On October 11, 1906, it was able to pressure the San Francisco school board to pass a resolution directing principals to transfer all Japanese and Korean children to the city's segregated Oriental School in Chinatown. The school board's decision, legal though unjust, adversely affected ninety-three Japanese elementary school students, sixty-five of whom were boys and twenty-eight of whom were girls.[79] Though twenty-five of these students were US-born citizens, they, too, had to attend the segregated school. According to the school board, segregation was necessary because Japanese were an uncivilized people given to licentious behavior. Young Japanese boys were undermining the morals of young American girls.[80] Evidently, the school board either forgot or did not care that earlier that year, the people of Japan had contributed $244,960 to the victims of the April 18 San Francisco earthquake, a sum greater than the total contributions from all other countries combined.[81]

California congressman Everis A. Hayes (Republican) supported the school board's decision, arguing that its action was a matter of states' rights versus federal power and was in keeping with long-approved precedents. In fact, the real issue was about California's desire to remain exclusively white. More broadly, the measure was intended to oppose the "Orientalizing" of the Pacific Coast.[82]

Unable to get the San Francisco school board to reverse its decision, the Japanese Association of America reported the matter to the press in Japan, where the news provoked public demonstrations against the United States for discriminating against Japanese and Japanese American children. Japanese outrage was expressed in calls for retribution for the many wrongs suffered by Japanese in America. Local Japanese community leaders appealed to Japan to exert pressure on the United States to reverse the school board's decision. The Japanese government officially registered a protest with the American government, calling the school board's action an insult as well as a violation of the 1894 American-Japanese Treaty of

Commerce and Navigation that assured Japanese the right to immigrate to the United States, where they were entitled to enjoy equality in American society.

There was saber rattling in both countries. News stories with headlines such as "War certain for Yankees and Japs" and "Hawaiian Islands may be seized by Japan" predicted a conflict between the two nations.[83] There were rumors that the Japanese were working night and day to prepare for war and unfounded stories about fifth-column Japanese in Hawaii drilling by moonlight to assist an invading Imperial Army.[84] The Colorado National Guard was put on a war footing.[85] It was said that Colorado would be able to send a well-equipped regiment into the field within a week. School board supporter Congressman Hayes confidently declared, "If we are going to have war with Japan, let's have it right away! We're ready, they ain't."[86] With cries for war on both sides of the Pacific, President Theodore Roosevelt sought a solution to the school board controversy.

AN AGREEMENT BETWEEN GENTLEMEN

Out of respect for Japan's recent victory over Russia during the Russo-Japanese War and a belief in a laissez-faire immigration policy, President Roosevelt personally interceded in the school board controversy. From the start, Roosevelt made it evident to all concerned that he sided with the Japanese. In his annual message to Congress in 1905, Roosevelt had advocated a nondiscriminatory immigration policy; in 1907, he was even more vigorous in his defense of the Japanese, noting that the San Francisco School Board's decision was absurd, wickedly so, and asking that the Japanese be treated as fairly as Germans or Englishmen, Frenchmen, Russians, or Italians.[87] In addition, he expressed concern about protecting America's relationship with Asia.[88] He threatened to exercise his executive authority if necessary to fulfill America's obligations to other nations.

In February 1907, President Roosevelt invited San Francisco mayor Eugene E. Schmitz and members of the school board to Washington to discuss the matter. He was willing to work with Schmitz even though he personally detested him and his corrupt administration, considered by many to be worse than New York's Tammany Hall. Schmitz was a reluctant participant in the negotiations but ultimately cooperated, probably in order to divert public attention from his ongoing legal problems. Roosevelt's challenge was to end the agitation against the Japanese while finding a face-saving diplomatic solution to smooth relations with Japan without appearing to appease it.

Mayor Schmitz, however, was under instruction from the league to hold out for an exclusion law as stringent as the one applied to the Chinese.[89] League president O. H. Tveitmore sent a wire to Schmitz urging him not to betray whites: "If the President wants to humiliate the American flag let him tell California's Governor and Legislature to repeal the law, but he cannot coerce free Californians to bow in submission to the will of the Mikado. Roosevelt's power will not make one white man out of all the Japs in the Nipponese Empire. California is the white man's country, and not the Caucasian graveyard!"[90] Schmitz, however, disappointed the league, settling for something less than the banning of Japanese from America. After a week of discussions, Roosevelt, Schmitz, and other negotiators crafted a compromise that rescinded the resolution to segregate Japanese children, allowing them to return to their regular schools. The reversal was part of a much broader agreement to curtail but not end Japanese immigration to America.

The agreement led to the Immigration Act of 1907 and the issuance of a Presidential Executive Order prohibiting Japanese from migrating to American shores via Mexico, Canada, and, most importantly, Hawaii, which was the principal route to America for Japanese not arriving directly from Japan. The act authorized Roosevelt to enter an entente with Japan to curtail immigration to America, a provision that resulted in the secret Gentlemen's Agreement (1907–1908). According to its terms, the Japanese government agreed to restrict its people from going to the United States by refusing to issue them passports. By so doing, Japan hoped to safeguard its newly acquired reputation as a world power and to avoid the humiliation of an American legislative ban on Japanese immigration similar to the Chinese Exclusion Act.

Realizing that a drastic reduction in immigration to America was imminent, Japanese expedited their departure to America: 9,948 emigrated from Japan in 1907, and 7,250 in 1908.[91] Once the ban went into effect, however, emigration from Japan fell precipitously, to 3,275 in 1909.[92] Immigration was not ended because the Gentlemen's Agreement was only a partial ban. Passports could still be issued to workers who wanted to resume residence in America, and to travelers, merchants, students, and members of society other than the working class. Also, a crucial proviso allowed for family reunification. The Japanese government could and did provide passports to wives and children who wanted to join their husbands and fathers in the United States. The most significant result of this was that it allowed women to immigrate to America, usually as "picture brides."

PICTURE MARRIAGES

The picture bride practice requires explanation since it was a controversial but essential element in the growth of the Japanese American community.[93] As the name of the practice indicates, Japanese men selected brides from their native land through photographs. Because the matches were arranged at a distance, it was a fraught process for all concerned. And because the men were abroad, they had almost no choice other than to accept or reject their proposed spouse based on the photograph and accompanying information about her. Since the procedure actually involved an exchange of pictures, it is more accurate to call the custom "picture marriages." Japanese society regarded the marriages as legally binding when the wife's name was entered into the husband's family registry. The American government, however, considered the marriages illegal, so it was necessary for Japanese wives to participate in a mass wedding ceremony immediately after arriving in America.

As a rule, Japanese women acquiesced to these marriages in deference to their parents; they accepted them as a way to improve their families' economic circumstances. Often, Japanese women mistakenly thought they were marrying prosperous men, which would enable them to remit money to their families once they were established in America. In many instances, the men's descriptions of themselves and their circumstances in America were exaggerations, if not outright lies. Deceit notwithstanding, these marriages proved to be enduring, in no small degree due to the perseverance of the women themselves. It is estimated that the divorce rate for such couples was only 1.6 percent, a remarkable statistic then and certainly now.[94]

Japanese women agreed to participate in this practice for reasons other than just the material benefit to their families. In a feature article in the *Colorado Times*, Shika Takaya, herself a picture bride, listed wealth as only one of the reasons why Japanese women went to America.[95] While Japanese women rarely got rich, going abroad at least afforded them an opportunity to get away from their families and the concomitant daily social obligations they had to fulfill. Being overseas also provided them with the possibility of enjoying freedoms denied them in Japanese society.

These women were an essential element in the stability and growth of the Japanese American community. Between 1909 and 1923, they constituted nearly two-fifths of the Japanese admitted into the United States. Between 1908 and 1920, over ten thousand Japanese women arrived in the American mainland.[96] This influx of women helped to redress the gender imbalance among Japanese and enabled the first generation to found families. This raised the morale of men and curbed, if not necessarily ended, some of their premarital vices, like gambling. As for American farmers in general, having a family provided Japanese American farmers with the additional labor necessary to make a homestead viable. Thus, many Japanese men were able to avoid the fate of their Chinese counterparts, who were condemned to a life of bachelorhood. Families gave them reasons to become permanent residents and inspired them to become something more than common laborers. This, of course, was the very thing that the Japanophobes were afraid would happen.

Picture brides were essential in producing a second generation of Japanese in America—the Nisei. Equally important, they instilled in the Nisei traditional values like obligation to family and community. By the time the Japanese government stopped issuing passports to picture brides in 1920, the Japanese in America had produced thirty thousand children.[97] The majority of these second-generation Japanese Americans were born between the signing of the Gentlemen's Agreement and the eve of World War II.

Whites looked askance at picture marriage as a deviant practice at variance with American values. Such marriages lacked the quality of romantic love, which was regarded as the necessary precursor to and sustainer of married life in the West since the late nineteenth century. The picture-bride marriages were suspected of being shams, and the wives were thought to be prostitutes, which is hardly surprising given earlier attitudes toward Chinese women. Labor unions thought that Japanese wives would enter the workforce and threaten the livelihoods of Americans. Once more, insinuations were made about a secret Japanese plan to infiltrate America to betray it. California Exclusion League leader and newspaper publisher Valentine S. McClatchy declared that picture brides were part of a "conspiracy" by Japanese loyalists to surreptitiously take over the United States and "secure upon the continent a foothold for their race, not as individual units to be absorbed and assimilated in the great American melting pot, but as a compact body of loyal subjects of the Mikado to serve his interests in every way possible."[98] California senator James D. Phelan (Democrat) considered the custom uncivilized, "a throwback . . . to barbarism by which women were married off without regard to love or morality."[99] He tried to exploit the practice politically, making it part of his 1920 reelection campaign ("Keep California White" was one of his slogans).

In order to maintain harmonious relations with the United States, Japan, once again, took action at the expense of the Nikkei. In 1920, despite protests from Japanese in America, the Japanese government accepted the recommendation of Consul Ota Tamekichi to discontinue providing passports to picture brides. Ota thought that this would deprive Japanophobes of an issue around which they could rally people to ban all Japanese. However, this act of appeasement did not change the fact that it was their race rather than their culture that made the Japanese objectionable. Agitation against Japanese in America continued without letup. The failure to end these anti-Japanese activities caused Japan to accuse the United States of bad faith.

ANTI-JAPANESE VIOLENCE

Japanophobes continued to press for the complete exclusion of Japanese from the United States, and in some places the movement took a vicious turn. In Colorado, one of the worst instances of violence against the Japanese was associated with the infamous Ludlow massacre. In September 1913, when the Trinidad coalfields became the scene of a protracted strike, Japanese brought in as strikebreakers found themselves in the midst of a struggle between militant coal miners and ruthless coalfield managers.

Many Japanese miners were reluctant to become strikebreakers. They even sided with the union and considered seeking admission to the United Mine Workers of America (UMWA). UMWA Japanese miners at Kemmerer in southern Wyoming appealed to their Colorado compatriots *not* to become strikebreakers.[100] But Kawabata Minoru, a labor contractor working for the CFI, believed that it was in the interest of Japanese miners to side with the coal operators.[101] This became the tacit position of the Japanese Association of Colorado. At least one Japanese worker, however, argued that Kawabata and other labor contractors were merely pursuing their own selfish interests in advocating support for the coal operators.

The irony was that, except in rare instances, the labor movement

FIG. 6.2. Bubba, Uyado, and Matsumoto, Japanese Coloradan UMWA coal miners in Tioga, Huerfano County, Colorado, July 20, 1915. Denver Public Library, Western History Collection, X-60401.

had opposed the inclusion of Asians in their ranks. For union members, racial prejudice usually trumped working-class solidarity. When the union in southern Wyoming accepted Japanese miners in 1907, it did so for calculated short-term advantage. As Iwata noted, when Asians were permitted to join the local union, it was so that the union could deprive the company of nonunion workers and potential strikebreakers. The union's long-term objective, however, was to prevent the entry of large numbers of Japanese into the Wyoming coal mines.[102]

Meanwhile, during the Colorado coalfield strike of 1913–14, Japanese labor contractors opportunistically began supplying strikebreakers when they saw that the tide of the labor struggle had turned in favor of the mine owners. At that time, labor contractors recruited about one hundred Japanese miners to work in the southern coalfields: forty at Oakview, eleven at Green Canyon, twenty-four at Forbes, and the rest at other mines.[103] These strikebreakers were singled out for harassment.

On September 29, 1913, unidentified assailants fired on the living quarters of the Japanese miners and the office of the Oakdale mine (in Oakview), which was some twenty miles west of Walsenburg. Most of the gunfire was directed at the boardinghouse and segregated huts where the Japanese lived.[104] Though the union denied that striking miners had done the shooting, this incident, along with others, convinced the authorities that the situation was beyond the power of local sheriffs to control and that the state militia (Colorado National Guard) needed to be called in to restore law and order. The arrival of the state militia contributed to the escalation of violence that led to the infamous Ludlow massacre. On April 20, 1914, the state militia and company guards fired machine guns and rifles into the striking workers' tent colony at Ludlow, killing nineteen people, including twelve children and two women.

The worst instance of violence against Japanese miners occurred in the aftermath of the Ludlow massacre. As revenge, the striking workers sought to destroy the operators' mines, wrecking company buildings and killing or expelling strikebreakers and company guards at the various mining camps. One of their major retaliatory attacks occurred nine days later at the mining camp at Forbes, the Rocky Mountain Fuel Company's coal camp between Trinidad and Ludlow. On April 29, 1914, about three hundred armed miners, mostly Greeks, attacked the camp and set twelve buildings afire. Eleven men were killed at the Forbes camp: one striker and ten mine guards and strikebreakers, including four Japanese miners. In keeping with the biases of the era, the Japanese victims were barely mentioned in the news coverage. They were Itō Kotarō, Hino Tetsuji, Murakami Jōbei, and Niwa Masukichi.[105]

Eventually, federal troops were brought in to end the bitter labor dispute and to restore order. Meanwhile, Japanese miners withdrew from the southern coalfields.

Japanese who arrived to replace the diminishing numbers of Chinese workers sought unsuccessfully to separate themselves from their predecessors. Japanese hoped to be treated like their European counterparts who were arriving at the same time. But as far as their enemies were concerned, no exceptions were to be made among Asians. Japanophobic forces were determined to prevent the Japanese from entering the country.

SEVEN

YELLOW PERIL: FROM THREATENING CHINAMEN TO TREACHEROUS JAPAN

NTI-JAPANESE SENTIMENT IN COLORADO WAS FED BY FEARS OF the "Yellow Peril." But the idea of the Yellow Peril was not developed from apprehensions about Japan alone. It was a metaphor for a larger, shape-shifting threat from Asia that was felt to endanger Western civilization. It was a myth rooted in racial anxiety. As historian John W. Dower astutely observes, the "vision of the menace from the East was always more racial rather than national. It derived not from concern with any one country or people in particular, but from a vague and ominous sense of the vast, faceless, nameless yellow horde: the rising tide, indeed, of color."[1] This specter has been a staple of American culture right up to the present. It might be said that ever since the Huns and the Mongols invaded Europe, in the fourth and thirteenth centuries, respectively, the threat of an Asian onslaught has been an archetypal Western angst.

By the late nineteenth and early twentieth centuries, dread of the Yellow Peril had become deeply ingrained in American culture. As discussed earlier, many Americans subscribed to the mistaken belief that Chinese and Japanese immigration endangered the livelihood of white workers, so a ban was necessary. Once Asians were statutorily forbidden to enter the country and to intermarry with whites, their disappearance from the United States was assured through natural attrition.

IMITATION HUMANS

Labor leaders, politicians, and journalists regularly promoted the myth of the Yellow Peril to advance their own careers. In doing so, they drew support from an unexpected quarter. Christian missionaries, who served simultaneously as mediators of Western civilization and critics of Eastern civilization, were regarded as authoritative sources of knowledge about Asians. Their pejorative judgments about Asian societies were widely accepted. Their stereotypes of Asian peoples, often offered on the basis of limited understanding, were racist in effect, if not necessarily in intent.

In the case of China, no one had more influence on molding public opinion than Arthur H. Smith, missionary of the American Board of Commissioners for Foreign Missions and author of several books that supposedly demystified the Chinese. Smith was sympathetic to Chinese people, spoke out against female infanticide, and was credited with persuading President Theodore Roosevelt to use the Boxer Uprising indemnity to pay for Chinese students to study in the United States. Still, Smith fell into the trap of what historian Charles W. Hayford calls Sino-myopia, that is, misrepresenting the Chinese based on false cultural assumptions about them.[2] This misrepresentation was most evident in Smith's well-known work *Chinese Characteristics* (1894), a collection of essays originally published in 1890 in the Shanghai *North-China Daily News* and reprinted in American newspapers, including the *Rocky Mountain News*.[3]

The importance of Smith's work in shaping perceptions about the Chinese cannot be overstated, as it set the terms according to which Chinese would be judged. President Theodore Roosevelt considered it the best book concerning the Chinese he had ever read. The characteristics that Smith admires—industriousness, habits of domestic economy, the capacity for endurance, and even skill in cooking, among other traits—receive due consideration in his book. But Smith's goal, as he explains in his introduction, is to improve the Chinese. To this end, Smith cannot overlook the grave defects in their character, and these receive the lion's share of his attention.

Smith evaluates the Chinese from the perspective of middle-class American values and Christian religion, and finds them wanting. His essential error is to characterize the common limitations of a people living in an underdeveloped country as peculiar cultural deficiencies. For instance, he finds fault with impoverished Chinese for focusing on physical survival to the exclusion of the mental and spiritual aspects of life. With the same disconnect, he cites as an instance of immeasurable foolishness their tendency to postpone medical care in times of serious need because they happened to be busy or the treatment was too costly.[4] Smith begins the book with chapters disparaging Chinese social virtues such as the regard for "saving face" (an irrational obsession) and politeness (a matter of ritual technicalities). Later chapters survey the rest of what is wrong with the Chinese, with the greatest inadequacy being their "Polytheism, Pantheism, and Atheism."

What gave Smith's work a certain cachet was its attempt to analyze the Chinese in light of theories that were popular at the time, such as the doctrine of Nordic supremacy that believed in the innate superiority of the Anglo-Saxon race. This made his book one of the most frequently quoted about China at the turn of the century, though Pearl S. Buck's *The Good Earth* (1931) eventually superseded it as the book to read about the Chinese.

Smith's portrayals influenced attitudes toward Chinese workers in the United States. One of his most widely accepted characterizations was that Chinese were nerveless automatons who were able to work tirelessly all day, in contrast to whites; this view was featured in the *Rocky Mountain News* (RMN) in 1898.[5] According to Smith, it is a physiological "fact" that Chinese lack the sensitivities that distract Westerners. This trait enables Chinese to perform repetitive tasks for as long as twelve hours at a time without needing rest, food, or exercise. Like machines, they can sleep wherever they are left. They do not need fresh air, nor do they require quiet to rest, so they can sleep in the most crowded and noisy environments. By nature they are passive. This is evident from birth: infants typically lie motionless in their mothers' arms, and children readily sit, stand, or squat for long periods of time without protest. Also, they remain impassive while enduring physical pain or facing personal extinction. Smith suggests that in any struggle between East and West in which the outcome was determined by the Darwinian principle of the survival of the fittest, the Chinese, precisely because of their nervelessness, would have an important advantage over Europeans.[6]

Smith's identification of Chinese with automatons was not accidental. The Chinese fondness for machine-driven devices was well known. Clocks, watches, mechanical birds, and other automata were popular European exports to the Chinese market; a Chinese emperor's obsession with his mechanical nightingale was the subject of a popular fairy tale by Hans Christian Andersen.[7] However, Smith's transmogrification of the Chinese into mechanical men was significant because it lifted judgments of them out of the moral sphere into a supposedly scientific realm, in which Chinese could be appraised objectively. Chinese may have been inherently defective humans who would remain forever a puzzle, as Smith says, but they somehow came into clear focus for Americans as quasi-machines. As robots, they could be regarded as secondary creations with limited functionality. An automaton, as literary scholar Norma Rowen says in her discussion of nineteenth-century interest in such inventions, "could never be taken for a human being. Rather, he was always clearly nothing more than an imitation of the human, a kind of secondary or parallel creation whose likeness to humanity was evident but who raised no ideas or expectations that he possessed any real human life."[8]

The image of the Chinese as incompletely human dovetailed with the racial theories of the day that relegated Asians to second-class status, making for a potent combination. Smith's pseudoscientific analysis provided further support for the contention that Chinese posed an economic threat to Americans and should therefore be banned.

Though worries about Chinese and Japanese "coolies" eventually lessened after the immigration restrictions were put into place, concerns about the Yellow Peril persisted as attention swung from Asian workers to Asian nations. In the early twentieth century, the focus was on the danger that China and Japan posed to the United States and its interests in Asia. Dire predictions were made about an inevitable conflict between the rising nation of Japan and the preeminent power in the Pacific—the United States. Although we cannot know for sure, such prophecies probably influenced policies that led to the Pacific War (1941–45), which was an integral part of World War II. What is certain is that belief in the Yellow Peril colored the social discourse on Asian Americans and contributed to the decision to imprison Japanese Americans during World War II.

METAPHOR REVEALED

Kaiser Wilhelm II is mistakenly credited with coining the term "Yellow Peril" after the First Sino-Japanese War (1894–95). István Türr, a Hungarian architect and engineer who was involved in the ill-fated initial attempt at building the Panama Canal, first used it in mid-1895. Wilhelm's association with the metaphor can be traced to the drawing he commissioned titled "Völker Europas, wahrt eure heiligsten Güter" (Peoples of Europe, protect your most sacred possessions). The picture is an allegorical representation of his anti-Asian phobias, chief among which was the dread that an Asian horde would devastate Europe. Long before Samuel P. Huntington wrote his seminal work on the clash of civilizations, Wilhelm used the drawing to warn Europeans of the danger that Asians posed to Western civilization.

FIG. 7.1. *"Völker Europas, wahrt eure heiligsten Güter"* (Peoples of Europe, guard your most sacred possessions), also nicknamed "The Yellow Peril," by Hermann Knackfuss, 1895, *Harper's Weekly.* On a cliff overlooking a peaceful valley is the archangel Michael with his sword unsheathed, warning the rest of Europe (represented by women warriors) about Asia. The sign of the cross shining above them suggests that the struggle is between the Christian West and the pagan East. Denver Public Library, Western History Collection.

The picture became a popular poster used to encourage European cooperation against Asia and was rechristened "The Yellow Peril."

Others distrustful of Japan's rapid progress toward modernity shared Kaiser Wilhelm's paranoia. They feared that a powerful Japan would pose a danger to the West. Halford J. Mackinder, the renowned geographer, underscored the potential threat in his seminal article "The Geographical Pivot of History."[9] Mackinder argues that world domination would ultimately be achieved by the power that controlled the world's geographic heartland, currently occupied by Russia. But a Sino-Japanese alliance would create a formidable geopolitical rival combining the advantages of "oceanic frontage" and the resources of a great continent. Such an empire would endanger the world's freedom, and Russia was the only country that stood in the way of this.[10]

A detailed Japanese plan to achieve world domination by harnessing China's strategic resources eventually surfaced decades later in the form of the "Tanaka Memorial," first translated into English and published in the United States in 1934. This document supposedly came out of a Far East Conference convened in 1927 by Prime Minister Baron Tanaka Giichi to prepare a comprehensive plan for world domination for Emperor Hirohito. The memorial was a fake, similar to "The Protocols of the Elders of Zion," an anti-Semitic hoax purporting to describe a Jewish plan for world domination that was distributed widely in the United States in the 1920s with Henry Ford's support. Among the speculations surrounding the Tanaka Memorial was that it was a ploy by the Soviet Union to sow anti-Japanese feelings in the United States. If that was the purpose, it was successful. The Tanaka Memorial strengthened many Americans' belief in the existence of a Yellow Peril.

In the midst of the Russo-Japanese War (1905–1906), various pundits evoked the myth of the Yellow Peril. In Colorado, headlines such as "Wily Japs hate whites and await day when Mongols rule the world" and "Race must prepare to meet Asia's yellow horde" appeared to awaken the public about an impending war with Asia.[11] Stern warnings—especially from foreign correspondents living in Europe—could be found in the pages of the RMN. In a special report from Paris, Paul Villiers informed people that the French government intended to enlist the aid of other European powers as well as the United States "to call a halt" to the Japanese invasion of Siberia, put the Japanese in their place, and thwart Japanese "Pan-Mongolism" while it is still possible to do so.[12] Writing from Berlin, Malcolm Clarke issued a warning to his fellow Americans about their complacency toward the Yellow Peril. He said that the Japanese intended to establish an Asian Monroe Doctrine and expel Europeans and Americans from China.[13] He prophesized that the English would regret their alliance with the Japanese (in the Anglo-Japanese Treaties of 1902 and 1905) and their celebration of Japanese victories against the Russians when the Japanese eventually drove the English out of Asia, the French out of Indochina, and the Americans out of the Philippines. Also, the Japanese would take revenge on the United States for its treatment of the Chinese.[14] Such pronouncements played an important role in turning public opinion against the Japanese.

What Villiers, Clarke, and others worried most about was a military conflict with Asia in which whites would have to face a superior enemy. Japan's military prowess combined with China's vast population would provide Asia with a significant advantage in any such confrontation. Villiers even predicted that within a decade, war would come—a war in which hundreds of thousands of Chinese soldiers, drilled and organized by Japanese officers, would fight for Japan. Such an alliance was a prerequisite for world conquest. Some people agreed that to meet such a danger, Anglo-Saxons and Slavs (that is, Russians) would have to overcome past differences. This would be an apocalyptic contest for ascendancy in Asia— as one grandiloquent commentator put it, "a sanguinary struggle between antipodal types of civilization."[15]

In Colorado, attitudes toward Japan were divided during the Russo-Japanese War. Certainly, Coloradans, like many other Americans, felt uneasy as they pondered the implications of an Asian nation defeating a European nation. A Japanese triumph would at the very least undermine assumptions about the natural superiority of whites and the innate inferiority of colored people in Asia, Africa, and Latin America. Local commentators aired ambivalent views of Japan: admiration for Japan's modernization was tempered with misgivings about what a Japanese victory would portend for the West.[16] Sympathy for Japan's opposition to Russia's pan-Slavic ambitions was combined with concerns about an ascendant Japan becoming a future threat to the United States.[17] The unexpected battlefield successes of the doughty Japanese gave rise to admiring stories about their culture, with particular emphasis on their martial virtues. There were limits to this appreciation, however. Though the Japanese were capable warriors, they were thought to be no match for Americans, and thus harmless to the United States and its Philippine colony. To the extent that Coloradans thought Japan was a danger, it was as a commercial rather than a military one. As one Summit County writer put it, the concern was that the United States would lose the competition in trade with Japan, ending up with the dubious privilege of furnishing it with raw materials for Japanese-made goods that would be sold to Americans for a healthy profit.[18]

Japanese leaders countered negative views of Japan with reassurances intended to allay Western anxieties. These also found their way into Colorado newspapers. Playing on the words used against them, the Japanese argued that they were a "Yellow Blessing."[19] Japanese people had the capacity to adopt the best that the West had to offer, as shown through their enlightened attitudes, democratic institutions, and economic progress. This was in contrast to Czarist Russia, an autocratic empire that was tyrannical in the treatment of its own people, devoid of liberal impulses, and prone to religious bigotry. As Count Okuma observed, it was Russia, not Japan, that posed a threat; thus, it was the "height of folly [for statesmen in the West] to lay so much stress upon the difference in color" rather than other attributes.[20] If nothing else, the Russo-Japanese War proved that Asians were not inferior morally or physically to Europeans, or in terms of democratic principles and humanitarian concerns.

Later, as one of the victorious allies in World War I (1914–18), Japan sought to claim its rightful place as an equal with Western nations and also to end discrimination against its nationals in America and elsewhere. During the Versailles Peace Conference, the Japanese delegates tried unsuccessfully to include a clause in the Covenant of the League of Nations guaranteeing equal treatment for the people of all nations.[21] The motion to include the equality clause passed, only to be blocked by President Woodrow Wilson. Even though a majority of the representatives had voted for it, he ruled that because the vote was not unanimous, the proposal could not be adopted. This was a violation of established procedure as well as of the lofty moralism that Wilson professed.

Wilson took this contradictory step because he thought the proposal would alienate anti-Asian constituents in the United States. Japanophobic groups were concerned that the acceptance of the equality clause in the league's charter would lead to the revision of US immigration laws, opening the floodgates to Asians. California senator John D. Phelan (Republican) had already sent a telegram to the American delegation of the league warning that his constituents were alarmed about the prospect of free immigration and land purchases by Japanese (prohibited in California through legislation in 1879 and 1913) that were likely to result from such an agreement.[22] Some Allied nations were also opposed, including Australia, with its White Australia policy, and New Zealand, which placed severe restrictions on Asian immigration.[23]

A MATTER OF NATIONAL SECURITY

In the early twentieth century, the specter of a global race war, anticipated by Mackinder's geopolitics, cast a shadow on America's relations with Asia. The worry was that Japanese militarists were moving to assemble an

Asian empire to challenge Western interests. If the Japanese succeeded in mobilizing China's millions for this purpose, the West faced a real threat. The *New York Times* reported that Japanese agents were distributing tracts and disseminating the idea that Asia should be for Asians, asserting that no European power had rights in Asian territories or to trade with Asian countries.[24]

In assessing Japanese ambitions, the United States felt that much hung on the outcome of the Russo-Japanese War. It was said that Russia was fighting for all of Europe, while Japan was fighting for all of Asia. If Japan became a world power, there would be little to prevent it from emulating the expansionist West. As the well-known writer Jack London put it, "Just as the West was engaged in an adventure to expand its power around the world, what would prevent the Japanese and Chinese peoples from having similar dreams of wealth and conquest?"[25] London's story "The Unparalleled Invasion" (1910) portrays such a scenario. Set in the future, the story tells how America counters an imminent threat in 1976 by introducing a plague germ into China to exterminate all the Chinese—this is the "unparalleled invasion."[26] London's grim fantasy about the use of biological weapons of mass destruction as a military tactic is especially chilling because it comes only a few years before World War I and the use of chemical weapons.

After Japan's victory in the Russo-Japanese War, attitudes toward Japanese Americans shifted subtly. Japanophobes such as California's Senator Phelan began to argue that, because Japan now represented a military danger to the country, it was necessary to establish large army garrisons in America's Pacific possessions.[27] Inasmuch as Japanese immigrants were an extension of that threat, they should be excluded from the country for reasons of national security. Meanwhile, the American labor movement continued to play the race card to advance its agenda but packaged it differently for public consumption.

Labor leaders sought to take advantage of the growing unease about Japan's military might to heighten worries about Japanese workers as an economic threat. They claimed that Japanese in Japan and Japanese in America were all of a piece—their first allegiance was to the Japanese emperor. Labor leaders emphasized the potential risk that such a population posed to the nation, repeating the charge made by the Asiatic Exclusion League that Japanese would serve as a fifth column in any future war with Japan (see chapter 5). This groundless allegation resurfaced before, during, and after the 1941 attack on the Pearl Harbor naval base in Hawaii, with disastrous consequences for Japanese Americans.

The hardening of views about Japanese in Colorado in the aftermath of the Russo-Japanese War is suggested by the narrowing of the range of public opinions expressed by local contributors to a workers' forum in the RMN. On January 6, 1907, the pro-labor newspaper devoted its regular forum to the so-called Japanese invasion.[28] At the center of the broadsheet is an innocuous drawing of a Japanese face, which has a neutral expression rather than a sinister or slavish one, as was typical of Japanese caricatures. The sketch is titled "Yellow Peril" and captioned "A study of the Little 'Brown' Man," referring to a popular designation for the Japanese at the time. The discussion itself begins with the idea that the status of Japanese has risen due to their victory in the Russo-Japanese War, so they can no longer be considered subordinate. However, there are still irreconcilable differences between whites and Japanese that should be acknowledged. These dissimilarities, plus the standard litany of complaints about Japanese and other Asians, are presented in several short articles following. What sets these succinct pieces apart from the usual anti-Japanese diatribes is their appearance of balance and objectivity. Each puts forward a particular perspective on the Japanese problem, but all lead to the same conclusion: Japanese should be kept out of the country. Taken as a whole, these essays provide an inventory of local attitudes illustrating how the interests of different groups coalesced around anti-Japanese themes.

The first article, by George L. Knapp, offers a historian's argument that the Japanese are unassimilable. History teaches that the Japanese are "inferior in some things" but "superior in endurance, in loyalty, in tenacity of an idea, [and] in willingness to die for [their] convictions, religious or otherwise." Unfortunately, the list of things that Japanese lack—"initiative," "inventiveness," "broad sympathy," and "many of the things which give value to Caucasian life"—are so important to American identity that the Japanese will remain forever foreigners in the country. In a subsequent article, John M. O'Neill speaks for socialists in castigating American capitalists for taking advantage of cheap Japanese labor; he also praises the anti-Chinese demagogue Dennis Kearney as a prophet. Industrialists come in for criticism in a complementary piece by E. J. Chambers, who presents the "Democratic citizen's" outlook. Chambers complains that captains of industry are importing Japanese to Colorado because they are cheap, humble, and submissive, and now five or six hundred of these "little brown men" in Pueblo are voting for Republican gubernatorial candidate Henry A. Buchtel (1907–1909). An unnamed Denver merchant argues that immigration needs to be restricted to protect trade but hastens to add that he does not personally dislike the Japanese; on the contrary, he likes them even though (and here his impartiality begins to slip) they are frugal in the extreme, clannish to the detriment of whites, and a fundamentally dishonest people. Paying a backhanded compliment to the Chinese, the merchant offers a memorable comparison: "A Chinese hardly ever cheats. A Japanese hardly does anything else."

Finally, the last contributor, Otto F. Thum, offers the longest article, titled "Seventy-five per cent of the labor in Hawaii is now performed by the Japs." He provides the labor union perspective, raising alarms about the Asian colonization of America. Using the Hawaiian Territory as an example, Thum explains his theory of how Asians will take over the United States. His evidence is a March 6, 1906, report from the Department of Commerce and Labor that purportedly shows the "Orientalization" of the islands, along with the attendant negative consequences. Asians gained control of Hawaii by clinging to their lower standard of living, which made them unfair competitors with white and indigenous wage earners, including those in skilled trades. Also, Asians' strong competitiveness and ethnic solidarity as small businessmen caused considerable harm to their white rivals. Furthermore, Asian control of the Hawaiian economy had ruinous social effects because Asians lacked the civic capacity necessary to build a self-governing American commonwealth. Thum concludes on an "optimistic" note, however. While it was too late to save the Hawaiian Territory from Asians, the American mainland could still be saved.

Thum was hardly the first to warn about the danger that Japanese in Hawaii posed. He was recycling a decade-old argument about them outcompeting whites and taking over the islands by force of numbers.[29] In the mid-1890s, whites had worried that Japanese laborers, who were chafing under the onerous working conditions of the sugar plantations and unfair disenfranchisement by the Hawaiian government, might rise in revolt to take over the Hawaiian Islands.[30] Their disquietude was similar to the unease that Southerners had felt about a possible black slave revolt during the antebellum period. White planter oligarchs who ruled Hawaii were concerned that the ever-increasing numbers of Japanese laborers might eventually encourage Japan to assert dominance over the islands and annex them outright.[31] If apprehension about Japan did anything, it probably sped up American annexation of the Hawaiian Islands in July 1898.[32]

ROAD TO TOTAL EXCLUSION

To stop the flow of Asians to the United States, anti-Asian foes lobbied for additional restrictions. A step toward the goal of total exclusion was the passage of the Literacy Act of 1917. This measure required adults, defined as those over sixteen years old, to demonstrate basic English reading comprehension to gain entry into the United States. It also created an Asiatic Barred Zone, banning immigration of people from Turkey and Saudi Arabia in the West to the Polynesian Islands in the East. Japan, the Philippines, and China were not included in the zone: the Japanese were exempt because the earlier Gentlemen's Agreement (1907) had limited their immigration to the United States; the Filipinos, because they were American subjects and could travel freely to the United States; and the Chinese, because they were prohibited from entering the United States under the exclusion laws.

The Literacy Act did not satisfy those who also wished to severely curtail the arrival of new emigrants from Southern and Eastern Europe or to totally end emigration from Japan. They were finally able to achieve their goals with the Johnson-Reed Act (May 26, 1924), an immigration bill that established a hierarchy for emigrants, with those from Eastern and Southern Europe at the bottom. It also included a gratuitous Japanese exclusion clause to end emigration from Japan.

Washington State congressman Albert Johnson (Republican) was the chief architect of the 1924 immigration bill that bears his name. Johnson was a dyed-in-the-wool nativist with an unfeigned dislike of foreigners in general and a hatred of Japanese and Jews in particular. In an earlier effort to suspend the immigration of Jews, Johnson had appended a report on their character from American consuls abroad. In the report, he described them as an "abnormally twisted" and "unassimilable people," "filthy, un-American, and often dangerous in their habits," who were prepared to flood the United States in large numbers.[33] As is by now evident, the language here echoes that used to describe Asians and other undesirable immigrants of the time. It was part of the same nativist discourse.

Johnson also was the leader of the Eugenics Research Association, a group that opposed interracial marriage and supported the forced sterilization of the mentally disabled. In an appeal to those with similar convictions, his bill was presented as a way to stem the tide of alien blood flowing into America that threatened to pollute white bloodlines. Such thinking relied on specious theories emphasizing white purity and supremacy, which were used to shore up the existing system of dominance over people of color.[34] Eugenics theories have had a long, shameful pedigree of providing pseudoscientific justification for racist policies and practices. As early as the eighteenth century, scholarly research was based on questionable methodology, such as measuring the conic shape of Chinese heads to supply the rationale for classifying them as a grotesque type.[35] In constructing a taxonomy of human types, scholars relied on such analysis to place Chinese in the category of *Homo monstrosus*, which was distinct from *Homo sapiens*, the classification to which normal people belonged. Included in this aberrant category were also Patagonians, Hottentots, Native Americans, and assorted other Third World peoples. These fallacious theories eventually lost their currency in the second half of the twentieth century.

Johnson and others like him were deeply disturbed by the changing character of immigration to the United States during the late nineteenth and early twentieth centuries and its transformative effect on the country. This concern was evident in a 1905 RMN editorial over the numbers and kinds of new immigrants:

Formerly, Irish, Germans and Scandinavians formed the overwhelming majority; today the Mediterranean, Oriental and Slavic races predominate. . . . During the past three years Italy has sent to this country 602,300, Austro-Hungary enough people to populate another city as large as Boston, and Russia more than enough to fill Cleveland. Our total immigration . . . has amounted to about 3,570,000. . . . Since their war with Russia commenced the Japanese have been coming to us only at the rate of a trifle over 14,000 a year, whereas, just previously, 20,000 were arriving annually. In our Chinese immigration, on the other hand, there has been an increase of 100 per cent in the past year, 4,300 entering in 1900.[36]

Such figures were distressing to those who sought a racially homogeneous United States.

Among those who shared this concern was future president Franklin D. Roosevelt. He, too, was perturbed about the country's increasing diversity.[37] In the spring of 1925, as a guest columnist for the *Macon Telegraph*, Roosevelt wrote nine columns on a variety of subjects, including the temporary restriction of Europeans (April 21) and the exclusion of Japanese (April 30). While his thoughts regarding which Europeans to restrict were vague, he was clearly opposed to admitting people whom the United States would be unable to "digest" or who would be "poisonous" to American society. Among such undesirables, Roosevelt included Asians in general and the Japanese in particular. Roosevelt thought that the essential reason to exclude Asians from the country was not to protect American livelihoods but to prevent Asians from contaminating white bloodlines. Roosevelt wrote that the prospect of miscegenation with Asians filled him with "repugnance": "Anyone who has traveled in the Far East knows that the mingling of Asiatic blood with European or American blood produces, in nine cases out of ten, the most unfortunate results. . . . In this question, then, of Japanese exclusion from the United States, it is necessary only to advance the true reason—the undesirability of mixing the blood of the two peoples."[38] This statement reflected popular attitudes toward Asians as well as some of Roosevelt's personal experiences in the Far East, where, he said, Eurasians were "looked down upon and despised" by both whites and Asians.

ASIANS AS A PEOPLE OF COLOR

With Congressman Johnson leading the way, the Japanophobes were able to incorporate the exclusion of Japanese into the growing national campaign to curtail the immigration of Southern and Eastern Europeans. Nativists considered these groups, especially Italians and Poles, to be culturally backward and as difficult to "digest" as Asians. American studies professor David Roediger notes that in accordance with the race-based logic of the period, Southern and Eastern Europeans were perceived as people who were, at best, racially in-between.[39]

There was, however, no longer any doubt that Asians were people of color. Precedent-setting court cases confirmed this. In Takao Ozawa v. United States (1922), the Supreme Court ruled against University of California student Takao Ozawa's application for citizenship because he was not Caucasian and therefore not white, even though he was light in complexion. As a person of color, he was thus ineligible to apply for citizenship, which was a white-only privilege. A year later, in the case of United States v. Bhagat Singh Thind (1923), the High Court ruled against Thind's application for citizenship as well. In this instance, it determined that even though Thind, an Asian Indian, was of Aryan blood and thus a Caucasian, he was nevertheless *not* a white person as it was commonly understood. So far as the High Court was concerned, although all whites were Caucasian, not all Caucasians were white.

With the Thind decision, the US Supreme Court summarily reversed previous lower court decisions that had classified Asian Indians as Caucasians, allowing them to become US citizens and to intermarry with whites. This decision adroitly circumvented the ethnological debates about who was white and who was not by relying on public opinion to make that determination. In so doing, the High Court deprived Asians of any chance of attaining citizenship and acquiring the political power needed to safeguard their interests in the United States.

Though the Ozawa and Thind cases were ultimately flawed legal decisions, they were consonant with the sentiment of the times and should be understood as part of the period's effort to maintain existing racial boundaries. These rulings showed the close connection between whiteness, citizenship, and being an American. Among the unfortunate consequences of these legal decisions, Asian Indians who had previously been naturalized were stripped of their citizenship, and Asian American veterans of World War I were disqualified from becoming naturalized citizens, which they otherwise would have been entitled to because of their wartime service.[40]

With the passage of the Johnson-Reed Act, the existing national immigration quotas were reduced to 2 percent of the foreign-born residents from that country according to the 1890 census. In effect, the act encouraged emigration from Northern and Western European countries, while drastically limiting emigration from Southern and Eastern Europe. After its passage in 1924, emigration from the latter countries dropped dramatically. The number of immigrants who returned to these countries exceeded the number of those who came from them.

What made the Johnson-Reed Act fatal to Asian immigration was its provision forbidding the entry of any alien who, by virtue of race or nationality, was ineligible for citizenship. That meant that Asians who had previously been allowed to enter the United States were no longer allowed to do so. This included the Japanese as well as people from the Asia-Pacific Triangle area, comprising East Asia, Southeast Asia, and South Asia. Filipinos alone remained exempt from this restriction because they lived in American territory. Consequently, as Asian workers in agriculture and other sectors of the American economy were shut out of the country, Fili-

pinos replaced them, at least until the Philippines was granted commonwealth status in 1934.

Opponents of Johnson-Reed realized that the act was inimical to US
interests. Secretary of State Charles Evans Hughes thought it violated the
earlier Gentlemen's Agreement (1907), which had for all practical purposes
effectively halted Japanese immigration. Hughes also believed that the act
would undermine diplomatic relations with Japan. His appraisal proved
correct. Fifteen major newspapers in Japan published a joint condemnation
of the immigration bill.[41] Uchimura Kanzo, a leading Christian evangelist
in Japan, also thought that grave consequences would follow from what he
considered a mad and thoughtless measure. After the act was passed, a Japanese citizen committed suicide outside the American Embassy in Tokyo
in protest. On his person were two letters: one addressed to the American
ambassador and American people, requesting the withdrawal of the Japanese exclusion clause, and another addressed to the nation of Japan, calling on it to avenge the insult. The Japanese press seized on the suicide to
predict a race war between the United States and Japan.

A SELF-FULFILLING PROPHECY

The long-awaited war that both Japanese and American pundits predicted years earlier turned out to be the Pacific War. As historian John W.
Dower shows in his seminal study, *War without Mercy: Race and Power in
the Pacific War,* the war exposed the underlying racism that contributed
to the cruelty of the conflict. Following Japan's preemptive strike at Pearl
Harbor, both sides were inflamed with feelings of mutual injury. Professor Earl Swisher, a contemporary authority on the Far East at the University of Colorado who later served in the US Marine Corps during World
War II, noted that the Japanese remembered American affronts, such as
the denial of Japan's request for an equality clause in the Treaty of Versailles ending World War I and the enactment of the Reed-Johnson Act in
1924. The immigration act was considered so great an insult that Japanese
wanted "revenge up to the hilt."[42] After Pearl Harbor, Americans were
also thirsting for revenge. For the Americans, the decision to focus on
defeating their Axis enemies in Europe was not simply a matter of sound
strategy; it was also intended to enable them to devote their undivided
attention to the complete and utter destruction of Japan.[43]

How the Pacific War between the United States and Japan began is often forgotten or misunderstood. The Pacific War has been overshadowed by the larger conflict of World War II. Earlier fears about the Yellow Peril and an apocalyptic clash between East and West were swallowed up in the sprawling struggle against Nazi Germany, Fascist Italy, and militarist Japan, which played out in multiple theaters of war. The American perspective on World War II is that it was a death match to defend freedom and democracy against the threat of tyranny and dictatorship. In that sense, the war was straightforward, and until recently, Americans felt little need to take a more nuanced look at the events and actors who were involved in this momentous conflict.

The Japanese perspective was markedly different. Japanese militarists wanted to project Japan's power in the region, but they rationalized their expansion into the rest of Asia in terms of Pan-Asianism, the belief that Asians should unite against Western imperialism. It was an old idea. Originally, Pan-Asianism was a response to the coming of the West. In the early twentieth century, idealists like Miyazaki Torazō had worked with Dr. Sun Yat-sen to advance what they considered Japan and China's common interests.[44] They hoped that by working together, the two countries would unify Asia, liberate it from Western aggression, and, in the process, regenerate the region.

During World War II, Japanese militarists perverted the idea of Pan-Asianism, using it as a propaganda ploy. They tried to convince Asians that the conflict was a war against their white oppressors and that the invasion of China and Southeast Asia was actually meant to free them from generations of white domination. The effect of Western imperialism was such that the Japanese militarists managed to attract support from key Asian nationalist leaders, such as Ba Maw, Subhas Chandra Bose, and Wang Jingwei, who sought independence for Burma, India, and China, respectively.[45] These men were willing to work with the Japanese to accomplish their goals and later suffered opprobrium for it.

The Japanese militarists offered Asians the opportunity to be part of the Greater East Asia Co-Prosperity Sphere, a name that implied mutual benefit for the nations that joined them. In 1943, Japanese leaders convened the Greater East Asia Conference to showcase this idea, demonstrate Japan's commitment to Pan-Asianism, focus attention on its role as liberator of Asia from Western imperialism, and celebrate the end of colonialism in Asia. However, the Co-Prosperity Sphere turned out to be little more than a cloak for Japanese ambitions to gain control over Asia. It never masked

the fact that the puppet governments established by the Japanese throughout Asia were intended to assist them in exploiting the peoples of Asia
rather than promoting their welfare.

From its inception, the Japanese call for a Greater East Asia Co-
Prosperity Sphere was flawed, because it was based on the belief that the
Yamato race (that is, the Japanese) was superior to all others. The Japanese saw themselves as presiding over a racial hierarchy in which they
had ascendancy. Whatever legitimacy Pan-Asianism and the Greater East
Asia Co-Prosperity Sphere possessed quickly dissipated with the brutality
of wartime occupation. Japanese soldiers' atrocious behavior in the conquered areas of Asia undercut their appeal for regional solidarity.

Arguably, the Japanese militarists were doomed to fail from the beginning. Like the Yellow Peril, Pan-Asianism proved to be a myth because
Asians identified themselves in distinct ethnic and national terms rather
than in broad racial and regional terms. The diversity of Asia made bringing Asians together in a common cause against a common enemy a difficult, if not impossible, task. Moreover, Japan's incursions in Asia had
generated strong opposition. This was certainly the case in Korea, where
the people had been resisting Japanese colonialism since 1905, when the
country first came under Japan's influence. Ever since Japan colonized
Korea, Korean Americans had been active in a movement to liberate their
ancestral home. Similarly, Japan's attempts to reduce China to a Japanese
protectorate with its "Twenty-One Demands" in January 1915 were continuously challenged by Chinese at home and abroad. Both Korean Americans and Chinese Americans lobbied Washington and the international
community to support their native lands.

Japan's Western opponents, however, took the idea of Pan-Asianism
seriously. They understood it best in the familiar language of the Yellow
Peril. American military commanders such as Admiral Ernest King worried that Japan's victories early in the war would have grave repercussions
for the nonwhite world. Admiral William Leahy feared that Japan might
actually succeed in mobilizing Asians against whites.[46] In addition, American politicians such as William Philips, President Franklin D. Roosevelt's
personal emissary to India, sent back deeply pessimistic reports about a
rising "color consciousness." Roosevelt worried about the threat posed by
a billion Asian enemies.[47] For American leaders, it seemed the Yellow Peril
might become a frightening reality.

The Japanese attack on Pearl Harbor had devastating consequences for Japanese Americans, but not just for them. Anger toward Japan spilled over to Asian Americans in general. White Americans, who were unable or unwilling to differentiate Japanese Americans and Japanese resident aliens from other Asian Americans, indiscriminately subjected all of them to varying degrees of harassment and violence. The problem was sufficiently severe to move *Life* magazine to publish an illustrated article two weeks after the attack on Pearl Harbor titled, "How to tell Japs from the Chinese." With the subtitle "Angry citizens victimize allies with emotional outburst at enemy," the essay tried to halt the violence against Asian Americans.[48]

As a matter of self-defense, other Asian Americans immediately began wearing badges declaring that they were Chinese Americans or Korean Americans to protect themselves from assaults. In Denver, Chinese Americans wore lapel pins with American and Chinese flags bearing the words "American Chinese" to emphasize the Sino-American alliance as well as their American nationality. To avoid being mistaken for a Japanese, a Denver Chinese American high school student, copying actions taken by some Chinese in Seattle, pinned a sign on his jacket that read, "Don't Shoot, I'm a Chinaman."[49] The words "Don't Shoot" resonate with the slogan used by demonstrators to protest the August 2014 shooting of Michael Brown, an African American, in Ferguson, Missouri. Though the Ferguson saying was directed at the police and the World War II message was meant for civilians, both were generated by fears of racially motivated violence against racial minorities.

Chinese Americans, Korean Americans, and other Asian Americans supported the mass imprisonment of Japanese Americans during World War II as a way of affirming their identification with the United States and with their ancestral homelands.[50] This was a misguided attempt to prove that their loyalties were with the United States. What they showed instead was that they were not any more capable than other Americans of distinguishing Japanese Americans from Japanese nationals. And like their fellow Americans, they enthusiastically embraced Japanophobic rhetoric and employed epithets against Japanese Americans.

What these Asian Americans failed to understand was the racial underpinnings of the mass imprisonment of Japanese Americans in concentration camps. Some officials, such as Lieutenant General John L. DeWitt, believed in the innate perfidy of Japanese Americans. In a letter to Secretary of War Henry L. Stimson, DeWitt claimed: "In the war in which we are now engaged racial affinities are not severed by migration. . . . The Japanese race is an enemy race and while many second and third generation Japanese born on United States soil, possessed of United States citizenship, have become 'Americanized,' the racial strains are undiluted."[51] Such thinking led DeWitt and other Japanophobes to conclude that racial inheritance made Japanese Americans natural-born traitors, spies, and saboteurs, suggesting how deeply repeated claims about Japanese disloyalty had rooted themselves in American thinking since they were first given a public stage in the early 1900s. DeWitt and others perceived Japanese Americans as the enemy and treated them as such.

EIGHT

A CONCENTRATION CAMP IN THE CENTENNIAL STATE

THE IMPERIAL JAPANESE NAVY'S PREEMPTIVE STRIKE ON THE American Pacific fleet at the Pearl Harbor naval base in Hawaii sparked an outburst of hostility toward the Japanese in the United States, especially on the West Coast. December 7, 1941, the day that will live in infamy, stretched into "years of infamy" for Japanese Americans, to use former concentration camp prisoner Michi Nishiura Weglyn's phrase, when America made them pay for the attack.[1]

From the outset, many Americans were afraid that the Pearl Harbor attack would be followed by an invasion of the US mainland. In this anxious atmosphere, some looked for a scapegoat and found one in the Japanese American community. Because of an inability or unwillingness to distinguish Japanese Americans from Japanese nationals, all ethnic Japanese were exposed to abuse. In Denver, after news of the attack spread, an angry mob gathered outside the Japanese Methodist Church, yelling epithets and breaking the church's stained glass windows. As a matter of protection, the church quickly renamed itself the California Street Methodist Church. Other acts of vandalism were committed, but in the immediate aftermath of Pearl Harbor there were no calls for restrictions on Japanese Americans.

Once war had been declared against the Axis powers, the US Department of Justice took the standard safety precautions. The Federal Bureau of Investigation (FBI) began arresting suspicious persons, usually ethnic community leaders who had been previously identified as potential risks to national security, and confiscating their personal possessions, such as cameras and weapons, which were now declared contraband. By December 19, practically all suspect aliens had been placed in custody. Ultimately,

FIG. 8.1. "Waiting for the Signal from Home...," by Dr. Seuss, February 13, 1942. During World War II, Dr. Seuss's anti-Japanese editorial cartoons had a decidedly racist character to them. Here, he portrays Japanese Americans as all looking alike, with duplicitous smiles and bespectacled, slanted eyes. It is this sort of publicity that encouraged the public clamor for the forced removal of Japanese Americans from the West Coast and their imprisonment in concentration camps. Dr. Seuss Collection, University of California, San Diego.

the FBI detained 1,291 Japanese, 857 Germans, and 157 Italians living in Hawaii and the United States.[2]

For the Japanese American community, this was only the beginning of its travails. As the Japanese military offensive achieved victory after victory in Southeast Asia and the Pacific, many Americans became increasingly worried about the enemy landing on their shores. The much-feared "Yellow Peril" was becoming a reality, at least in their minds. Panic spawned stories about Japanese American subversion, even though there was none. According to the perverse logic of some leaders, the lack of subversion was suspicious in itself. Lieutenant General John L. DeWitt, head of the Western Defense Command, argued that "the fact that we have [not even] sporadic attempts at sabotage clearly means that control is being exercised somewhere."[3] In other words, the very absence of sabotage proved there was a conspiracy afoot to commit such acts when the moment was right. In the face of such irrational thinking, there was little hope of making a reasonable case for tolerance.

Some people blamed Japanese Americans for the destruction of the Pacific fleet, accusing them of aiding and abetting the attack. Without a shred of evidence, they assumed that Japanese Americans had engaged in fifth-column activities undermining the nation's security. Indeed, it became an article of faith that not only did a fifth column exist, but that immediate action was necessary to prevent it from doing any further damage.

EXECUTIVE ORDER 9066

In the context of widespread war hysteria and racial prejudice, which had existed since the late nineteenth century, people began to demand that something be done about Japanese Americans. Within the White House, views were divided. Secretary of War Henry L. Stimson favored mass removal as an emergency measure even though he was aware that in doing so the government was violating the US Constitution.[4] Attorney General Francis Biddle opposed it on constitutional grounds. In this matter, none other than FBI director J. Edgar Hoover sided with Biddle. No civil libertarian himself, Hoover nevertheless considered the uprooting of the Japanese American community unnecessary. UK prime minister Winston Churchill proposed an alternative. Finding himself in the midst of a conversation about the Japanese problem at the White House, Churchill suggested the British approach of creating local boards to evaluate the loyalty of enemy aliens and separate the sheep from the goats.[5] This suggestion, however, was never taken up. The Western Defense Command rejected loyalty board hearings as too time consuming and probably ineffective in identifying disloyal elements.

President Franklin D. Roosevelt was one of those who drew no distinction between loyal and disloyal Japanese Americans. To Roosevelt, their Japanese ancestry made them untrustworthy in any war against Japan, so they needed to be isolated and contained. On February 19, 1942, Roosevelt signed Executive Order 9066, transferring responsibility for internal security from the Justice Department to the War Department. This politically expedient act allowed the War Department to designate any part of the country as a military area from which any or all persons could be removed.

Implementation of the order was placed in the hands of the previously mentioned General DeWitt. His prejudice toward Japanese Americans can be summed up in his comment "'A Jap's a Jap.' It makes no difference whether he is an American citizen or not." However, his public report on the removal of the Japanese Americans stated that the action was a matter of military necessity rather than a result of racial beliefs.[6] On March 2, 1942, DeWitt declared a restricted zone covering the entire West Coast and the southwest half of Arizona.

It soon became evident that the vaguely worded Executive Order 9066 was aimed primarily at the Japanese, rather than at the Italians and Germans living on the West Coast. The order authorized the forced removal of men, women, and children of Japanese descent living there. No distinction was made between the first-generation immigrants who were resident aliens and second-generation citizens who were born in the United States. This amounted to what the American Civil Liberties Union at the time condemned as the worst wholesale violation of the civil rights of citizens in the nation's history.[7] The race-based determination dramatically altered the lives of West Coast Japanese Americans and destroyed their communities. It was not applied to Japanese Americans living elsewhere. Although Hawaii was clearly vulnerable to further Japanese attack and even invasion, the Japanese Americans living there were spared because imprisoning 37 percent of the population was impractical and would severely dislocate the local economy.

AMERICAN REFUGEES

Between February 19 and March 27, 1942, Japanese Americans were given an opportunity to voluntarily leave the restricted zone and move inland before the executive order went into effect. Most of them were understandably reluctant to leave. After all, they were being asked to abandon their homes even though they had done nothing wrong. However, during those few weeks, an estimated 1,963 Japanese Americans resettled in Colorado. They chose Colorado, first, because there was already a sizable Japanese American community there. As of 1940, some 2,734 Japanese Americans were living in Colorado, more than in any other Western inland state.[8] But the second and perhaps more compelling reason for moving to Colorado was that its governor, Ralph L. Carr, invited them to come. His reasons for doing so are discussed below. All other Western states were openly against accepting them. Kansas even posted police on its border to keep them out.

Many Coloradans were alarmed by Carr's open-door policy. Various groups across the state, such as the Denver Cooperative Club, the Daughters of Colorado, the Order of Moose in Rifle, the Independent Order of Odd Fellows of Alamosa, and the County Commissioners of Bent County, opposed the coming of Japanese Americans. Many business, labor, and farm leaders grudgingly agreed to accept the West Coast Japanese only if they were under some type of government control. A common concern was that once the Japanese Americans arrived in Colorado, they would compete for jobs and, perhaps worse, buy land and stay. Unlike many other states, Colorado had no alien land laws to prevent this.

Some Japanese Americans chose to go to Colorado because family or friends there could provide shelter and employment. Nancy S. Miyagishima, for example, went to work on her Aunt Doris Nakata's farm in Fort Lupton, Weld County, in northern Colorado.[9] Eventually, fifteen other West Coast families chose to relocate to Greeley, the main city in Weld County. Many others moved to small, rural communities, such as Blanca, Fort Garland, and Jaroso in Costilla County, and to the comparatively large city of Alamosa in the San Luis Valley in southern Colorado, where they worked on farms.[10]

Other refugees, such as George H. Kato, had neither family nor friends in Colorado but went there anyway. As he explained, "With only three days to be out . . . we had to practically give away our belongings. . . . We didn't want to settle in a large city, nor too small a town. We looked at the map and Fort Morgan seemed to fit the bill."[11] Kato was one of several hundred who settled in Morgan County, in northeastern Colorado, where workers were needed to harvest the sugar beet crop. For Kato, who had been a gas-station worker, this proved to be a fortunate choice. After the war, he became a successful farm owner and was later profiled in the intermountain magazine *Western Farm Life* (Denver) as "Agriculture's Horatio Alger."[12]

Miyagishima, Kato, and other Japanese who moved to Colorado had to adjust to a new normal that included being monitored by the state's security agencies. Upon their arrival, highway patrol and port-of-entry officers searched them to look for contraband items such as shortwave radios and weapons. They were also required to register with the US District Attorney's office to obtain permission to take trips away from home. If they had thought they might escape prejudice by moving to relatively remote areas of Colorado, they were mistaken. In some places, health care workers refused to treat them, theaters forced them to sit in segregated sections, and churches made them feel unwelcome at religious services. In violation of their First Amendment right to peaceful assembly, they were forbidden to participate in exclusively Japanese American gatherings, including those held by religious congregations and social organizations.

Not least of their difficulties was a less-than-warm welcome from Japanese Coloradans, who were worried about rising anti-Japanese sentiment. Japanese Coloradans had always depended on the sufferance of the white majority. As Joe Masaoka, regional director of the Japanese American Citizens' League (JACL) of Denver, explained: "A group whose position because of the war was made precarious naturally looked askance and even with resentment toward the influx of newcomers with their identical physical characteristics. They felt that the larger numbers would be looked upon with suspicion and that consequently their own assailable position in the community would be endangered."[13] That is to say, Japanese Coloradans feared that the sudden arrival of refugees would strain white tolerance. Japanese American farmers living in Fort Lupton, Weld County, in northern Colorado, expressed a similar concern that "if anything happened, it would be [a] reflection upon them in the public mind and they did not wish to see any such risks taken."[14] Those living in the Grand Valley, on Colorado's Western Slope, tried to distance themselves from potentially suspect "Japanese aliens" for exactly that reason.[15] Even if they did not actively disavow the new arrivals, many Japanese Coloradans, unnerved by the resurgence of anti-Japanese sentiment in the local community, were reluctant to extend a helping hand.

Clarence Iwao Nishizu's fruitless odyssey through Colorado and neighboring states in search of a place to resettle illustrates the difficulties. In early March 1941, in the last weeks before the narrow window for the voluntary departure of West Coast Japanese Americans closed, Clarence, his younger brother John, and Clarence's friend Jack Tsuhara drove their Chevy nonstop from their home in Orange County, California, to Littleton, Colorado, to see the head of a seed company about getting jobs, only to be turned away. They then drove south to the San Luis Valley, looking for work in San Luis, Costilla County, and also nearby La Jara, Conejos County, where the hoped-for help from one of the oldest Japanese American farmers in the state never materialized. He did not want to get involved with any outsiders.

Giving up on Colorado, Clarence and crew drove south into northern New Mexico to visit relatives and family friends who had already been locked up in a prison for "alien enemies" in Santa Fe. They were discouraged from settling in southern New Mexico by a local Japanese American businessman (the self-styled "Japanese Chili King of Las Cruces"); threatened by a white customer at a bar in Deming, New Mexico, who said, "I can't tell the difference between a [good] Chinese and a bad Jap"; and given a decidedly unfriendly reception at a Chinese restaurant in El Paso, Texas.[16] As they were leaving the restaurant, they found a knife under one of their tires. Driving northwest to Chandler, Arizona, they were stopped and harassed by a highway patrolman purporting to check their travel permits. During their four-state trip, they found no refuge for their family. After returning home to California, they were no longer allowed to leave.

On March 29, 1941, General DeWitt forbade all persons of Japanese ancestry from leaving the restricted zone. Then he began issuing civilian exclusion orders for the mandatory mass removal of Japanese Americans from the West Coast. In May 1941, Clarence I. Nishizu and his family were deported to the Heart Mountain concentration camp in northwestern Wyoming, one of eight such facilities in the American West built to confine Japanese Americans. The Nishizu family and nearly 120,000 other Japanese Americans, two-thirds of them citizens, were imprisoned in camps.[17] In contravention of the law, the US Census Bureau provided personal information about Japanese Americans to surveillance agencies, facilitating their roundup and imprisonment.[18] The Census Bureau gave out the names and addresses of Japanese Americans living in Washington, DC, and neighborhood data about them in other parts of the country, including Colorado. Once more, Japanese American civil rights were violated in the name of national security.[19]

The instructions accompanying the Civilian Exclusion orders allowed

Japanese Americans to take only what they could carry. They were forced to sell their property—including their principal possessions, such as land, homes, and cars—at fire-sale prices to other Americans, who were more than willing to profit from their plight. Almost all Japanese American families suffered severe economic losses.

A PROFILE IN COURAGE

During this dark chapter in American history, Colorado had a shining light—Governor Ralph L. Carr. In a nation gripped by war hysteria, Carr stood virtually alone among public officials in his opposition to the wholesale incarceration of Japanese Americans in concentration camps. In doing so, he defended the civil rights of all Americans. With singular moral courage and at the cost of his political career, he affirmed anew the American pledge of liberty and justice for all. Yet, except to the Japanese Americans whom he helped and students of Colorado history, Carr remains largely unknown.[20]

Carr's decision to speak out on behalf of Japanese Americans was made in a climate of fear and anger. Like many others at that time, Carr thought that some Japanese Americans had in fact assisted in the attack on Pearl Harbor; he believed that there were "thousands of persons who are not friendly to those things [called] American" living on the Pacific Coast.[21] As is known now, none of this was true. However, although Carr shared the widespread belief that there were fifth columnists in American society, he still took a stand on behalf of Japanese Americans. But why? Even with the benefit of hindsight, there is nothing about his public life that would have predicted this.[22]

After receiving his undergraduate and law degrees from the University of Colorado, Carr worked as an attorney specializing in irrigation and interstate river law. Widely regarded as one of Colorado's outstanding attorneys, he was drafted as the Republican gubernatorial candidate in 1938, easily won the election, and, after rescuing the state from insolvency, was reelected in 1940, once more by a sizable margin.[23] On the eve of America's entry into World War II, he had developed a reputation as a fiscally conservative but socially progressive governor. As events unfolded in the early days of the war, Carr proved to be a courageous governor as well.

To understand Carr's stand on behalf of Japanese Americans, one must look at his early years in rural Colorado *and* his ideals of Ameri-

FIG. 8.2. Governor Ralph Lawrence Carr, c. 1940. History Colorado, Stephen H. Hart Library and Research Center, 10028117.

canism. Together, they shaped his character, providing him with a moral compass to guide both his words and his actions. Carr came from modest circumstances. The son of a Scotch-Irish miner, he was raised in mining camps near Cripple Creek, Colorado. His outlook was influenced by his early experiences in the small settlements of Colorado, where he developed compassion for ordinary people. During a 1942 interview with Lee Taylor Casey of the *Rocky Mountain News* (RMN), Carr expressed the hope that, as a two-term governor, he had not lost touch with "my fellows because, when I do, I shall cease to be the human being I've always been since those peculiar but interesting days in that great Colorado mining camp [Cripple Creek]. My life has been spent in close contact with people. I love people. I sense their feelings when I'm around them."[24] His empathy for people was probably enhanced by his stint as a journalist. He worked for several newspapers and press associations, and edited a newspaper. Carr counted among his close friends a former journalistic competitor, Lowell Thomas, who grew up in Victor and Cripple Creek near Carr and later became a famous author, world traveler, and news commentator.

Among the Coloradans Carr enjoyed being with were people of color. He was fluent in Spanish and was close to the Latino community of the San Luis Valley, especially in Antonito, where he helped many with their legal problems. He was also familiar with the small Japanese American community of La Jara, about fourteen miles north of Antonito. As a result of his contacts with Japanese Coloradans, Carr refused to see them as tools of the emperor of Japan.[25] Japanese Coloradans such as longtime La Jara resident Noboru Ashida, who earned two Bronze Stars and a Purple Heart while fighting for his country in the European Theater, proved Carr right.[26]

It may have been Carr's interaction with the state's people of color that developed his appreciation of America as a culturally pluralist country. In a stirring radio address to Coloradans three days after Pearl Harbor, Carr reminded them that the United States was a nation of immigrants, the great "melting pot" of the modern civilized world.[27] Perhaps mindful of his own family's Scotch-Irish ancestry, he observed: "From every nation of the globe people have come to the United States who sought to live as free men here under our plan of government. We cannot test the degree of a man's affection for his fellows or his devotion to his country by the birthplace of his grandfathers. All Americans had their origins beyond the border of the United States."[28] From his own experience, Carr was acutely aware that people of color were often victims of prejudice. When the first Japanese Americans arriving in the spring of 1942 at the Amache concentration camp in southeast Colorado were threatened with violence, Carr confronted the mob and told them: "If you harm them, you must first harm me. I was brought up in small towns where I knew the shame and dishonor of race hatred. I grew up to despise it because it threatened the happiness of you, and you and you," indicating members of the crowd.[29] Carr understood the toxic effects of such beliefs on society at large.

IDEALS OF AMERICANISM

Perhaps even more crucial to the development of Carr's character were his ideals of Americanism.[30] He realized that the concept of Americanism was by nature elusive and difficult to put into words, though specific aspects could be described in different ways.[31] Unfortunately, "Americanism" was a word with which many liberties were taken, as George Norlin, president of the University of Colorado (1919–39), noted.[32] What was evident to Carr was that, ever since the founding of the Republic, Americans had recognized that they lived in a unique place, different from the native lands from whence many of them had emigrated. Yet neither Carr nor anyone else had articulated a clear, coherent, and universally accepted philosophy of Americanism that could be embraced by one and all to explain that difference.

To guide his understanding of Americanism, Carr relied on Abraham Lincoln, with whom he identified personally.[33] With Lincoln, he shared three personal qualities: a compassion for others, a sense of humor, and a commitment to a cause. Above all, Carr appreciated Lincoln's adherence to the ideals of the Republic during the Civil War. These were the ideals expressed in the nation's founding documents, notably the US Constitution, with its Bill of Rights. The core ideals were the principles of liberty and democracy, which served as the cornerstones of the country. Carr believed that these principles were what distinguished Americans from others in the world. In other words, he believed in what is often called American exceptionalism. As political scientist Jürgen Gebhardt puts it, "The United States has no meaning, no identity, no political culture or even history apart from its ideals of liberty and democracy and the continuing efforts of Americans to realize those ideals."[34] Carr believed that these ideals impressed themselves on the consciousness of Americans regardless of their perspective. To defend them, Americans were fighting overseas, and it was because of these ideals that they would triumph over their enemies.

On the eve of World War II, Carr framed Americanism as a stark contrast to two popular ideologies of the time, Communism and Fascism. On February 25, 1936, in a speech to the Alamosa Junior Chamber of Commerce, Carr said that Americanism "does not subjugate the individual to the point where, as under certain systems of government existing in Europe at this time . . . in order that the ruling power may be absolutely free to work its own will, every subject of that rule is, in effect, a slave, stripped of every right, not only of the right to liberty and the pursuit of happiness, but the right of life itself."[35] Carr was determined that the sort of tragedy unfolding in Europe not happen in the United States. Adopting the perspective of classical liberalism, Carr argued that the quest for freedom was part of the natural evolution of mankind: "Regardless of origin, and no matter how humble the condition in life, there smolders in every human breast a feeling of hostility against circumstances which tend to hinder and obstruct a man's individual initiative and enterprise. And that declaration . . . is the embodiment of mankind's final protest against the forces of dictatorship, of the supremacy of government, and the subjugation of the individual for the good of the state."[36]

For Carr, Americanism was essentially a way of life rooted in the principle that individual rights and responsibilities were inviolable. He objected to the government's incarceration of Japanese Americans because it trampled on the freedom of individual Japanese Americans, who were being held collectively responsible for any negative actions committed by members of their ethnic group. Carr steadfastly refused to condemn the entire group, as others were doing. As early as January 1942, he published a statement of support in the *Pacific Citizen*, the official newspaper of the national Japanese American Citizens League (JACL), the largest and most influential Japanese American civil right organization in the country.[37]

On February 29, 1942, Carr publicly declared that Colorado was willing to provide temporary quarters for Italian, German, and Japanese refugees from the West Coast. He admonished Coloradans against engaging in attacks on these groups and pointed out, "They are as loyal to American institutions as you and I. Many of them have been born here—are American citizens, with no connection with or feeling of loyalty toward the customs and philosophies of Italy, Germany, and Japan."[38] They were, in a word, trustworthy.

To show in a personal way that he meant what he said, Carr invited a Japanese American into his Denver home. He hired Wakako Domoto to work as his house girl.[39] She was an exemplary student at Stanford University before being forced to leave with her family for Amache. Initially, she refused to accept the position with Carr because of fears about leaving Amache and facing angry Coloradans, who might abuse, beat, or even lynch her, a treatment some Coloradans suggested for all "Japs."[40] To allay her forebodings, Carr personally went to Union Station to escort her to his home. He also arranged for her to take courses at the Emily Griffith Opportunity School and provided room and board, as well as a salary of thirty-five dollars a month.

Carr's willingness to accept Japanese Americans into Colorado subjected him to intense public pressures. He regularly received hate mail. As Carr confided to his friend James F. Lockhart in Los Angeles, he got "oodles" of scathing letters that "took [his] hide off."[41] Some writers accused him of being Japanese or "merely" in love with them.[42] Critics demanded that he use force to prevent them from entering Colorado. His political nemesis, US senator Edwin "Big Ed" Johnson (Democrat), wanted him to use the National Guard to close the borders to Japanese American migrants, whether citizens or not.[43] (Having himself used the National Guard earlier to block the entrance of migrant sugar beet workers when he was governor of Colorado, Johnson knew that it could be done.)[44]

Governor Carr's perspective on the treatment of Japanese Americans was complex. While he was ambivalent about the questionable orders of the president and American military authorities to imprison Japanese Americans and restrict their freedoms, he nonetheless followed those directives for the same reason that he defended the rights of Japanese Americans— loyalty to the country and the ideals of Americanism.[45]

He was acutely aware of the injustice of imprisoning Japanese Americans in concentration camps without a fair hearing.[46] Carr saw the clamor for incarcerating Japanese Americans for what it was—intolerance. He recognized that they were entitled to equal protection under the law. Besides the inherent immorality and illegality of such treatment, he understood the appalling implications of the federal government's action. The failure to defend the rights of the Japanese Americans would imperil the rights of all Americans. In explaining his offer to welcome the West Coast refugees, Carr warned: "I am not talking on behalf of Japanese, of Italians, or of Germans as such when I say this. I am talking to . . . all American people whether their status be white, brown or black and regardless of the birthplaces of their grandfathers when I say that if a majority may deprive a minority of its freedom, contrary to the terms of the Constitution today, then you as a minority may be subjected to the same ill-will of the majority tomorrow."[47]

The onslaught from Carr's political opponents was ferocious. Democrats used his stand on behalf of Japanese Americans as an opportunity to denounce him while garnering personal support. In places like Cañon City and Poncha Springs, Carr was accused of inviting the Japanese to Colorado in order to obtain their votes.[48] Senator Edwin Johnson made a more serious allegation: that Carr had invited Japanese Americans to Colorado to exploit their labor, knowing that they were desperate. According to Johnson, the governor had thus placed Coloradans at risk of potential violence from Japanese Americans, who, as he put it, were under great emotional duress. At the same time, the jobs of Coloradan workers had been placed in jeopardy. Johnson publicly questioned Carr's motives: "Was patriotism and cooperation with the Federal Government, and preservation of civil liberties, and humanitarianism Colorado's motive? Indeed it was not! The motive was the desire to exploit distressed Japanese labor."[49] In a state that was still suffering the effects of the Great Depression, Johnson's claim that cheap Japanese American labor would threaten the livelihood of Colorado workingmen was damaging. Carr was vulnerable on this score because he was known as a businessman's governor. He had shown this in 1940 when he called out the National Guard to end a violent labor dispute at the Green Mountain Dam in western Colorado.[50] The ongoing lobbying efforts by sugar beet growers in northern Colorado and the intermountain region to bring in Japanese American workers to meet labor shortages lent credence to Johnson's allegations.

While it is true that Carr wanted Japanese American workers, it was to meet Colorado's agricultural labor shortage rather than to assist the sugar beet companies. As he told the Colorado Defense Council in July 1942, the state's real test of patriotism would come in the fall, when it was faced with the problem of the harvest.[51] Carr had the foresight to realize that an important part of the struggle would be waged on the home front, where American workers, including Japanese Americans, would have to provide the wherewithal to fight the war. Given the level of anti-Japanese sentiment in Colorado, he also realized that it would be imprudent to say so publicly. However, Carr did share his thoughts on the subject in a letter to his friend James F. Lockhart: "There won't be many [Japanese Americans] coming into Colorado at the best and, while I don't dare to mention it in public, we will probably need all who come to replace the men who have been called in the draft. There's going to be an awful shortage of labor in the beet and potato fields and also among the fruit raisers."[52] As Carr foresaw, the labor of Japanese Americans was needed in agriculture as well as other sectors of the state's economy. Their contributions to the domestic wartime effort are discussed in chapter 9.

POLITICAL DEFEAT, MORAL VICTORY

When Carr made his decision to defend the Japanese Americans, he knew the political risks involved. Indeed, after issuing his order to allow them into Colorado, he said, "If I am wrong in the eyes of the people I can be told so at the polls in the next election."[53] Coloradans did just that.

In 1942, much to the surprise of his supporters, Carr lost his bid to replace his archrival Edwin Johnson in the US Senate. His loss occurred in an election where Colorado voters had favored Republicans.[54] As one supporter said to Carr, "All of the other Republican candidates, some of whom are almost unknown to the electorate, won by a tremendous plurality, and yet you, the most outstanding candidate which the state has produced in several decades, lost to a mediocre man. It is almost unbelievable."[55] One supporter remarked, "I have never seen such a campaign of hatred as was manifested among certain classes of the population over that Japan lie that Johnson cultivated so carefully."[56] Contributing to Carr's defeat may have been the lost votes of another minority group whom he championed— Latinos.[57] They blamed Japanese Americans for the Latino casualties at the Battle of Bataan (January 7–April 9, 1942) in the Philippines and the infamous Bataan Death March that followed it. Some felt betrayed by the man whom they had affectionately referred to as "Rafaelito" for allowing Japanese Americans into Colorado, and some publicly called him a "Jap lover."[58]

It was one of the closest senatorial races ever held in Colorado. Carr lost by a mere 3,642 votes out of 375,000, a defeat that many of his supporters attributed to anger over his stand on behalf of the Japanese Americans.[59] However, Carr himself was not convinced; in any case, he said that if he had to defend the Japanese Americans all over again, he would have.[60] Carr accepted his loss graciously, taking some personal consolation from the title "Human Governor" bestowed on him by one of his constituents.[61]

Fifty years after the war, Carr's actions were publicly vindicated. In the spring of 1996, the Colorado General Assembly passed a resolution honoring Carr for his efforts to protect Japanese Americans during World War II. Three years later, the *Denver Post* (DP) declared him Colorado's "Person of the Century" for his "humanity and decency" in one of America's—and Colorado's—most troubled times.[62]

RESISTANCE TO INJUSTICE

And troubled times they were, indeed. Paralyzed by fear, most Japanese Americans offered no resistance to the government's persecution. However, two individuals who later moved to Colorado were exceptions—James "Jimmie" Matsumoto Omura and Minoru "Min" Yasui. Both Omura and Yasui were concerned about the racialization of Japanese Americans as well as the violation of their civil rights. Like many other Japanese Americans, they placed their experience in the larger context of the country's history. This is foremost in Omura's reflections on the consequences of a proposed

FIG. 8.3. James "Jimmie"
Matsumoto Omura, editor,
Rocky Shimpo, 1944. Photo
courtesy of Frank Abe.

Japanese American evacuation: "The forceful evacuation of citizen Americans on the synthetic theory of racial fidelity—'Once a Jap, always a Jap'—would be an indictment against every racial minority in the United States. It would usher in the bigoted and misguided belief that Americanism is a racial attribute and not a national symbol. The scar that will be left will be broad and deep—a stigma of eternal shame."[63] Omura's and Yasui's actions in defense of their community were quintessentially American, embodying the spirit of individualism and dissent that gave birth to the United States. Their protests took very different forms, however. And as is often the case, both paid a high personal cost for their actions.

Jimmie Omura was an outspoken journalist and activist. On February 23, 1942, in testimony before the Select Committee to Investigate the Interstate Migration of Destitute Citizens in San Francisco, he denounced the forcible removal of Japanese Americans from the West Coast and their confinement in concentration camps. He challenged the committee itself to answer the questions "Has the Gestapo come to America? Have we not risen in righteous anger at Hitler's mistreatments of the Jews? Then, is it

FIG. 8.4. Minoru "Min" Yasui, 1946. Auraria Library Special Collections and Digital Initiatives, Minoru Yasui Collection.

not incongruous that citizen Americans of Japanese descent should be similarly mistreated and persecuted?"[64]

On March 29, 1942, Omura and his wife joined other Japanese Americans who left San Francisco for Denver to avoid being sent to the camps. A year later, Omura opposed the War Department's decision to conscript Japanese Americans and to establish a segregated Japanese American army unit—in effect, reversing its earlier decision to classify them as unfit for service. After inmates in the Heart Mountain concentration camp in Wyoming formed a Fair Play Committee to oppose being conscripted until their rights as citizens had been restored, Omura, then editor of the newly established Denver newspaper *Rocky Shimpo,* wrote news stories and editorials supporting the resisters. For his support of the draft resistance movement, Omura, along with seven leaders of the Fair Play Committee, was secretly indicted for unlawful conspiracy to counsel, aid, and abet violations of the draft.[65] At their joint trial, the Fair Play Committee leaders were sentenced to jail, but Omura was acquitted because the judge ruled that he had the right as a journalist to publish what he thought appropriate.

When Omura returned to editing the *Rocky Shimpo* from May to December 1947, he made JACL policies one of his chief targets. He took the organization to task for its complicity in the removal and imprisonment of Japanese Americans, and for encouraging cooperation with the federal government in the hope of future considerations. Mike Masaoka, JACL executive secretary, responded by dubbing Omura the organization's "Public Enemy Number One."[66] The JACL blacklisted him and made it difficult for him to make a living.

Min Yasui also fought against the government's violation of Japanese American civil rights. His defiance was markedly different from Omura's, however. As a lawyer, Yasui took a legalistic approach. He has the distinction of being the defendant in the first of what became known as the Supreme Court internment cases challenging the constitutionality of Executive Order 9066. As political scientist Peter Irons states in his study of these cases, Yasui was in many ways an unlikely candidate to challenge the government, because he had been trained as an American Army officer, educated as a lawyer, employed in a Japanese consular office, and was actively involved in the JACL.[67]

Though Yasui accepted the basic legality of President Roosevelt's Executive Order, he decided to test the constitutionality of General DeWitt's 8:00 P.M. to 6:00 A.M. curfew for all enemy aliens and all Japanese Americans within restricted areas. He focused on the fact that DeWitt's order made distinctions between citizens on the basis of ancestry—that is, the curfew targeted a specific minority group, which was an infringement on their fundamental rights as American citizens. So Yasui deliberately violated the curfew and was arrested. In doing so, he also provoked Mike Masaoka, who branded him a renegade and a self-styled martyr. Masaoka was concerned that Yasui's actions might inspire Japanese Americans to violate not only the curfew but also the removal orders, when he and the JACL had already assured the government of their compliance. Eventually, Masaoka and Yasui reconciled.

In a contorted ruling on the case, Judge James Alger Fee concluded that the laws targeting a race were unconstitutional when applied to citizens, but he found that Yasui had forfeited his citizenship when he had demonstrated his loyalty to Japan by defying the curfew, so he sentenced him to a year in jail—spent mostly in solitary confinement—and fined him five thousand dollars. Yasui appealed his case all the way to the US Supreme Court, where he lost. The High Court ruled unanimously that the government did have the authority to restrict the lives of citizens during wartime. After his release from jail, Yasui was imprisoned in the Minidoka concentration camp in Idaho, but he was freed in 1944 to work as a laborer in an ice plant in Chicago, and then moved to Denver.

Following this experience, it would have been natural for Yasui to continue to oppose the federal policies toward Japanese Americans, but instead, he assisted the government in carrying them out. After his release from Minidoka in 1944, he worked with the JACL to try to squelch the Heart Mountain draft resistance movement and came into conflict with Omura on this. Yasui felt his actions were consistent with his commitment to the US Constitution and the rights and obligations of citizens. He thought that the draft offered Japanese Americans the chance to fulfill their obligations of citizenship alongside members of other races. He adhered to the JACL position that participation in the armed forces would facilitate resettlement from the camps and deter discrimination against Japanese Americans. Regrettably, as is discussed in chapter 10, neither belief proved to be true.

In their efforts to defend Japanese Americans, Ralph Carr, Jimmie Omura, and Min Yasui took a morally courageous stand for democracy.

CONCENTRATION CAMPS, USA

During the spring and summer of 1942, the US Army collected, guarded, and transported Japanese Americans to one of the fifteen "assembly centers" in the West Coast, located as far north as Puyallup, Washington, and as far south as Mayer, Arizona. Most of these centers were former fairgrounds or racetracks. As Peter Ota, who was fifteen at the time, recalls the atmosphere of confusion in which Japanese Americans were sent away, "We didn't know where we were going, how long we'd be gone. We didn't know what to take. A toothbrush, toilet supplies, some clothes. Only what you could carry." Ota and his family ended up in the "Santa Anita assembly center," a former racetrack, where the stables had been quickly converted into living quarters. As Ota remembers, "The people in the stables had to live with the stench. Everything was communal. We had absolutely no privacy. When you went to the toilet, it was communal. It was very embarrassing for women especially."[68]

Later, Peter Ota and other Japanese Americans were transported in cattle cars to what were euphemistically called "relocation centers," where they were confined without benefit of a trial. Management of the camps was in the hands of the newly created War Relocation Authority (WRA), which had as its ostensible aim the "resettlement" of Japanese Americans in the Interior West. Milton S. Eisenhower, an administrator from the Department of Agriculture, headed the WRA. Eisenhower envisioned these facilities to be similar to the subsistence homesteads that had been established in the rural areas during the New Deal era. According to this view, the centers were to serve as temporary places that Japanese Americans would pass through on their way to employment in the private sector. Unfortunately, Eisenhower's plans were derailed by the public loathing of Japanese Americans.

On April 7, 1942, in Salt Lake City, Eisenhower met with the governors and other officials of the Western states to seek their cooperation. He soon discovered that, with the sole exception of Governor Ralph L. Carr, the group was opposed to the presence of Japanese Americans in their states. Carr was willing to cooperate because he felt that it was the "American thing," the "patriotic thing," and the "decent thing" to do.[69] The failure of the other governors to follow Carr's lead took the mass removal of Japanese Americans in a tragic direction. Had they done so, things would have been very different. While Japanese Americans would still have been forced to leave the West Coast, they might have been integrated into the inland economy. But the prevailing anti-Japanese sentiment in the Western states ensured that Japanese Americans would be allowed there only under lock and key.

From the Salt Lake City meeting, Eisenhower learned that the governors perceived the Japanese Americans as a menace—and not just because of the war. Wyoming governor Nels Smith declared that his constituents simply disliked Asians and would not stand for being California's dumping ground. Indeed, Smith warned Eisenhower, "If you bring Japanese into my state, I promise you they will be hanging from every tree."[70] Smith and the other governors shared a common concern that the Japanese Americans might settle permanently, acquire property, and compete with local workingmen. They insisted that the Japanese Americans be deported from their states after the war. In the face of such antipathy, Eisenhower concluded that it was necessary to confine the Japanese Americans in camps. It took the government nearly a year to accomplish this, at a cost of nearly ninety million dollars, money that could have been spent fighting America's real enemies in Europe and the Pacific.[71]

MAP 8.1. Assembly camps and concentration camps.

The Japanese Americans were incarcerated in concentration camps situated in some of the most isolated places in the United States. They were located in Poston and Gila River, Arizona; Jerome and Rohwer, Arkansas; Manzanar and Tule Lake, California; Granada, Colorado; Topaz, Utah; Minidoka, Idaho; and Heart Mountain, Wyoming. The eight camps in the Western states were built in semiarid lands, the two in Arkansas next to swamplands. All of them were placed in remote areas with extreme climates, torrid in the summer and frigid in the winter.[72] Dr. Yamato Ichihashi, former professor of history at Stanford University, describes the inhospitable Granada site as "a desolate prairie. . . . The only creatures which seem to feel at home here are jackrabbits, rattlesnakes and turtles."[73]

Remarkably, the conditions at these camps were worse than those at the prisoner-of-war (POW) camps set up for captured German and Italian soldiers. Not only were the POW camps located in more congenial places, such as Camp Carson, near Colorado Springs, but the captives were also generally better regarded by the authorities and by local residents.[74] The disparity in treatment reflected the fact that the enemy soldiers were European, and thus white, and the Japanese Americans were not. Racial affinity proved to be more important than national identity during the war.

Life in the camps was as harsh as the surroundings, with inmates living in hastily built tar-papered barracks lacking comfort and privacy, eating meals that until 1943 fell below minimum army standards, and working at jobs that paid less than the minimum wage. Furthermore, the camps initially lacked schools and medical facilities. The camps were all enclosed by barbed wire and guarded by armed soldiers. There were instances of soldiers shooting unarmed inmates trying to escape and beating so-called troublemakers.

Between eight thousand and twenty thousand Japanese Americans were confined in each camp. Inmates found incarceration debilitating. Besides the physical privations, there was the psychological trauma of being locked up for no other reason than their race. Even after they were released, many of them suffered from posttraumatic stress disorders. This condition had severe consequences for the Japanese American community as a whole and for individual families. Imprisonment caused their world to become topsy-turvy, dislocating the community's long-established traditions and undermining families' interpersonal relationships.

Perhaps the most deep-rooted damage was that done to the integrity of Japanese American families, as children became estranged from their parents and wives from their husbands. Living in barracks adversely affected family unity. Seemingly innocuous requirements, such as having the inmates eat in communal mess halls rather than in their own homes, eroded the authority of parents over their American-born children, who began to congregate among themselves.[75] The influence of the Japanese immigrant generation was further compromised, as camp administrators relied on their second-generation children because of their fluency in the English language and familiarity with American culture.

In anger and frustration over the injustice of it all, some inmates resisted their incarceration and engaged in demonstrations and strikes.[76] But while there was an underlying tension in the camps, it rarely flared up into violence. On the contrary, life was peaceful to the point of boredom. Such was the case at Amache, which the WRA considered a model camp.[77]

FIG. 8.5. Japanese American family en route to the Amache concentration camp, May 1942. Denver Public Library, Western History Collection, X-6557.

COLORADO PURGATORY

"The strangest city in Colorado"—that was how Lee Casey, the well-known *RMN* columnist, described Amache after a visit in November 1942. The camp was located fourteen miles east of Lamar and twenty miles west of the Kansas border in the Arkansas River Valley. It was an apt description for what became the tenth-largest city in Colorado, where as many as 7,567 Japanese Americans were exiled.

The official name of Amache was the Granada Relocation Center in Colorado. Some other name was needed to distinguish the camp from that in the nearby town of Granada for the purpose of mail delivery. The name Amache stuck after Mayor R. L. Christy of Lamar, Colorado, suggested it as a way of honoring the daughter of Onichee, the Cheyenne chief who had been killed in the Sand Creek Massacre in 1864. Amache proved to

FIG. 8.6. Overview of the Amache Concentration Camp, December 12, 1942. Photo by Tom Parker. Denver Public Library, Western History Collection, X-6570.

be a boon to Granada. On the eve of World War II, Granada was a rural backwater. With establishment of the camp, it once again became a boomtown. Like present-day Colorado communities with prisons in their midst, it benefited from the infusion of people and money into the area.

Amache was built on a rectangular, ten-thousand-acre patch of prairie. Construction began in March 1942 under the direction of the US Army

Corps of Engineers. Even though over a thousand people were employed to build it, the camp was only half completed when it officially opened on August 29, 1942. With the assistance of the prisoners themselves, it was finally finished in November 1942, at a cost of over four million dollars.[78]

More than anything else, Amache resembled a military base. It was laid out in twenty-nine blocks, each block containing twelve barracks, each barrack divided into twelve one-room units, and each unit housing a family of up to seven people. Every inmate was issued a canvas cot with a cotton pad and comforter but no sheets or bedding. Exacerbating the poor living conditions was the high-plains weather, with its sharp extremes. The combination of inadequate heating and inadequate clothing made it bitterly cold in the winter. In the summer, the poorly ventilated buildings were unbearably hot, and the stifling atmosphere was made worse by dust storms that covered everything with sand and dirt. The Japanese American inmates had to endure these harsh conditions for several years.

James G. Lindley, Amache's respected administrator, and his staff governed the prisoners with the assistance of a community council consisting of second-generation Japanese Americans, who policed the compound. Over 130 soldiers were assigned to watch the prisoners, patrolling the perimeter of the compound, manning thirty-foot wooden guard towers at the edge of the compound, and operating searchlights throughout the night. Their primary assignments were to prevent unauthorized arrivals and departures and to inspect parcels for contraband items.

Most of the Japanese Americans imprisoned at Amache came from California. Among them was the Shigekuni family, who had been transferred from the Santa Anita Assembly Center near Los Angeles. Tom Shigekuni, who was twelve years old at the time, recalled the unsettling trip and shock of their first sight of the Colorado landscape at Amache:

> When the soldiers loaded us onto the train at Santa Anita, they still wouldn't tell us where we were going. They just told us not to look outside. . . . And when the trains stopped or were sidetracked and they let us walk around for a few minutes outside, the soldiers kept their guns aimed at us as if they expected that we might try to run away. Here we were in the middle of the desert or the mountains, in places where there was nothing in sight for miles. Where did they think we were going to run? . . . No one knew where we were going. . . . The first impression I had when we got to the camp was that it was . . . bleak, very, very bleak. No trees. No grass. Nothing. Just a bare hill with a bunch of barracks on it and lots of sagebrush and other Japanese.[79]

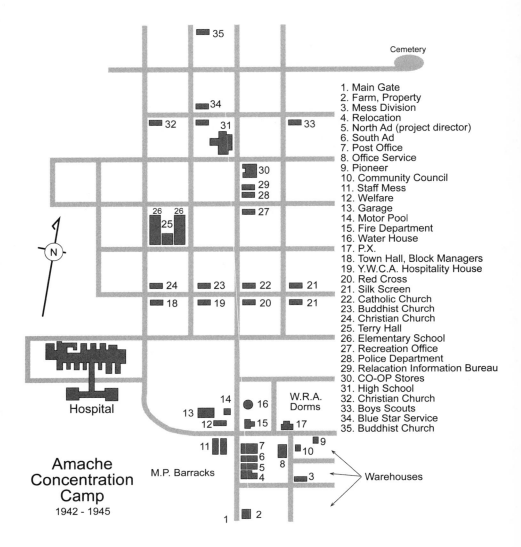

1. Main Gate
2. Farm, Property
3. Mess Division
4. Relocation
5. North Ad (project director)
6. South Ad
7. Post Office
8. Office Service
9. Pioneer
10. Community Council
11. Staff Mess
12. Welfare
13. Garage
14. Motor Pool
15. Fire Department
16. Water House
17. P.X.
18. Town Hall, Block Managers
19. Y.W.C.A. Hospitality House
20. Red Cross
21. Silk Screen
22. Catholic Church
23. Buddhist Church
24. Christian Church
25. Terry Hall
26. Elementary School
27. Recreation Office
28. Police Department
29. Relacation Information Bureau
30. CO-OP Stores
31. High School
32. Christian Church
33. Boys Scouts
34. Blue Star Service
35. Buddhist Church

MAP 8.2. Amache concentration camp, 1942–1945. Based on a map by Eddie Kubota, a high school student at Amache.

The Amacheans were equally divided between rural and urban dwellers. Tensions developed between the two groups, resulting in occasional disturbances during the early months of incarceration. In terms of occupational background, about 40 percent of them had engaged in agricultural work, while about 10 percent were professionals and managers, 15 percent were domestics, 13 percent were clerks and salespeople, 16 percent were skilled workers, and 6 percent were unskilled workers.[80] Most Amacheans who chose to work spent their time in agricultural pursuits. In their capable hands, the camp farm became a highly productive enterprise. In their first year, they produced nearly four million pounds of vegetables, valued at over $190,000.[81] In addition to producing enough for their own needs, they were able to ship sixteen railroad-car loads of vegetables to other concentration camps. This was an even more remarkable achievement considering that many of them had volunteered to become migrant workers outside the camp.[82]

AMACHEANS: "NEITHER CODDLED NOR MISTREATED"

In spite of the Amacheans' contribution to the war effort, considerable public criticism was leveled at the camp during its existence.[83] Critics focused on the way it was managed or, as they believed, mismanaged. Perhaps the most serious allegation made against the camp was that it coddled the prisoners. On the floor of the US Senate, Colorado senator Edwin Johnson railed against the Amache administration for what he characterized as its lavish support of the Japanese Americans at public expense. Tom Cavett and Gene Hagberg, investigators for the notorious Dies Committee, the precursor to the House Un-American Activities Committee, lent credence to such accusations when they reported that Amache was planning to build a concrete swimming pool at a cost of fifty thousand dollars.

Public anger was aroused in the controversy surrounding the WRA's construction of a school complex at Amache. In 1942, the school dispute erupted when the WRA planned to build three one-story schools at a cost of $308,498 ($172,612 for a high school and $135,886 for two elementary schools). The cost was considered outrageous. The RMN had a valid point when it noted that "the sum of $308,000 is wholly out of proportion in view of the usual cost of country schools in Colorado and the additional fact [that] the building will be for temporary use."[84]

The Amache school plans were also opposed by those who were concerned that current shortfalls were putting existing Coloradan schools in jeopardy. While arguments about the school construction project at Amache were going on, the Colorado Education Association was seeking legislation to bolster the precarious financial situation of state schools, arguing that "thousands of boys and girls in the state may be denied the opportunity of attending school without more funding."[85] Some people felt that, since schools were closing in Costilla and Conejos Counties because of insolvency, Amache students should be similarly deprived.[86] And residents of nearby Lamar asked, "Why should the Japanese center have schools that cost more than those afforded our own American children in Lamar?"[87] They felt that it was unfair for the "foreign" students at Amache to get an education while their "American" students did not.

Following a familiar pattern, racialist objections were cloaked in patriotic rhetoric. The level to which such criticism could sink is illustrated by the Denver Building Trades and Construction Council, which declared that it was a "patriotic duty to oppose the squandering of any money on such things as schools for Japs . . . [instead] every effort should be to kill these slant-eyed back stabbers instead of educating them, and we are of the opinion that the only education that will do this race of people any good is the kind that is supplied by bullets and bayonets."[88] What the critics all had in common was the belief that Amache's prisoners, children included, belonged to an enemy race, even though most were American citizens.

Among public officials, Senator Johnson was the foremost foe of the school construction project. Having received numerous complaints about it, he condemned the project as an extravagance, raising the issue with the WRA and with his colleagues on the Senate floor. However, the Amache camp administrators strongly opposed him.

Relocation officials argued that the United States had a moral obligation to educate Japanese American children. James G. Lindley, the Amache administrator, believed that it was a matter of fairness.[89] Moreover, he thought it was to the country's own advantage that the youngsters should be educated, and in the American way.[90] Joe McClelland, who served on Lindley's staff, pointed out that educating and training Japanese Americans to become better able to serve their country was probably the most important WRA goal, certainly in terms of their future in the United States.

The end result was a compromise. Senator Johnson and his allies, including other Colorado members of Congress, such as Representative Edgar Chenoweth (Republican), were able to get the original construction contract renegotiated. The construction of the half-completed high school was allowed to continue, but the building of the elementary schools was halted, and remodeled barracks were substituted.

The school controversy and other allegations made Amache a center of media attention. An open-house tour was organized for journalists who came to ferret out the truth for themselves. The camp became the subject of feature articles in newspapers in four states. Most journalists wrote impartial reports that neither condemned nor condoned what was going on in it, but the consensus was that the accusations were baseless. As the Amache semiweekly newspaper, the *Granada Pioneer*, noted with satisfaction, "Reports that the Japs have a $350,000 school, [with a] beautiful swimming pool, and are fed the best food in the state" were discredited as malicious and false.[91] Jack Carberry of the *Denver Post*, however, consciously sought to stir up suspicions about the camp, creating the impression that it was a foreign settlement:

> All conversations I heard were in Japanese—this included the talk that was going on in the newspaper office where a staff of more than twenty people turns out the camp paper. . . . I asked the officials about this. I was told I was mistaken, that most conversation is in English. I was told that many of the younger group cannot speak Japanese. I listened carefully after that—both in the camp and in the towns where I saw groups of camp residents going about on their pass leaves. . . . I never heard a single conversation among camp residents in English."[92]

While it is possible that Carberry never encountered an English-speaking Japanese American during his visit to Amache, it is also likely that he needed an article to suit the DP's anti-Japanese bias.[93] From the beginning, the paper had cast the war as "not merely a war between the American and Jap governments," but also—with the added emphasis of uppercase lettering—"A FIGHT TO THE DEATH BETWEEN THE AMERICAN PEOPLE AND THE JAP PEOPLE."[94] Student journalists at the University of Colorado writing for the *Silver and Gold*, the school newspaper, decried the DP's hate campaign against Japanese Americans: "Now that the *Denver Post* has embraced Hitler's doctrines of race and Aryan superiority, now that the Post has converted this war from a battle of principles or even nations into a battle of peoples, now that the Post has declared war on the Japanese Americans in our cities and internment camps, it's about time we college students registered our protests against such fascist techniques in our midst."[95] The *Granada Pioneer* welcomed the *Silver and Gold*'s editorial and also condemned the DP attitude that "once a Jap, always a rat." This remained the DP's prevailing perspective until Amache was closed for good.[96]

The federal government took four years to close the concentration camps. It was a complicated procedure that lasted until 1946, extending beyond the end of the war itself. In 1942, the government began releasing various categories of prisoners, beginning with college students whose educations had been disrupted by their expulsion from the Pacific Coast. Under the aegis of the National Japanese American Student Relocation Council, over four thousand students were eventually released from the camps and read-mitted into some six hundred colleges and universities beginning in May 1942.[97] Because of Governor Carr's willingness to accept Japanese Americans into Colorado, 505 applicants were admitted to the state's institutions of higher learning (University of Colorado, University of Denver, the Denver Art Institute, the Colorado State College of Education, and the Colorado State College of Agriculture and Mechanical Arts), which was about half of all those accepted in the Great Plains states.

As will be discussed in the next two chapters, after the students, other inmates were released temporarily to produce the food necessary to sustain the war effort, and still others left to serve in the armed forces. Their participation in the war would change them, how they perceived themselves, and how they perceived their place in America. They returned from the war with a deeper determination to end racial inequality and social injustice.

As early as April 1943, some members of Congress called for the closing of the camps, arguing that they were expensive as well as unjust. Kentucky senator Albert B. Chandler (Democrat) observed that freeing the Japanese Americans would save the government an estimated fifty million dollars in operating costs. Moreover, those released would increase the number of people available to work in the nation's military, industrial, and agricultural sectors.[98] Imprisoning them for the duration of the war cost the government money that it could ill afford. In addition, the government had assigned the Army Corps of Engineers the task of building the camps and had deployed thousands of soldiers to guard them, even though the engineers and soldiers were sorely needed elsewhere.

Besides wasting valuable resources, the US government was also unwittingly aiding its adversaries by providing them grist for their propaganda mills. As part of their campaign to win the hearts and minds of other Asians, the Japanese militarists claimed that the Pacific War was a race war and exploited the racial conflicts in the United States to prove it. They drew attention to the fact that whites had discriminated against Asians in much the same way they had against blacks. Blacks may have been treated as second-class citizens, but Asians were denied the privilege of citizenship as well as the right to immigrate to the United States. Imprisoning Japanese Americans played into enemy hands. The imperial Japanese government reported on this folly as an example of how the American people and their government mistreated the Japanese.

Some of President Roosevelt's advisers, including two cabinet members, called for the release of Japanese Americans. On December 30, 1943, Attorney General Francis Biddle wrote to President Roosevelt, "The present practice of keeping loyal American citizens in concentration camps on the basis of race for longer than is absolutely necessary is dangerous and repugnant to the principles of our Government."[99] President Roosevelt, however, chose to ignore these calls for the closing of the camps in order to avoid alienating the people of California and elsewhere on the West Coast and thus jeopardizing his bid for an unprecedented fourth presidential term in the November 7, 1944, election. In effect, he prolonged the injustice for political advantage.

After Roosevelt's victory, on December 17, 1944, the military rescinded DeWitt's orders, which had forcibly removed Japanese Americans from the West Coast two and a half years earlier. War Department officials concluded that the need for their imprisonment had ended. Thirty-eight years later, in 1982, the bipartisan congressional Commission on Wartime Relocation and Internment of Civilians concluded that the decision to incarcerate the Japanese Americans was never a matter of military necessity. Instead, it was the result of racial prejudice, wartime hysteria, and a failure of political leadership.[100]

The federal government allowed Japanese Americans to return to their homes on January 2, 1945. When Japanese Americans were permanently freed from the camps, they were given a standard relocation allowance of twenty-five dollars per individual and fifty dollars per family, along with a train ticket. Because of continuing Japanophobia on the West Coast, many chose to settle in other parts of the country, establishing new Japanese American communities in such cities as New York and Chicago and reinvigorating the one in Denver.

The war continued for another nine months, ending finally on September 2, 1945, known as V-J Day, or Victory over Japan Day, when the

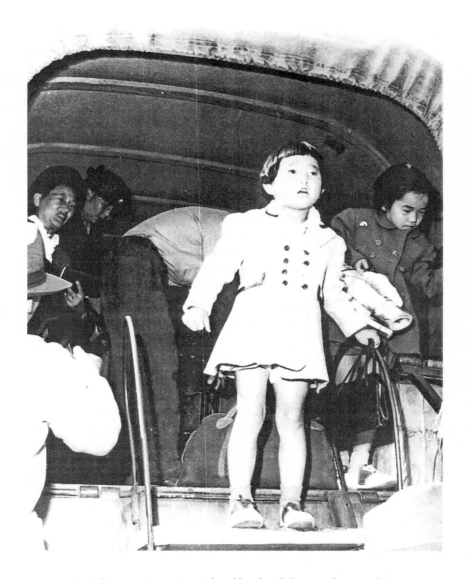

FIG. 8.7. A Japanese American girl and her family leaving the Amache concentration camp, c. autumn 1945. Returning to the West Coast was almost as stressful and traumatic as the forced removal years earlier. Many of those leaving the concentration camps were scarred psychologically, and most were unwilling to talk about the experience with anyone who had not been in the camps. Amache Preservation Society, prepared by Dr. Robert Fuchigami.

Japanese government formally surrendered aboard the battleship USS Missouri. It was only with the end of World War II that the War Relocation Authority began shutting down the concentration camps. Except for Tule Lake, all of them were closed by December 1945. Amache closed its gates on October 15, 1945, becoming just another Colorado ghost town that had outlived its purpose.

Imprisoning Japanese Americans in concentration camps during World War II is now recognized as one of America's worst mistakes. Noted cultural historian John M. Blum calls it the most blatant mass violation of civil liberties in American history.[101] There were few heroes in this sorry episode. Ralph L. Carr, Jimmie Omura, and Min Yasui were three of them. They proved to be kindred spirits in their defense of the US Constitution and the democratic principles it embodies. "Liberty and Justice for All," the inscription on the entryway to the new Ralph L. Carr Colorado Judicial Center in Denver, completed in 2013, sums up the essence of what they stood for. All three men believed that Japanese Americans were loyal to the country, and when the Japanese Americans were given a chance to prove this, they did so time and again. Japanese Americans supported the war effort in the farm fields of northern Colorado and on the battlefields in Europe and the Pacific. As the *Granada Pioneer* noted, many of them made the sacrifices they did to "attain the ideals of Americanism."[102] But as will be discussed in the next chapter, their experience during World War II was more complicated than the prevailing narrative of patriotic Japanese Americans seeking to prove their loyalty to a country that had betrayed them.

NINE

LOYALTY AND BETRAYAL
ON THE HOME FRONT

BECAUSE OF THE WORKFORCE NEEDS OF THE WAR, SOME GOVERN-ment leaders were forced to rethink the wholesale imprisonment of West Coast Japanese Americans. Within months of moving them into concentration camps, officials realized that it was a mistake to imprison able-bodied Japanese American men and women who could be out work-ing to support the war effort. In May 1942, officials created seasonal leave, a short-term program that temporarily released Japanese Americans to work on the home front to meet labor shortages resulting from the war. Approximately ten thousand prisoners applied to the War Relocation Authority (WRA) for release from the assembly centers and concentration camps to be employed in the civilian economy. Employers agreed to pro-vide transportation and housing as well as protection for them. Although less attention has been focused on these activities, their importance should not be underestimated because it was, after all, America's economic might more than anything else that won World War II.

Japanese American involvement in this aspect of the war fits easily into the national narrative of home front unity. According to this account, during the "Good War," ordinary people of all races, creeds, and religions transcended their differences to work together to defeat the Axis foe. In doing so, the participants advanced the cause of their own equality, or at least set precedents that eventually benefited their children decades later. This is one of the country's enduring myths about World War II. In reality, there was dissension on the home front during the war, and prewar dis-crimination continued to dog various groups long after the war.

Certainly for the Japanese Americans who were released from Amache for domestic war-related service, such work was more complicated than simply participating in a patriotic campaign. The Amache prisoners were themselves divided over whether to join the war effort. Many of them refused to take part, preferring to sit out the war to passively protest their imprisonment. Others declined because they were ill equipped for the positions that needed to be filled. Also, given the real concerns about encountering violence outside the camp, remaining in the bleak but safe confines of Amache seemed a rational choice for some. Indeed, many inmates who volunteered for such assignments experienced exploitation and prejudice. In the end, for those who did participate, the rewards were modest, though some individual Japanese Americans forged lasting friendships with the people with whom they worked.

STARTING OVER

The agricultural sector benefited the most from the release of Japanese Americans from the camps. In accounts of Japanese American contributions to the World War II effort, little attention has been given to their participation in the Food for Freedom program, a national effort to increase farm production to feed troops and civilians. Farm workers became increasingly scarce as more and more men were inducted into the military, left for better-paying defense industry jobs, or migrated to urban areas in search of greater economic and social opportunities. Colorado farmer Ed Christensen, a former neighbor of Governor Ralph L. Carr, sent the governor a letter explaining the problem. Christensen's three sons were army-bound, and he could not work his 240-acre farm without them because he found it impossible to hire farmhands. He ended his letter with a plea that many farmers agreed with: "I'm willing to do all I can to help our country but I believe the boys can do more good on the farm than they can in the Army as there has got to be food raised for the Army to eat."[1] Because of their increasing importance to the war effort and through the efforts of the powerful farm lobby, farm workers were granted Selective Service draft deferments beginning in the fall of 1942 and paid higher wages to keep them on the farms to meet crop production goals.

During the first months of the war, the government found itself unable to overcome the problem of decreasing agricultural laborers at the same time that the demand for food to feed civilians, soldiers, and allies was increasing dramatically. Because of labor shortages, Japanese Americans were now considered an asset rather than a liability, at least by officials concerned about having an adequate labor supply to sustain the economy, by farmers who needed field laborers, by factory owners who needed assembly line workers, and by many other employers.[2] Perhaps the most significant advocate for employing Japanese American workers was the sugar beet lobby.[3] Growers, refiners, and state farm bureaus also wanted to make camp prisoners available to farmers to ensure that sugar beets were harvested.

Among government officials concerned about labor scarcity were the governors of the Western states who had originally opposed the coming of West Coast Japanese Americans into their states. Now the governors thought better of their earlier opposition. They wanted them in their states as farm laborers. They even wanted the WRA to serve as a de facto employment agency to assign them to wherever they were needed.[4]

The average citizen, however, was not prepared for such an about-face in government policy. A blunt *Denver Post* (DP) opinion column expressed how many Coloradans felt about the idea: "Colorado's answer to suggestions that this state import thousands of Jap aliens and give them jobs in the sugar beet fields should be: 'TO HELL WITH THE JAPS! KEEP COLORADO AMERICAN.'"[5] As the distinction between "Japs" and "Americans" indicates, Coloradans were not ready to welcome Japanese Americans any more than they were before the latter were locked up.

When the call for workers came, Japanese Americans responded, though not in overwhelming numbers and not with much enthusiasm. They were fully aware of their ambiguous status—too dangerous to remain on the West Coast but harmless enough to work in Colorado and other intermountain states. If there was any danger in the area, it came from organizations that declared "open season" on them and issued "Jap Hunting Licenses." One man in southern Colorado reportedly bought ammunition from a sporting goods store to go "Jap huntin' . . . if any of 'em wander too far from camp [Amache]."[6]

To the prisoners at Amache and the other camps, it was as if their history in the United States had been turned upside-down. They were essentially being asked to start where most of their parents and grandparents had begun life in the United States—as laborers. By dint of hard work, their forebears had climbed America's socioeconomic ladder to become farm owners rather than farm workers, businesspeople rather than farmers, and professionals rather than merchants. With President Roosevelt's signing of Executive Order 9066, however, West Coast Japanese Americans lost all that had been attained by earlier generations and were now forced to do work for which they had neither experience nor inclination. This was in marked contrast to other Americans, including members of other minority groups and women, who were enjoying unprecedented opportunity for social and economic advancement during the war.

However, Japanese Americans did have reasons for becoming laborers. For some, doing so was one of the few paths open to them to fulfill their civic responsibilities, a chance to demonstrate that they, too, were devoted citizens willing to make the sacrifices necessary to win the war. In this, they had the support of the Japanese American Citizens League (JACL), whose "Japanese American Creed" required members to pledge, "I actively assume my duties and obligations as a citizen, cheerfully and without any reservations whatsoever, in the hope that I may become a better American in a greater America."[7] The JACL appealed to imprisoned Japanese Americans to show what they could do when given the opportunity.

Most volunteered because they wanted to earn some money, since they had lost everything in their forced removal.[8] It is estimated that relocation caused the Japanese American community to suffer a staggering loss estimated at $67 to $116 million (or $942 million to $1.6 billion in 2012 dollars).[9] The money they made as laborers hardly compensated them for their losses, but it did allow them to save something for when they were permitted to return home. They were paid the prevailing wages for the work they did.

Perhaps the strongest motive for volunteering was to be free of the camp, to regain some sense of personal autonomy. For many Amacheans, doing something constructive outside the barbed wire enclosure was preferable to doing nothing meaningful inside it. This was particular true for the young, who were languishing in the camps just when they should be thriving. Esther Nishio and Florence Tsunoda, for example, accepted temporary jobs to escape the boredom of Amache. Both fared well. Nishio became a house girl for a family in Boulder and gained a sense of freedom, while Tsunoda worked at a YMCA camp in Pueblo, where she picked green beans and red beets, earned some spending money, and enjoyed being away from her parents.[10]

During the war, Amache prisoners served as a mobile workforce who could be employed as seasonal or temporary workers in a variety of industries and institutions, such as food-processing canneries, munitions factories, railroad lines, university campuses, and hospitals. In Denver, forty-two of them worked at US foundries producing parts for warships.

They were found to be loyal, efficient, and unusually adaptable to foundry work.[11] (For obvious reasons, reports on Japanese American workers in wartime occupations often made it a point to note their trustworthiness as well as their efficiency.) Other inmates were released to work as nurses at the University of Colorado School of Medicine and other area hospitals, allowing such medical facilities to stay open to the public when they would otherwise have been closed, due to the shortage of trained personnel.[12] Since 40 percent of the Amacheans had agricultural backgrounds, most were recruited to harvest sugar beets in Colorado.[13]

SUGAR BEET FARMERS, AGAIN

After Pearl Harbor, overseas supplies of sugar, on which Americans had relied, were curtailed or even cut off. Previously, sugar was imported from Hawaii and the Philippines in the Pacific, and Puerto Rico and Cuba in the Caribbean. Enemy naval activity, particularly submarine warfare, made the importation of sugar from abroad unreliable just as the need for it increased. Besides its use for flavoring food, sugar was an important ingredient in the production of vital war matériel. Sugar could be converted into industrial-grade alcohol, which was an indispensable ingredient in the manufacture of the smokeless powder used in military ordnance. Sugar was also required for the mass production of synthetic rubber. The latter was necessary when, in the early months of the Pacific War, the Japanese conquered what are now Indonesia and Malaysia, where most of the world's supply of natural rubber was produced.

As the demand for sugar surpassed the supply, it became one of the first foodstuffs to be rationed to civilians in the spring of 1942. To replace its lost overseas sources, the government turned to the domestic production of sugar beets, focusing on expanding production principally in the Interior West, where 85 percent of the sugar beets were produced. The federal government relied on six western states, including Colorado—the leading sugar beet–producing state in the nation since 1909—to meet national needs. The sugar produced in the West was intended to relieve critical shortages on the Atlantic seaboard and throughout New England. To ensure that this would be the case, on March 31, 1942, the War Production Board allocated 15 percent of the sugar beet production for distribution east of Chicago.

The government tried to boost the production of sugar beets by raising prices and subsidizing transportation costs. But the shortage of laborers remained a persistent problem. Sugar beets required the greatest amount of work and the largest number of workers of any crop. As mentioned earlier, the federal government changed Selective Service rules to keep men on farms, but many were simply unavailable. Among those who were available, not many were willing to do this kind of work. Robert A. Baer, chairman of a local USDA War Board that was responsible for overseeing production, complained that the problem was not so much the shortage of personnel as the fact that "many farm laborers would rather sit by the fire than work [and] get in where it was warm and wouldn't work in the cold and mud."[14] Before the war, farmers relied mainly on migrant workers from Mexico to do the stoop labor necessary to harvest sugar beets, but during the war, these laborers left to work on construction projects and in other industries, where the wages were higher and conditions better.

Harvesting sugar beets was considered one of the most physically disagreeable, demanding jobs in the agricultural sector, attractive only to those with the lowest social status.[15] To collect sugar beets in the spring, workers had to get down on their hands and knees, crawl between rows of plants, and methodically cull the plants with short-handled hoes. To pick the sugar beets in the fall, they had to pull them from the ground and use a sharp knife to cut off the crown and toss it into a truck. And after a day of such backbreaking work, they slept in nearby shelters that were rude, makeshift, crowded, and unsanitary. The majority of Amacheans who took jobs outside the camp did this work and under these conditions.[16]

Farmers in the northern and southern parts of the state appealed to the government to release the prisoners from Amache to help with their crops.[17] Hundreds of Amacheans were recruited to bring in sugar beets and other crops. In 1942, the camp newspaper the *Granada Pioneer* reported that over one thousand were harvesting sugar beets and potatoes.[18] For the Amacheans, their most notable achievement as farm laborers was the eleventh-hour rescue of the 1942 Colorado sugar beet harvest, which was in danger of being lost to an early frost. In the fall of 1942, in Prowers County, where the camp was located, Amacheans joined high school students to save what proved to be the largest sugar beet crop in years. An estimated sixty thousand tons of beets would have been lost without their assistance.[19] C. V. Maddux, labor commissioner of the Great Western Sugar Company, praised the Amacheans for their accomplishment, adding, "If I were offhand to set an efficiency rating, I would not set it below 90

FIG. 9.1. Amacheans working in an onion field, c. autumn 1942. Because of labor shortages, students, including those in elementary school, participated in farm work during World War II. Amache Preservation Society, prepared by Dr. Robert Fuchigami.

FIG. 9.2. Amache prisoner Takayuki Tushima topping sugar beets, c. autumn 1942.

per cent, and that in our experience is a high rating for any group as large as this one."[20]

In 1943, working on farms in Denver, Adams, Jefferson, and Arapahoe Counties, seven hundred Amacheans harvested an estimated 65,300 tons of sugar beets, yielding 18,666,200 pounds of sugar.[21] Besides sugar beets, the Amacheans aided in the harvesting of head lettuce, root vegetables, tomatoes, celery, potatoes, and other crops. Nearly two hundred Japanese Americans picked Elberta peaches along the Colorado River in Palisade, Colorado, for example.[22] Often they worked alongside Mexican migrant workers and German prisoners of war (POWs).

In sum, working for such companies as the Great Western Sugar Company, Amacheans and other Japanese Americans produced the millions of pounds of sugar needed for the war effort.[23] As seasonal laborers, they were essential in sustaining agricultural output in Colorado and elsewhere in the American West. Reviewing their achievements, economist Leonard Arrington noted, "Despite the injustice and psychological shock of the evacuation, these Issei (Japanese-born) and Nisei (American-born) were among the most industrious and intelligent workers who ever labored in the region."[24]

However, the work release program had an unanticipated effect on many of the volunteers and their families.[25] Separations resulting from it sometimes undermined family relationships, especially between husbands and wives, who divorced each other with increasing frequency. This was evident in the story of the Shitara sisters, which follows.

ANOTHER UNTOLD STORY

Among the Amacheans participating in the work release program were the Shitara sisters, whose lapse in judgment resulted in their being tried for treason.[26] Their trial has been all but forgotten in Asian American annals, and understandably so. Their story is a complex one, disrupting the dominant narrative of Japanese American victimization. As law professor Eric Muller notes, this narrative is one of uncomplicated loyalty and monolithic innocence.[27] The behavior of the Shitara sisters challenges this account. To protect that interpretation and the reputation of the Japanese American community, the trial of the sisters has been left out of the retelling of the concentration camp experience.

The treason trial had its beginnings on the evening of October 16, 1943, when two German soldiers, formerly of Rommel's Afrika Korps, escaped from the US Army's Trinidad POW camp in southern Colorado. Heading south, the two reached Watrous, New Mexico, where local authorities captured them. On their persons were found photographs of German soldiers embracing Japanese women. In the course of interrogating the captured fugitives, a Federal Bureau of Investigation (FBI) agent discovered that the women were married Japanese Americans from Amache. In the midst of a bitter conflict with Germany and Japan, the American public was affronted at the gall shown by these Japanese American women in assisting German prisoners to escape.

The trial—the third treason trial of World War II—and the jury's verdict reveals much about the federal government's treatment of Japanese Americans as well as the conservative mores of Coloradans at the time. The government indicted the three sisters for treason and conspiracy to commit treason. The trial that followed was filled with ironies and inconsistencies. As the DP reported at the end of it, "The case had become historic in Washington. The justice department had gone before Congress with it to show that the law of treason should be altered to fit cases like it."[28]

Ultimately, the jury found the sisters innocent of treason but guilty of conspiring to commit treason, an illogical verdict that caused the youngest of the three to wonder: "How come they can find us guilty of conspiracy? We didn't do that because we didn't do treason."[29] The answer to her question can be found by looking at attitudes toward race and sex in World War II–era Colorado.

THREE NISEI SISTERS

Tsuruku "Toots" Wallace, Shivze "Flo" Otani, and Misao "Billie" Tanigoshi hardly fit the current image of Asian Americans leading lives of socioeconomic success. Toots, Flo, and Billie, as they were called throughout the trial, were three of five sisters born into the Shitara family, who earned their living as farmers in Inglewood, California. The defendants had attained a modest education and led commensurate working-class lives. Toots, the oldest, thirty-four at the time of the incident, was considered the leader of the trio. She had graduated from Inglewood High School and worked as a waitress at Mio's Café on Terminal Island in Los Angeles. Flo, who was thirty-one, had attained only a grammar-school education and worked as a packer at the French Sardine Company. Billie, who at thirty

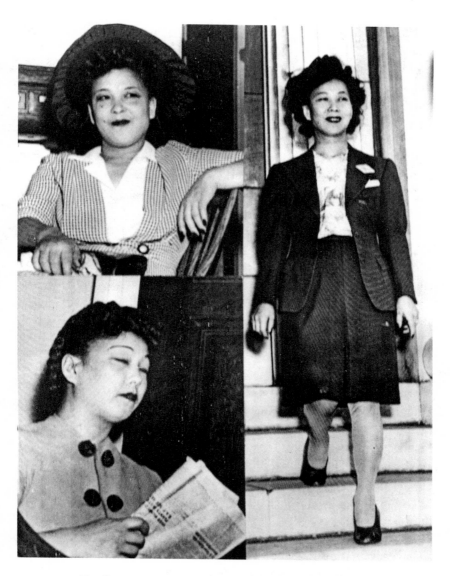

FIG. 9.3. The Shitara sisters: Misao "Billie" Tanigoshi (right), Shivze "Flo" Otani (upper left), and Tsuruku "Toots" Wallace (lower left), August 8, 1944. Wofford College, Broadus R. Littlejohn, Jr. Collection.

was the youngest of the three, had managed to complete two years of high school and worked as a waitress at the Inside Grill in Los Angeles.

The trial in no small measure turned on the interpretation of the Shitara sisters' character. The August 18, 1944, presentence report noted that the sisters had a generally poor reputation in Los Angeles. During the trial, the prosecutors sought to use that to their advantage, pointing out that the sisters were known to consort with bad people.[30] In the parlance of the day, they were women of questionable virtue who drank too much and talked in a rough manner. Among other things, the prosecutors called Toots a "well-known water-front character," insinuating that her job meant that she had low morals.[31]

To counter these characterizations, the defense called on two of the sisters' neighbors, Mrs. Wilma Ann Readman, of Bloomington, California, and Mrs. Ethel N. Sherman, of Compton, California, to testify to their good character. Readman offered that all the Shitara sisters had been "baptized Christians in the Church of the Brethren" and that "Toots had the highest athletic honors in high school."[32] Perhaps more important, Readman and Sherman reported that before the incident, they had received letters from the defendants declaring that they wanted to help the United States, that they did not feel like Japanese, and that they were Americans.

The Shitara sisters led lives that were clearly different from those of other Japanese American women. Some of them had married men outside the ethnic community. Toots's second husband was a white man named Virgil Cleo Wallace. Flo, however, had married Harry Otani, the only Japanese among the husbands. Billie married William Tanigoshi, who was half Japanese and half white. Their sisters Kazumi and Lily had married a Korean American and a black man who was then serving as a lieutenant in the US Army, respectively.

Despite various investigations of Shitara family members, nothing of a subversive nature was uncovered. In the panic following the attack on Pearl Harbor, along with many Japanese American families, the Shitaras fell under a cloud of suspicion. At the instigation of neighbors who found the comings and goings of Japanese to the house suspicious, the FBI investigated Toots, only to discover that her home was used by a Japanese school. But later the FBI noted that Toots associated with Japanese naval and merchant marine officers as well as American sailors. This was hardly surprising, since she worked as a waitress in a harbor café, the owner of which had pro-Japan sentiments.

During the trial, the defense characterized these FBI reports as "old women's gossip," arguing that, if anything, they indicated that some Californians had been biased for years against and had spread false rumors about Japanese Americans.[33] To prove that Toots was a law-abiding citizen, the defense pointed out that she had, of her own volition, informed US immigration authorities of the illegal entry of Japanese into the United States.

In the spring of 1942, the Shitara family was incarcerated in Amache. Less than a year later, they were released to harvest onions on the six-hundred-acre Winger farm near Trinidad, Colorado. They worked alongside German soldiers from the nearby POW camp. While working on the farm, the Shitara sisters met Corporal Heinrich Haider. He convinced Toots to help him escape from the Trinidad POW camp. What motivated Toots and her sisters to do this is unclear, since they were never called to testify in court and tell their side of the story. Instead, various men spoke for and about them during their trial. They were characterized as weak-willed women who were easily manipulated by men. But their actions hardly fit the popular perception of fragile and irresolute Japanese women. On the contrary, they were independent-minded and daring women willing to plan and execute a jailbreak.

THE "GREAT" ESCAPE

Though the Trinidad POW camp was known in army circles as a tough facility, escaping from it was a comparatively easy thing to do. On the evening of October 16, 1943, equipped with civilian clothes, road maps, train schedules, a flashlight, and money that the sisters had left behind a bush on the Winger farm, Haider and fellow prisoner Corporal Hermann August Loescher cut through a wire fence using the pliers they had acquired earlier and made their break. Along the highway near Trinidad, they rendezvoused with the sisters, who drove them south until they had trouble with the car's water pump. Haider and Loescher got out at Wagon Mound, New Mexico, making their way to the town of Watrous on foot. After the evening's adventure, the sisters returned to the Winger farm undetected the next morning.

Meanwhile, at Watrous, Haider and Loescher went to the nearby train station to ask about arrivals and departures. A suspicious station agent called the state police. Chief Nolan Utz of the Las Vegas, New Mexico, police department and state police officers arrested Haider and Loescher at a local watering hole, where they were drinking beer and conversing with some Mexican women.

In their initial account of their escape to the police, Haider and Loescher omitted the role of the Shitara sisters. That would have been the end of it except for the discovery of the photographs on Haider that Flo had taken of Toots with Haider and of Billie with another German POW named Backus, in what were considered compromising positions. Soldiers, even German soldiers, with pictures of themselves embracing women normally would not have attracted much attention or comment. But the fact that these were Japanese women was another matter.

On October 24, the DP published the incriminating pictures as part of an article titled "German Prisoners Spooned with Jap Girls in Trinidad."[34] Two of the photos, which were printed with a caption that began with the phrase "Allies in Arms," showed a German POW with his arm around a Japanese woman. The third photo was the most damaging, since it showed a couple wrapped in each other's arms, engaging in a kissing fest. The *Associated Press* subsequently circulated the photographs, giving rise to stories about "Japanazi Romances," which proved embarrassing to the authorities, particularly the military, who were accused of pampering prisoners.

These titillating photographs aroused public interest as well as indignation. The suggestion of sex between enemies of the United States, along with the whiff of seduction and adultery, proved an irresistible combination. The anti-Japanese DP ran a series of stories with sensational headlines, such as "German and Jap Spooning Still Unexplained" and "Five Jap Women Quizzed on Nazi Love Interludes." It demanded an explanation for this unseemly fraternization.[35] The FBI sent an agent to interrogate the two German POWs. After learning of the Shitara sisters' complicity in the escape attempt, the government decided to indict them for the high crime of treason and the lesser crime of conspiracy to commit treason.

COMMUNITY APATHY

Though the affair of the Shitara sisters attracted both national and local attention, Japanese Americans at Amache and elsewhere in the nation offered little public reaction. Why they displayed such an apparent lack of interest in the indictment and trial is worth considering. The Japanese American community might have been expected to rally around the Shitara sisters, providing them support in their time of need, if for no other reason than ethnic solidarity; or, at the very least, they might have been expected to show some curiosity about a trial involving three of their own people. Instead, the Japanese American community effectively disowned the Shitara sisters.

Of course, to have publicly supported individuals accused of treason would have been unwise, since it would have raised suspicions of treachery. Japanese Americans may have considered it more prudent to display loyalty to their country than loyalty to members of their own ethnic group whose behavior was very un-Japanese. As it turns out, Japanese Americans hardly talked about the case and certainly made no effort to defend the sisters.

The Amache newspaper, the *Granada Pioneer,* remained largely silent about the case. It covered the case in a perfunctory manner, reporting on what it understood to be the facts of the indictment and trial while avoiding any editorial comment. The newspaper's main concern seems to have been how the sisters' actions would affect the Japanese American community's image. In the November 3, 1943, issue, it published a story under the headline "FBI Releases Nisei Women Who 'Spooned,'" noting that "some of the Japanese families, also at work in the farming district, have voiced their desire to have the case investigated, saying that the affair, as it now stands, is a reflection upon all the Japanese in that area."[36] The implication was that the Japanese families found the affair shameful.

At the end of the trial, the *Granada Pioneer* reprinted without comment the August 12, 1944, *Rocky Mountain News* (RMN) editorial "The Treason Trial Verdict," from four days earlier, implying that it agreed with the RMN's interpretation of the verdict. The RMN touted the verdict as "a credit to the country, to its Constitution and to its system of criminal jurisprudence."[37] Given the inherent inconsistencies of the verdict, it is hard to see how this was a vindication of the American judicial system.

Though embarrassing, the headlines and stories themselves cannot fully account for the Japanese American community's indifference toward the Shitara sisters. Instead, this indifference may have been due largely to the sisters' reputation as women with "loose morals." James G. Lindley, director of the Amache camp, probably mirrored the community's impressions when he described the sisters as being a bit on the "wild side." In addition, H. F. Halliday, Lindley's assistant, noted that the Shitara family, "from a strictly Japanese view-point, were lower caste and generally ignored by most of the other Japanese at the center [that is, Amache]."[38] Given the conservative nature of the prewar Japanese community, the camp's reaction may have had something to do with the sisters' unconventional lifestyle. They crossed ethnic boundaries by marrying men outside of their ethnic group. Perhaps by marrying outsiders, they hoped to transcend the limitations on their lives imposed by their community, only to end up being ostracized by it.

Another consideration in the Japanese American community's reaction to the plight of the sisters might be the nature of their offense. On November 3, the *Granada Pioneer* editor, Sueo Sako, reported in his "Just Incidentally" column that a Japanese American working at the veterans' hospital in Hines, Illinois, had "griped" about the sisters. Writing to James Lindley, the Illinois resident said: "How about this? Is this on the level? I've seen and heard many a man go crazy over some stupid woman but this beats them all. While our buddies are fighting and dying in Italy against the Germans and to find some of our girls at home are making love to German war prisoners. That is enough to make any good man go batty."[39] The emotion behind this response suggests that some Japanese American men may not have been indifferent at all. With a few lines, the writer manages to convey his feeling that, though some Japanese American women are "stupid," they are nevertheless "our girls"—that is, their sexuality belongs to Japanese American men. So when the women slept with white men— and worse yet, white men who were the enemy—they were guilty of being disloyal to Japanese American men twice over.

In the end, the Japanese American community probably judged the sisters as severely as the white community did, accepting the punishment as necessary as well as just.

DEMOCRACY ON TRIAL

In retrospect, the affair of the Shitara sisters might have been regarded as a minor matter. After all, the sisters' crime consisted of nothing more than providing aid and comfort to two German POWs. Yet the authorities chose to make a federal case out of it, garnering headlines from coast to coast. Newspaper accounts of the Shitara sisters' trial considered it a major event, though they focused on the sensational aspects of the trial: the romantic involvement of Japanese American women with German POWs, the fact that the witnesses for the prosecution were their erstwhile

German lovers (one of whom claimed to be anti-Nazi), and the nature of treason itself.

Both the prosecution and the defense wanted to show that the four-day trial was an impartial one, showcasing the fairness of American democracy while the United States fought a war against authoritarian dictatorships. The press duly pointed this out with a self-congratulatory tone. On the third day of the trial, August 10, 1944, the DP quoted chief prosecutor Thomas Morrissey as emphasizing that the sisters had the benefit of a spirited defense.[40] "That is as it should be," Morrissey said. "That is the American way. That is what we are fighting for." On the following day, RMN writer Jack Foster observed with satisfaction that the trial was an exemplary forum, "where reason, judgment and deliberation was taking place in wartime—the only place in the world, with the exception of England, where such a scene can now take place . . . in an American court."[41] Foster went on to record defense attorney Kenneth Robinson as saying in his summation to the jury, "You are proving today, gentlemen, that democracy is not going out. You are vindicating the highest hopes of that democracy. You are standing firm against rabble-rousing talk."[42]

Still, the issues of race and gender permeated the trial, influencing its outcome. From the beginning of the trial there was confusion over the national identity of the accused. They were almost always identified as Japanese. US district judge J. Foster Symes himself referred to the sisters as Japanese Americans only once during the entire proceedings, though presumably he knew the difference between Japanese and Japanese Americans. After passing sentence on them, Symes felt it necessary to add that the Japanese sisters are American sisters and had received an impartial trial.

The court tried to ensure that the jury had no bias against Japanese, even eliminating prospective jurors who had relatives fighting in the Pacific Theater, in case they harbored anti-Japanese sentiments. Each of the twelve male jurors chosen claimed to have no prejudice toward Japanese. None of them had a son in the armed forces. Though seven of them had relatives in the armed forces, there was no indication that this fact affected their judgment.

Everyone involved appreciated that this was the third treason trial of World War II. In the earlier treason trials, two German-born naturalized Americans had been convicted for assisting enemy agents who had entered the country to commit acts of sabotage. In both cases, the defendants were found guilty of treason. They were sentenced to life imprisonment and fined ten thousand dollars each.

This was the first time that Japanese Americans had been put on trial for treason. The prosecution and defense prepared accordingly, bringing to the trial impassioned arguments that played to a packed courtroom of about three hundred spectators, most of whom were women. Perhaps the women were there because they sympathized with the Shitara sisters' situation, admiring their adventurous or romantic spirit. Or perhaps they were there simply because they were interested in the sisters' fate. If found guilty of treason, the Shitara sisters could be sentenced to a term of five years to life imprisonment, or even executed. The less serious charge of conspiracy to commit treason could bring them a maximum sentence of two years' imprisonment and a fine of five thousand dollars each.

THE TREASON TRIAL

To successfully convict the sisters, Morrissey had to meet the high standard for treason set forth in the Constitution, including having two witnesses who could testify in court that the sisters had provided aid and comfort to enemies of the United States. Much to the surprise of everyone, and to the chagrin of the sisters, the witnesses for the prosecution were the German soldiers.

The prosecution wanted the soldiers to limit their testimony to describing how the sisters had assisted them to escape so that they could return to Germany to fight against the United States. Haider, however, confounded the prosecution when he told a dramatic story that implied that the sisters were motivated by their patriotic love of America rather than any romantic love for him. He told the jury that he had been a member of the Austrian underground and hated the Nazis. For his anti-Nazi sentiments, he had been imprisoned for two years in a concentration camp in Bavaria, where Stormtroopers abused him. Later, he was conscripted into the German Army. In addition, he said that he feared for his life in the Trinidad POW camp, where a German sergeant might kill him for his anti-Nazi sentiments. Finally, Haider claimed that all he wanted was to return to Germany to join the Austrian Legion or the Czechoslovakian Legion to fight against Hitler. In spite of Toots's efforts to discourage him from trying to escape and risk being shot, he pressured her into helping him.

Though, on the face of it, Haider's story might seem preposterous, it did cast doubt on the case against the sisters, since the prosecution had to prove that, in assisting the German soldiers to escape, the sisters were endangering the country's security. Assuming that Haider was telling the truth, his escape would have been injurious to Germany rather than to the United States.

Loescher, whom Haider also claimed detested the Nazis, told a simpler story. As reported in the RMN, Loescher testified as follows: "May I say this: I guess my comrade told you that Germany had violated Austria," he said.[43] "As for myself, I was wounded, and I could not fight again. I have no interest in renewing the fight again. I just wanted my freedom."[44] With his freedom, Loescher had planned to make his way first to Mexico and later to South America. He stated that he did not know the sisters previously and literally went along for the ride. In court, he even had trouble identifying the sisters, since he had seen them only at night, though he recognized them from the pictures in the newspapers.

Obviously, as witnesses for the prosecution, Haider and Loescher proved to be less than ideal. Though they affirmed that the sisters had assisted them in their escape from Trinidad, it was not for the purposes of fighting against the United States but rather to fight against Germany, in Haider's case, and not to fight at all, in Loescher's. Haider and Loescher undermined the prosecutor's case by attributing to the sisters motives that were far from treasonous. Instead, Haider effectively argued that they were being patriotic. Consequently, the prosecution had to challenge the credibility of its own witnesses, disputing Haider's assertion that he was anti-Nazi. The prosecution argued that whether Haider was a Nazi or anti-Nazi was irrelevant; he was a German soldier who fought for Nazi Germany and would have done so again had his escape been successful. In spite of the testimony of their witnesses, the prosecutors continued to insist that the sisters were nothing more than traitors to their country, "little Benedict Arnolds in skirts."[45]

Because the sisters pleaded poverty and were unable to afford attorneys to represent them, the court appointed Kenneth W. Robinson, one of Denver's most outstanding criminal lawyers. He mounted what the press referred to as the "love defense," in which he argued that the sisters were motivated by love for the German soldiers rather than disloyalty to their country. Robinson offered a two-pronged argument: first, he tried to demonstrate to the judge and jury that the prosecution had failed to prove that the Shitara sisters had intended to injure the United States or to help the

Third Reich and that such intent was essential in order to find his clients guilty; second, he tried to persuade the jury that his clients' actual motivation was romantic.

To support his defense, Robinson argued that the German soldiers had seduced the sisters. Since the sisters never took the witness stand in their own defense and Robinson offered no details, it is unclear how they were seduced. It is, however, imaginable that Haider could have taken advantage of their victimization by the US government, appealing to their shared status as fellow prisoners to establish an emotional bond with them. If he had done so, Haider might have been able to manipulate the sisters for his own selfish purposes.

In any case, a letter that Loescher had written on November 5, 1943, supported Robinson's contention that the sisters had been seduced into helping the soldiers, but it was not delivered to Judge Symes until the time of sentencing, so it did not affect the outcome of the trial.[46]

Robinson's main aim was to persuade the jurors that the sisters might be guilty of a crime, but it was not treason; therefore, they should acquit his clients. To win acquittal, he was prepared to make racist and sexist appeals to the jury. He adroitly placed his own spin on the evidence that the prosecution had presented. He sought to show that the incriminating pictures proved that the sisters were comfortable only with white men.

Even though the Shitara sisters showed that they had the strength, daring, and courage to pull off the escape of the POWs, Robinson painted them as weak and timid. Moreover, he argued that they had a particular weakness for white men, and he built his case on the notion that their sympathy for the German soldiers was in part a reaction to their being incarcerated with Japanese. In his presentation, Robinson asked the jury to see beyond the sisters' physical appearance and argued that they were essentially non-Japanese:

> Remember that these women, all their lives did not associate with Japs. Their entire association was with Caucasians. Imagine the horror that must have been theirs as they were sent from California to the camp at Amache, there surrounded by Japs. Imagine how happy they must have felt when they went to the farm near Trinidad, away from the Japs in the camp, and then came three, white, Cacausian [sic] men. Oh, I know these women were married. I am not a judge of morals—I have lived too long for that. But you know, gentlemen, the way of a woman. I say to you, gentlemen, "Frailty, thy name is woman."[47]

Playing to the all-male perspective of the jurors, Robinson recast the stories told by Haider and Loescher, characterizing the former as "a man of smooth and oily tongue" who seduced Toots with his tale of being a member of the Austrian underground opposed to the Nazis. In his impassioned summation, Robinson repeatedly called his clients fools while appealing to the jurors' masculinity. He rhetorically asked the jury: "How far did this go? None has said. But it is indicated it went pretty far. I say again, to you, 'FOOLS.' But what, gentlemen of the jury, does any woman do who finds herself in this condition? Why, that heart of hers—that heart of a woman—that big heart of this woman foolishly responded and unthinkingly, she helped to take him away. It is, I say, the old, old story of woman. It is the old, old story of what a man can do to a woman who likes him."[48] In describing his clients as stereotypical women who were emotional, irrational, and vulnerable to male manipulation, Robinson deprived the Shitara sisters of personal agency and reduced them to a cliché. But would it be sufficient to save their lives?

Robinson's strategy proved successful. After deliberating for ten hours, the jury found the sisters guilty only of conspiracy to commit treason. The jurors had decided that, when the sisters helped the German soldiers, they did so without the intent of injuring the United States or helping Germany. Then the jurors decided that the sisters were guilty of the lesser offense of conspiracy to commit treason, even though Judge Symes had earlier instructed them that the matter of intent went to the crime of conspiracy the same as to the crime of treason.

Judge Symes, nevertheless, agreed with the verdict.[49] He sentenced Toots Wallace to two years' imprisonment and Flo Otani and Billie Tanigoshi to twenty months' imprisonment in the women's reformatory at Alderson, West Virginia, and fined them each one thousand dollars. Presumably, the lesser sentences for Flo and Billie was due to his sense that their involvement in the affair was more a matter of their loyalty to Toots and devotion to one another as sisters rather than anything to do with the POWs. An RMN editorial on the verdict recognized that the jury had arrived at a compromise verdict, in effect evading the issue of treason. The editorial noted that the jurors probably were in agreement with the feelings of the average citizen, who believed that the death penalty was too severe in view of the nature of the offense. However, they felt that some penalty should be imposed.[50]

The Shitara sisters were being punished, but for what offense? The women had clearly committed a crime, though not the one specified in the indictment. Legally, they should have been found innocent of the treason charges and tried for a lesser criminal charge. But equally important, in engaging in adultery, the sisters had violated their marital vows, a serious matter in conservative Colorado. In a sense, the jury's verdict was really a social judgment, rather than a legal one. Miscegenation may have also weighed in the judgment. After their tryst with the German soldiers, the sisters needed to pay for breaking the taboo against interracial relationships. Since some sort of punishment was warranted, the jury accepted the only option available to them, the minor charge of conspiracy to commit treason.

THE SHITARA SISTERS REMEMBERED

The story of the Shitara sisters has been retold in Ann Howard Creel's novel *The Magic of Ordinary Days* (2001) and in a made-for-TV movie of the same name with a teleplay by Camille Thomasson, produced for the Hallmark Hall of Fame (2005).[51] In both works, the sisters are portrayed sympathetically. No longer silent, as they were in real life, they are given a chance to express their innermost feelings. From these fictionalized accounts, we see the sisters as ingenues whose motives were pure. But the novel and film imagine very different outcomes.

In an interview about her novel, Creel explains that she was first drawn to the Shitara sisters' story by the expression on their faces in the photos of them with the POWs: "One thing that caught my attention was a photo of a young Japanese woman with one of the [German] soldiers. On their faces was a look of such youthful innocence. It is a great story; tragic, sad, and understandable in many ways and definitely motivated by love."[52] Where people in 1944 saw a lewd display of promiscuity, Creel saw innocent love. This formed the basis for a retelling of their story to develop feminist themes.

In the novel, the plot revolves around Olivia Dunne (aka Livvy), a white University of Denver graduate student, who becomes pregnant out of wedlock and is forced into an arranged marriage with Ray Singleton, a bean farmer living in Otero County, Colorado. On Singleton's farm, Livvy befriends the sisters Rose and Lorelei Umahara, former UCLA undergraduates, who are incarcerated in Amache. Together, the three women share feelings of loss, dislocation, and estrangement while reflecting on the unfairness of life. Livvy's friendship with the Umahara sisters allows the novel to raise thoughtful questions about the legitimacy of the mass removal and incarceration of Japanese Americans and provide glimpses of life in Amache.

Later, the Umahara sisters trick Livvy into helping their boyfriends, two German POWs, to escape from Colorado. Though Livvy was deceived, she forgives the sisters anyway, because she understands that anger over their unjust imprisonment and falling in love with the German soldiers drove them to commit this terrible mistake. Livvy predicts that society will make them pay for this. In a clear allusion to the fate of the Shitara sisters, Livvy says: "Rose and Lorelei would be painted in the newspapers and on the radio as traitors by people who'd never met them, by people who could never understand what torments and desires had driven them to their sad, ill-fated decision. . . . And would the world ever count Rose and Lorelei among the casualties of the war? Perhaps someday they could be forgiven for their mistake, too."[53] Insofar as the Umahara sisters embody Livvy's own yearnings, the novel suggests Livvy will also face humiliation if she ever seeks to claim personal happiness. The Umahara sisters' fate stands as a warning to Livvy that society will always punish women for wanting love. By this interpretation, the Umahara sisters are presented as casualties of a larger war against women continuing up to the present.

The subversive message of the Creel novel is completely erased in Thomasson's teleplay. In the film version, the story has a happy ending. None of the women are punished. Instead, the characters ultimately find happiness by complying with prevailing social norms. To reach this conclusion, the film simplifies matters all along the way, making do with fewer characters and emphasizing conventional morality. There are still only two Umahara sisters. However, they are called Rose and Flo. Flo, the one with bad judgment, has a German soldier boyfriend, who she helps escape from the POW camp. Realizing that she is abetting the escape of a POW, Livvy acts decisively to have him recaptured. Furthermore, Livvy shields the Umahara sisters, as well as herself, from being named as accomplices in his escape. Thus, instead of being tried for treason, the sisters remain free and are last seen attending Livvy's baby shower. The final scene suggests that all women have been rehabilitated socially and will find happiness in conventional social roles. They need not suffer the consequences of their actions. As such, the movie has a Hollywood ending that departs even further from actual events than does the novel.

The Shitara sisters' treason trial might have served as a vehicle for confronting the government's violation of the civil rights of Japanese Americans when it interned them in concentration camps. If the defense attorney Kenneth W. Robinson had placed the legality of the mass removal and imprisonment of the Japanese Americans itself on trial, he might have turned the sad affair of the Shitara sisters into one that dealt with significant constitutional issues. He might have been able to discuss how the federal government had betrayed American ideals. Instead, he contested the federal government's charge that the sisters had betrayed the country when they assisted the German soldiers in escaping. As attorneys are expected to do, Robinson placed the interest of his clients ahead of the broader interest of the Japanese American community. The verdict vindicates Robinson's decision, since his strategy saved the sisters from being found guilty of treason.

Once the trial was over, the Shitara sisters faded into the recesses of historical memory. To the extent that the sisters are remembered, it will probably be the romantic fictional accounts rather than the ambiguous historical one. Those aware of the story are likely to evoke the novel and film interpretations, understanding the women's actions in terms of the emotions generated by their exile in a strange land. As such, the story of the Shitara sisters adds another facet to the tragedy that befell Japanese Americans during World War II.

TEN

ASIAN COLORADO'S
GREATEST GENERATION

URING WORLD WAR II, COMPARATIVELY FEW ASIAN COLORADANS were available for military service. Immigration and miscegenation laws limited the number of men of enlistment age. Those who had enlisted or were conscripted served in both regular and segregated units commanded by mainly white officers. In addition to the hardships they endured with other troops, they also shouldered the burden of racial discrimination in the most hierarchical institution in the country. Those incorporated into regular units were often relegated to menial tasks, such as mess duty, that is, working in the kitchen. As members of segregated units, they were disparaged by regular units.

Asian Coloradans overcame any ambivalence they had to participate in the war effort. They took part for a mix of reasons. For Chinese Coloradans, enlisting was a way to fight Japanese aggression against their ancestral homeland, China, and to affirm their claim to their adopted homeland, America.[1] For Japanese Coloradans, it was a way to demonstrate that they were Americans by taking up arms against Japan, which had, through its attack on Pearl Harbor, destroyed so much of what their parents and grandparents had accomplished in the United States. For both groups, military service was an affirmation of their American identity as well as a fulfillment of their civic responsibility. What could be more patriotic than engaging in military service to show their loyalty to the country? Such service was an expression of their commitment to the ideals of equality implicit in the US Constitution. Through their sacrifice, they proved the truth of President Franklin D. Roosevelt's words, that "Americanism is not, and never was, a matter of race or ancestry."[2]

Along with those who labored on the home front, Chinese and Japanese American soldiers can be considered Asian America's greatest generation (to borrow Tom Brokaw's term) for not only doing their duty but doing it in spite of discrimination against them. Rather than looking at the past or even the present, they looked to the future, believing that their service would contribute to a better life in the postwar period. In demonstrating their dedication to the country, they hoped to be accepted as equal members of it. Reviewing the progress of Asian Americans in recent decades, many are convinced that they succeeded. Larry S. Tajiri, the wartime editor of the Japanese American newspaper *Pacific Citizen*, credits the heroism of Japanese American soldiers and the victory over Japan with the collapse of the anti-Asian movement in the United States.[3] Historians Robert A. Wilson and Bill Hosokawa also see World War II as a watershed for Japanese Americans. They claim that the wartime accomplishments of Japanese Americans in uniform were the single largest factor in changing the status of their people from a despised, discriminated-against minority to "near-total acceptance" as full-fledged Americans.[4]

Appropriately enough, this shift occurred first in the military. In 1948, in recognition of the contributions of Asian Americans and other people of color during World War II, President Harry S. Truman issued Executive Order 9981, which integrated the armed forces. Now that the United States had defeated the Nazis, who publicly promoted racial segregation, the maintenance of segregated American military units that denoted the inferiority of servicemen of color was one contradiction too many to bear. It has only been since Truman's executive order that people of color have been accepted on anything like an equal basis in the military.[5]

By contrast, significant change was slow to come in society at large. It did not occur in the immediate aftermath of the war or for many years afterward. To use Wilson and Hosokawa's equivocal phrase, to reach the point of "near-total acceptance," it took the civil right's movement's demand for racial equality for African Americans in the 1960s—and the demands raised by other ethnic consciousness movements that were inspired by it— to awaken American society to the need to keep its promise of inclusion.

Thus, to their chagrin, Asian Coloradans continued to experience prejudice in the postwar period, when the American public was most aware of their wartime service. This was disheartening for returning veterans, who had expected to be treated with respect for what they had achieved on battlefields around the world. Members of the storied 442nd Regimental Combat Team bitterly remembered the hostility they encountered upon returning home to the United States. Though they wore their military uniform, whites were still unable to see past their racial uniform. Their wartime heroism did not necessarily make them equal in the eyes of whites. World War II, nevertheless, proved to be a critical event that had important implications for their future and their families' future in the United States. It became *the* catalyst for societal changes.

For Asian Coloradans, the war changed everything, but not overnight. The war brought into sharp relief contradictions within American democracy that were, of course, reflected in Colorado. When America defeated its Axis enemies, it may have discredited racism abroad and aroused compassion for its victims, but it did not diminish the belief that many Americans had about the inferiority of races and ethnicities different from their own.

CHINESE COLORADANS AT WAR

Of the Chinese Americans who put on US military uniforms in World War II, 61 percent were born in the United States. Altogether, approximately fifteen to twenty thousand of them, or 19 to 25 percent of the Chinese American community, either enlisted or were drafted into the armed forces. This was a higher percentage than the 11.5 percent of the general population who served in the military. The Chinese American enlistees represented 22 percent of all Chinese American men in the country, and they came mainly from the West or East Coasts, where there were significant populations. In New York City, the percentage was extraordinarily high. As many as 40 percent of all Chinese American men between eighteen and thirty-six enlisted or were drafted—the highest ratio among any ethnic group in the country.[6] They represented the youngest, best-educated, and most able-bodied segment of their community.[7] Ironically, Chinese American men were more liable to be conscripted than their white counterparts because the selective service system emphasized men without dependents and the country's discriminatory laws had created a Chinese American community of dependent-less bachelors.

Seventy percent of Chinese American soldiers were integrated into the US Army, serving in various infantry divisions in Europe and the Pacific, and 25 percent served in the US Army Air Force. Many of those in the US Army Air Force went on to serve with the 14th Air Force as members of the segregated 14th Air Service Group (ASG).[8] The 14th ASG was formed in the summer of 1942 from a civilian Chinese American support team employed at Patterson Field air base in Ohio. The group agreed to serve as a bilingual team of specialists to support American forces in the China-Burma-India Theater under the command of General Joseph W. Stillwell, deputy Allied commander in China, and General Claire L. Chennault. Chennault was the creator and leader of the famous Flying Tigers unit, comprised of volunteer pilots from the American armed forces and recruited under presidential authority, and subsequent commander of the 14th Air Force. The 14th Air Force was the only American unit to carry out active combat duty in China itself.

The contributions of the 14th ASG remain largely unknown. Its special mission was to assist American Flying Tiger pilots and to train Chinese ground crews. It proved to be an invaluable frontline unit, thereby becoming an enemy target. Members of the 14th ASG flew over the Hump (the lower range of the Himalayas), drove on the legendary Burma Road, performed troop transport, and recovered and repaired battle-damaged planes. They coordinated with Chinese air force personnel to maintain aircraft operating in the China Theater of operations. They contributed significantly to Allied success by maintaining aerial operations from airfields across China. In sum, the 14th ASG kept the 14th Air Force in the air, and in so doing, kept Japanese troops in China rather than being transferred to the Pacific to fight American forces.

There were several other bilingual Chinese American units under the 14th Air Force, such as the 407th Air Service Squadron, which provided administrative, engineering, and other technical support, and the 987th Signal Company of the US Army Signal Corps, which provided communications support. Among other things, this involved sending out small two- and four-man field teams, primarily on horseback, to remote locations to assist American Army Infantry Liaison teams working with Chinese Army units that were deployed in Japanese-occupied French Indochina. In addition to coordinating ground and ground-to-air communications throughout their area of operations, they coordinated communication for long-range reconnaissance patrols that penetrated deep into Japanese-held territory.

Among the Chinese Coloradans who served in the US Army Air Force are three who have positive memories of their time in the military. These men's stories are remarkable in that they are so normal. Their wartime experience anticipates the direction in which American society ultimately moved in its treatment of Asian Americans, demonstrating that equality was possible decades before it was realized in civilian society.

Edward and William Chin, great-grandchildren of the pioneer Chin Lin

FIG. 10.1. Sergeant Edward L. Chin, 964th Air Engineering Squadron, 235th US Army Air Force, 1943. Courtesy of Carolyn G. Kuhn.

Soo, were airmen.[9] As a result of his score on the military's IQ test, Edward Chin was selected for aircraft school. He rose to the rank of sergeant, participating in the North African and Italian campaigns. Afterward, he was reassigned to the United States, where he trained aerial gunners for B-29s and worked with remote-controlled aircraft. Edward Chin was the only Asian American in his unit of five hundred airmen.

His brother, William Chin, was a second lieutenant who worked as a communications officer, training radiomen to serve on heavy bombers. In 1943, he was ordered to China, where he served with the 23rd Fighter Group of the 14th Air Force, the aforementioned Flying Tigers unit. In China, he was put in charge of ground communications and worked as a cryptographic security officer. He recalled his time in the Flying Tigers fondly and was pleased to have been ordered to China. He recalled that, "as a Chinese-American US serviceman in China during World War II, [he] was pleasantly surprised for the opportunity to see the 'old country' as a guest of the United States Army."[10]

FIG. 10.2. First Lieutenant William C. Chin, 23rd Fighter Group, 14th Air Force (Flying Tigers), c. autumn 1942. Courtesy of Carolyn G. Kuhn.

Like his brother, William never experienced any difficulties with the men with whom he served. On the contrary, he recalled that "the officers and enlisted personnel always gave courtesy and respect to an officer, even a lowly lieutenant." Neither Edward nor William recalled being discriminated against, except when they were mistaken for Japanese. Problems of discrimination came during the postwar period.

After the war, William Chin continued his involvement with the military, becoming the first commander of Denver's American Legion Cathay Post 185. Cathay Post 185 was comprised almost entirely of Asian Coloradan veterans. In 1963, it launched a campaign to raise money for a war memorial to honor the Japanese American servicemen from the Rocky Mountain region who had died in World War II.[11] The memorial, designed by Floyd Hideo Tanaka, was erected in the military section of the Fairmount Cemetery in Denver. The co-chairs of the campaign were Yoshiaki Arai and John T. Noguchi, who had served in the 442nd Regimental Combat Team in Europe and military intelligence in the Pacific, respectively. It is important to note that the memorial was initiated by the Asian Coloradan veterans of the Denver chapter of the American Legion rather than the national organization. The American Legion, the nation's largest wartime service organization, had previously opposed Japanese immigration and called for the imprisonment of Japanese Americans in concentration camps.

Another Chinese Coloradan who served with the Flying Tigers was John Yee.[12] Unlike the Chin brothers, who were born in Denver, Yee was born in Zhaotong, Yunnan Province. John Yee abandoned his studies at Southwest Union University in China to work with the Flying Tigers as a translator, serving with the communications section to translate intelligence about the movement of Japanese fighters and bombers to determine where and when American forces could intercept them. In 1944, he worked as a translator for Chinese pilots training in the United States.

After the war, Yee remained in the United States to pursue a better life. But with the status of an illegal immigrant, he was vulnerable to deportation. With the support of wartime friends, including General Chennault, Yee applied for and was granted political asylum. If Yee had returned to China, where the Communists had won the civil war, he would have been persecuted for collaborating with the American military during World War II. In 1952, he became a naturalized citizen and then resumed his long-interrupted college studies at the University of Denver, eventually earning his master's degree in social science from the University of Colorado before commencing a career teaching social studies in the Aurora public school system. Yee stayed close to his wartime comrades, regularly attending Flying Tiger reunions and serving as president of the Colorado chapter of the China-Burma-India Veterans Association. Despite his former service as a member of the Flying Tigers, he was denied veteran status and deemed ineligible for veterans' benefits. With a stoic attitude born of experience, Yee simply says, "I think what I've done speaks for itself."[13] Indeed, what Yee and other Asian Coloradans achieved during the war was something that no one would ever be able to take away from them.

JAPANESE COLORADANS AT WAR

In the aftermath of Pearl Harbor, approximately thirty-five hundred Japanese Americans who had been drafted into the army were summarily reclassified as either 4-C, enemy aliens, unacceptable for military service because of their nationality or ancestry, or 4-F, unfit for military service.[14] Other Japanese Americans already serving in the armed forces were arbitrarily discharged because of their race.[15] As Wilson and Hosakawa report, the latter were understandably resentful at being dismissed in this manner.[16] In the course of the war, the government realized that it had erred and sought to recruit Japanese Americans. As was the case with Chinese Americans, proportionally more Japanese Americans served in the military than members of the general population.

The government was particularly interested in recruiting Japanese Americans to serve in the newly founded 442nd Regimental Combat Team. On January 28, 1943, Secretary of State Henry L. Stimson announced the decision to create this unit, and three days later President Roosevelt issued a ringing endorsement of it: "No loyal citizen of the United States should be denied the democratic right to exercise the responsibilities of citizenship, regardless of his ancestry. . . . A good American is one who is loyal to this country and to our creed of liberty and democracy. Every loyal American citizen should be given the opportunity to serve this country wherever his skills will make the greatest contribution—whether it be in the ranks of the armed forces, war production, agriculture, government service, or other work essential to the war effort."[17]

This was a fine speech. However, instead of rousing Japanese Americans in the concentration camps to enlist in the armed forces, it raised questions. Roosevelt, after all, had signed Executive Order 9066, which had sent them to the camps in the first place. In the camps themselves, there was considerable controversy over serving in the military, because the inmates were just as concerned about their rights as citizens as they were about their responsibilities.

The dissension over serving in the armed forces came to a head with the so-called loyalty questionnaire, copies of which were distributed on February 10, 1943, a little over a week after President Roosevelt's public statement. The four-page government questionnaire to be completed by all imprisoned Japanese Americans seventeen years of age or older provoked heated arguments. Answering it generated considerable conflict within families, broke up couples, and estranged parents from their children. The questions that were the focus of contention were 27 and 28:

No. 27—"Are you willing to serve in the armed forces of the United States on combat duty, wherever ordered?"

No. 28—"Will you swear unqualified allegiance to the United States of America and faithfully defend the United States from any or all attack by foreign or domestic forces, and forswear any form of allegiance or obedience to the Japanese emperor, or any other foreign government, power or organization?"

The questions had different implications for first-generation (Issei) and second-generation (Nisei) Japanese Americans.

Question 27 clearly indicated that the government had done a complete about-face on its position regarding the eligibility of second-generation Japanese Americans for military service. Second-generation Japanese Americans realized that a "yes" answer qualified them to be drafted into an army that kept their families prisoners in concentration camps. Ambivalence notwithstanding, 494 men interned at Amache answered "yes" to questions 27 and 28 and were thus directly inducted into the armed forces. Eventually, a total of six hundred Amache internees entered the armed forces. This made Amache the camp with the highest percentage of its men in the American military.

Question 28 posed a different set of problems. The government had imprisoned Japanese Americans en masse, reasoning that it was impossible to distinguish loyal from disloyal Japanese Americans, in spite of the earlier efforts by many to prove their allegiance to the country and the absence of any evidence to the contrary. Now the government had decided to use question 28 as a way to determine the loyalty of individual Japanese Americans.

For first-generation Japanese Americans, question 28 posed a dilemma. A "yes" would make them stateless, for it involved renouncing the only citizenship they had (Japanese) while simultaneously swearing allegiance to a country (the United States) that had denied them citizenship. The second generation found the question merely obnoxious, since it assumed an allegiance to Japan that they did not have. Nevertheless, the vast majority of Japanese Americans chose to affirm their allegiance to the United States, answering "yes" to question 28. At Amache, 99.8 percent of the inmates answered "yes," the highest percentage of all the camps.

Of the 75,000 Japanese Americans who eventually filled out the loyalty questionnaire, only 6,700 answered "no" to both questions. They were classified as disloyal, and most of them were transferred to the Tule Lake concentration camp in Northern California to isolate them. From Amache, there were only 125 "no-no boys," as the members of this group were called.[18] Japanese Americans, such as the "no-no boys," who resisted the government's military policies, did so in pursuit of their civil liberties and in the name of human dignity. Their protest was a deeply American act. They were prepared to risk even harsher imprisonment than they currently endured for the sake of principle. Their example challenges the dominant image of Japanese Americans as stoic (some would say passive and quiet) victims of the government's misguided policies.[19]

The young men who answered "yes" to questions 27 and 28 did not necessarily rush to enlist in the armed forces. On the contrary, the vast majority of them did not volunteer, forcing the War Department to fill the ranks of the newly established 442nd Regimental Combat Team with recruits from Hawaii who had not been imprisoned in concentration camps.[20] Eventually, as many as twelve hundred camp inmates enlisted, a remarkable number considering the bitterness that pervaded the camps because of the circumstances and conditions of the inmates' imprisonment. Many young men enlisted without the approval of their parents, resulting in a generational divide that would not be bridged for a long time, if ever. Those from Amache and the other camps who volunteered or were drafted into the armed forces served with high distinction.[21] They not only suffered the privations of war but also had the additional burden of proving their trustworthiness. Altogether, about thirty-three thousand Japanese Americans served in the military. Like Chinese Americans, Japanese Americans took part in the war effort for a variety of reasons, which ranged from seeking gainful employment to fulfilling their patriotic duty. For many of the young prisoners, the war offered an opportunity to express their idealism and a chance to do something exciting, even if it meant getting in harm's way. In general, the most commonly expressed purpose was to obtain better treatment for themselves and their families after the war. For example, James Kanazawa, one of the first Amacheans to enlist, said he did so to "fight for his children's place in society—so that they would hold up their heads, so that they too would feel that their place, their rights were worth fighting for."[22] Japanese Colorado veterans outside of Amache had similar sentiments. Sam Terasaki, who was born in Denver and served with the 100th Battalion, concluded that Japanese Americans' military service did make a difference to subsequent generations, granting opportunities to them that his generation did not have.[23]

When Japanese Americans joined the armed forces for the sake of their families, they realized that they were also leaving their families behind to an uncertain fate. While they fought their country's enemies, their families were exposed to harassment and even violence. Even toward the end of the war, after Japanese American soldiers had distinguished themselves in combat against the enemy, there were anti-Japanese incidents. Citing one such case in April 1945, the *Rocky Mountain News* (RMN) noted that two Japanese American soldiers had asked the US government to protect their parents from terrorists engaged in shooting incidents. The soldiers reported that shots had been fired into the home of their invalid father from an automobile that had driven past the house. The newspaper condemned the attacks as an example of misplaced anger at Japan: "Because Japan is our enemy and guilty of atrocities, some think we should take it out on these Americans of Japanese ancestry. Fortunately, they don't try to punish Americans of German ancestry for Nazi barbarism. But they think that Japanese Americans somehow are different."[24] What is left unsaid is that the "somehow" factor differentiating Japanese Americans was race. The article ends with a call for justice and the preservation of American ideals, and a demand that law officers protect the equal rights of all citizens, regardless of ancestry.

The views expressed in this article are significant. In one sense, the position taken by the RMN is consistent with its customary denunciations of acts of mob violence and vandalism against members of the public, even acts against Asian Americans, which its own inflammatory editorials and articles had encouraged in the past. As expected, the newspaper condemned such acts because they disrupted public order. But in another, important sense, the newspaper's stance was different. There was something new here, an acceptance of Asian Americans as citizens that was not evident at an earlier time. This adjustment reflects the evolution in thinking that was under way in Colorado.

Japanese Americans participated in the war effort in many ways. Because of the classified nature of their work, those who were employed by the Naval and Military Intelligence Services have received the least attention.[25] Yet they were key to achieving victory in Asia and the Pacific. Because of their knowledge of Japanese language and culture, Japanese Americans were recruited to serve with the Naval Intelligence Service as language instructors and in the Army's Military Intelligence Service as translators, interpreters, interrogators, analysts, and propagandists. As Mark Murakami says, the irony of the situation was not lost on the participants themselves: "[On] the one hand the Japanese Americans were condemned for having the linguistic and cultural knowledge of Japanese, and on the other hand the knowledge they had was capitalized on and used as a secret weapon by the Army and Naval Intelligence."[26] The Army and Naval Intelligence showed different tolerances for Japanese Americans and utilized them in different ways.

Before the navy could find the necessary instructors for its naval language school, it first had to overcome its aversion to working with Japanese Americans and its traditional policy of restricting people of color to the most menial chores. So far as the navy was concerned, the necessity of relying on Japanese Americans to train its white officers for intelligence work in the Pacific Theater was an unfortunate wartime exigency.[27] The navy recruited its instructors both directly from the concentration camps and also from outside of them, through advertisements in publications such as the *Colorado Times*, an ethnic newspaper published in Denver for Japanese living in the American West. The navy employed mostly Japanese Americans and whites (usually those who had grown up in Japan) to serve as instructors in Japanese-language schools, which were housed at Harvard, the University of California at Berkeley, and finally at the University of Colorado at Boulder from 1942 to 1946. Twenty-seven of the forty-seven new instructors who taught at the University of Colorado's Boulder campus were recruited directly from Amache.[28] They helped to equip over eleven hundred non-Japanese-speaking men and women with the Japanese language proficiencies needed to perform a range of intelligence tasks in the Pacific Theater.

The army's Military Intelligence School also trained students for intelligence work in the Pacific Theater. However, in contrast to the short-sighted navy, the army trained Japanese Americans themselves for intelligence work, tapping a cadre of capable, motivated individuals to serve as intepreters for officers and officials, translators of captured enemy documents, and interrogators of Japanese prisoners of war (and in some cases, propagandists who persuaded enemy soldiers to surrender). Two graduates of the army's school, Shiro Omata and Kan Tagami, served as interpreter-aides to General Douglas MacArthur, supreme commander for the Allied Powers Southwest Pacific and later supreme commander for the Allied Powers during the postwar occupation of Japan.[29] As translators and interrogators of Japanse prisoners of war, the intelligence officers accompanied combat units in the field, facing the added risk of "capture by the enemy which would have meant slow death for themselves and cruel reprisals against any relatives still living in Japan," according to one study.[30] They served with about 130 different army, navy, and marine units, as well as units of Allied nations. Their work gave American military commanders strategic and tactical advantages, such as anticipating enemy action and evaluating enemy strengths and weaknesses. Their achievements included the translation of Operation Z documents, which contained Japanese strategy in the Central Pacific, leading to Allied victories in the Mariana Islands Campaign.

Military leaders who worked with Japanese American intelligence specialists testified to the important part the latter played in winning the war against Japan. Colonel Sidney F. Mashbir, who was in charge of the Allied Translator and Interpreter Section, an inter-Allied agency, was emphatic on this score: "The United States owes a debt to these men and to their families which it can never fully repay. At a highly conservative estimate, thousands of American lives were preserved and millions of dollars in materiel were saved as a result of their contribution to the war effort."[31] His superior, Lieutenant General Charles Willoughby, MacArthur's chief of intelligence, credited the Japanese Americans who served in the Military Intelligence Service with helping to shorten the war by two years, saving many American lives.[32]

Probably the best-known Asian American servicemen were those who served in the acclaimed 100th Battalion, made up mostly of Hawaiian Japanese Americans, and the 442nd Regimental Combat Team, which included second-generation Japanese Americans recruited directly from the concentration camps.[33] The 100th and 442nd were segregated military units that some people ridiculed as "Jap Crow" units, after the Jim Crow laws that had segregated blacks and whites in American society. During the North African campaign, the 100th Battalion was originally assigned to guard supply trains but was later allowed to fight in the grueling Italian campaign, landing at Salerno to join in the assault on Monte Cassino. Had the men of the 100th not been ordered to halt ten miles from Rome, they would have had the honor of being the first Americans to liberate the Italian capital. Later, the 100th and 442nd were merged. Together, they fought in Italy before being reassigned to the invasion of southern France. The 522nd Field Artillery Battalion of the 442nd was among the first to liberate Dachau, the oldest Nazi concentration camp in Germany.

The 442nd Regimental Combat Team became the most decorated

FIG. 10.3. Japanese Americans of the 442nd Regimental Combat Team guarding captured Germans soldiers, Orciano area, Italy, July 15, 1944. Courtesy of the National Archives and Records Administration, Number 4304-SC, 192069S; Photographer Musser.

unit in US military history for its size and length of service. In less than two years, it participated in seven major campaigns in Italy and France, received seven Presidential Unit Citations (five in a single month during combat in the Vosges). The 442nd also suffered a shocking casualty rate of 314 percent in the war, with 9,486 wounded and 800 killed in action, including 31 from Amache. For their bravery, the soldiers received over 18,000 decorations, including a Congressional Medal of Honor, 47 Distinguished Service Crosses, 350 Silver Stars, 810 Bronze Stars, and 3,600 Purple Hearts.

Fifty years after World War II, the Pentagon found that many Asian American veterans had been denied the Congressional Medal of Honor because of wartime prejudice. To correct this inequity, the Pentagon upgraded twenty-two of the forty-seven Distinguished Service Crosses to Congressional Medals of Honor, the highest military award.[34] Among

FIG. 10.4. Private First Class Kiyoshi K. Muranaga, US
Army, Congressional Medal of Honor recipient, c. 1943.
Muranaga was killed on June 26, 1944, in Suvereto, Italy.
Fallen Heroes Project, http://www.fallenheroesproject.org.

those to have their award upgraded were two Japanese Coloradans—
Private First Class Kiyoshi K. Muranaga and Private George Taro "Joe"
Sakato. Both Muranaga and Sakato were originally from California.
Muranaga had volunteered for service at Amache along with his brothers
Kenichi and Yoshio. Muranaga proved his loyalty to his country with the
only thing that was left to him—his life. In 1944, he was killed in action
near Suvereto, Italy, protecting his comrades.

FIG. 10.5. Private "Joe" Sakato, U.S. Army, Congressional Medal of Honor recipient, second from the left. Easy Company, 442nd Regimental Combat Team, marching to Bruyères, France, c. late 1944. Denver Public Library, Western History Collection, US Army Signal Corps, National Archives, Record Group 111-SC.

Sakato's experience in the war not only reveals his personal commitment to the highest standards of bravery but also offers insight into the ethos of the segregated Japanese American fighting unit with which he served. Sakato was born and raised in San Bernardino County, California, and moved with his family to Glendale, Arizona, during the voluntary evacuation period.[35] When he tried to enlist in the military for the first time, he was rejected as an enemy alien. Later, when the government allowed Japanese American to serve, he volunteered for the air force, which tended to exclude Japanese Americans.[36] Sakato ended up as a replacement in the 100th Infantry Battalion, which was nicknamed "The Purple Heart Battalion" for its high number of casualties.

While in eastern France, Sakato and his comrades were ordered to rescue the "Lost Battalion," as the seemingly doomed 1st Battalion of the 141st
(Alamo) Regiment, 36th (Texas) Division came to be known. Cut off and
surrounded by German forces, the 211 survivors were trapped on the bald
top of a thickly forested ridgeline for a week, facing certain death.[37] Two
earlier attempts to save the Texans had failed. Why the 442nd Regimental
Combat Unit was selected for this seemingly impossible mission, rather
than another unit, is controversial. Some thought that General Clayton
Dahlquist had assigned them this job because he considered them expend-
able cannon fodder. Others thought it was simply a matter of sending the
best, and the 442nd was the best.

The rescue mission was one of the bloodiest battles in US Army history.
After four days of murderous combat in the rugged Vosges Mountains, the
442nd broke through the reinforced German lines to save the Texans. One
of the lieutenants of the Lost Battalion who survived the ordeal remarked,
"We men who came off the hill know that the Nisei aren't just as good as
the average soldier—they're better."[38] In the course of the battle, the 442nd
suffered more than a thousand casualties, including two hundred killed in
action or missing and over eight hundred seriously wounded. Their dead
and injured far exceeded the number of Texans they saved. It was for this
battle that Private Sakato was awarded the Congressional Medal of Honor
for extraordinary heroism. After the war, he moved to Denver, where he
worked for the US Postal Service.

The distinguished service of Kiyoshi Muranaga, Joe Sakato, and other
Japanese Americans prompted General "Vinegar Joe" Stilwell to say: "They
bought an awful hunk of America with their blood.... [Y]ou're damn
right those Nisei boys have a place in the American heart, now and forever.
We cannot allow a single injustice to be done to the Nisei without defeating the purposes for which we fight."[39] As Stilwell recognized, those who
discriminated against Japanese Americans were thwarting World War II's
larger goals—freedom and justice for all. But while the war reshaped opinions in the military, many Americans back home still clung to their prewar
views.

COMING HOME

For returning Japanese Coloradan veterans, the persistence of prejudice
in the state was galling. Veteran Dick Momii of the 442nd Infantry Regi-

ment was dismayed to discover that many Coloradans' feelings toward Japanese Americans had not changed, in spite of what he and others had gone through:

> Well, I was surprised by the first experience I had when we stopped in a small town. We had on our military uniforms and battle ribbons and we saw people and they said, "What are those Japs doing in here?" And, you know, we got out of there as quick as we could. That really shocked me, that kind of prejudice, even though there was publicity about Japanese Americans being so loyal to the country and being in one of the best units in the whole United States Army. When I got back to Denver and was going to medical school, shortly after we got married, we wanted to get an apartment down there, 1951, near Denver General [Hospital]. And I wanted to rent an apartment and I said, "Well, if it makes any difference, I'm a Japanese American." And he said, "We don't rent to Japs."[40]

But not all Coloradans were like this. Momii also recalled being invited to a block meeting for a political caucus. When he asked the organizer, "Does it make any difference that I'm Japanese American?" he was told, "You're an American." It was "a great boost," Momii said, "that people didn't put that Japanese part before the American."[41] This was the direction in which postwar Colorado eventually moved, as thinking changed.

It also took the war to make Chinese Americans acceptable members of society. They benefited directly from changing perceptions of Chinese and China. During the war, Chinese American identity was reconstructed through wartime service, and the image of China was similarly reformed around its role as America's ally. The public was encouraged to see Chinese as courageous comrades confronting a common enemy, rather than as coolies or heathens. China was no longer regarded as the "sick man of Asia" but rather extolled as one of America's three major allies, along with Great Britain and the Soviet Union.

The change is evident in public condemnations of acts of discrimination against Chinese military visitors in social situations involving ordinary Coloradans during the war. In 1942, when Captain C. C. King, a Chinese national who was at Lowry Field in Denver to study aerial techniques, was refused admission to the ballroom at Lakeside Park, the RMN criticized his treatment as ungrateful. After all, Captain King was a representative of China, a nation that had for nearly five years "fought heroically and unflinchingly against a barbaric power" in its single-handed War of Resistance against Japan, which began with the invasion of China in 1937.[42] The Chinese were one ally who deserved Americans' respect.

Similarly, in another such incident in 1944, when staff at an Estes Park café placed a large sign on the table that read "White Trade Only" and refused to serve a Chinese official, his wife, and two children, the act was roundly criticized as unpatriotic. In Weld County, the *Ault Progress* declared that the staff's conduct was an affront to all the Chinese airmen training in Colorado and the many Chinese students studying at the University of Colorado. Evoking the racialist "Yellow Peril" bogeyman once again, the newspaper warned readers that things would be very different for the United States if China had decided to ally itself with Japan as America's enemy: "China could have saved millions of lives and much suffering by joining Japan in a racial war and that attitude, such as shown in Estes Park, aids the Japanese greatly in their campaign: 'The Orient for the Orientals.'"[43] In other words, discriminating against Chinese was tantamount to helping the enemy; it was unwise to give China a reason to regret its choice of allies.

Changes in feelings about China influenced American immigration policy as well. With China now an ally of the United States, the exclusion laws became an embarrassment. Despite opposition from the American Federation of Labor and other Sinophobic forces, on December 17, 1943, Roosevelt signed the Chinese Exclusion Repeal Act, better known as the Magnuson Act after its sponsor, Washington State congressman Warren G. Magnuson (Democrat). The Magnuson Act ended the ban on Chinese immigration. Now, small numbers of Chinese could immigrate to the United States, and for the first time, some Chinese who were already US residents could apply for citizenship.

The Magnuson Act was a compromise bill. Though it allowed Chinese to enter the country, it was highly restrictive, limiting immigrants to a quota of 105 new entry visas per year. This paltry number was based on the Immigration Act of 1924, which restricted the number of immigrants from eligible countries to 2 percent of those already living in the United States in 1890. For that reason, the Magnuson Act represented a change in immigration policy more symbolic than real. Still, the Magnuson Act was a significant reform since it marked the first time since the Naturalization Act of 1790 that any Asians were allowed to become naturalized citizens. At the same time, the Magnuson Act upheld discriminatory policies against Asians regarding property rights. It provided for the extension of state bans against Chinese American ownership of property and businesses. In many states (not including Colorado), Chinese Americans, including US citizens, were denied property-ownership rights either de jure or de facto until the Magnuson Act itself was fully repealed in 1965.

Such limitations notwithstanding, the Magnuson Act was an impetus for changing other immigration laws. One lesser-studied reform that had a dramatic effect on the development of the Chinese American community was the Chinese War Brides Act (August 9, 1946). This act amended previous legislation limiting Chinese immigration, including the recently passed Magnuson Act. It enabled Chinese veterans to legally bring their wives over from China as non-quota immigrants.[44] The effect of this act can be seen in the fact that, between 1946 and 1952, almost 90 percent of all Chinese immigrants were women. The admission of Chinese women without regard to the annual quota of 105 visas as required by the Immigration Act of 192 represented a historic reversal of the Page Law of 1875, which had excluded Chinese women from entering the United States under the pretext of keeping out prostitutes. This and other reforms in immigration policy during the postwar period resulted in a threefold increase in the Chinese American population, transforming Chinatowns from bachelor communities to family communities.

Socioeconomic changes also came to the expanding Chinese American community. Before the war, few employment opportunities in the mainstream economy, especially white-collar jobs, were open to Chinese Americans, but things changed during the war. Due to workforce shortages, Chinese Americans were no longer restricted to menial jobs in the ethnic economies of local Chinese communities but found better-paying positions in the wartime economy. This was particularly true of the burgeoning defense industry, which could ill afford to discriminate on the basis of race or, for that matter, gender.

The nature of the prewar–postwar shift is illustrated by the contrast in the experiences of different siblings in the Chin family seeking employment in Denver. Wawa Chin, granddaughter of Colorado Chinese pioneer Chin Lin Sou, describes the climate of prewar employment discrimination:

> Before the war, I couldn't even get an application to work at the dime store!
> They took my application but as soon as I left they threw it in the basket!
> After I got out of high school, I couldn't get a job anyplace, so I went to a
> Chinese restaurant and worked as a waitress. While I was working there, this

Jewish man came in and said to me, "What are you doing here? You've got an education and everything." And I said to him, "Nobody is willing to give me a job; that's why!" And he said, "You come see me tomorrow; I'll give you a job." So, I went to see him the next day; he put me to work right away and I became the secretary to the purchasing agent and the shipping department [of the Winter-Weiss Company trucking firm.][45]

Wawa's brothers, Edward and William Chin, experienced no such problems after returning from the war. They found comparatively good jobs, moving from one better-paying position to the next. They felt that circumstances had improved considerably due to subsiding discrimination. Edward Chin believed that, "if you could meet their qualifications and [were] capable of doing the work assigned, you could be hired."[46] He worked as an electronics technician for Decimeter, a small firm that made radar-receiving units for the navy. Later, he worked for the US Postal Service, then moved to United Airlines as a radio-electrical mechanic, and finally to Martin Marietta, where he was a quality-control inspector for the Titan missile until his retirement in 1982.

Similarly, William Chin held a variety of jobs, including working as a mechanic for the Bell Music Company, which made jukeboxes. The position he enjoyed most was as a production foreman for the Burroughs Corporation, which was building its first electronic computer at that time. As a production foreman, he supervised seventy-five employees who worked as cablers, assemblers, and final assembly workmen, among other jobs. He attributed his success to improved government stances toward Chinese Americans because of their war service, and the "many job opportunities for Asian Americans to a grateful US government who decided that Asian Americans deserved a better life in the USA. . . . After all, there were 20,000 Chinese Americans serving in the armed forces of the USA."[47]

Gender difference played a significant role in the reception that these three siblings received. Job opportunities for women were severely restricted both before and after the war; they were not comparable to those available to men. However, the Chins' accounts suggest a shift in racial perspectives not only in society at large but also in Chinese Americans themselves. In Wawa's recollection, before the war, race mattered more than individual capability. As Edward and William saw it, after the war, personal capability mattered more; their race no longer held them back. The world seemed to have changed—or had it? Did the brothers' denial of racial discrimination reflect the new social reality of the workplace or the firm desire of Asian American veterans to see it this way? Society's perceptions of Chinese Americans may have changed, but so had the siblings' sense of personal agency. The one thing that remained constant was their sensitivity to being judged by mainstream society and the importance they attached to being accepted or not. It would take another two generations for Asian Americans to begin to define themselves not in terms of others' judgments, but as they themselves wanted to be seen.

While the Chin brothers were being integrated into the workforce, they admitted that they still faced residential segregation that thwarted them from being able to live wherever they wanted to in Denver. Edward Chin recalled looking at several housing possibilities only to be told, "Well, we won't sell to you because if we sell to you, then white people won't buy here."[48] Eventually, he was able to circumvent this problem and acquire property in the exclusive Park Hill area by working with an enterprising realtor who was willing to buy the land and then turn it over to him. The Chins were prevented from buying homes in preferred residential neighborhoods in Denver through a combination of threatened boycotts of real estate agents, public pressure, and zoning ordinances. They came up against gentleman's agreements that commonly prevented Asian Americans, other people of color, and Jews from purchasing homes in certain places. Some property deeds even carried specific "Oriental exclusion" clauses.[49] In 1949, the US Supreme Court ruled such restrictive covenants unenforceable.

For Japanese Americans, the situation was different and improvements occurred more slowly. Japanese Americans were essentially displaced persons seeking asylum in their own country. After being released from the concentration camps, many of them chose not return to the Pacific Coast. An estimated fifty thousand remained in the Interior West.[50] For them, Colorado was a popular destination.[51] More former camp inmates resettled in the Centennial State than any other in the Intermountain West. By the end of the war, the number of Japanese Coloradans had quadrupled. In May 1944, about 2,507 Japanese Americans who had been freed from the camps had settled in Colorado, while only 385 had migrated to Wyoming and 293 to Montana.[52] Of those who went to Colorado, an estimated 1,144 gravitated toward Denver's Japantown.[53]

Denver became a mecca for released prisoners. It was considered the unofficial Japanese American capital of the United States, a distinction that had been held previously by Los Angeles. In 1940, there were 323 Japanese Americans in Denver (out of 2,734 in the entire state of Colorado); in 1945 and 1946, the population of Japanese Americans in Denver swelled temporarily to four to five thousand. The rest were dispersed throughout the state.[54] Given their agricultural background, many of them were eventually drawn to rural areas. Of the estimated 3,200 Japanese Coloradans in the rural areas, half were former camp inmates.

For the new arrivals, it was the immigrant experience all over again, except this time it was the second-generation Japanese Americans who bore the burden, and their place of origin was not foreign but somewhere else in the United States. These mostly single men and women were in the vanguard of the resettlement process. Once they found a job and a place to live, the rest of their family joined them. They opened businesses to serve the growing Japanese Coloradan community. No longer able to acquire ethnic food products either from Japan or from the West Coast, these entrepreneurs began to manufacture and distribute their own goods. Opening their own businesses was also a matter of necessity, because whites declined to serve them. Even though the war was over, whites still harbored racial hatred. Japanese Coloradans were regularly refused service and denied goods, and they were also segregated in public facilities, such as the bathhouse on Twentieth and Curtis Streets.

In 1940, there were 46 Japanese Coloradan businesses; by 1946, there were 258. Most of them were located in and around Japantown, with only about 10 percent located in the better areas of the city. At the center of Japantown was the Granada Fish Market, founded in 1944, which was named after the town of Granada near Amache. Besides wanting to be near their customers, Japanese American businesspeople were also limited in where they could operate. They were restricted to Denver's Japantown because of the city's licensing practices and their de facto exclusion from other parts of the state. According to one study, many Coloradan communities kept Japanese American businesses from buying or leasing property, or obtaining licenses to operate their stores in desirable locations.[55]

Finding housing was also a challenge. Residential segregation in Denver was particularly prevalent. Harold S. Choate, an administrator responsible for relocating Japanese Americans from the concentration camps, noted, "It is an unwritten law among Denver realty houses that rentals, leases and sales shall not be to persons of Japanese ancestry, so housing is difficult for them to find."[56] Gentlemen's agreements restricted Japanese

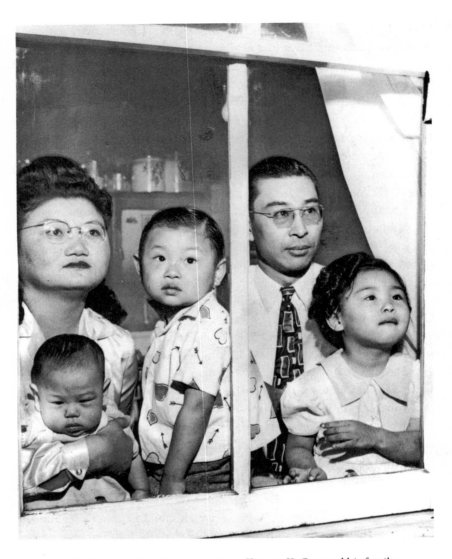

FIG. 10.6. Japanese American war veteran Katsuto K. Gow and his family were barred from moving to their prospective new home at 2718 Gaylord Street, Denver, by a restrictive covenant, c. 1946. From left to right: Mrs. Tomoe Gow, Gale (six months old), Larry (three years old), Mr. Katsuto K. Gow, and Patsy (four years old). History Colorado, Stephen H. Hart Library and Research Center, 10038890.

Americans to a triangle north of Eighteenth Street and West of Champa Street, running to the Platte River.[57] In its 1943 pamphlet *Japanese in Our Midst*, the Colorado Council of Churches documented how neighbors and real estate groups forced Japanese Americans from various parts of Denver and across the state into the poorer section of the city.[58] Besides being patently unfair, these restrictions were shortsighted since Japanese businesses tended to improve the area in which they were located. Their presence in the lower downtown district of Denver helped to revitalize it.

In addition to settling in Denver and other urban areas, Japanese Americans also settled in rural communities. Some Amache farmers moved to the irrigated areas of the Arkansas Valley, where they contributed to its agricultural development.[59] A few of them purchased farms, but most worked as tenant farmers. They engaged in small-scale truck farming, producing dozens of different crops that had seldom been seen in the lower valley before and doing so in large quantities. This was in marked contrast to the other farmers in the area, who tended to engage in large-scale farming that focused on only a half dozen different crops. Their presence in southeastern Colorado was more accepted than in other rural locales, which had banned new Japanese American arrivals in 1944.

YELLOW PERIL, REDUX

Japanese American resettlement in rural Colorado stirred up prejudices that flowed easily in the old channels of the Yellow Peril myth. In December 1943, Weld County and Morgan County farmers protested after the War Relocation Authority (WRA) announced plans for the "extensive" resettlement of Japanese truck farmers in northeastern Colorado and Nebraska.[60] In January 1944, amid reports that "several farms" had already been sold for good money to Japanese Americans in western Colorado, hundreds of farmers in Mesa County organized to take action to prevent Japanese Americans from buying any Western Slope farmland.[61] A general panic ensued. Reports abounded of a "Japanese land grab" under way by prisoners who were being rapidly released from camps and given generous WRA loans and other government assistance to resettle in Colorado, Utah, Idaho, and elsewhere. Echoing the rhetoric of decades past, one Western Slope rancher, noting that Colorado had already been saddled with "thousands" of Japanese whom the West Coast did not want, warned that a further influx of inmates would be disastrous for farming families: "If Colorado must absorb them, in a few generations our best lands will be Japanese settlements. The infiltration now is a grave menace and our Americans, living the American way, cannot compete with them."[62] As usual, these anti-Japanese outcries were either groundless or an exaggeration of the facts. Some charged that three thousand Japanese had purchased land in Adams County, when only twenty-three actually had.[63] Within weeks, towns across the state enacted resolutions protesting further land sales to Japanese Americans and organized petitions calling for a statewide ban.

The most serious response to this imaginary threat was an effort to enact state legislation to prevent Japanese farmers from settling in Colorado. After a proposed bill to ban land purchases by "Japanese aliens" failed in February 1944, one of its proponents, State Senator Willard B. Preston (Republican, Adams County), rallied support to put a broader alien land law on the ballot in November as an amendment to the state constitution.[64] Italian truck farmers in Adams County, where the largest number of Japanese Americans lived and worked, pressured Republican governor John Charles Vivian to call a special session of the Colorado General Assembly to discuss the proposed amendment.[65]

Among those testifying for the proposal was Brighton mayor J. W. Wells. His speech captured the emotions that inspired many advocates of the ban. Wells depicted Brighton as a proud American community that was now "being overrun with Japanese who, with plenty of money, are buying our farm-lands, businesses and residences in increasing numbers." Wells said that to allow this invasion to continue was a betrayal of the sacrifices that American servicemen were making to defeat Japan. While drawing a distinction between Japanese Americans and enemy combatants, Wells emphasized the link between them: "Some are American-born, yes; but they have parents who still pay homage to the emperor of Japan. . . . The people who committed the atrocities to Americans on Bataan are not the same as those buying our land, but they are tied by blood and upbringing. What will our soldiers think when they come back and find Japanese owning our farms and business establishments?[66] Everyone who heard Wells speak knew that his son had been captured at the Battle of Bataan.[67]

The amendment was opposed by other speakers who saw it as a contradiction of America's fundamental ideals of freedom and democracy. Among them was Japanese American army sergeant James Gozawa of Camp Carson, Colorado, "an American citizen by birth and an American soldier by choice." Gozawa took Wells's message about the nobility of the American war sacrifice but elevated it above race, placing it on the altar of democracy: "Tens of thousands of Americans" were presently "dying for democracy," he said, "not because they were white, or black, or yellow, but because they feel democracy is worth dying for. . . . Our training for the battlefield has kept us on maneuvers for 48 hours with our only food a piece of bread. That bread was heaven sent. Your democracy is too— don't tamper with it."[68] Gozawa's brief statement honored the sacrifices made by Wells's son and other veterans but transmuted them from sacrifices exacted in a race war to sacrifices freely given for a value that unified Americans.

In the end, the vote on whether to place the amendment on the ballot was close but was defeated on a split vote (in the House of Representatives, forty-eight to fifteen for; in the Senate, fifteen to twelve against).[69] Having failed with the bill and legislative-endorsed amendment, proponents then organized a citizens' petition drive to get the amendment before the voters. Adoption of Amendment No. 3, as it was called, would have denied "Filipinos, Koreans, and immigrants from India, as well as the Japanese, the rights accorded German or Italian aliens," but it was mainly an effort to prevent Japanese Americans from purchasing property.[70] One critic of the initiative, Senator Robert G. Bosworth (Republican), aptly described it as a hypocritical amendment that was nothing more than a Japanese exclusion act.[71]

The campaign to pass the amendment was spearheaded by the anti-foreign American League of Colorado, led by Mayor Wells and supported by groups such as the Colorado Veterans of Foreign Wars, who agreed with Wells that American fighting men would not tolerate their land being bought up by the "Japs" while they were overseas defending it.[72] The decidedly anti-Japanese *Denver Post* lent support by running stories with such headlines as "Experts says Jap land-owners drive out American farmers" and recommending a "yes" vote.[73]

A Citizens' Emergency Committee emerged to organize a grassroots campaign to oppose the amendment, arguing that "the fundamental issue at stake [is] the maintenance of the principles and practices upon which America was founded."[74] The committee's slogan was "Keep Colorado American; Vote 'No' on Amendment No. 3." A variety of groups rallied around it. Religious organizations were in the vanguard. As early as the summer of 1942, the Colorado Council of Churches had recognized that "one of the fundamental issues in this world-wide war is that of race equality or inequality," and it sounded a warning that "democracy will go down first of all on the rocks of racial prejudice and discrimination."[75] Among the media supporters were the *Rocky Mountain News*, the *Pueblo Star Journal* and *Chieftain*, and ethnic publications including the *Intermountain Jewish News*, and the *Colorado Statesman* and *Star* (both African American newspapers). Together, these various groups engaged in a campaign to educate the public about the amendment's true intent. At the core of the conflict between the Citizens' Emergency Committee and the American League was the important issue of what the United States was as a nation. Was it a nation that stood for racial equality, or one that stood for racial inequality? On the eve of the election, the answer to that question was uncertain.

Among the opponents, there was considerable pessimism that Coloradans would approve the amendment. As the voting unfolded, it was evident that it was proceeding in part along ethnic group lines. In Denver, the black and Jewish precincts voted "no" while the Italian and Spanish precincts voted "yes." However, what may have made the crucial difference in the final result was the soldier vote against the amendment. It is difficult to know why the soldiers voted against it. Perhaps soldiers and their families realized that the intent of the amendment was to deny Japanese Americans land for no other reason than their race, while the soldiers themselves were fighting a war against those who promoted racial inequality and even genocide. Perhaps it was simply because the soldiers realized that the amendment was aimed at their fellow veterans and their families, who deserved better than that. In any case, among the three amendments on the ballot, only Amendment No. 3 failed. That made Colorado one of the only states in the Interior West that declined to enact an alien land law. In 1952, all such laws were declared unconstitutional.

CITIZENS AT LAST

At the same time that the US Supreme Court was eliminating alien land laws from the statute books, Congress was updating the country's naturalization laws by enacting one of its most important pieces of postwar legislation—the McCarran-Walter Act of 1952, sponsored by Senator Pat McCarran (Democrat, Nevada) and Congressman Francis Walter (Democrat, Pennsylvania). McCarran himself was no liberal. He was one of the leaders of the anti-Communist witch-hunt during the McCarthy era and a staunch nativist who was opposed to opening America to a flood of Asian immigrants. In his view, the United States was facing a double threat, from both outside and within its borders. One threat came from immigrants wanting to come to America and the other came from immigrants already in America who had refused to assimilate, along with their descendants. America was endangered by what he called "indigestible blocs."[76]

While the McCarran-Walter Act reaffirmed the use of discriminatory quotas in the Immigration Act of 1924, it also began the liberalization of American immigration policy by ending race-based denials of admission to the country. As a result, Japan was assigned an annual quota of 185 entry visas, and countries within the so-called Asia-Pacific Triangle, such as India and the Philippines, were granted a quota of 100, similar to the limited quota of 105 that had been previously allotted to China by the Magnuson Act (1943). The McCarran-Walter Act also abolished the naturalization statutes that had restricted citizenship to free white persons. Most of the Japanese who had immigrated to Colorado before or immediately after the war became US citizens.[77]

The McCarran-Walter Act was passed despite the veto of President Harry S. Truman, who opposed the continuation of immigrant quotas, which he thought were un-American as well as discriminatory. Truman realized that such quotas reflected badly on the United States, hampering its ability to counter the Soviet Union and its Communist allies. The continuation of such policies and practices within America's borders undermined its claim to the moral high ground and diminished its appeal for support among nonaligned nations, especially Third World countries that had been liberated from colonialism. Changes needed to be made.

Under Truman, the federal government issued "To Secure These Rights: The Report of the President's Committee on Civil Rights" (October 1947), a study showing that many minorities, including Asian Americans, were still experiencing prejudice. Discrimination was especially acute among blacks, who suffered the most from bigotry. Truman took a significant step to address this problem when he desegregated the federal workforce and the military through Executive Orders 9980 and 9981, paving the way for the subsequent integration of other institutions. Segregated Asian American military units, such as the 14th Air Service Group and the 442nd Regimental Combat Team, were now a thing of the past.

It would take a sustained campaign to generate the public pressure necessary to substantially improve the plight of America's racial and ethnic minorities. This came with the civil rights movement (1954–68), a black-led social movement characterized by acts of nonviolent protest and civil disobedience. After spending most of its first two hundred years keeping races separate, the government finally agreed that segregation was inherently unequal and detrimental to society. Beginning with the US Supreme Court's Brown v. Board of Education of Topeka (1954) decision, the government began enacting legislation to dismantle the legal structures maintaining white supremacy.[78] In effect, these reforms made the immortal words "all men are created equal" a matter of racial equality, and American identity something more than being white.

World War II was a watershed in American history and culture, changing how Americans thought about race. For decades, Americans had been preparing for a life-and-death struggle with an Asian enemy and, with the attack on Pearl Harbor, it finally came to pass. Though World War II started as a race war, it did not end that way. In the course of the conflict, Americans began to define themselves in contrast to their Axis enemies, for whom racial supremacy was the ideological goal. For Americans, the war became something nobler—it became a war for an ideal that united all Americans—a war for democracy. This ultimately reshaped American postwar identity.

COMING TO AMERICA, AGAIN

FOR ASIAN AMERICANS, THE MOST MEANINGFUL STEPS THE COUN-
try took to become more equitable after World War II were to institute
an impartial immigration policy and to abrogate miscegenation laws.
During the Cold War (1945–91), political leaders needed an immigration
policy that proved to other nations, especially those in the Third World,
that Americans were fair-minded. Business leaders realized that the existing policy hurt their interests since it impeded the inflow of people who
were necessary for the country's future growth in the emergent global
economy.

The United States addressed the need for a fairer immigration policy
with the passage of the Hart-Celler Act (the Immigration and Nationality
Act of 1965), a comparatively liberal law. While the United States never
returned to the free immigration policy of the eighteenth and early nineteenth centuries, Hart-Celler eliminated many of the discriminatory features of past laws that had created a hierarchical system of quotas giving
preference to emigrants from Western and Northern Europe while excluding those from Asia. With the passage of Hart-Celler, considerations of
race, gender, and country of origin were ruled out of naturalization and
immigration decisions, and immigrants with family in the country, refugee status, or needed skills were given preference. After nearly half a century, the country once again opened its borders to Asians. Many more
arrived than expected. Between 1960 and 2009, the Asian-born population
in the United States mushroomed from fewer than five hundred thousand
to over 10.6 million.

As in the past, a variety of push-pull factors were at play in the emigrants' departure from Asia, arrival in America, and subsequent journey

to Colorado. The main driving force continued to be economic. With the advent of a global community, the United States increasingly turned to Asia to take advantage of its rapid economic development. With greater interconnection and interdependence with Asia came not only capital, goods, and services but labor as well, especially in the form of skilled workers. Since the enactment of the Hart-Celler Act, the government has awarded a large proportion of its entry visas to Asians with professional qualifications, technical expertise, and advanced educational attainments. By the end of the first decade of the twenty-first century, approximately 75 percent of the computer systems analysts and programmers in the United States were from Asia.[1] This Asian influx played an important role in the country's transformation from an industrial economy into an information economy. A new generation of Asians brought the energy, enterprise, and skills needed for the United States to compete in the world economy. As of 2014, in Silicon Valley alone, Asian Americans formed the majority of the technical workforce (the main countries of origin being China, India, Japan, Korea, the Philippines, Vietnam, Thailand, Taiwan, and the Pacific Islands); Asian Indian Americans by themselves were responsible for founding a third of the Silicon Valley's start-ups.[2]

In addition to economic factors, the other major driver of Asian immigration was political. As part of America's Cold War containment strategy to counter its Communist adversaries, the Soviet Union and the People's Republic of China, the United States established numerous military bases in Asia and fought two so-called limited wars in Korea (1950–53) and Vietnam (1965–75), creating the conditions for more Asians to go to the United States. Beginning in 1950, Korean women began immigrating as war brides; as of today, nearly a hundred thousand Korean women have immigrated as military wives. The Vietnam War resulted in a flood of Asian refugees who washed up on American shores and were resettled throughout the United States under the provisions of the Indochina Migration and Refugee Assistance Act of 1975. A first wave (1975–77) of largely well-educated refugees (175,000) was followed by a much larger wave of indigent "boat people" and ethnic minorities, including the Hmong, who arrived mainly from 1978 to the mid-1980s, bringing the total to about 760,000 by 2002.

While the dramatic increase in immigration by Asians since the 1970s can be directly attributed to the Hart-Celler Act, the US Supreme Court's decision in Loving v. Virginia (1967), though lesser known, was arguably more meaningful in its long-term implications for ending discrimination against Asian Americans and other people of color in the United States. At the end of World War II, thirty-eight of the forty-eight states had miscegenation laws prohibiting interracial marriage, including Virginia's "Racial Purity Act" (1924). The High Court unanimously struck down these laws as unconstitutional. As a result, intermarriage has steadily increased, with a concomitant change in attitudes toward interracial relationships. A quiet revolution has been in the making. Between 1970 and 2010, the percentage of interracial marriages in the United States increased substantially, from 2.1 percent to 15.1 percent. The rate of interracial marriage among Asian Americans has gone even higher: a full 31 percent of Asian Americans who married in 2008 married non-Asians. Though the percentage dropped to 28 percent in 2010 (with 36 percent of Asian women and 17 percent of Asian men outmarrying), Asian Americans are still more likely to outmarry than other ethnic groups.[3]

Both the Hart-Celler Act and the Loving v. Virginia decision have gradually transformed the character of the country and of Colorado. As one of the new growth states after World War II, the Centennial State has attracted its share of Asian immigrants and refugees.[4] However, they are no longer limited to low-wage occupations and hard physical labor to build the state's infrastructure. Now, Asian Coloradans can be found across the entire socioeconomic spectrum of the state. They have started successful small businesses. In 1982, they owned more than 1,817 such enterprises; in 1988, that number had nearly doubled, to 3,500.[5]

The Asian Coloradan population has changed dramatically. It comprises an ethnically diverse group of people who generally mirror the distribution of Asians throughout the Interior West and the nation as a whole. According to the 2010 decennial census, Colorado's six largest Asian ethnic groups are Chinese (25,215), Vietnamese (20,899), Koreans (20,433), Asian Indians (20,369), Filipinos (14,448), and Japanese (11,097).[6] Sixteen other separate Asian ethnic groups were counted in the census, with several of the smallest grouped together in a residual category called "Other Asian."[7] Besides economic immigrants, recent Colorado Asians include refugees seeking asylum, such as Hmong and Burmese. Asian Coloradans live throughout the state, though most prefer to live in urban areas. The most popular places for them are the Denver metropolitan area and Colorado Springs. In the metropolitan area, Aurora has been a magnet for Asian immigrants and refugees ever since it began expanding in the 1950s.

As the census data indicates, the Chinese have come back to the Centennial State even though there is no longer a Denver Chinatown for them to return to. Once again, they are the largest Asian ethnic group in Colorado. In contrast, the Japanese are now the smallest of the six major Asian ethnic groups, a reversal from the World War II period, when they were the most numerous Asians in the state. Hardly any Japanese have immigrated to Colorado in recent years because there are fewer factors, such as economic deprivation, that would motivate them to leave. Combined, the Chinese and Japanese now make up about 25 percent of all Asian Coloradans.

Asian Coloradans still remain a small minority. In 1990, they constituted only 1.7 percent of the state's population; in 2000, they grew to 2.2 percent; and by 2010, they reached 2.8 percent, totaling an estimated 143,760 people.[8] At 2.8 percent, the percentage of Asian Coloradans is lower than the 4.8 percent of Asian Americans nationally.[9] When the length of time that Asians have been in the United States is considered, even the national percentage may seem surprisingly small. This is, of course, due to past discriminatory laws that hindered the growth of the community.

Asian Americans are making up for lost time. By 2010, they had become the fastest-growing racial group in the country and in Colorado. The Asian population increased more than four times, growing by 43.3 percent while the rest of the nation grew by only 9.7 percent. Even with this comparatively high rate of growth, it is doubtful that they will ever catch up to or surpass other racial and ethnic groups. Their contribution to the country will have little to do with their numbers. Instead, it will be because they share the same characteristic of past Asian Coloradans—true grit.

It is a profound historical irony that Asian Americans are no longer condemned as an unassimilable group to be chased from the country, but are now praised as a "model minority" to be emulated by others.[10] At present, they are found to possess exemplary cultural characteristics that have allowed them to achieve success in the United States.[11] Calling them a model minority, however, simply promotes another stereotype. Just like negative stereotypes, positive ones serve political purposes. In this case, the image of Asian Americans as a model minority invites invidious comparisons with other people of color in America. The implication is that, given how well Asian Americans have done materially (they have exceptionally high median household incomes) in spite of a history of persecution, the failure of other people of color to advance is their own fault rather than the product of structural causes that have traditionally held them back and the institutional racism that continues to dog them today. Asian

Americans' achievements are attributed to their discipline and hard work, while blacks', Latinos', and Native Americans' failures are said to be due to the dysfunctional beliefs and behaviors that are part of their biological inheritance. In the minds of many, Asian Americans are now considered "honorary" whites in America's contemporary racial hierarchy and are separated from other people of color by a wide chasm.

While Asian Americans are faring better than their pre–World War II predecessors, a contemporary socioeconomic portrait shows a bimodal distribution within and between Asian ethnic groups. In most discussions of Asian Americans, the less-successful segment of the community, such as Hmong Americans, is often overlooked. Asian Americans point out that not all of them are academically successful or have high-level jobs or incomes, and that the "model minority" image is just another social construction created to prevent some Asian Americans from obtaining assistance to meet their educational, economic, health, and human service needs.[12] Even those who are considered successful continue to face a "glass ceiling" that has prevented their advancement, and they are paid less than their white counterparts with the same position and education.[13]

Along with changing public perceptions of Asian Americans, there has been an absence of widespread anti-Asian campaigns of the sort that led to their exclusion from the country. Mainstream groups such as organized labor no longer agitate against Asian Americans to recruit union members, political parties no longer oppose them to garner votes, and newspapers no longer stoke hostility toward them to enlarge their readership. However, there continues to be violence against individual Asian Americans.[14]

Underlying race resentment often returns with a vengeance when a crisis erupts. Asian nations, such as Japan in the 1980s and China in the early twenty-first century, have been made scapegoats for America's economic problems. China has also been demonized as a military threat. American antipathies toward Asian nations have also had negative consequences for Asian Americans, who bear the brunt of any backlash. Asian Americans have been mistaken for Asian nationals and have been subject to misdirected anger. The most famous example is the Vincent Chin case. On June 19, 1982, two unemployed Detroit autoworkers mistook Vincent Chin, a Chinese American, for a Japanese and bludgeoned him to death with a baseball bat to make him pay for the decline of the auto industry.[15] Compounding the tragedy, his two murderers were sentenced to a mere three years' probation and fined a paltry $3,780.

More recently, following the terrorist attack of September 11, 2001, a spate of incidents against Asian Indian Americans has occurred. The government has reported eight hundred instances of violence against those perceived to be Middle Easterners, resulting in serious injury and death, as well as threats, vandalism, and arson against their homes, businesses, and places of worship. Being deemed a foreigner in the United States can be very dangerous. Four days after 9/11, Balbir Singh Sodhi, an Asian Indian American, was fatally shot outside his gas station in Mesa, Nevada, because, like other Sikhs, he wore a turban, which many Americans associate with terrorists.

A crucial difference between the past and present is that racially motivated acts of violence have been criminalized.[16] In 1990, when three white men used baseball bats to beat six Japanese students attending Teikyo Loretto Heights University in Denver, they were prosecuted under Colorado's new ethnic intimidation statute. The two brothers who perpetrated this crime were each sentenced to seventy-five-year prison terms.[17] After 9/11, federal charges were brought against fifty-four perpetrators of hate crimes, with forty-eight convictions thus far.[18] Mindful of what had occurred in the aftermath of the attack on Pearl Harbor, political leaders, including President George W. Bush, have spoken out against blaming Muslim Americans and their religion for the 9/11 tragedy. And there have been no public demands for their mass imprisonment in concentration camps.

Asian Americans are now in a better position to deal with racism. Besides self-identifying as Chinese Americans or Japanese Americans, they have also embraced a broader identity as Asian Americans, with a common history that transcends that of their individual ethnic group. While primacy is still given to the needs of their particular group, Asian Americans cooperate, communicate, and interact with other racial and ethnic groups to pursue common goals. Together they have engaged in advocacy and outreach activities to promote their common interests. They have decried media portrayals that have stereotyped and degraded them. They have joined coalitions to fight for political empowerment, social justice, and racial equality. It is evident that they have evolved along with the rest of the American people, and that is cause for cautious optimism about the future.

While it is far too early to declare that racism is a relic of the past, it appears that racism is far less acceptable today. Members of the Millennial

Generation (those born after 1980 and before 2000) are able to recognize more readily that the racial categories of the past reflect social constructs rather than innate characteristics. Millennials, who are estimated to number at least eighty million, are said to be the most diverse generation in American history and seem to have as their bedrock values equality and fairness.[19] Their highest value seems to be empathy, that is, open-mindedness and openhearted connection to others, which is essential for a more tolerant society.[20] They are quite willing to have real encounters and relationships with individuals belonging to different racial and ethnic groups. With the Millennials and their descendants, individual-level racism will continue to decline, if not necessarily end.

At the beginning of the twentieth-first century, the rise of previously marginalized groups is transforming the United States into a pluralistic society with an increasingly multiracial mainstream through the process of intermarriage. As noted earlier, among people of color, Asians have the highest rate of intermarriage, with close to a third of them marrying non-Asians. That trend is likely to increase as bias decreases in the new century. A sense of how rapidly that is occurring can be gathered from the fact that, in 2001, 24 percent of the general population still disapproved of a family member marrying an Asian American, but by 2009, the number had dropped to 11 percent.[21] Intermarriage will lead to ever-increasing numbers of multiracial Asian Americans. It is projected that, by 2020, one out of five Asian Americans will be multiracial; by 2050, one out of three will be.[22]

Demographic forces are eroding American racism. These changes help make an American identity something more than being white. That has made a few people nervous, engendering resentment among some whites who feel they are losing their privileged place in society and their links with the nation's past, when they were once absolutely dominant. There is evidence that some even believe that discrimination against whites has become as big a problem as discrimination against people of color.[23] Whether this is enough to cause a significant backlash is doubtful, but rising frustrations about their position in a changing country will probably need to be released somehow, sooner or later.

What is certain is that it is premature to proclaim that the United States has entered a post-racial period, as some did following the historic election in 2008 and reelection in 2012 of Barack Obama, the country's first black president.[24] His presidency has confounded some people, who regard it as counter to their understanding of where blacks should be in America's racial hierarchy. What is clear is that his presidency represents "the changing demographic nature of America, the browning of America."[25] But a brown America is far from being a color-blind America. As the *New York Times* journalist Charles M. Blow notes, "Race remains a frame for inequality in this country."[26] Racial inequalities can be expected to continue into the foreseeable future even as officially sanctioned racism declines.

To achieve equality, Asian Coloradans and their fellow Americans will need to actively challenge entrenched racial divisions that continue to impede social progress. The sooner people accept that we are living in an increasingly pluralistic society, the sooner a color-blind society will be a reality. Americans will need to embrace the change that is coming rather than to oppose it.

ABBREVIATIONS

ADT	*Aspen Daily Times*
CR	*Colorado Republican*
CT	*Colorado Tribune*
DCCR	*Daily Central City Register*
DDT	*Denver Daily Tribune*
DEP	*Denver Evening Post*
DMR	*Daily Miners' Register*
DP	*Denver Post*
DR	*Denver Republican*
DRC	*Daily Register-Call*
DT	*Denver Times*
FS	*Fairplay Sentinel*
GP	*Granada Pioneer*
GT	*Greeley Tribune*
KR	*Knight Ridder/Tribune Business News*
NYT	*New York Times*
PC	*Pacific Citizen*
PUC	*Pueblo Chieftain*
RMN	*Rocky Mountain News*
RMS	*Rocky Mountain Sun*
TMR	*Tri-Weekly Miners' Register*
WCCR	*Weekly Central City Register*
WRC	*Weekly Register-Call*
WRMN	*Weekly Rocky Mountain News*

OTHER SOURCES

Baker transcript: Sources identified by this tag refer to selected transcripts made by Black Hawk historian Roger Baker of Central City *Register* newspapers (the *Tri-Weekly Miner's Register, Weekly Miner's Register, Daily Central City Register,* and

Register-Call) from 1862 to 1919, focusing on Chinese miners in Gilpin County but including other references to Chinese, kindly supplied to the author in 2002.

CHS index: Sources identified by this tag refer to the Colorado Historical Society Subject Index, held in the Stephan H. Hart Library and Research Center. This index includes transcripts, excerpts, and photocopies of articles, as well as lists of articles about topics in Colorado history, drawn from a variety of newspapers, magazines, books, and other publications. The sources were not restricted to the library's own collection. The index began as a Civil Works Administration project in 1933 and was continued by many different volunteers over the decades.

NOTES

PROLOGUE

1   While Asian Americans have made considerable progress in gaining acceptance as Americans, they are still defined in many respects as "others." Committee of 100 and Harris Interactive, "Still the 'Other?': Public Attitudes toward Chinese and Asian Americans" (New York: Committee of 100, 2009), 21.

2   *True Grit,* directed by Henry Hathaway (Paramount Pictures, 1969), was filmed in Ouray County, Colorado. In 2010, Paramount Pictures produced a remake of this classic film.

3   Charles Portis, *True Grit* (New York: Overlook Press, 1968), 61.

4   Ibid., 64.

5   Colorado is nicknamed the Centennial State because it entered the union on August 1, 1876, twenty-eight days after the centennial of the United States.

6   Rose Hum Lee, *The Growth and Decline of Chinese Communities in the Rocky Mountain Region* (New York: Arno Press, 1978), 101.

7   Marion R. Casey, "How waves of Irish became Americans," NYT, November 16, 2012.

8   Reginald Horsman, *Race and Manifest Destiny: The Origins of American Racial Anglo-Saxonism* (Cambridge, MA: Harvard University Press, 1981), 4.

9   Mary Roberts Coolidge, *Chinese Immigration* (New York: Henry Holt, 1909), 40.

10 See Noel Ignatiev, *How the Irish Became White* (New York: Routledge, 1995), and David R. Roediger, *Working toward Whiteness: How America's Immigrants Became White, The Strange Journey from Ellis Island to the Suburbs* (New York: Basic Books, 2005), for a discussion of how this transformation occurred.

11 "Race antipathies," NYT, November 28, 1879.

12 Alleyne Ireland, "Commercial Aspect of the Yellow Peril," *North American Review* 171 (September 1, 1900), http://archive.org/stream/jstor-25105061/25105061_djvu.txt. Ireland points out that most Chinese live in the same climate as French, Germans, Austrians, Americans, and British.

13 Gunther Barth, in *Bitter Strength: A History of the Chinese in the United States, 1850–1870* (Cambridge, MA: Harvard University Press, 1964), for example, places the blame on the Chinese themselves.

14   Kay J. Anderson, "The Idea of Chinatown: The Power of Place and Institutional Practice in the Making of a Racial Category," *Annals of the Association of American Geographers* 77, no. 4 (1987): 580–598.

15   "A reconstruction of some Oriental literature is very humiliating to our western and nineteenth century pride in showing how far the Chinese had gone in civilization when Europe was barbarian and America unknown," DMR, October 13, 1867.

16   "John Chinaman and his troubles," DMR, February 21, 1865; "The Chinaman's pigtail," DCCR, November 13, 1868; and "A Chinaman disgusted," DCCR, July 31, 1869.

17   "Celestial sinners. Caucasian against Mongolian—the survival of the fittest," RMN, October 31, 1880.

18   *Mining Review,* May 15, 1876.

19   "The Chinese in California," TMR, August 18, 1862; "The thievish habits of the San Francisco Chinamen are accounted for not from 'pure cussedness' or even greed of gain, but in order to get the wherewithal to gratify their love for opium," RMN, June 26, 1875; and "A shrewd Chinaman," RMN, August 17, 1877.

20   Carl Abbott, Stephen J. Leonard, and Thomas J. Noel, *Colorado: A History of the Centennial State,* 4th ed. (Boulder: University Press of Colorado, 2005), 210.

21   Charles Leland Sonnichsen, *Roy Bean: Law West of the Pecos,* cited in *Asian Texans: Our Histories and Our Lives,* ed. Irwin A. Tang (Austin, TX: The It Works, 2007), 49–72.

22   Since World War II, the term "concentration camps" has been associated with the Nazis and connotes "death camps." For that reason, some people take exception to using it to refer to the facilities that incarcerated Japanese Americans even though they were called that by President Franklin D. Roosevelt and other government officials. The euphemism "relocation camps" fails to adequately describe the conditions of these detention centers. Historically, it is more accurate to use "concentration camps" since officials fully realized that the government was forcibly removing and imprisoning Japanese Americans in facilities where they lived under harsh conditions.

23   "United States: Demographics & Social," Migration Policy Institute, 2013, www.migrationpolicy.org/data/state-profiles/state/demographics/US.

ONE. IMPERIALISM, NATIONALISM, AND THE COMING OF ASIANS TO COLORADO

1   Frank Ninkovich, *The United States and Imperialism* (Malden, MA: Blackwell, 2001), 9.

2   Harold R. Isaacs, *Scratches on Our Minds: American Views of China and India* (Armonk, NY: M. E. Sharpe, 1958), 71.

3   June Mei, "Socioeconomic Origins of Emigration: Guangdong to California," *Modern China* 5, no. 4 (October 1979): 463–501.

4   Hsin-yun Ou, "Mark Twain, Anson Burlingame, Joseph Hopkins Twichell, and the Chinese," *ARIEL* 42, no. 2 (April 2011): 43–74.

5   "Minister Wu in praise of Lincoln. Also speaks in Brooklyn of Burlingame and his work in China," NYT, February 13, 1901.

6   See Frederick W. Williams, *Anson Burlingame and the First Chinese Mission to Foreign Powers* (New York: Charles Scribner's Sons, 1912), for information about Burlingame and his mission.

7   Hugh Borton, *Japan's Modern Century: From Perry to 1970*, 2nd ed. (New York: Ronald Press, 1970), 82–83.

8   John E. Van Sant, *Pacific Pioneers: Japanese Journeys to America and Hawaii, 1850–80* (Urbana: University of Illinois Press, 2000), 62–63.

9   Bill Hosokawa, *Nisei: The Quiet Americans*, rev. ed. (Boulder: University Press of Colorado, 2002), 37.

10   Matsudaira Tadaatsu died in 1888 and was buried in Denver's Riverside Cemetery, where a tombstone was erected in memory of the "First Japanese Resident of Colorado."

11   "Journeying Japs. A party of them arrive in Denver en route for Yale College," RMN, October 18, 1883.

12   "Japanese capitalists, N. Sumitomo and party will arrive in Denver Friday," DEP, May 5, 1897. Some other stories about Japanese businessmen and experts include "Japanese smelter men. They will inspect the big establishments of Denver," RMN, May 8, 1897, and "Japanese railway men. Investigating transportation system of America," RMN, April 15, 1896.

13   "Visitors from Japan. Prominent Japanese mining engineers visit Denver," RMN, October 18, 1896.

14   "Want a steel plant. Japs arrive with money in their clothes," DEP, November 9, 1896, and "Japanese invester [*sic*], Janani Sam will look over Colorado with a view to placing several bags of Japanese money," DEP, May 7, 1899.

15   "Will invest in oil. Japanese capitalists interested in Florence," DEP, July 21, 1896, and "Leased oil fields. Japanese investor becomes interested in Florence properties," DEP, July 24, 1896.

16   Ninkovich, *The United States and Imperialism*, 38.

17   Moon-Ho Jung, *Coolies and Cane: Race, Labor, and Sugar in the Age of Emancipation* (Baltimore: John Hopkins University Press, 2006), 223. Jung believes that the term *coolie* is a controversial one and that "it is far more instructive to argue that no one in the United States or the Caribbean was

really a 'coolie,' a racialized and racializing figure that denied Asian migrants the liberal subjectivity that 'immigrants' presumably possessed." Moon-Ho Jung, "Coolie," in *Keywords for American Cultural Studies*, ed. Bruce Burgett and Glenn Hendler (New York: New York University Press, 2007), 64–66.

18   Lynette Holloway, "Re-enslaved: How African-American Bondage Came Back after Emancipation," *Humanities* 34, no. 2 (March-April 2013): 38.

19   "The fraternization of races," RMN, July 28, 1869.

20   "Frederick Douglass," RMN, October 17, 1887.

21   Ibid. In contrast to Douglass, W. E. B. DuBois saw Chinese, Japanese, and Koreans as belonging to the same side of the color line as he did. See Kwame Anthony Appiah, "Race in the Modern World: The Problem of the Color Line," *Foreign Affairs* 94, no. 2 (March-April 2015), 2.

22   Irwin A. Tang, "The Chinese Texan Experiment," in *Asian Texans: Our Histories and Our Lives*, ed. Irwin A. Tang (Austin, TX: The It Works, 2007), 30.

23   Ibid., 29.

24   Ibid., 28–29.

25   Andrew Gyory, *Closing the Gate: Race, Politics, and the Chinese Exclusion Act* (Chapel Hill: University of North Carolina Press, 1998), 31.

26   "Memphis labor convention," RMN, July 15, 1868.

27   Jung, *Coolies and Cane*, 102.

28   "Chinese in Louisiana," DCCR, May 21, 1871.

29   DCCR, August 21, 1869, Baker transcript.

30   "John Chinaman in Colorado," RMN, April 24, 1874.

31   Ibid. Also see "The assertion that the Chinese do not invest their earnings in this country is well answered by the Sacramento Union," DCCR, December 21, 1870.

32   "Idaho Territory," *Wikipedia,* last modified July 3, 2015, http://en.wikipedia .org/w/index.php?title=Idaho_Territoryoldid=626058796. George Everett, "Butte's Far Eastern Influences," 2004, www.butteamerica.com/fareast.htm.

33   "One of our enterprising democratic fellow-citizens sends us the following communication," DCCR, September 3, 1872.

TWO. CHINESE PIONEERS

1   "The first John Chinaman arrived in Denver yesterday," CT, June 29, 1869. Another report can be found in "John Chinaman arrived in town today," RMN, June 30, 1869.

2   Mike Flanagan, "Early migrants face mob rule, legal bigotry," DP, March 27, 1988.

3   "Our Chinamen are spreading out," CT, November 30, 1870.

4   Roger Daniels, *Asian America: Chinese and Japanese in the United States since 1850* (Seattle: University of Washington Press, 1988), 33–34.

5   "Chinese cheap labor," RMN, April 5, 1876.

6   Renny Christopher, *The Viet Nam War/The American War: Images and Representations in Euro-American and Vietnamese Exile Narratives* (Amherst: University of Massachusetts Press, 1995), 123.

7   "Chinese laborers," RMN, November 30, 1869.

8   Ibid.

9   "Changes in labor and trade," RMN, July 1, 1869.

10   Ibid.

11   "Chinese laborers."

12   "Changes in labor and trade."

13   Ibid.

14   Ibid.

15   "The fraternization of races," RMN, July 28, 1869.

16   Governor Edward M. McCook, "Female Suffrage," in "Message to the Colorado Legislature, January 4, 1870," in *Council Journal of the Legislative Assembly of the Territory of Colorado, Eighth Session* (Central City, CO: David C. Collier), 19.

17   Ibid., 21.

18   Ibid., 20.

19   Ibid., 21.

20   Governor Edward M. McCook, "Conclusion," in "Message to the Colorado Legislature, January 4, 1870," in *Council Journal of the Legislative Assembly of the Territory of Colorado, Eighth Session* (Central City, CO: David C. Collier), 23.

21   Governor Edward M. McCook, "Emigration," in "Message to the Colorado Legislature, January 4, 1870," in *Council Journal of the Legislative Assembly of the Territory of Colorado, Eighth Session* (Central City, CO: David C. Collier), 20–22.

22   Ibid.

23   Ronald Skeldon, "Reluctant Exiles or Bold Pioneers: An Introduction to Migration from Hong Kong," in *Reluctant Exiles? Migration from Hong Kong and the New Overseas Chinese*, ed. Ronald Skeldon (Armonk, NY: M. E. Sharpe, 1994), 7. Thomas Archdeacon provides a similar set of figures in *Becoming American: An Ethnic History*, cited in Harry H. L. Kitano and Roger Daniels, *Asian Americans: Emerging Minorities*, 3rd ed. (Upper Saddle River, NJ: Prentice Hall, 2001), 22.

24   Jean Pfaelzer, *Driven Out: The Forgotten War against Chinese Americans* (New York: Random House, 2007), xxv.

25   Elmer Clarence Sandmeyer, *The Anti-Chinese Movement in California* (Urbana: University of Illinois Press, 1939).

26 "Cannon fears Chinese," RMN, December 26, 1897.

27 Mary Roberts Coolidge, *Chinese Immigration* (New York: Henry Holt, 1909), 22.

28 "Chinamen and Chinese labor," DMR, August 2, 1867.

29 Unless otherwise indicated, statistical data on the Chinese population (as well as on the Irish and Italians) is based on *A Compendium of the Ninth Census, June 1, 1870* (Washington, DC: Government Printing Office, 1872); *Statistics of the Population of the United States,* vol. 1 of the Tenth Decennial Census (Washington, DC: Government Printing Office, 1883); *A Compendium of the Tenth Census, June 1, 1880* (Washington, DC: Government Printing Office, 1883); *Statistics of the Population of the United States,* vol. 1, part 1 of the Eleventh Decennial Census (Washington, DC: Government Printing Office, 1895); and *Compendium of the Eleventh Census, 1890* (Washington, DC: Government Printing Office, 1892).

30 "Chinaman's New Year," RMN, February 6, 1875.

31 "The Heathen Chinee. What the Celestial economists are doing in the way of solving the labor problem in Colorado," RMN, July 19, 1873.

32 Ibid.

33 "The labor employed the past year has been Chinese," FS, reported in the GT, October 28, 1874.

34 RMN, August 19, 1869, CHS index.

35 "The Chinese," DRC, November 8, 1880.

36 "About thirty Chinamen have just arrived from the West to reinforce Camerontown, making in the neighborhood of 150 Celestials at that camp," DCCR, January 14, 1874.

37 "Some claim-owners over south, encouraged, no doubt, by Cameron's success in importing cheap laborers, propose bringing in a lot of Chinese miners next spring," DCCR, November 7, 1873.

38 "The *Tribune* has at length heard that the Cameron placer mine, on North Clear Creek, is to be worked by Chinamen," DCCR, January 17, 1873.

39 DCCR, August 8, 1873, Baker transcript.

40 DCCR, September 17, 1873, Baker transcript.

41 "The Heathen Chinee," RMN, April 4, 1874.

42 Ibid.

43 DRC, August 9, 1890, Baker transcript.

44 "The labor employed the past year has been Chinese."

45 Ibid.

46 Richard White, *"It's Your Misfortune and None of My Own": A New History of the American West* (Norman: University of Oklahoma Press, 1991), 288.

47 "Chinamen robbed," DDT, September 24, 1878. For another robbery, in Silver Plume, see DCCR, June 19, 1878, Baker transcript. Sometimes the Chinese were

the ones doing the robbing. See, for example, "Arrested and locked up," DRC, October 26, 1883; "Black Hawk," RMN, November 3, 1883; "Central," RMN, January 16, 1884; and DRC, February 22, 1884, Baker transcript.

48 DRC, March 3, 1882, Baker transcript.

49 "Chinese vs. whites," RMS, October 1, 1881.

50 "A Chinese bandit. Mi Gow, a heathen desperado, here from Central City," DEP, January 13, 1897.

51 "Celestial sinners. Caucasian against Mongolian—the survival of the fittest," RMN, October 31, 1880.

52 "Social pests who are invading the soil of the country corrupting the morality of its life and ruining the recompense of labor," RMN, October 29, 1880.

53 "Driving off Chinamen," WCCR, April 8, 1874, and "City and vicinity," RMN, March 6, 1874.

54 "Driving off Chinamen."

55 "The Nederland troubles," April 1, 1874, and WCCR, March 30, 1874, CHS index.

56 "The Heathen Chinee."

57 "Driving off Chinamen."

58 "No Chinese in Leadville," DDT, May 8, 1879.

59 Robert G. Athearn, *The Coloradans* (Albuquerque: University of New Mexico Press, 1976), 178.

60 "Justice of the Peace in early Leadville," *Steamboat Pilot*, December 3, 1936.

61 "John Chinamen," DRC, August 2, 1880.

62 Ibid., citing the *Alpine True Fissure*.

63 "The advent of a lot of Chinamen into Breckenridge," WRC, May 21, 1880.

64 LeRoy R. Hafen, ed., *Colorado and Its People: A Narrative and Topical History of the Centennial State*, vol. 2 (New York: Lewis Historical Publishing, 1948), 110.

65 Ibid.

66 Leonard Dinnerstein and David M. Reimers, *Ethnic Americans,* 3rd ed. (New York: Harper and Row, 1988), 48–49.

67 Thomas Guglielmo, "'NO COLOR BARRIER': Italians, Race, and Power in the United States," in *Are Italians White? How Race Is Made in America,* ed. Jennifer Guglielmo and Salvatore Salerno (New York: Routledge, 2003), 30.

68 Kent G. Sieg, "The Chinese Community in Park County, as Indicative of the Chinese Experience in the Western Mining Areas" (unpublished student paper, University of Colorado, Boulder), 20.

69 Ibid., 21.

70 The *New York Times* gives another account based on personal interviews with

Thayer, who is elevated to heroic stature. "Race hatred in the West," NYT, November 24, 1879.

71 "'Chinese Must Go': Battle cry of the Italian miners at Como," RMN, November 23, 1879.

72 There are conflicting accounts of this incident. See, for example, "Holocaust: Several Chinese reported burned to death at Como," RMN, August 1, 1893; "Chinese must go: The Celestials of Como are given a house warming," RMN, August 2, 1893; and "Chinese laundry and house burned in Como," *Fairplay Flume*, August 3, 1893.

73 "Opening of a long conflict," RMN, November 26, 1879.

74 "Chinese cheap labor: A workingman's protest against the invasion of the heathen hordes," RMN, December 2, 1879.

75 "Chinese cheap labor. Governor Evans explains the recent troubles at Como and defends his employment of the 'Heathen Chinee,'" RMN, November 25, 1879.

76 "Introducing Chinese," RMN, November 29, 1879.

77 Ibid.

78 Ibid.

79 "A Chinese organ," RMN, December 2, 1879.

80 Edna Bonacich, "A Theory of Ethnic Antagonism: The Split Labor Market," in *From Different Shores: Perspectives on Race and Ethnicity in America*, 2nd ed., ed. Ronald Takaki (New York: Oxford University Press, 1994).

81 According to Xi Wang, "Chinese in Denver: A Demographic Perspective, 1870–1885," *Essays and Monographs in Colorado History* 12 (1991), the Italians were "given the most menial jobs when blacks and Chinese were not available." After the Chinese were excluded from the country and no longer posed a threat, some people began to prefer them to the Italians. When the Santa Fe Railway planned to establish Italian colonies in Arizona and California, local residents vehemently protested and even said, "Chinese would be much more acceptable than the Italians, the Orientals always proving to be quiet, peaceable neighbors, and adept in agriculture and horticulture," DT, July 11, 1901.

82 "The Chinese conquest: The Italian miners at Como are paid off and discharged," RMN, November 25, 1879.

83 Lynn Perrigo, "The Cornish Miners of Gilpin County," *Colorado Magazine* 14 (May 1937).

84 Ibid., 97–98.

85 Ralph Mann, *After the Gold Rush: Society in Grass Valley and Nevada City, California, 1849–1870* (Stanford, CA: Stanford University Press, 1982), 188.

86 "Boulder University Commencement Exercise," DDT, June 19, 1879.

87 Ibid.

1   "Deadly opium," RMN, October 9, 1880.

2   "Fumes from the Orient, midnight prowl through Denver's opium joints,"
      RMN, March 28, 1880. Other RMN articles include: "Celestials corralled. The
      police make a raid on the opium joints," October 12, 1880, and "Horrible habit.
      Arrest and trial of Chinese for opium practices," February 6, 1881.

3   See the political cartoon portraying Wo Jim, with the caption "Hatchet man
      calm in security of city jail," DR, August 11, 1903, for an example of the way
      Chinese were perceived by the public.

4   "Oriental Denver. Tragedy, comedy and romance of the quaint followers of
      Confucius," RMN, August 10, 1902.

5   Forbes Parkhill, *The Wildest of the West* (New York: Henry Holt, 1951), 110.
      Though much was made of violence in Chinatown, there were very few
      recorded homicides and these were between Chinese. See *Murder Book of
      Detective Sam Howe, 1860–1921*, Sam Howe Collection, Stephen H. Hart Library
      and Research Center, History Colorado Center, for the specific instances.

6   "'Hop Alley' to be knocked off map of Denver, says chief," *Fort Collins Courier*,
      January 10, 1922.

7   S. A. Meyer, DT, December 7, 1909.

8   Murray Sperber, "*Chinatown* 'Do as Little as Possible' Polanski's Message and
      Manipulation," *Jump Cut: A Review of Contemporary Media* 3 (1974).

9   *Deadwood* is a Western television series that was created, produced, and largely
      written by David Milch, and aired from March 21, 2004, to August 27, 2006.

10   Alex Witchel, "The man who can make Bruce Lee tall," *New York Times
      Magazine*, November 7, 2012.

11   Gerald E. Rudolph, "The Chinese in Colorado, 1869–1911" (master's thesis,
      University of Colorado, 1964), 91n1.

12   Robert G. Athearn, *The Coloradans* (Albuquerque: University of New Mexico
      Press, 1976), 179.

13   "Oriental Denver."

14   "A Chinese Consul for Colorado," DRC, January 6, 1881, and "When rogues fall
      out. Chin Poo, a prominent and wealthy Washee man, makes the accusation,"
      RMN, July 12, 1889. It should be noted that Chin Poo was not above paying
      money to William A. Glasson, who managed a private detective agency to protect
      the members of his faction from police harassment. Clark Secrest, *Hell's Belles:
      Prostitution, Vice, and Crime in Early Denver, with a Biography of Sam Howe,
      Frontier Lawman*, rev. ed. (Boulder: University Press of Colorado, 2002), 118.

15   "Chinamen alert. Imposing religious rites. Evil spirits conjured and sent
      chasing the Mikado. China bound to finally win," RMN, July 31, 1894.

16   "Chinese are going. Old quarters on Wazee Street to be abandoned for more

healthy accommodations. The fever-breeding hive filled with pestilential germs of fifteen years' growth to be razed," RMN, August 14, 1889, and "Took forty-five. A big raid on John Taylor's Chinamen last night," RMN, June 19, 1891.

17 "Chinese colonies. The outlook is for numerous sudden calls for the police ambulance," DEP, November 25, 1897.

18 "Fighting factions. Chinese interpreter frightened into silence by threats of instant death," RMN, January 4, 1890, and "A Chinese vendetta. Little Ho Juey used simply as an instrument in the hands of cunning rascals," RMN, January 5, 1890.

19 "Chinese colonies."

20 "Chinese are going."

21 "Oriental Denver."

22 This is probably the group that Rudolph, in "The Chinese in Colorado," 91, identified as the "Horn Boy faction."

23 "Frisco highbinders. Denver's Chinatown excited and aroused over the proposed importation of Celestials," RMN, November 15, 1892, and "Job lot of gods causes a bitter factional fight in Chinatown," DP, February 3, 1901.

24 "Chinese are going."

25 "A Chinese boycott. Celestials decline to give countenance to San Toy," DP, February 6, 1903.

26 "The Chinese must go. So say the property owners on Wazee Street," RMN, August 23, 1882.

27 Tom Sherlock, *Colorado's Heathcare Heritage: A Chronology of the Nineteenth and Twentieth Centuries* (Bloomington, IN: iUniverse, 2013), 1:221.

28 Carl Abbott, Stephen J. Leonard, and Thomas J. Noel, *Colorado: A History of the Centennial State,* 4th ed. (Boulder: University Press of Colorado, 2005), 225–227.

29 Ibid., 197.

30 "Chinamen corralled. A large number of Mongolians arrested for making pest hole of Chinatown," RMN, December 7, 1883 and "Pleaded guilty," RMN, December 9, 1883.

31 "The Chinese must go."

32 "Hotbed of disease. Businessmen unanimously favor an early removal of the Chinese quarter," RMN, February 23, 1889.

33 "Denver's Chinatown will be forced to clean up," RMN, May 31, 1900.

34 Jeannine Natsuko Shinozuka, "From a 'Contagious' to a 'Poisonous Yellow Peril'? Japanese and Japanese Americans in Public Health and Agriculture, 1890s-1950" (PhD diss., University of Minnesota, 2009), 41.

35 Ibid., 29.

36 Patricia Ourada, "The Chinese in Colorado," *Colorado Magazine* 29, no. 4

(October 1952): 280, says that from May to September 1870, there were forty-two Chinese (twenty-nine men and thirteen women) living in thirteen small houses between Wazee and Wiwata Streets in Denver's Chinatown.

37   Xi Wang, "The Chinese in Denver: A Demographic Perspective, 1870–1885," *Essays and Monographs in Colorado History* 12 (1991).

38   Parkhill, *Wildest of the West*, 109.

39   "Clear Creek echoes. Dr Young Bong," RMN, January 1, 1881.

40   "No Ticket, No Washee! That is the song the Chinese washman chants," RMN, April 1, 1880.

41   See Wolfgang Mieder, "No Tickee, No Washee," *Western Folklore* 55, no. 1 (Winter 1996): 1–40, www.jstor.org/stable/1500147; and Terry Abraham, "'No Tickee No Washee': Sympathetic Representations of the Chinese in American Humor," University of Idaho, July 2003, www.uiweb.uidaho.edu/special -collections/papers/notickee.htm.

42   Rudolph, "The Chinese in Colorado," 103.

43   *Colorado Bureau of Labor Statistics, Second Biennial Report, 1889–1890* (Denver: Collier and Cleveland Lithography Company, 1890), 57. Also, for a typical view of "washee-washee" as the cause of economic ruin for washerwomen and their families, see James Amaziah Whitney, *The Chinese and the Chinese Question*, 2nd ed. (New York: Tibbals, 1888), 124.

44   "Laundrymen. Object to the Chinese wash houses and want them closed on Sundays," DEP, June 4, 1897.

45   *Ouray Times*, July 16, 1881.

46   "Two Coolies," DEP, February 18, 1898.

47   "White Chinaman. Death of Chung Ling Sou. A pioneer of the Chinese colony, and one high in the estimation of his race," RMN, August 13, 1894.

48   Among the Chinese in nineteenth-century Colorado, Chin Lin Sou is the only person for whom there is any appreciable knowledge. He is included in John H. Monnett and Michael McCarthy, *Colorado Profiles: Men and Women Who Shaped the Centennial State* (Niwot: University Press of Colorado, 1996), 75–81. In addition to the occasional vignettes and newspaper articles about Chin Lin Sou, his descendants have honored his memory by compiling materials about his life as well as those of other members of his family. William Jung Jr. gathered these materials in *Biography of Chin Lin Sou*, a portfolio of pertinent information deposited in the Chin Lin Sou Collection (collection number 113) at the Stephen H. Hart Library and Research Center, History Colorado Center, Denver. In the portfolio is an essay by Chin's granddaughter, Ruth Chin, with the help of Miss Mary Van Deren, Teacher Presbyterian Church, entitled "The Story of a Colorado Pioneer," and an essay by his great-great-granddaughters Carolyn and Linda Jew, entitled "Chin Lin Sou."

49   WRC, 1877, Baker transcript.

50   Monnett and McCarthy, *Colorado Profiles*, 79–80.

51   Carolyn and Linda Jew, "Chin Lin Sou," in *Biography of Chin Lin Sou*, 8.

52   Sucheng Chan, *Asian Americans: An Interpretive History* (Boston: Twayne, 1991), 47. Chin was not the only Chinese to become an American citizen, but he was one of the first. In Denver, it was reported that there were as many as a hundred Chinese who were naturalized citizens and exercised the right to vote. "Chinamen who vote," RMN, October 12, 1891.

53   Elaine Abrams Clearfield, *Our Colorado Immortals in Stained Glass* (Denver: Mountain Bell, 1986), 64.

54   Rose Hum Lee, *The Chinese in the United States of America* (Hong Kong: Hong Kong University Press, 1960), 175.

55   Caroline Bancroft, *Gulch of Gold: A History of Central City, Colorado* (Denver: Sage, 1958), 260. See "Great conflagration in Central City," RMN, May 22, 1974, and Corinne Hunt, "The Chinese Miners of Gilpin County," *Colorado Gambler* 3, no. 24 (August 18–31, 1994).

56   DCCR, May 24, 1874, Baker transcript.

57   It was also reported that the conflagration might have originated in Morgan's blacksmith shop, which adjoined the building where the Chinese lived. DCCR, May 21, 1874, Baker transcript.

58   Clearfield, *Our Colorado Immortals in Stained Glass*, 64.

59   Chin, "The Story of a Colorado Pioneer," in *Biography of Chin Lin Sou*.

60   After receiving permission from the Chin family, Ida Kruse McFarlane donated money for a bronze plaque on the chair, which was inscribed with the words "Chin Lin Sou, 1871." "Opera House," in *Biography of Chin Lin Sou*, 33.

61   "White Chinaman."

62   "Frontier Sketches," in *Denver Field and Farm,* Dawson Scrapbook, IX, Stephen H. Hart Library and Research Center, History Colorado Center, Denver.

63   Clearfield, *Our Colorado Immortals In Stained Glass*, 64–67.

64   Interview with Linda S. Jew, Denver, August 14, 2002. See William Wei, "Five Generations in Colorado: An Interview with the Descendants of Chin Lin Sou," *Colorado Heritage* (Autumn 2002): 14–16.

65   Jean Pfaelzer, *Driven Out: The Forgotten War against Chinese Americans* (New York: Random House, 2007), 103. See Susan Lee Johnson's *Roaring Camp: The Social World of the California Gold Rush* (New York: W. W. Norton, 2000) for a reassessment of gender roles in California during the gold rush period.

66   David G. Atwill and Yurong Y. Atwill, *Sources in Chinese History: Diverse Perspectives from 1644 to the Present* (Upper Saddle River, NJ: Prentice Hall, 2010), 5–6.

67 Millard F. Everett, "Early Denver boasted flourishing Chinatown," *Denver Catholic Register*, February 13, 1941.

68 "Chinamen in the pageant, they will play an important part in the Festival," RMN, September 18, 1987.

69 See chapter 26, "Polytheism, Pantheism, Atheism," in Arthur H. Smith, *Chinese Characteristics*, 4th ed. (New York: Fleming H. Ravell Company, 1894).

70 Harte's poem, "Plain Language from Truthful James," was intended as satire but was widely read as an anti-Chinese text and reprinted under the title "Heathen Chinee." Francis Bret Harte, "Plain Language from Truthful James," Bartleby.com, 1870, www.bartleby.com/102/200.html.

71 "A Chinese church. Opening of a Joss house on Wazee Street last evening—grand feast this afternoon," RMN, April 24, 1884.

72 "The NEWS, as the organ and champion of the Salvation army, regrets very much," RMN, February 6, 1889.

73 "Fighting for Joss. Chinese factions find a new subject to engage attention," RMN, March 20, 1890.

74 "Frisco highbinders."

75 "New Chinese temple. Denver Chinamen plan for a place of worship," DEP, August 26, 1896.

76 "A Chinese church," RMN, April 24, 1884.

77 "Chinamen alert" and "Devil's festival," RMN, October 12, 1894.

78 "Their bones go home. Lively trade in the shipment of dead Chinamen," DEP, August 19, 1896.

79 See "Buried with banners," RMN, November 19, 1882, for an account of the funeral of Chin Ping Quock, and DT, November 25, 1902, for a description of the funeral of Kong Ring, who is described as the king of Chinese gamblers and one of Denver's most famous pagans.

80 "Mobbed a funeral. Heartless desecration at a big Chinese burial, " RMN, March 19, 1894.

81 "Chinese hotel to be opened here. The only one between 'Frisco and the East," DR, July 17, 1901.

82 See "Christian Chinamen," RMN, February 18, 1882, and Wilbur Fiske Stone, ed. *History of Colorado*, vol. 2 (Chicago: S. J. Clarke Publishing Company, 1918), 610–611, for information about the Stoddards.

83 Helen Webster, "The Chinese School of the Central Presbyterian Church of Denver, Later Known as The Oriental Mission," *Colorado Magazine* 40, no. 1 (January 1963): 57–63, and 40, no. 2 (April 1963): 132–137.

84 "What Dr. Westwood says of the riot," DR, November 2, 1880.

85 "Christian Chinamen watched," RMN, January 29, 1894.

86   "One reason for conversion. Christian Chinese among the most artful smugglers," RMN, October 26, 1897.

87   Ibid. According to W. H. Chamberlain, a special officer of the government investigating the presence of illegal Chinese immigrants in Denver, "The only oath a Chinaman feels under obligation to respect is an oath taken in a graveyard over the head of a chicken. Any Chinaman will acknowledge that an oath taken under such circumstances is binding."

88   "Oriental Denver."

89   According to the DP, July 22, 1963, police began raiding Chinatown gambling and opium dens periodically beginning in 1910 and closed them down in 1927.

90   See Diana L. Ahmad, *The Opium Debate and Chinese Exclusion Laws in the Nineteenth-Century American West* (Reno: University of Nevada Press, 2007), for a discussion of the important role that opium played in stimulating Sinophobic propaganda and calls for the exclusion of Chinese from the country. Also see Secrest, *Hell's Belles*, for a description of the sale and consumption of opium in Denver, and of the opium dens themselves, including racially segregated ones for white and black customers. The so-called "black and tan saloons" were closed down in 1913 as part of a general cleanup before some conventions came to Denver. Secrest, *Helles Belles*, 117.

91   "The opium pipe, the Heathen Chinee and the narcotic of death. How John smokes his pipe. The interior of a Chinese house in Denver," RMN, September 17, 1873.

92   "Growth of the opium habit in Denver," DT, February 1, 1999.

93   "Fumes from the Orient."

94   "The Chinese cop. Our Mongolian policeman in the interviewer's hands," RMN, December 8, 1881. In addition to having the first Chinese policeman, Denver also has the distinction of having employed the first Chinese detective, Moy Gop, in the United States in 1900. Secrest, *Helles Belles*, 116.

95   "Opium plot discovered. Denver Celestials are engaged in illegitimate manufacturing," RMN, December 10, 1894.

96   Occasionally, white opium smokers were identified in the public press. "All he wanted to know. The Chinese furnished the convicting evidence," DEP, March 14, 1898. According to Chinese police officer Louis Johnson, white patrons, generally variety actors and actresses, and sporting men and prostitutes, were allowed to come into the opium dens at two or three in the morning. "The Chinese cop."

97   *Denver Saturday Night,* May 26, 1936. This clipping can be found in the Western History Collection, Denver Public Library.

98   "Chinatown war settled for $3.80 and peace reigns in alley again," RMN, April 22, 1915.

99   Ed Quillen, "Of course the Drug War is bigotry in action. What else is new?" DP, June 11, 2000.

100   Ed Quillen, review of *Menace in the West,* by Henry O. Whiteside, *Colorado Central Magazine,* November 1997, http://cozine.com/1997-november/menace-in-the-west-by-henry-o-whiteside/.

101   Ibid.

102   Ed Quillen, "Of course the Drug War is bigotry in action," DP, June 11, 2000.

103   James T. Smith, *Eighth Biennial Report of the Bureau of Labor Statistics of the State of Colorado, 1901–1902* (Denver: Smith Brooks Printing Company, 1902), 299.

104   The sociologist Rose Hum Lee predicted as much in her study, "The Growth and Decline of Chinese Communities in the Rocky Mountain Region" (PhD diss., University of Illinois, December 1947), which was reprinted by Arno Press in 1978; 345-351.

105   See table 5 in Rose Hum Lee, *The Growth and Decline of Chinese Communities in the Rocky Mountain Region* (New York: Arno Press, 1978), 34. The Denver population was 322,412.

106   "Report to the Foreign-Born Committee, Chinese Women," in Kent G. Sieg, "The Chinese Community in Park County, Colorado as Indicative of the Chinese Experience in the Western Mining Areas" (unpublished student paper, University of Colorado, Boulder).

107   Robert L. Perkin, "Denver's Chinatown fades away," RMN, July 1, 1951.

FOUR. IMPORTING CHINESE PROSTITUTES, EXCLUDING
CHINESE WIVES

1   "The *Tribune* adds to the current news by saying a new importation of female Celestials has reached Denver," DCCR, June 30, 1870.

2   Lucie Cheng, "Free, Indentured, Enslaved: Chinese Prostitutes in Nineteenth-Century American Sexual Borderlands," in *Sexual Borderlands: Constructing an American Sexual Past,* ed. Kathleen Kennedy and Sharon Ullman (Columbus: Ohio State University Press, 2003), 141.

3   Ibid., 141–142. Cheng notes that only four such contracts, dating from 1873–99, can be verified from original sources. The contract in Herbert Ashbury, *The Barbary Coast* (New York: Pocket Books, 1957), 130, though widely quoted, has no clear provenance and may not be authentic.

4   Mainly because of Ruthanne Lum McCunn's biographical novel *Thousand Pieces of Gold* (Boston: Beacon, 2004), first published in 1981, the best-known Chinese prostitute in nineteenth-century America is Polly Bemis (also known as "China Polly," Lalu Nathoy, or Gung Heung). In 1991, a film of the same

name was produced, starring Korean American actress Rosalind Chao as Polly Bemis. Another well-known prostitute is Ah Yuen (also known as "China Mary"). According to her obituary, she had worked in San Francisco, Denver, and Park City. See "'Riches to rags' career ends for China Mary, Full century of life closes for Evanston character, once toast of her countrymen and possessor of riches," *The Evanston News and Advertiser*, January 17, 1939. For information about Chinese prostitution, see Benson Tong, *Unsubmissive Women: Chinese Prostitutes in Nineteenth-Century San Francisco* (Norman: University of Oklahoma Press, 1994).

5   Unless otherwise noted, references to "A Chinese Romance" are from a typescript of "A Chinese Romance," *Daily Denver Tribune*, June 1, 1874, in the file "Ethnic Groups—Chinese," Colorado Historical Society, Denver, Colorado. Also see "Marriage licenses were granted yesterday to three Chinamen who have their habitation in Denver," RMN, May 30, 1874.

6   "Chow Chow. How some almond-eyed Celestials had nuptials tied—A bride thrown in prison—release after a few hours incarceration—interesting scenes in the Justices' courts—a riot threatened—a sequel and some comments," RMN, May 31, 1874. The faux Chinese phrase "Chow Chow" is the name given to the mixed collections of music popular at the time. Here it probably refers here to the mélange of events in the story.

7   J. P. C. Poulton, Third Lecture: "Frontier Peculiarities and Wild Western Scenes," 36–38, in the J. P. C. Poulton Papers, 1870–1876, Denver Public Library, Western History Collection.

8   "The Chinese cop. Our Mongolian policeman in the interviewer's hands," RMN, December 9, 1881.

9   See table 6.3 in Cheng, "Free, Indentured, Enslaved," 43.

10 "Chow Chow" identified the principals as Fung Leung and King Yok, and Low Quong and Gime Yow.

11 In "Chow Chow," Judge Whittier is referred to as Judge Walker.

12 Jan MacKell, *Brothels, Bordellos, and Bad Girls: Prostitution in Colorado, 1860–1930* (Albuquerque: University of New Mexico Press, 2004), 195.

13 Henry Yu, "Reflections on Edward Said's Legacy: Orientalism, Cosmopolitanism, and Enlightenment," *Journal of the Canadian Historical Association/Revue de la Société historique du Canada* 17, no. 2 (2006): 17. www.erudit.org/revue/jcha/2006/v17/n2/016588ar.pdf.

14 Edward W. Said, *Orientalism* (New York: Vintage, 1979), 290. His chapter 3, "Orientalism Now," discusses the phenomenon in the context of the United States and the American West.

15 MacKell, in *Brothels, Bordellos, and Bad Girls*, 274n13, observes that in Cripple Creek and Silverton there were "Mikado parlor houses."

16 Sheridan Prasso, in *The Asian Mystique* (New York: Public Affairs, 2005), 10, notes that the myth about Asian women having horizontal vaginas has been around since the Korean War. The myth was probably started much earlier than that.

17 The typographical errors in the typescript of "A Chinese Romance" may have been in the original newspaper article.

18 J. P. C. Poulton Papers, Western History Collection, Denver Public Library, 38.

19 Vincent Canby, "The Screen: *McCabe and Mrs. Miller*: Miss Christie portrays prostitute in West, Beatty is a gambler in Altman's film," NYT, June 25, 1971.

20 Said, *Orientalism*, 6. Said actually says very little directly about women, earning for himself the sobriquet of "accidental feminist." Sondra Hale, "Edward Said—Accidental Feminist: Orientalism and Middle East Women's Studies," *Amerasia Journal* 31, no. 1 (2005): 1–5.

21 George Anthony Peffer, *If They Don't Bring Their Women Here: Chinese Female Immigration before Exclusion* (Urbana: University of Illinois Press, 1999).

22 Anne M. Butler, *Daughters of Joy, Sisters of Misery: Prostitutes in the American West, 1865–1890* (Urbana: University of Illinois Press, 1985), 6.

23 "The *Tribune* adds to the current news."

24 "A Chinese Romance" and William E. Roberts, "The Chinese Riot in Denver, Colorado, October 31, 1880," in Denver Veteran Volunteer Firemen's Association Papers, 1873–1946, 11.

25 MacKell, *Brothels, Bordellos, and Bad Girls*, 6. According to Cheng, "Free, Indentured, Enslaved," Chinese prostitutes, unlike their white counterparts, were able to leave their past behind after getting married. Chinese prostitutes were able to do this because the Chinese community did not attach the same stigma to prostitution that whites did.

26 Cheng, "Free, Indentured, Enslaved," 136–140.

27 A discussion of the opium problem and the Chinese can be found in Diana L. Ahmad, *The Opium Debate and Chinese Exclusion Laws in the Nineteenth-Century American West* (Reno: University of Nevada Press, 2007), and Henry O. Whiteside, *Menace in the West: Colorado and the American Experience with Drugs, 1873–1963* (Denver: Colorado Historical Society, 1997).

28 Sucheng Chan, "The Exclusion of Chinese Women, 1870–1943," in *Entry Denied: Exclusion and the Chinese Community in America, 1882–1943*, ed. Sucheng Chan (Philadelphia: Temple University Press, 1991), 138. According to Ian Buruma and Avishai Margalit, *Occidentalism: The West in the Eyes of Its Enemies* (New York: Penguin, 2004), 127, in the non-Western world, the West is held responsible for perverting sexual morality.

29 Stanford Lyman counted fourteen states, many of them in the American West and in the American South, with miscegenation laws preventing Asian–white

marriages. See Stanford Lyman, *Chinese Americans*, cited in "Multi-racialism and Asian Americans," Dartmouth, http://www.dartmouth.edu/~hist32/ History/Multi-racial.htm.

30   Ida Pruitt, *A Daughter of Han: The Autobiography of a Chinese Working Woman* (Stanford, CA: Stanford University Press, 1945), 239.

31   See Kerry Abrams, "Polygamy, Prostitution, and the Federalization of Immigration Law," *Columbia Law Review* 105, no. 3 (April 2005), for a discussion of the Page Act as an unprecedented federal immigration law to prohibit the entry of immigrants deemed undesirable.

32   Eithne Luibhéid, *Entry Denied: Controlling Sexuality at the Border* (Minneapolis: University of Minnesota Press, 2002), 31.

33   Abrams, "Polygamy, Prostitution, and Federalization," 642.

34   Cited in Peffer, *If They Don't Bring Their Women Here*, 67. The quotation is repeated and annotated on 108–109.

35   Ibid., 67.

36   George Anthony Peffer, "Forbidden Families: Emigration Experiences of Chinese Women under the Page Law, 1875–1882," *Journal of Ethnic History* 6, no. 1 (Fall 1986): 28–46.

37   Luibhéid, *Entry Denied*, 37.

38   Peffer, *If They Don't Bring Their Women Here*, 103.

39   Eunhye Kwon, "Interracial Marriages among Asian Americans in the U.S. West, 1880–1954" (PhD diss., University of Florida, 2011).

40   "Marrying Chinamen," *New York Herald*, reprinted in the RMN, September 21, 1879. The article also mentions that a Chinese had married a "colored woman," which was rarer still.

41   Ibid.

42   Ibid.

43   "The Chinese cop."

44   Ibid.

45   Unless noted otherwise, information about Leo Latt Sing and Nellie Mershon comes from the following DT accounts: "Tried to marry a Chinaman," June 11, 1902; "Chinaman and the white woman are freed in court," June 12, 1902; "Refused to marry Chinaman," June 13, 1902; "Sing weds Mrs. Mershon, June 15, 1902; and "She is finally Mrs. Sing," June 14, 1902.

46   DCCR, June 13, 1902, Baker transcript.

47   "She is finally Mrs. Sing."

48   "Chinaman and the white woman are freed in court," DT, June 12, 1902.

49   "Sing weds Mrs. Mershon."

50   "White neighbors try to drive away Chinaman," DT, December 30, 1909; "A Rapid Jap, Dr. Hara, who married Miss Gay, said to have another wife," DEP,

March 11, 1898; and Alice Rohe, "American woman arrested for stealing cheap kimono. Weeps in her cell while she tells of alleged conspiracy to keep her from her beloved Japanese husband." The latter article is in the Japanese American clipping file, Western History Collection, Denver Public Library Japanese American clipping file.

51 Bosley Crowther, "Screen: Sea adventure: Under Ten Flags on new double bill," NYT, September 16, 1960.

52 Roger Ebert, "The Ballad of Little Jo," *Sun Times*, September 10, 1993.

53 "Superbly solid! Grand Democratic demonstration last night," RMN, October 31, 1880.

54 Roberts, "Chinese Riot in Denver," 3.

55 Ibid.

56 Ibid.

57 Ibid., 10 and 11.

58 Buruma and Margalit, *Occidentalism*, 19.

FIVE. THE DENVER RACE RIOT AND ITS AFTERMATH

This chapter is based on William Wei, "The Anti-Chinese Riot in Denver, 1880: A Reconsideration," read at "Asians in America: A Conference for Scholars," Auraria Campus, Denver, Colorado, April 3, 1993; and "Denver Race Riot: Destruction, Reconstruction, and Disappearance of an Ethnic Enclave," read at the American Historical Association Pacific Branch meeting, Denver, Colorado, August 8–10, 2013.

1 Jean Pfaelzer, *Driven Out: The Forgotten War against Chinese Americans* (New York: Random House, 2007), xxv. *Driven Out* places the Denver race riot in the context of the ethnic cleansing of Chinese from the American West. Other works that have dealt with the riot include Roy T. Wortman, "Denver's Anti-Chinese Riot," *Colorado Magazine* 42, no. 4 (Fall 1965), which provides an early scholarly treatment, and Liping Zhu, *The Road to Chinese Exclusion: The Denver Riot, 1880 Election and the Rise of the West*, (Lawrence: University of Kansas Press, 2013), which interprets it as a political riot.

2 Richard Hogan, *Class and Community in Frontier Colorado* (Lawrence: University Press of Kansas, 1990), 46. See also GT, November 3, 1880, and *Colorado Sun*, November 6, 1880, for other newspaper accounts of the Denver race riot.

3 DCCR, September 21, 1876, Baker transcript.

4 "Utes and Chinese. Sensation caused by both becoming republican voters," RMN, October 6, 1880.

5 DCCR, September 21, 1876, Baker transcript.

6 "NOT A FORGERY!" RMN, October 31, 1880.

7   See Zhu, *Road to Chinese Exclusion,* for a discussion of the political significance of the Morey letter, its authorship, and the trial of the perpetrator for fraud.

8   "Garfield's record. His repeated votes in favor of cheap labor," RMN, October 31, 1880.

9   William E. Roberts, "The Chinese Riot in Denver, Colorado, October 31, 1880," in Denver Veteran Volunteer Firemen's Association Papers, 1873–1946, 1.

10   "About the row. . . . The outrageous throwing of water caused it all," RMN, November 1, 1880.

11   Robert L. Perkins, *The First Hundred Years: An Informal History of Denver and the Rocky Mountain News* (Garden City, NY: Doubleday, 1959), 352.

12   "Consistent or inconsistent, the News favors the white race against the Chinese," RMN, February 29, 1880.

13   "John Chinaman—the pest of the Pacific Coast . . . Workmen starving and women following prostitution through the competition of the wily heathen," RMN, October 23, 1880.

14   "A broad view. A mine owner who can profit by Chinaman but will not curse the state with them," RMN, October 30, 1880.

15   Unless otherwise noted, the description of the pro–Democratic Party parade and quotes from the various speakers are from "Superbly solid! Grand Democratic demonstration last night," RMN, October 31, 1880.

16   "Garfield convicted. The proof adduced by Hon. T. M. Patterson," RMN, October 31, 1880.

17   "Gilpin's glory," RMN, October 31, 1880.

18   Perkins, *The First Hundred Years,* 353.

19   Roberts, "The Chinese Riot," 1.

20   "Only Denver mob attack on Chinese came in 1880," RMN, April 22, 1934. Diamond Jubilee edition, 1859–1934.

21   John Asmussén's testimony during the coroner's inquest in *Executive Documents, 47th Congress, 1st Session, 1881–82, v. 1, Foreign Relations, no. 1, pt. 1, 2009* (Washington, DC: Government Printing Office, 1882) (hereafter referred to as FRUS), 332–333.

22   According to Mark M. Pomeroy, the mob consisted of about three thousand. This is the figure usually used in most reports about the riot. However, in his March 25, 1881, reply to Chinese minister Chen Lan Pin (aka Chen Lanbin), Secretary of State James G. Blaine referred to Frederick Bee's investigation and cited "an enraged mob numbering over 5,000."

23   Statement of M. M. Pomeroy, October 31, 1880, FRUS, 333–334.

24   DT, November 19, 1880.

25   "About the row."

26 "The radical split," RMN, October 31, 1880.

27 Mrs. W. M. Cole's testimony during the coroner's inquest, FRUS, 331. It should be noted that Mrs. Cole, along with Mrs. Bradbury, bravely waded into the hostile mob to rescue Look Young.

28 Stephan J. Leonard, "The Irish, English, and Germans in Denver, 1860–1890," *Colorado Magazine* 34, no. 2 (1977): 126–153.

29 "Ching Lee. A thrilling incident in connection with the Chinese riots," RMN, August 5, 1885.

30 Ibid.

31 Roberts, "Chinese Riot," 2. The RMN also blamed the riot on the hosing of the crowd with cold water, saying, "This naturally created great indignation and caused all that followed." "About the row," RMN, November 1, 1880.

32 Statement of M. M. Pomeroy.

33 "About the row."

34 Nicholas G. Kendall's testimony during the coroner's inquest, FRUS, 326.

35 Dr. O. G. Cranston's testimony during the coroner's inquest, FRUS, 328.

36 Frederick A. Bee to the Chinese Ministers, FRUS, 324.

37 A decade after the Denver race riot, three Chinese were lynched at Military Park, Denver. DCCR, July 26, 1890, Baker transcript. For the details that led to the lynching, see "Curran's odd ways, Jerking up Chinamen with a rope for the purpose of getting information," RMN, July 13, 1890, and "Outraged Chinamen," WRC, July 18, 1890.

38 Equal Justice Initiative, "Lynching in America: Confronting the Legacy of Racial Terror" (2015). www.eji.org/.../EJI%20Lynching%20in%20America%20SUMMARY.pdf.

39 Alex. Ealy's testimony during the coroner's inquest, FRUS, 329.

40 Geo. C. Hickey's testimony during the coroner's inquest, FRUS, 330.

41 Roberts, "Chinese Riot," 5.

42 Ibid., 6.

43 "Big demonstration in Denver," *Leadville Daily Herald*, November 2, 1880.

44 "The Last Word. Immense parades by the friends of both parties," *Leadville Daily Herald*, November 2, 1880.

45 "Clear Creek echoes: Central. Dr Young Bong," RMN, January 1, 1881.

46 Denver County (Early Arapahoe County) District Court Criminal Case Files (hereafter referred to as DCCC), nos. 2133, 2137, 2139, 2151–2154, 2167, 2168, 2184, Colorado State Archives. See chapter 5, "Justice Denied," in Zhu, *Road to Chinese Exclusion*, for a description of the trial.

47 DCCC, no. 2132.

48 FRUS, 326–333.

49 According to Ah Sin (aka Ah Sing), it was too dark for him to recognize any

of the assailants. Besides, by that time the mob had placed a rope around his neck and had dragged him out of the house. "Ah Sing (through Chee Quong, interpreter) testimony during the coroner's inquest," FRUS, 332.

50   Dr. C. C. Bradbury's testimony during the coroner's inquest, FRUS, 327.

51   Zhu, *Road to Chinese Exclusion*, 283–285.

52   DCCC, no. 2132.

53   Evarts's response reflects the legal quandary in which the federal government found itself. It was responsible for protecting aliens under international law, yet was unable to take the necessary steps to do so under the US Constitution, which makes it the state's responsibility to protect and compensate its residents. Jules Alexander Karlin, "The Indemnification of Aliens Injured by Mob Violence," in *Anti-Chinese Violence in North America*, ed. Roger Daniels (New York: Arno Press, 1978).

54   Evarts to Chen, December 30, 1880, FRUS, 319.

55   Ibid.

56   Ibid.

57   "Estimate of losses sustained by Chinese residents during the riot in Denver," October 31, 1880, FRUS, 325.

58   "Testimony before the coroner's jury sitting on the body of Sing Lee (aka Look Young)," FRUS, 326.

59   This is from the congressional record of the 45th Congress, cited in Catherine Lee, "Prostitutes and Picture Brides: Chinese and Japanese Immigration, Settlement, and American Nation-Building, 1870–1920" (Working Paper 70, Center for Comparative Immigration Studies, University of California at San Diego, February 2003).

60   Blaine to Chen, March 25, 1881, FRUS, 335.

61   A transcript of the Chinese Exclusion Act (1882) maybe be found at Our Documents, www.ourdocuments.gov/doc.php?doc=47.

62   Roger Daniels, *Coming to America: A History of Immigration and Ethnicity in American Life*, 2nd ed. (New York: Perennial, 2002), 271.

63   Delber L. McKee, *Chinese Exclusion versus the Open Door Policy, 1900–1906: Clashes over China Policy during the Roosevelt Era* (Detroit, MI: Wayne State University Press, 1977).

64   "House Passes Rep. Judy Chu's Resolution of Regret for the Chinese Exclusion Act," June 19, 2012, press release, Congresswoman Judy Chu's website, http://chu.house.gov/press-release/house-passes-rep-judy-chu's -resolution-regret-chinese-exclusion-act.

65   *Ouray Times*, May 20, 1882.

66   See Alexander Saxton, *The Indispensable Enemy: Labor and the Anti-Chinese Movement in California* (Berkeley: University of California Press, 1971), for

an analysis of how unions used Chinese workers as a scapegoat for the plight of American workers and a convenient recruitment tool for the nascent labor movement.

67 See Craig Storti, *Incident at Bitter Creek: The Story of the Rock Springs Chinese Massacre* (Ames: University of Iowa Press, 1991), for a recent study of the Rock Springs massacre; for eyewitness accounts, see George L. Erhard, "Labor Day— Fiftieth anniversary of the Chinese riot. Vivid recollections of Rock Springs residents of Wyoming's major race riot of September 2, 1885," *Wyoming Labor Journal*, August 30, 1935 (a typescript of the article can be found in the Chinese clipping file, Western History Collection, Denver Public Library); for an official account, see "Special Report of the Governor of Wyoming to the Secretary of the Interior Concerning Chinese Labor Troubles, 1885," Western History Collection, Denver Public Library.

68 According to one account, their arrival created tension in the already-crowded Chinese laundry business. See "Moon-eyed Mongolians. A number arrive from Rock Springs and are threatened with extermination by Denver Chinese," RMN, September 21, 1885.

69 Xiaoyan Zhou, "Qing Perceptions of Anti-Chinese Violence in the United States: Case Studies from the American West" (master's thesis, University of Wyoming, Laramie, 20008), 33.

70 "It is reported that 500 white coal miners at Carbon, Wyoming, and 200 at Louisville, Colorado, have quit work because the Union Pacific Railway company retains Chinese miners at Rock Springs, Wyoming," RMN, October 3, 1885.

71 "A large number of the coal miners employed by the Union Pacific in Colorado have refused to obey the recent order of the Knights of Labor to quit work," RMN, October 8, 1885.

72 "Chinamen must go. Inspector William O'Malley will ship out all Celestials having violated the Geary law," RMN, February 12, 1896.

73 Sometimes the crimes against the Chinese were a result of avarice rather than racism. Charles Cobb and W. B. Strickland were arrested for brutally assaulting and robbing Yee Hi, an aged Chinese laundryman, in Georgetown, Colorado. Cobb and Strickland hanged him three times to force him to reveal where he hid his money. RMN, February 17, 1907. Another concerned a Chinese man who died suddenly while traveling on the Colorado and Southern passenger train from Trinidad to Denver. His corpse was robbed of three thousand dollars. RMN, February 1, 1907.

74 *Denver Tribune*, June 20, 1900.

75 This phenomenon was evident in other places in the Intermountain West. When it was rumored that Chinese were going to be brought in to work on a

waterworks project in Nebraska, the executive committee of the local labor union began arming its members to deal with the arrival of "pigtails." See "A Chinese sensation in Omaha," DRC, November 3, 1880.

76   Jennifer Jung Hee Choi, "The Rhetoric of Inclusion: The I.W.W. and Asian Workers," *Ex Post Facto: Journal of the History Students at San Francisco State University* 8 (1999), http://userwww.sfsu.edu/epf/journal_archive/volume_VIII,_1999/choi_j.pdf.

77   "They expect trouble, Chinese laborers appear in Idaho Springs," RMN, January 22, 1895, and "Against Chinamen miners. Chinamen contractors take a job on the Wallace and stopped for work," *Daily Mining Record*, January 23, 1895.

78   "Two coolies, Chinese cheap labor in a state institution," DEP, February 18, 1898.

79   See chapter 8, "The Dog Tag Law," in Pfaelzer, *Driven Out*, for a detailed discussion of the Geary Act. For a California perspective on the Geary Act, see Elmer Clarence Sandmeyer, *The Anti-Chinese Movement in California* (Urbana: University of Illinois Press, 1973), 103–105.

80   Philip Chin, "Enforcing Chinese Exclusion Part 3: The Geary Act 3: Senate Debates," 7, www.chineseamericanheroes.org/history/Enforcing%20Chinese%20Exclusion%20Part%203%20-%20The%20Geary%20Act%203.pdf. A paraphrase of Hitt's remarks were published in "Chinese must go," RMN, May 5, 1892.

81   See Robert A. Bickers and Jeffrey N. Wasserstrom, "Shanghai's 'Dogs and Chinese Not Admitted' Sign: Legend, History and Contemporary Symbol," *China Quarterly* 142 (June 1995), for a discussion of the symbolism of this sign to Chinese.

82   "Chinese inspector dead. William P. O'Malley seized with an affection of the heart while at home," RMN, February 18, 1897. There may have been a bounty on Chinese who had violated the exclusion laws that encouraged the kidnapping of some of those living in Mexico, who were then turned over to the federal authorities in the United States. "Rather strange story, United States marshals accused of kidnapping Chinamen," RMN, November 25, 1892.

83   "Chinese in trouble. Inspector O'Malley keeps the Denver colony busy showing certificates," RMN, January 8, 1897; and "Raid on Chinatown, Inspector after Chinese without certificates," DEP, January 7, 1897.

84   "Sent back to China. Marshal Israel left this morning with the first two Chinamen to be deported," RMN, March 15, 1897.

85   "Black Friday in the Chinese calendar. Federal authorities haul into court all the Mongolians to be found to ascertain if they were properly provided with

certificates," RMN, October 23, 1897, and "Herded Johns. Chinese rushed to the Marshal's office on order of examination," DEP, October 22, 1897.

86   "Beware the Yellow Peril," *Aspen Democrat*, June 16, 1901.

87   Peter Kwong and Dušanka Miščević, *Chinese America: The Untold Story of America's Oldest and Newest Community* (New York: New Press, 2005), 126.

88   "Union miners banish cheap Asiatic labor," RMN, February 13, 1902.

89   "Chinese residents of Silverton ask protection. Seventy of them ordered to leave town by March 1—Secretary Hay calls on Governor Orman to inform him of the situation," DT, February 12, 1902.

90   "Chinese run out of Silverton with guns," DP, May 13 1902, and "Chinks quit Silverton," DP, May 15, 1902.

91   "Chinese trouble at Silverton is over, says Orman," DT, May 16, 1902.

92   "Miners against Chinese. Fight begun to drive Mongolians out of mining camps," NYT, March 9, 1902.

93   "Ouray citizens meet and discuss Chinese," DT, March 7, 1902, and October 22, 1902.

94   George Hamlin Fitch, "Chinese no longer menace labor," RMN, March 21, 1897.

95   "Importing Asiatic labor," RMN, May 6, 1900.

96   "Conspiracy against free labor," RMN, May 13, 1900.

97   "Union miners banish cheap Asiatic labor," RMN, February 13, 1902.

98   "Asiatic horde driven out of Colorado mining camps and promise is given that no further importations will be made," DP, February 13, 1902.

99   See House Joint Resolution No. 2, introduced by Representative Max Morris of Arapahoe County and approved on March 12, 1902, *House Journal (extra session), Thirteenth General Assembly of the State of Colorado* (Denver: Smith Brooks Printing Company, 1902), 181.

SIX. JAPANESE IMMIGRANTS

1   For a comparison between the two Asian groups, see chapter 7, "The Chinese and Japanese," in Robert A. Wilson and Bill Hosokawa, *East to America: A History of the Japanese in the United States* (New York: William Morrow, 1980).

2   Sucheng Chan, *Asian Americans: An Interpretative History* (Boston: Twayne, 1991), 9.

3   "The thrifty Japanese. A race of industrious people who are simple in their tastes," RMN, November 8, 1893.

4   "The Jap face. Unlike the face of other Asiatics, and deserving of study," DEP, May 14, 1895.

5   Occasionally, famous Japanese like Yamagata Aritomo, father of the modern Japanese Army, visited Denver. "A Japanese General," DEP, March 30, 1896.

6   Yuji Ichioka, *The Issei: The World of the First Generation Japanese Immigrants, 1885–1924* (New York: Free Press, 1988), 191.

7   Ibid., 190.

8   Ibid.

9   Ibid.

10 Ibid., 191.

11 Wilson and Hosokawa, *East to America*, 113.

12 Yamato Ichihashi, *Japanese in the United States: A Critical Study of the Problems of the Japanese Immigrants and Their Children* (Stanford, CA: Stanford University Press, 1932), 231.

13 Harry A. Millis, *The Japanese Problem in the United States*, cited in Ichihashi, *Japanese in the United States,* 229.

14 US Immigration Commission, *Immigrant in Industries*, Part 25, *Japanese and Other Immigrant Races in the Pacific Coast and Rocky Mountain States* (Washington, DC: US Government Printing Office, 1911), 307.

15 Russell Endo, "Japanese of Colorado: A Sociohistorical Portrait," *Journal of Social and Behavioral Sciences* 31, no. 4 (Fall 1985).

16 Masakazu Iwata, *Planted in Good Soil: A History of the Issei in United States Agriculture*, Issei memorial edition (New York: Peter Lang, 1992), 1:130.

17 Ibid., 1:178.

18 Kiyoshi Karl Kawakami, *Asia at the Door: A Study of the Japanese Question in Continental United States, Hawaii, and Canada* (New York: Fleming H. Revell, 1914).

19 "No Japanese are wanted. Laboring men hold a meeting to protest yellow men," RMN, December 20, 1897.

20 Ibid.

21 "Vile smells as weapons. Chemicals used to drive patrons from a Japanese restaurant," RMN, December 24, 1897; "The anti-Japanese movement. Meeting at Coliseum Hall to arouse sentiment against them," DEP, December 20, 1897; "Against the Japanese restaurants," DEP, December 8, 1897.

22 "New menace," DEP, January 10, 1898.

23 Clark Secrest, *Hell's Belles: Prostitution, Vice, and Crime in Early Denver, with a Biography of Sam Howe, Frontier Lawman*, rev. ed. (Boulder: University Press of Colorado, 2002), 116.

24 U.S. Immigration Commission, *Immigrants in Industries*, cited in Kara Mariko Miyagishima, "Colorado's Nikkei Pioneers: Japanese Americans in Twentieth Century Colorado" (master's thesis, University of Colorado at Denver, 2007), 88.

25 "The menace of Japanese restaurants, Cooks and Waiters' Union making a determined effort to prevent coolie methods from spreading in Denver— Trailing the Japs customers," RMN, December 21, 1897.

26 "The Japs deride the union. Say they will remain in business and get supplies without bother," RMN, December 8, 1897.

27 "Boycott will be declared illegal, Federal Court will decide Japanese case against the unions," DT, December 11, 1901.

28 Endo, "Japanese of Colorado," 102.

29 See Iwata, *Planted in Good Soil*, 2:665n15 for more information on Hokazono.

30 Willa Kane, "Japanese labor was essential to Garfield County," *Post Independent/Citizen Telegram/Grand Junction Free Press*, April 1, 2014. http://www .postindependent.com/news/10844257–113/japanese-brothers-harris-colorado.

31 Bill Hosokawa, *Colorado's Japanese Americans: From 1886 to the Present* (Boulder: University Press of Colorado, 2005), 77, 124.

32 Ibid., 35.

33 Bill Hosokawa, *Nisei: The Quiet Americans*, rev. ed. (Boulder: University Press of Colorado, 2002), 76.

34 Hosokawa, *Colorado's Japanese Americans*, 94.

35 "Arrow Head Japs may be deported," RMN, February 4, 1905.

36 Iwata, *Planted in Good Soil*, 2:641.

37 "Takes contract for Japanese labor," DT, March 13, 1903; and Iwata, *Planted in Good Soil*, 2:631.

38 Richard W. Roskelley, "The Japanese Minority in Colorado following Evacuation," *Agriculture in Transition*, Proceedings of the Western Farm Economics Association annual meeting (1944): 259–265.

39 "San Luis Valley Japs," *The Creede Candle*, December 13, 1924.

40 Carl Abbott, Stephen J. Leonard, and Thomas J. Noel, *Colorado: A History of the Centennial State*, 4th ed. (Boulder: University Press of Colorado, 2005), 173–175.

41 "Colorado is first," RMN, March 27, 1905, and "Sugar beet fields attract colonists," RMN, April 23, 1905.

42 "Contract labor for sugar growing," RMN, January 19, 1900, and David R. Roediger, *Working toward Whiteness: How America's Immigrants Became White* (New York: Basic Books, 2005), 18.

43 "Colorado beet sugar workers will oppose importation of Japanese," DT, March 26, 1903.

44 Ichihashi, *Japanese in the United States*, 169.

45 U.S. Immigration Commission, *Immigrants in Industries*, 72.

46 Hosokawa, *Nisei*, 61.

47 Iwata, *Planted in Good Soil*, 2:662.

48 Ibid., 2:661.

49 William Wei, "Americans First: Colorado's Japanese-American Community during World War II—An Interview," *Colorado Heritage* (Winter 2005): 18–20.

50   Iwata, *Planted in Good Soil*, 2:646.

51   For details of Nakamura Shingo's life, see chapter 6, "One Man's Story," in Hosokawa, *Colorado's Japanese Americans*.

52   Iwata, 2:663.

53   Wei, "Americans First."

54   Roskelley, "The Japanese Minority in Colorado following Evacuation," 259.

55   "Cheap labor on railroads give poor satisfaction," RMN, May 14, 1900.

56   "Bitter against the Japanese," RMN, May 18, 1900.

57   "Cheap labor on railroads," RMN, May 14, 1900.

58   "Importing Asiatic labor," RMN, May 6, 1900.

59   Robert G. Athearn, *The Coloradans* (Albuquerque: University of New Mexico Press, 1976), 193.

60   Ronald C. Brown, *Hard-Rock Miners: The Intermountain West, 1860–1920* (College Station: Texas A & M University Press, 1979), 159.

61   "Serious crises approaching in the industrial world, Western labor union will act on the coming of Japanese labor," RMN, May 14, 1900.

62   House Joint Resolution No. 2, introduced by Representative Max Morris of Arapahoe County and approved on March 12, 1902, *House Journal (extra session) Thirteenth General Assembly of the State of Colorado* (Denver: Smith Brooks Printing Company, 1902), 181.

63   "Japanese laborers must leave Fremont. Fremont County miners hold an enthusiastic mass meeting and decide not to permit yellow labor in mines," DP, February 12, 1902. See also "Victor Fuel Company shut down mines at Chandler today" and "Japanese laborers leave in a body rather than fight," DP, February 13, 1902. As part of their opposition to Japanese labor, the Victor Miner's Union voted to request that Congress exclude not only the Chinese but the entire Mongolian race from the United States, not just for a limited time, but for all time. Mark Wyman, *Hard Rock Epic: Western Miners and the Industrial Revolution, 1860–1910* (Berkeley: University of California Press, 1979), 39.

64   Thomas Andrews, *Killing for Coal: America's Deadliest Labor War* (Cambridge, MA: Harvard University Press, 2008), 100–101.

65   Carroll D. Wright, *A Report on Labor Disturbances in the State of Colorado, from 1880 to 1904, Inclusive, with Correspondence Relating Thereto* (Washington, DC: Government Printing Office, 1905), 63. In this context, the expression "work for their bacon and beans" implies that the company pays them low wages, so they subsist on humble fare.

66   Andrews, *Killing for Coal*, 101.

67   Wyman, *Hard Rock Epic*, 39.

68   According to the RMN, February 11, 1907, the Denver Trades and Labor

Assembly estimated the number employed at the Colorado Fuel and Iron Company to be 1,100.

69 Ichihashi, *Japanese in the United States*, 145.

70 "500 added to Jap colony at Pueblo in two weeks," RMN, February 11, 1907.

71 Andrews, *Killing for Coal*, 105.

72 In 1908, the US Immigration Commission surveyed the composition of the workforce and found that there were only sixty-six Japanese miners, though it noted that many Japanese had already left the mines to work in other industries or in agriculture. Ichioka, *The Issei*, 126.

73 Cited in Hosokawa, *Nisei*, 75. Barron B. Beshoar, *Out of the Depths: The Story of John R. Lawson, a Labor Leader* (Denver: The Colorado Labor Historical Committee of the Denver Trades and Labor Assembly, 1942).

74 The following editorials in the RMN address this issue: "Labor is alarmed," May 10, 1900; "House makes inquiry," May 11, 1900; "Asiatic menace," May 13, 1900; and "Japanese threat," May 19, 1900.

75 "Grievances go to the polls," RMN, May 19, 1900.

76 Proceedings of the Asiatic Exclusion League, San Francisco, April 1908, published by Organized Labor Print, 15 (seq. 39), retrieved from the Harvard University Library.

77 "Grievances," RMN, May 19, 1900.

78 Proceedings of the Asiatic Exclusion League.

79 Ichihashi, *Japanese in the United States*, 238.

80 Ibid., 239.

81 Payson J. Treat, *Japan and the United States: 1853–1921*, cited in Ichihashi, *Japanese in the United States*, 244.

82 Everis A. Hayes, "Japanese Exclusion," Speech in the House of Representatives, March 13, 1906, http://pds.lib.harvard.edu/pds/view/4579712, and "The Treaty-Making Power of the Government and the Japanese Question," Speech in the House of Representatives, January 23, 1907, http://pds.lib.harvard.edu/pds/view/4579741.

83 "War certain for Yankees and Japs" and "Hawaiian Islands may be seized by Japan," RMN, February 1, 1907.

84 "Japs working night and day at arsenals," RMN, February 4, 1907.

85 "Guard officers ordered to begin recruiting at once," RMN, February 4, 1907.

86 *Los Angeles Times*, September 19, 1906, cited in Gilbert P. Gia, "States' Rights, T.R., and Japanese Children, 1907," 2012, Historic Bakersfield & Keern Co., www.gilbertgia.com/hist_articles/civRights/States_rights_%20tr_japanese_children_1907_%20v1_civ.pdf.

87 President Roosevelt's December 3, 1907, message to the U.S. Congress, cited in Ichihashi, *Japanese in the United States*, 240.

88 Raymond Leslie Buell, "The Development of Anti-Japanese Agitation in the United States, *Political Science Quarterly* 37, no. 4 (December 1922), 619.

89 "Schmitz goes down to defeat," RMN, February 16, 1907.

90 San Francisco Call, February 11, 1907, cited in Buell, "Anti-Japanese Agitation," 630.

91 Ichihashi, *Japanese in the United States,* 247. Wilson and Hosokawa, *East to America*, 125, provide significantly higher figures for these two years.

92 Wilson and Hosokawa, *East to America,* 125.

93 See Evelyn Nakano Glenn, *Issei, Nisei, War Bride: Three Generations of Japanese American Women in Domestic Service* (Philadelphia: Temple University Press, 1986), for personal perspectives on being a picture bride.

94 Harry H. L. Kitano, *Japanese Americans: The Evolution of a Sub-culture,* 2nd ed. (Englewood Cliffs, NJ: Prentice-Hall, 1976), 42.

95 Mei T. Nakano with OKAASAN by Grace Shibata, *Japanese American Women: Three Generations 1890–1990* (Berkeley, CA: Mina Press, 1990), 26.

96 Kei Tanaka, "Japanese Picture Marriage and the Image of Immigrant Women in Early Twentieth-Century California," *Japanese Journal of American Studies* 15 (2004).

97 Catherine Lee, "Prostitutes and Picture Brides: Chinese and Japanese Immigration, Settlement, and American Nation-Building, 1870–1920," Working Paper 70, Center for Comparative Immigration Studies, University of California, San Diego, February 2003.

98 V. S. McClatchy, "Picture brides and their successors," *Sacramento Bee*, November 28, 1921, cited in Iwata, *Planted in Good Soil,* 1:52.

99 Roger Daniels, *Asian America: Chinese and Japanese in the United States since 1850* (Seattle: University of Washington Press, 1988), 173.

100 Ichioka, *The Issei,* 128. For an explanation of why and how the Japanese miners were admitted into the United Mine Workers of America, see Ichioka, *The Issei,* 123–125.

101 Ibid., 128.

102 Iwata, *Planted in Good Soil,* 1:129.

103 Ichioka, *The Issei,* 127.

104 Scott Martelle, *Blood Passion: The Ludlow Massacre and Class War in the American West* (New Brunswick, NJ: Rutgers University Press, 2007), 85–86.

105 Ibid., 202.

SEVEN. YELLOW PERIL

1 John W. Dower, *War without Mercy: Race and Power in the Pacific War* (New York: Pantheon Books, 1986), 156.

2   Charles W. Hayford, "Chinese and American Characteristics: Arthur H. Smith and His China Book," in *Christianity in China: Early Protestant Writings*, ed. Suzanne Wilson Barnett and John King Fairbank (Cambridge, MA: Harvard University Press, 1985), 153–174.

3   "Chinamen are not nervous," RMN, February 6, 1898. For informative period reviews of *Chinese Characteristics*, see *The Spectator*, March 12, 1892, and NYT, November 4, 1894.

4   Arthur H. Smith, *Chinese Characteristics*, 4th ed. (New York: Fleming H. Revell, 1894), 89.

5   "Chinamen are not nervous," RMN, February 6, 1898.

6   Smith, *Chinese Characteristics*, 90–97.

7   For the most recent edition of this 1843 fairy tale, see Hans Christian Andersen, *The Nightingale*, ill. Yegor Narbut (n.p.: Clap Publishing, 2015).

8   Norma Rowen, "The Making of Frankenstein's Monster: Post-Golem, Pre-Robot," in *State of the Fantastic: Studies in the Theory and Practice of Fantastic Literature and Film*, ed. Nicholas Ruddick (Westport, CT: Greenwood, 1992), 169–177, http://knarf.english.upenn.edu/Articles/rowen.html. Also see "The labor issue," RMN, October 31, 1880, quoting the *Louisville Courier-Journal*, California, which compares Chinese to machines.

9   Halford J. Mackinder, "The Geographical Pivot of History," *The Geographical Journal* 23 (April 1904).

10   Robert D. Kaplan, *The Revenge of Geography: What the Map Tells Us about the Coming Conflicts and the Battle against Fate* (New York: Random House, 2013), 188.

11   Malcolm Clarke, "Wily Japs hate whites and await day when Mongols rule the world," RMN, March 12, 1905, and Paul Villiers, "Race must prepare to meet Asia's yellow horde," RMN, April 3, 1905. Also see Paul Villiers, "A flourish of power in Cochin China against yellow peril," RMN, May 28, 1905.

12   Paul Villiers, "Mongol horde line up, every white man a foe, France points out danger to Caucasian race from heathens among whom a yellow face is the badge of bloodthirsty brotherhood—menace to the civilized world," RMN, April 3, 1905.

13   Malcolm Clarke, "Conquering Japan showing her teeth to hated white race and eager to fight whole world," RMN, March 9, 1905.

14   Villiers, "Mongol horde line up."

15   Frank G. Martin, "Foresees a Yellow Peril," NYT, March 10, 1904.

16   "Japan modern sure enough," RMN, March 1, 1905.

17   "Russo-Japanese War—Yellow Peril is now a reality: It is Japan," *Ouray Herald*, February 16, 1906.

18   "Real 'Yellow Peril' is competition in trade from Japan," *Summit County*

Journal, December 10, 1904, and "The Yellow Peril," ADT, April 19, 1904. Also see "Japs on top in Denver," RMN, June 13, 1896.

19 "The Yellow Blessing," CR, January 12, 1905.

20 Count Okuma, "The so-called Yellow Peril," ADT, June 1, 1904.

21 Mark Mazower, *Governing the World: The History of an Idea, 1815 to the Present* (New York: Penguin, 2012), 162–164.

22 Hugh Borton, *Japan's Modern Century, From Perry to 1970*, 2nd ed. (New York: Ronald Press, 1970), 330–331.

23 Mazower, *Governing the World*, 163.

24 "German distrust of Japan," NYT, December 4, 1904.

25 Daniel A. Métraux, "Jack London and the Yellow Peril," *Education about Asia* 14, no. 1 (Spring 2009): 29–33.

26 Jack London, *The Strength of the Strong* (New York: Macmillan, 1910).

27 Edward W. Pickard, "Congress decides an army of 175,000 is enough, despite 'Yellow Peril,'" *Akron Weekly Pioneer Press*, January 21, 1910.

28 All broadsheet articles and quotations are from the RMN, January 6, 1907.

29 "The Japs colonizing," DEP, May 12, 1897, and "The Japs and Hawaii," DEP, July 12, 1897.

30 "Ugly Japanese. The Hawaiian Republic has a serious difficulty to confront," RMN, January 22, 1895, and "In the balance. Japanese inhabitants of Hawaii threaten revolution," RMN, June 3, 1895.

31 Frank Ninkovich, *The United States and Imperialism* (Malden, MA: Blackwell, 2001), 29.

32 "Reply to Japan, State Department practically tells the Mikado to mind his business," RMN, June 24, 1897.

33 John Higham, *Strangers in the Land: Patterns of American Nativism, 1860–1925* (New York: Antheneum, 1974), 309. See Karen Brodkin, *How Jews Became White Folks and What That Says about Race in America* (New Brunswick, NJ: Rutgers University Press, 1998) for an insightful study of how Jews were able to achieve acceptance in America.

34 Roger Daniels, *Guarding the Golden Door* (New York: Hill and Wang, 2004), 55.

35 Jonathan Spence, "Western Perceptions of China from the Late Sixteenth Century to the Present," in *Heritage of China: Contemporary Perspectives on Chinese Civilization*, ed. Paul S. Ropp (Berkeley: University of California Press, 1990), 3; Lydia H. Liu, *The Clash of Empires: The Invention of China in Modern World Making* (Cambridge, MA: Harvard University Press, 2004), 62.

36 "A million immigrants," RMN, April 22, 1905. With the exclusion laws in place, it is doubtful that there was a 100 percent increase in Chinese immigration.

37 Greg Robinson, *After Camp: Portraits in Midcentury Japanese American Life and Politics* (Berkeley: University of California Press, 2012), 17.

38 "Franklin D. Roosevelt's Editorials for the *Macon Telegraph*," April 16–May 5, 1925, Georgia*Info: An Online Georgia Almanac,* http://georgiainfo.galileo.usg .edu/FDRedito.htm#anchor436644.

39 David R. Roediger, *Working toward Whiteness: How America's Immigrants Became White, The Strange Journey from Ellis Island to the Suburbs* (New York: Basic Books, 2005).

40 Cara Wong and Grace Cho, "*Jus Meritum*: Citizenship for Service," in *Transforming Politics, Transforming America,* eds. Taeku Lee, S. Karthick Ramakrishnan, and Ricardo Ramirez (Charlottesville: University of Virginia Press, 2006): 86n16.

41 Charles Johnson, "Did U.S. Racism Pave the Way for Pearl Harbor?" Real Clear History, December 10, 2011, www.realclearhistory.com/articles/2011/12/10/ what_might_have_prevented_pearl_harbor_3.html.

42 Adam Schrager, *The Principled Politician: Governor Ralph Carr and the Fight against Japanese Internment* (Golden, CO: Fulcrum, 2008), 105–106.

43 Paul Fussell, *Wartime: Understanding and Behavior in the Second World War* (New York: Oxford University Press, 1989), 120.

44 Marius B. Jansen, *The Japanese and Sun Yat-sen* (Stanford, CA: Stanford University Press, 1954), 58.

45 Rana Mitter, *Forgotten Ally: China's World War II, 1937–1945* (Boston: Houghton Mifflin Harcourt, 2013), offers an insightful discussion about Wang Jingwei's betrayal.

46 Dower, *War without Mercy,* 6.

47 Ibid., 7.

48 "How to tell Japs from the Chinese," *Life* 11, no. 25 (December 22, 1941), 81–82.

49 R. Douglas Hurt, *The Great Plains during World War II* (Lincoln: University of Nebraska Press, 2008), 292.

50 An exception was Walter Ching, who considered the "majority complex of the white race" to be the problem. "Chinese American warns on prejudice against Nisei," GP, March 15, 1944.

51 John L. DeWitt, *Final Report: Japanese Evacuation from the West Coast, 1942* (Washington, DC: Government Printing Office, 1943), 34–36.

EIGHT. A CONCENTRATION CAMP IN THE CENTENNIAL STATE

1 Michi Nishiura Weglyn, *Years of Infamy: The Untold Story of America's Concentration Camps* (New York: Morrow, 1976). At age fifteen, Weglyn was imprisoned in the Gila River concentration camp.

2 "Executive Order 9066," in *Personal Justice Denied: Report of the Commission on Wartime Relocation and Internment of Civilians,* December 1982, National

Park Service, www.nps.gov/parkhistory/online_books/personal_justice_denied/chap2.htm.

3   Roger Daniels, *Prisoners without Trial: Japanese Americans in World War II* (New York: Hill and Wang, 1993), 36.

4   "Japanese-Americans relive days of shame," DP, March 22, 1992.

5   Greg Robinson, *By Order of the President: FDR and the Internment of Japanese Americans* (Cambridge, MA: Harvard University Press, 2001), 7, 93, 161, and 243.

6   Paul M. Holsinger, "Amache: The Story of the Japanese Relocation in Colorado" (master's thesis, University of Denver, 1960), 14.

7   Joseph E. Persico, *Roosevelt's Secret War: FDR and World War II Espionage* (New York: Random House, 2001), 440.

8   This figure comes from the US War Department's *Final Report*, cited in Holsinger, "Amache," 22. According to Gordon F. Nicholson, the special agent in charge of the Denver FBI office, the 1940 census showed that the state's Japanese American population was 3,200, somewhat higher than the War Department's figure. Six months after the Pearl Harbor attack, the state's Japanese American population grew by an additional 30 percent, with most of that growth comprising American-born and agricultural workers. "Colorado Jap population up 30 percent," *Lamar Daily News*, June 13, 1942.

9   Kara Mariko Miyagishima, "Colorado's Nikkei Pioneers: Japanese Americans in Twentieth Century Colorado" (master's thesis, University of Colorado at Denver, 2007).

10 Ibid., 119n363.

11 Ibid., 119.

12 "From 25 cents an hour to $40,000 a year—Agriculture's Horatio Alger," *Western Farm Life*, April 1958, cited in Miyagishima, "Colorado's Nikkei Pioneers," 119n363.

13 Richard W. Roskelley, "The Japanese Minority in Colorado following Evacuation," *Agriculture in Transition*, Proceedings of the Western Farm Economics Association annual meeting (1944), 264.

14 Adam Schrager, *The Principled Politician: Governor Ralph Carr and the Fight against Japanese Internment* (Golden, CO: Fulcrum, 2009), 125.

15 Ibid.

16 Arthur A. Hansen, "Japanese Americans in the Interior West: A Regional Perspective on the Enduring Nikkei Historical Experience in Arizona, Colorado, New Mexico, Texas, and Utah (and Beyond): Part 1," October 16, 2009, Discover Nikkei, www.discovernikkei.org/en/journal/2009/10/16/enduring-communities/.

17 Doris Kearns Goodwin, "Franklin Delano Roosevelt: Runner-up," *Time*, December 31, 1999, 107.

18 J. R. Minkel, "Confirmed: The U.S. Census Bureau Gave Up Names of Japanese-Americans in WW II," *Scientific American*, March 30, 2007, www .scientificamerican.com/article.cfm?id=confirmed-the-us-census-b.

19 Representative Mike Honda (Democrat, California), who as a child was imprisoned in the Amache concentration camp, correctly called this breach of confidentiality an instance of racial profiling during World War II. "Rep. Honda outraged by Census confidentiality breaches," *US Federal News Service*, March 30, 2007.

20 Upon Ralph Carr's death, Hito Okada, national president, and Masao Satow, national director, sent the following telegram of condolence to his wife on behalf of the JACL: "All persons of Japanese ancestry in America will never forget Ralph Carr's courageous stand for democracy during their darkest days of World War Two when many Americans temporarily lost sight of what all of us were fighting for." "Memorials and Letters," scrapbook no. 3, Ralph L. Carr Papers, Western History Collection, Denver Public Library.

21 Ralph L. Carr, "Japanese Relocation," February 28, 1942, Ralph L. Carr Papers, Collection No. 1208, file folder 252, History Colorado Center, Stephen H. Hart Library and Research Center (hereafter referred to as the Carr Papers).

22 Biographical information on Carr is based on Jason Brockman, "Biography of Ralph L. Carr," in the Ralph L. Carr Collection, Colorado State Archives, June 16, 1997, www.colorado.gov/dpa/doit/archives/govs/carr.html; John S. Castellano, "Governor Ralph L. Carr: A Remembrance," *The Colorado Lawyer* 20, no. 12 (December 1991): 2475–2477; "Ralph L. Carr" in *Colorado and Its People: A Narrative and Topical History of the Centennial State*, ed. LeRoy R. Hafen (New York: Lewis Historical Publishing), 3:97; "Forgotten Hero: Ralph Carr," in *Pioneers and Politicians: 10 Colorado Governors in Profile*, by Richard D. Lamm and Duane A. Smith (Boulder, CO: Pruett, 1984), 136–145; and James E. Sherow, foreword to "An Inventory of the Papers of Governor Ralph L. Carr," April 1988, Carr Papers.

23 "Carr, a miner's son, worked his own way to the top," DP, September 23, 1950.

24 Carr to Lee Taylor Casey, April 23, 1942, Carr Papers, file folder 52.

25 Berny Morson, "Compassion in Colorado," RMN, September 27, 1987.

26 "Obituaries," *Valley Courier*, April 25, 2007. Jim Sheeler, "Guns mark turning points in man's life, Japanese-American fought in Europe with famed 442nd," RMN, May 28, 2004.

27 Carr, "Japanese Relocation." Israel Zangwill popularized the phrase "melting pot" in a 1908 play of that name.

28 Ralph L. Carr, "Speech delivered over stations KOA, KLZ, KFEL, and KMYR," December 10, 1941, Carr Papers, file folder 248.

29   Jane Harper, "Read all about it," *Colorado Editor*, September 1996, and "Ralph Carr dies!" RMN, September 23, 1950.

30   Ralph L. Carr, "Americanism," Carr Papers, file folder 282, is his only explicit statement on the meaning of Americanism. However, his papers make numerous references to it. In addition, there is an address on "Americanism" by Charles Moynihan, which provides the historical background for it. Charles Moynihan to Carr, July 8, 1940, Carr Papers, file folder 29. Carr sent a copy of the address to his friend Wendell Willkie.

31   Carr, "Americanism."

32   Charles J. Moynihan, "Americanism . . . A Definition, An Ideal, An Inspiration, and A Responsibility," a speech delivered at East Denver High School Auditorium, Denver, Colorado, on May 9, 1939, 2. A copy of this speech is in Carr Papers, file folder 29. Another of Carr's favorite words, *patriotism,* has also suffered the same fate. As Ed Quillen notes, "American patriotism has become the exclusive preserve of the right-thinkers, who employ all manner of twisted logic." Ed Quillen, "Patriotism needs to be rescued from the right-thinkers," *Denver Post Online*, August 2, 1999, www.edquillen.com/eq1998/19980705p.html.

33   According to Robert F. Carr, his father was "a great student of Lincoln." Gail Randall, "State Japanese-Americans honor memory of Gov. Carr," RMN, December 12, 1987. Unless otherwise noted, the comments about Carr and Lincoln are based on Carr, "What Would Lincoln do?," 1940, Carr Papers, file folder 188; "Abraham Lincoln," February 12, 1941, Carr Papers, file folder 215; and "Abraham Lincoln—The Union—Yesterday and Tomorrow" February 12, 1942, Carr Papers, file folder 251.

34   Jürgen Gebhardt, *Americanism: Revolutionary Order and Societal Self-Interpretation in the American Republic*, trans. Ruth Hein (Baton Rouge: Louisiana State University Press, 1993), 297.

35   Carr, "Americanism." Also see Ralph L. Carr, "Government and Individual Rights," January 17, 1939, Carr Papers, file folder 171.

36   Carr, "Americanism."

37   Ralph L. Carr, "A time that tries men's souls," PC, January 1942. Also see Stephanie Chang, "Side-by-Side: Japanese Americans and Colorado, 1941–1945" (undergraduate honors thesis, University of Denver, 1996), 34, and Paul M. Holsinger, "Amache: The Story of Japanese Relocation in America" (master's thesis, University of Denver, 1960), 24.

38   "Carr asserts state ready to take Japs," RMN, March 1, 1942. Also see the editorial "Right, Mr. Governor!" in the same issue.

39   Tom Noel, "Ralph Carr's principled protests," DP, February 23, 2013.

40   Ibid.

41 Carr to James F. Lockhart, March 5, 1942, Carr Papers, file folder 51.

42 Ibid.

43 Edwin C. Johnson, "Colorado and the Japs," Colorado State Federation of Labor, *1942 Year Book*, 21, Western History Collection, Denver Public Library.

44 Photostat copy of letter by William L. Lloyd to Coordinator of the Council of Defense, April 13, 1942, attached to Edwin C. Johnson to Ralph L. Carr, April 27, 1942, Carr Papers, file folder 52.

45 Ralph L. Carr, "Colorado's Part in the War Effort," Colorado State Federation of Labor, *1942 Year Book*, 17.

46 Ralph L. Carr, "Address to Organized Labor," 1942, Carr Papers, file folder 262.

47 Carr, "Japanese Relocation."

48 Note from Byrd R. Fuqua, undated, attached to Carr to Byrd R. Fuqua, April 14, 1942, Carr Papers, file folder 52. The vote-buying canard was so effective that it was used to harass his successor, Republican governor John C. Vivian (1943–47), who was accused of colluding with a Japanese American resettlement organization to provide favorable resettlement terms in exchange for guaranteed block votes. "Japs offer votes in trade for permanent homes in Colorado," DP, June 23, 1943.

49 Johnson, "Colorado and the Japs," 21.

50 According to Lowell Thomas, that action probably saved the lives of striking workers, because strikebreakers and their businessmen and farmer allies would have overwhelmed them. Lowell Thomas, "Carr, Colorado's political magician governor, is proposed as answer to Republicans' prayers," *Pittsburgh Press*, February 10, 1940.

51 "Gov. Carr says harvest will test patriotism," DP, July 9, 1942.

52 Carr to James F. Lockhart, April 6, 1942, Carr Papers, file folder 52.

53 "Carr stakes political future on Jap question," *Walsenburg World-Independent*, April 16, 1942.

54 DP, April 18, 1942, cited in Castellano, "Governor Ralph L. Carr."

55 E. L. Dutcher to Carr, November 6, 1942, Carr Papers, file folder 58.

56 J. H. Thomas to Carr, November 6, 1942, Carr Papers, file folder 58. Evidently, Johnson was willing to resort to some unseemly tactics to win this senatorial campaign. To Carr's credit, when a constituent offered to provide him with "ammunition with which to fight [Johnson]," he declined, saying, "I looked it over and felt that I didn't want to carry on the kind of campaign he did, and so I left it unused." Carr to Frederick P. Lilley, December 9, 1942, Carr Papers, file folder 59.

57 Childe Harold, "Ideas and comments," *Rocky Mountain Herald*, September 30, 1950.

58 Ibid.

59   Carr to Harold E. Stassen, Ed J. Thye, and Joseph H. Ball, September 9, 1942, Carr Papers, file folder 59.

60   Glenn Troelstrup, "Japanese Americans to honor late Gov. Ralph Carr," DP, December 14, 1975.

61   Carr to Lee Taylor Casey, April 23, 1942, Carr Papers, file folder 52.

62   Bill Briggs, "Century standout Gov. Ralph Carr opposed Japanese internment," DP, December 27, 1999.

63   James Omura, "In Spirit, We are Americans," updated November 19, 1998, http://resisters.com/Omura_Tolan.htm.

64   James Omura's testimony to the Tolan Committee, http://resisters.com/Omura_Tolan.htm.

65   Ibid.

66   Arthur A. Hansen, "James Omura," *Densho Encyclopedia*, http://encyclopedia.densho.org/James%20Omura/.

67   Peter Irons, *Justice at War: The Story of the Japanese American Internment Cases* (New York: Oxford University Press, 1983), 81. See Gil Asakawa, "Minoru Yasui," *Densho Encyclopedia*, http://encyclopedia.densho.org/Minoru%20Yasui/, for a short biography of Yasui.

68   Studs Terkel, *"The Good War": An Oral History of World War II* (New York: Pantheon, 1984), 29.

69   Carr to Mrs. Sam Rankin (April 30, 1942), Carr Papers, file folder 52.

70   Daniels, *Prisoners without Trial*, 53.

71   George Lurie, "A Legacy of Shame: The Story of Colorado's Camp Amache" (unpublished paper, 1985), 6.

72   Daniels, *Prisoners without Trial*, 66.

73   Gordon H. Chang, ed., *Morning Glory, Evening Shadow: Yamato Ichihashi and His Internment Writings, 1942–1945* (Stanford, CA: Stanford University Press, 1997), 260.

74   Christian Heimburger, "Life beyond Barbed Wire: The Significance of Japanese American Labor in the Mountain West, 1942–1944" (PhD diss., University of Colorado, 2013), 175.

75   R. Douglas Hurt, *The Great Plains during World War II* (Lincoln: University of Nebraska Press, 2008), 296.

76   Gary Y. Okihiro, in "Japanese Resistance in America's Concentration Camps: A Re-evaluation," *Amerasia Journal* 2, no. 1 (Fall 1973), and Arthur A. Hansen and David A. Hacker, in "The Manzanar Riot: An Ethnic Perspective," *Amerasia Journal* 2, no. 2 (Fall 1974), discuss resistance within the concentration camps.

77   See Robert Harvey, *Amache: The Story of Japanese Internment in Colorado*

during World War II (Lanham, MD: Taylor Trade Publishing, 2004), for a book-length study of the Amache concentration camp.

78   Holsinger, "Amache," 50.

79   Lurie, "A Legacy of Shame," 36–37.

80   Valerie Matsumoto, *Farming the Home Place: A Japanese American Community in California, 1919–1982* (Ithaca, NY: Cornell University Press, 1993), 123.

81   "Unsung heroes and heroines, GP, November 17, 1943; "Year's supply for 748,000 persons, Evacuees lauded in beet harvest," GP, November 3, 1943; "Center farm harvests field crops surpassing season's WRA quota," GP, November 17, 1943.

82   Matsumoto, *Farming the Homeplace*, 127–128.

83   Lee Casey, "Japs at Granada neither coddled nor mistreated," RMN, November 28, 1942. Countess Elsa Bernadotte, who had visited the camp, agreed with Casey. "Ex-countess finds no 'coddling' in Amache," GP, March 11, 1944.

84   "Waste at Granada," RMN, December 27, 1942.

85   "Financial aid for Colorado schools asked," DP, December 30, 1942.

86   Lee Casey's column, RMN, January 19, 1943.

87   Jack Carberry, "Amache center school program creates bad feeling in Lamar area," DP, February 18, 1943.

88   "The American way," GP, January 19, 1943.

89   "Granada Jap center school plan defended, Director says democratic fairness at stake," DP, December 30, 1942.

90   Ibid.

91   "Granada Center featured, evacuees are not 'spoiled, pampered, and coddled' write visiting newsmen," GP, July 24, 1943

92   Jack Carberry, "Amache center school program creates bad feeling in Lamar area." According to Bill Hosokawa, his colleague Jack Carberry was "a veteran reporter whose vivid imagination frequently obscured his view of the facts." Hosokawa, *The Thunder in the Rockies: The Incredible Denver Post* (New York: William Morrow, 1976), 192, 196,

93   Kumiko Takahara, *Off the Fat of the Land: The Denver Post's Story of the Japanese American Internment in World War II* (Casper, WY: Western History Publications, 2003).

94   William H. Hornby, *Voice of Empire: A Centennial Sketch of The Denver Post* (Denver: Colorado Historical Society, 1992), 30.

95   Editorial, *Silver and Gold*, April 27, 1943, cited in Jessica N. Arnston, "Journey to Boulder: The Japanese American Instructors at the Navy Japanese Language School (1942–1946)," in *Enduring Legacies: Ethnic Histories and Cultures of Colorado*, ed. Arturo Aldama et al. (Boulder: University Press of Colorado, 2011), 184.

96   "U. of Colorado, editor blasts *Post*'s "Fascist techniques,'" GP May 5, 1943.

97   Noriko Asato, "National Japanese American Student Relocation Council," *Encyclopedia of the Great Plains*, 2011, http://plainshumanities.unl.edu/encyclo pedia/doc/egp.asam.017.xml.

98   "Release recommended for 82,000 Japanese," GP, April 7, 1943.

99   Irons, *Justice at War*, 271.

100   Joan Z. Bernstein et al., Members of the Commission on Wartime Relocation and Internment of Civilians, and Angus Macbeth, Special Counsel, *Personal Justice Denied: Report of the Commission on Wartime Relocation and Internment of Civilians*, Part 2, *Recommendations* (Washington, DC: US Government Printing Office, 1983), 5. The commission recommended that the federal government officially apologize for its mistake, provide reparations of twenty thousand dollars to each survivor of the concentration camps, and set up a public education fund to ensure that such a tragedy would never happen again.

101   John Morton Blum, *V Was for Victory: Politics and American Culture during World War II* (New York: Harcourt Brace, 1976), 155.

102   Hafen, *Colorado and Its People*, 1:599.

NINE. LOYALTY AND BETRAYAL ON THE HOME FRONT

1   Adam Schrager, *The Principled Politician: Governor Ralph Carr and the Fight against Japanese Internment* (Golden, CO: Fulcrum, 2009), 104.

2   There were exceptions to this. Because of their deep-seated animosity toward Japanese Americans, Californians did not want any of them and sought to replace them with black and Mexican laborers. Moreover, they did not want any Japanese Americans to return after the war was over. "Racial tides," GP, November 6, 1943.

3   Ibid., 48.

4   Christian Heimburger, "Life beyond Barbed Wire: The Significance of Japanese American Labor in the Mountain West, 1942–1944" (PhD diss., University of Colorado, 2013), 53.

5   Schrager, *Principled Politician*, 117.

6   Heimburger, "Beyond Barbed Wire," 194

7   Mike Masaoka, "The Nisei creed," PC, April 1, 1941.

8   According to Leonard Bloom, "Transitional Adjustments of Japanese-American Families to Relocation," *American Sociological Review* 12, no. 2 (April 1947), 203, the primary motive was financial.

9   Frank Arnold et al., "Economic Losses of Ethnic Japanese as a Result of Exclusion and Detention, 1942–1946," cited in Greg Robinson, *A Tragedy of*

Democracy: Japanese Confinement in North America (New York: Columbia University Press, 2009), 124. According to Roger Daniels, *Prisoners without Trial: Japanese Americans in World War II* (New York: Hill and Wang, 1993), 36, the losses to the Japanese American community varied from sixty-seven to four hundred million in 1940s dollars. The losses to the Japanese American community would be from one billion to over six billion in 2015 dollars.

10 "Interview with Esther Nishio," in *REgenerations Oral History Project: Rebuilding Japanese American Families, Communities, and Civil Rights in the Resettlement Era, Chicago Region*, ed. Chicago Japanese American Historical Society (Los Angeles: Japanese American National Museum, 2000), 1:320–321; and "Florence Nakano Tsunoda—An Oral History," cited in Heimburger, "Beyond Barbed Wire," 141.

11 Letter from S. S. Cooke to J. R. McCusker (February 21, 1944), cited in Heimburger, "Beyond Barbed Wire," 110.

12 "Nurses of Japanese descent are proud of jobs in Colorado," RMN, 1943, cited in Heimburger, "Beyond Barbed Wire," 109n286.

13 Valerie Matsumoto, *Farming the Home Place: A Japanese American Community in California, 1919–1982* (Ithaca, NY: Cornell University Press, 1993), 123.

14 "Colorado farmers promise to attain record 1943 goals," RMN, December 18, 1942.

15 William John May Jr., *The Great Western Sugarlands: The History of the Great Western Sugar Company and the Economic Development of the Great Plains* (New York: Garland, 1989), 378.

16 Louis Fiset, "Thinning, Topping, and Loading: Japanese Americans and Beet Sugar in World War II," *Pacific Northwest Quarterly* 90, no. 3 (Summer 1999).

17 "Japs from Granada Center leave for work in the beet fields," DP, September 26, 1942, and "Use of Jap labor is discussed here," *Colorado Springs Gazette*, September 1942.

18 LeRoy R. Hafen, ed., *Colorado and Its People: A Narrative and Topical History of the Centennial State* (New York: Lewis Historical Publishing, 1948), 1:599.

19 "Holly farmers thank project beet workers," GP, December 24, 1942.

20 "Granada beet field workers lauded," GP, November 29, 1942.

21 "176 October relocatees swell grand total to 1411," GP, November 3, 1943.

22 Heimburger, "Beyond Barbed Wire," 105.

23 John Stephenson, "40 Jap-Americans arrive for Colorado farm work," RMN, May 15, 1943. Also see "Jap evacuees will be placed on farms," DP, February 18, 1943, and May, *The Great Western Sugarlands*, 378.

24 Leonard J. Arrington, *Beet Sugar in the West: A History of the Utah-Idaho Sugar Company, 1891–1966* (Seattle: University of Washington Press, 1966), 142.

25 Bloom, "Transitional Adjustments."

26 The section on the Shitara sisters is a revision of William Wei, "Sex, Race, and the Fate of Three Nisei Sisters," *Colorado Heritage* (Autumn 2007): 2–17.

27 Eric L. Muller, "Betrayal on Trial: Japanese American 'Treason' in World War II," *North Carolina Law Review* 82 (June 2004): 1759–1798.

28 "Three Jap girls convicted of plot to commit treason," DP, August 11, 1944.

29 Ibid.

30 Presentencing report in case file 10387, US v. Wallace, Otani, Tanogoshi, criminal case file, entry 32, District of Colorado, Records of US District Courts, National Archive at Denver.

31 "Jap girls given term in prison and $1,000 fines," DP, August 18, 1944.

32 Jack Foster, "Treason trial defense closes; none of Jap-U.S. sisters testifies," RMN, August 10, 1944.

33 "Jap girls given terms in prison and $1,000 fines."

34 "German prisoners spooned with Jap girls in Trinidad," DP, October 24, 1943.

35 "Five Jap women quizzed on Nazi love interludes," DP, October 28, 1943.

36 "FBI releases Nisei women who 'spooned'," GP, November 3, 1943.

37 "The treason trial verdict," GP, August 12, 1944.

38 Pre-sentencing report in case file 10387, US v. Wallace, Otani, Tanogoshi.

39 Sueo Sako, "Just incidentally," GP, November 3, 1944.

40 "Jap girls' fate put up to jury as treason arguments end," DP, August 10, 1944.

41 Jack Foster, "Denver treason jury returns a sealed verdict," RMN, August 11, 1944.

42 Ibid.

43 Jack Foster, "2d Nazi describes aid by U.S.-Jap girls," RMN, August 19, 1944.

44 Ibid.

45 "Jap girls' fate put up to jury."

46 Cpl. Hermann Loescher's letter to Judge J. Foster Symes, November 5, 1943, in case file 10387, US v. Wallace, Otani, Tanogoshi. "Jap girls given terms in prison and $1,000 fines."

47 "Jap girls' fate put up to jury."

48 Ibid.

49 "Three Jap girls convicted of plot to commit treason."

50 "Editorial: The treason trial verdict," and Jack Foster, "Three Jap-U.S. sisters convicted of plotting treason to ask retrial," RMN, August 12, 1944. Muller, in "Betrayal on trial," argues that the government presented no evidence proving that the Shitara sisters committed treason. Also see Eric L. Muller, "The Japanese American Cases: A Bigger Disaster than We Realized," *Howard Law Journal* 49, no. 2 (2006): 417–474.

51 Ann Howard Creel, *The Magic of Ordinary Days* (New York: Viking Penguin,

2001); *The Magic of Ordinary Days*, directed by Brent Shields (Hallmark Hall of Fame, 2005).

52   Review of Ann Howard Creel's *The Magic of Ordinary Days* by Kara Miyagi-shima, Colorado Book Review Center, 2002, www.coloradohistory.org/publications.

53   Ann Howard Creel, *The Magic of Ordinary Days*, 270.

TEN. ASIAN COLORADO'S GREATEST GENERATION

1   For information about Chinese American participation in World War II, see K. Scott Wong, *Americans First: Chinese Americans and the Second World War* (Cambridge, MA: Harvard University Press, 2005); Christina M. Lim and Sheldon H. Lim, "In the Shadow of the Tiger: The 407th Air Service Squadron, Fourteenth Air Force, CBI, World War II," *Chinese America: History and Perspectives* (1993), 25–27; Peter Phan, "Familiar Strangers: The Fourteenth Air Service Group Case Study of Chinese American Identity during World War II," *Chinese America: History and Perspectives* (1993): 75–108.

2   Roger Daniels, *Concentration Camps: North America, Japanese in the United States and Canada during World War II* (Malabar, FL: Krieger Publishing, 1989), 113.

3   "The decline of the Yellow Peril," *New Leader*, June 26, 1948, in Greg Robinson, ed., *Pacific Citizens: Larry and Guyo Tajiri and Japanese American Journalism in the World War II Era* (Urbana: University of Illinois Press, 2012), 201–203.

4   Robert A. Wilson and Bill Hosokawa, *East to America: A History of the Japanese in the United States* (New York: William Morrow, 1980), 243.

5   While segregation in the military has ended, the problem of racism has not. As the recent cases of Bruce I. Yamashita, who experienced racial discrimination while at Marine Corps Officers Candidate School, and Danny Chen, who suffered racial harassment and committed suicide while serving in the US Army in Afghanistan, show, prejudice against Asian Americans in the military persists to the present. Chen's case is a stunning testament to the persistence of racism, which originated 150 years earlier in America and followed him back to Asia, where he took his life. See Bruce I. Yamashita, *Fighting Tradition: A Marine's Journey to Justice* (Honolulu: University of Hawaii Press, 2003), and Miranda Leitsinger, "8 soldiers charged in alleged hazing death of GI; family seeks truth," *MSNBC.com*, April 25, 2012.

6   Victoria Moy, "Chinese American WWII vets remember Flying Tigers days," *Huffington Post*, October 3, 2011, and Julian Guthrie, "WWII all-Chinese American unit reminisces," *San Francisco Chronicle*, October 2, 2009.

7   Lim and Lim, "In the Shadow of the Tiger," 65.

8   For information about the role of Chinese American units in the 14th ASG and the 14th Air Force, see "CBI Order of Battle, Lineages and History: 14th Air Service Group," CBI History, updated September 2, 2010, www.cbi-history .com/part_vi_14th_asg.html.

9   William Wei, "Five Generations in Colorado: An Interview with the Descendants of Chin Lin Soo," *Colorado Heritage* (Autumn, 2002), and interviews with the members of the Chin family in Denver on August 14, 2002. Also see Jack Foster, "Chinese gave much to Denver," RMN, May 8, 1953. Information about the military service of Asian Coloradans can be found in their obituaries. For example, "Soon 'Charlie' Fong," PUC, June 4, 2000; "Yen G. Wong," PUC, October 17, 1973; and "Philip Hong Wong," PUC, June 28, 1974.

10   Wei, "Five Generations in Colorado." Similarly, Thomas H. Yee, another Chinese American veteran, summed up his time in the 14th ASG in the following manner: "I really enjoyed my Army stint. [There] was something about being in a special Chinese American unit serving in the land of your birth and in the service of your adopted county, plus I got an extraordinary opportunity to see the world, even during those conditions. It gave me a sense of pride and patriotism that I will never forget." Lim and Lim, "In the Shadow of the Tiger," 65.

11   "Nisei World War II Memorial urged by Legion in Denver," RMN, February 15, 1963. For a picture of the memorial, see Thomas J. Noel, "Fairmount Cemetery, Nisei War Memorial," 2010, Denver Public Library Digital Collections, http://digital.denverlibrary.org/cdm/ref/collection/p15330coll14/id/1623. For a picture of the memorial and the words inscribed on it, see "Nisei War Memorial—Denver, CO," November 28, 2010, Waymark, www.waymarking .com/waymarks/WMA7PK_Nisei_War_Memorial_Denver_CO.

12   Sara Burnett, "WWII Chinese translator denied U.S. veterans status but says record speaks for itself," DP, May 29, 2011, and Gary Massaro, "Lifetime of service bridges culture," RMN, September 14, 2005.

13   Burnett, "WWII Chinese translator denied veteran status."

14   This section on the loyalty questionnaire is based on William Wei, "'The Strangest City in Colorado': The Amache Concentration Camp," *Colorado Heritage* (Winter 2005).

15   Wilson and Hosokawa, *East to America*, 235.

16   Leonard Bloom, "Transitional Adjustments of Japanese-American Families to Relocation," *American Sociological Review* 12, no. 2 (April 1947), 204.

17   Daniels, *Concentration Camps*, 112–113.

18   Gordon H. Chang, ed., *Morning Glory, Evening Shadow: Yamato Ichihashi and His Internment Writings, 1942–1945* (Stanford, CA: Stanford University Press, 1997), 265.

19   See "Japanese American Resistance," in Gary Y. Okihiro, *The Columbia Guide to Asian American History* (New York: Columbia University Press, 2001), and Gary Y. Okihiro, "Japanese Resistance in America's Concentration Camps: A Re-evaluation," *Amerasia Journal* 2, no. 1 (Fall 1973).

20   Howard Schonberger, "Dilemmas of Loyalty: Japanese Americans and the Psychological Campaigns of the Office of Strategic Services, 1943–45," *Amerasia Journal* 16, no. 1 (1990), 22.

21   For testimonies of Japanese American military service, see chapter 10 of Joan Z. Bernstein et al., Members of the Commission on Wartime Relocation and Internment of Civilians, and Angus Macbeth, Special Counsel, *Personal Justice Denied: Report of the Commission on Wartime Relocation and Internment of Civilians* (Washington, DC: US Government Printing Office, 1982).

22   K. K., "Selfish? We're thankful," GP, December 16, 1942.

23   Tina Griego, "Special honors for Japanese-American WW II veterans' two-fronted battle against discrimination," DP, November 6, 2011.

24   "They are Americans, too," RMN, April 30, 1945.

25   "Editorial: Nisei heroes," GP, September 23, 1944, reprinted a news article from the *Washington Post*, September 10, 1944, about their contribution to the Pacific War.

26   Testimony to the Commission on Wartime Relocation and Internment of Civilians, Seattle, September 9, 1981, 39, quoted in Bernstein et al., *Personal Justice Denied*, 254.

27   Jessica Natsuko Arntson, "Journey to Boulder: The Japanese American Instructors of the Navy Japanese Language School (1942–1946)" (master's thesis, University of Colorado, 2003), 8.

28   Ibid., 167. Also see "Evacuees to teach at US Naval School," GP, November 29, 1942.

29   Kan Tagami, "Recollections of the Japanese Occupation," revised April 2005, Japanese American Veterans Association, www.javadc.org/Tagami.htm.

30   Ronald Spector, *Eagle against the Sun: The American War with Japan* (New York: Vintage, 1985), 459.

31   Wilson and Hosokawa, *East to America*, 242.

32   Bernstein et al., *Personal Justice Denied*, 256, and Ronald Takaki, *Strangers from a Different Shore: A History of Asian Americans* (Boston: Little, Brown, 1989), 400.

33   Robert Asahina, *Just Americans: How Japanese Americans Won a War at Home and Abroad* (New York: Gotham Books, 2007).

34   The army awarded the Congressional Medal of Honor to twenty Japanese Americans and two other Asian Americans, Staff Sergeant Rudolph B. Davila, a

Filipino American, and Captain Francis B. Wai, a Chinese American, for risk-
ing their lives above and beyond the call of duty in action against the enemy.

35 "Profile in courage: George Sakato and a belated Medal of Honor," *Denshō*,
November 11, 2009, and Joey Kirchmer, "World War II vet Joe Sakato, of
Denver, reflects on Medal of Honor," *YourHub* (DP), May 22, 2012.

36 A notable exception was Technical Sergeant Ben Kuroki, who earned three
Distinguished Flying Crosses during the war. A recruiter had decided that
Kuroki was a Polish name and signed him up. Ralph G. Martin, *Boy from
Nebraska: The Story of Ben Kuroki* (New York: Harper and Brothers, 1946).

37 "Rescue Lost Battalion," GP, November 15, 1944.

38 William Wei, "Americans First: Colorado's Japanese-American Community
during World War II—An Interview," *Colorado Heritage* (Winter 2005): 18–20.

39 Bernstein et al., *Personal Justice Denied*, 260.

40 Wei, "Americans First."

41 Ibid.

42 "Not Denver's way," RMN, June 11, 1942.

43 "Estes Park ban brings criticism," *Ault Progress*, January 27, 1944. This article
can be found in the "Clipping Files: Chinese Ethnic Group" of the Western
History Collection, Denver Public Library. Over three hundred Chinese
airmen, for example, were trained to fly the Consolidated B-24 heavy bomber
at the Pueblo Army air base during World War II. "The second class of Chinese
airmen graduated, May 1, 1944," PUC, May 2, 1944. Robert Strader, "The
Training of Chinese Air Force Crews at the Pueblo Army Air Base, 1944–45,"
courtesy of Maria E. Tucker, manager of Special Collections, Pueblo City-
County Library District.

44 See "1946 Chinese War Brides Act," US Immigration Legislation Online, http://
library.uwb.edu/guides/usimmigration/1946_chinese_war_brides_act.html, for
the legislation. Evidently, this special piece of legislation was deemed necessary
to reinforce the earlier War Brides Act (December 28, 1945), which was enacted
"to expedite the admission to the United States of alien spouses and alien
minor children of citizen members of the United States armed forces." See
"1945 War Brides Act," US Immigration Legislation Online, http://library.uwb
.edu/guides/usimmigration/1945_war_brides_act.html.

45 Wei, "Five Generations in Colorado."

46 Ibid.

47 Ibid.

48 Ibid.

49 "A City Looks at Its Minorities: An Abridgement of A Report on Minorities in
Denver by the Mayor's Interim Survey Committee on Human Relations: Toward
a Better Understanding of Race Relations," cited in Kara Mariko Miyagishima,

"Colorado's Nikkei Pioneers: Japanese Americans in Twentieth Century Colorado" (master's thesis, University of Colorado at Denver, 2007), 180n550.

50 "Japanese Americans may forsake the Pacific Coast—50,000 plan to remain east of the Sierras," GP, March 4, 1944. Article reprinted from the *San Francisco Chronicle*.

51 Pasquale Marranzino, "They have found asylum here," RMN, October 24, 1957.

52 "2,507 of released Jap camp residents settle in Colorado," DP, May 25, 1944. Colorado ranked second only to Illinois in the number of Japanese Americans settlers. About five thousand settled in Illinois, mainly in Chicago.

53 "2057 Japanese Americans now resettled in Colorado," GP, May 31, 1944, reprinted from the RMN, May 26, 1944.

54 Ibid.

55 Cited in Miyagishima, "Colorado's Nikkei Pioneers," 173.

56 Ibid., 179n547.

57 Ibid.

58 Ibid.

59 Ross Thompson, "Japanese have settled farms in Arkansas Valley and are introducing new agriculture," PUC, November 2, 1947.

60 "Opposition to plan for Japan settlement in county growing," *Ault Progress*, December 2, 1943.

61 "300 Lower Valley residents protest acquisition of land by Japanese at mass meeting," *Grand Junction Sentinel*, January 6, 1944.

62 "Threat to 'Burn Out Nips' heard on Western Slope: Rancher writes Vivian that he is sure citizens won't let Japs settle," DP, February 6, 1944.

63 "23 Japs, but not 3,000, buy land in Adams County," RMN, February 3, 1944. Similarly, Japanese Americans were reported to have purchased twenty-five farms in Crowley County in ten days. See "Jap aliens buying Crowley and Pueblo farms, Lions told," *Pueblo Star-Journal*, February 3, 1944. Additionally, a total of fifty-six families were said to have settled in the Grand Junction area. See "Committee draws up resolution opposing further relocation of Japanese, urges group meeting," *Grand Junction Sentinel*, January 14, 1944.

64 "New drive started to bar Japanese aliens," DP, February 10, 1944.

65 See chapter 6, "The Church Takes Political Action in Colorado," in *Beyond Prejudice: A Story of the Church and Japanese Americans,* by Toru Matsumoto (New York: Friendship Press, 1946), 88–96, for the details of the campaign to defeat the amendment to Colorado's constitution to prevent Japanese from owning real property in the state. According to Richard W. Roskelley, the move to enact an alien land law was precipitated by stories of wartime Japanese atrocities. See Roskelley, "The Japanese Minority in Colorado following Evacuation," in *Agriculture in Transition*, Proceedings of Western Farm

Economics Association annual meeting (1944): 259–265. See also Roy Yoshida, "Nisei farmers' outlook dark," GP, January 12, 1944.

66   DP, February 6, 1944, and RMN, February 6, 1944, cited in Roskelley, "Japanese Minority following Evacuation," 262nn21–22.

67   "Residents of Adams County protest Jap farm land buying," *Lamar Daily News*, January 7, 1944.

68   Roskelley, "Japanese Minority following Evacuation," 262.

69   Naturally, the inmates at Amache had a keen interest in the outcome of this vote. Sueo Sako, "Just incidentally," GP, February 12, 1944.

70   Roskelley, "Japanese Minority following Evacuation," 91.

71   Miyagishima, "Colorado's Nikkei Pioneers," 178.

72   "League to bar Jap aliens as owners is formed," RMN, May 26, 1944.

73   Matsumoto, *Beyond Prejudice*, 94–95.

74   Ibid., 92.

75   Ibid.

76   McCarran's speech is cited in "Immigration and Nationality Act of 1952," *Wikipedia*, last modified May 17, 2015, https://en.wikipedia.org/w/index .php?title=Immigration_and_Nationality_Act_of_1952.

77   Of the 1,616 Japanese Coloradan who were born abroad in Japan or elsewhere before 1980, 1,249 of them became naturalized US citizens. Data from US Census Bureau, "Year of entry by citizenship status in the United State (B05005)," 2006–2010 American Community Survey, American FactFinder.

78   Preserving the gains that were made during the civil right movement has been a challenge. In recent years, there has been some backsliding. For example, in the case of Shelby County v. Holder (2013), the US Supreme Court essentially eviscerated the Voting Rights Act of 1965 that prohibited racial discrimination in voting.

EPILOGUE

1   "H-1B Visa," *Wikipedia*, last modified June 25, 2015, http://en.wikipedia.org/ wiki/H-1B_visa#H-1B_demographics.

2   "Tech Immigrants: A Map of Silicon Valley's Imported Talent," *Bloomberg Business*, June 5, 2014, www.bloomberg.com/bw/articles/2014-06-05/ tech-immigrants-a-map-of-silicon-valleys-imported-talent.

3   Wendy Wang, "The Rise of Intermarriage: Rates, Characteristics Vary by Race and Gender," Pew Research Center Social and Demographic Trends, February 16, 2012, www.pewsocialtrends.org/2012/02/16/the-rise-of-intermarriage/. For a reaction to this study, see Jeff Yang, "The real reason why Asian Americans are outmarrying less," *Wall Street Journal*, April 16, 2012.

4   Burt Hubbard, "100 years change the face of Colorado. Census Bureau report adds new wrinkles to trivia, demographics," RMN, December 18, 2002.

5   "At home in Colorado. Doing business, Asian entrepreneurs abound," RMN February 25, 1990.

6   US Census Bureau, "2010 Demographic Profile Data," Geography: Colorado Table, American FactFinder.

7   Though these categories represent a specific Asian ethnic group, each of these groups may have many subgroups within it. The census category for Burmese masks the fact that it consists of different tribes. The ethnic-based community group called the "Burmese Community Rangers," for example, provides assistance to nine different tribes from Burma who are living in the Denver metropolitan area.

8   "New Americans in Colorado: The Political and Economic Power of Immigrants, Latinos, and Asians in the Centennial State," Immigration Policy Center fact sheet, July 2013. The Asian American population number is larger than the 2010 demographic data indicates because the statistic is based on the 2011 American Community Survey (1-Year Estimates), cited in note 14 of the fact sheet.

9   This is a conservative figure because it is based on the "Asians alone" census category, rather than the multi-race category, which takes into account those who have self-identified as belonging to an Asian group as well as another group. The multi-race category was offered for the first time with the 2000 census and continued with the 2010 census. The 4.8 percent figure also does not include those belonging to the Pacific Islander category, although in popular usage they are often combined with Asians, hence the designation "Asian Pacific Islanders." With the increase in intermarriages between Asians and other racial groups, particularly whites, the multi-race category has significant implications for the development of the Asian American community.

10   The term "model minority" was coined by William Petersen. See Petersen, "Success story: Japanese American style," NYT, January 9, 1966. An academic cottage industry has developed around the "model minority" theme, mainly challenging its validity and treating it as more myth than reality. For demythologizing studies, see "The Model Minority Stereotype Project," www.facebook.com/MMSProject.

11   To cite a recent example, Amy Chua and Jed Rubenfeld, in *The Triple Package: How Three Unlikely Traits Explain the Rise and Fall of Cultural Groups in America* (New York: Penguin, 2014), attribute Asian American success to cultural characteristics. Other minorities, including certain religious and ethnic groups, are said to possess the same traits. Suketu Mehta, in "The Superiority Complex," *Time*, February 3, 2014, 35–39, challenges Chua and

Rubenfeld's assertions. For an alternate explanation of Asian American success, see Jennifer Lee and Min Zhou, "The Success Frame and Achievement Paradox: The Costs and Consequences for Asian Americans," *Race and Social Problems* 6, no. 1 (March 2014).

12   Nestor Mercado, Elnora Minoza-Mercado, and Alok Sarwal, *Voices from Colorado: Perspectives of Asian Pacific Americans* (Denver: Mercado Information and Business Services, 2008), 309.

13   Committee of 100 and Harris Interactive, "Still the 'Other?': Public Attitudes toward China and Asian Americans" (New York: Committee of 100, 2009), 17.

14   Samuel Cacas, "Violence against APAs on the rise: Immigrant bias behind increase in anti-Asian hate crimes," *AsianWeek*, August 4, 1995.

15   William Wei, "An American Hate Crime: The Murder of Vincent Chin," Fight Hate and Promote Tolerance, Tolerance.Org: A Web Project of the Southern Poverty Law Center, June 14, 2002.

16   See "Hate Crime Laws in the United States," *Wikipedia,* modified June 24, 2015, http://en.wikipedia.org/wiki/Hate_crime_laws_in_the_United_States, for a discussion of the country's development of hate crime laws.

17   Robert Jackson, "Asian-Americans in Colorado confront racism, ethnic jealousy," RMN, August 9, 1992.

18   See the Civil Rights Division of the Department of Justice, www.justice.gov/crt/legalinfo/discrimupdate.php, for information on the prosecution of hate crimes.

19   Linda Feldman, "Millennials see themselves as 'post-racial.' What does that mean?" *Christian Science Monitor,* April 30, 2014.

20   Sam Tanenhaus, "Generation nice," NYT, August 17, 2014.

21   Committee of 100 and Harris Interactive, "Still the 'other?,'" 14.

22   Jeff Yang, "Mixing it up. Multiculturalism redefines Asian American identity," *SF Gate,* February 11, 2011.

23   Michael Kimmel, *Angry White Men: American Masculinity at the End of an Era* (New York: Nation Books, 2013).

24   Ibid.

25   Alan Greenblatt, "Race alone doesn't explain hatred of Obama, but it's part of the mix," *NPR: Code Switch,* May 13, 2014.

26   Charles M. Blow, "The Obamas, race and slights," NYT, December 17, 2014.

SELECTED BIBLIOGRAPHY

MANUSCRIPT AND ARCHIVAL COLLECTIONS

Colorado State Archives, Denver
 District Court Criminal Case Files
 Governor Ralph L. Carr Collection
Denver Public Library, Western History Collection, Denver
 Bill Hosokawa Papers
 Clipping Files: Asian Ethnic Groups
 Denver Veteran Volunteer Firemen's Association Papers, 1873–1946
 J. P. C. Poulton Papers, 1870–1876
History Colorado Center, Stephen H. Hart Library and Research Center, Denver
 Chin Lin Sou Collection
 Colorado Subject Collection, Asian Ethnic Groups
 Ralph L. Carr Papers
 Sam Howe Collection
National Archives and Records Administration, Broomfield, Colorado
 Records of U.S. District Courts, District of Colorado

ARTICLES

Abrams, Kerry. "Polygamy, Prostitution, and the Federalization of Immigration Law." *Columbia Law Review* 105, no. 3 (April 2005): 641–716.

Andersen, Hans Christian. *The Nightingale.* Illustrated by Yegor Narbut. Clap Publishing, 2015.

Anderson, Kay J. "The Idea of Chinatown: The Power of Place and Institutional Practice in the Making of a Racial Category." *Annals of the Association of American Geographers* 77, no. 4 (1987): 580–598.

Appiah, Kwame Anthony. "Race in the Modern World: The Problem of the Color Line." *Foreign Affairs* 94, no. 2 (March-April 2015): 1–8.

Arnold, Hazel C. "Sun Yat-sen in Denver." *Colorado Magazine* 19, no. 5 (September 1942): 197–198.

Arnston, Jessica N. "Journey to Boulder: The Japanese American Instructors at the Navy Japanese Language School (1942–1946)." In *Enduring Legacies: Ethnic Histories and Cultures of Colorado,* edited by Arturo Aldama et al., 175–193. Boulder: University Press of Colorado, 2011.

Bickers, Robert A., and Jeffrey N. Wasserstrom. "Shanghai's 'Dogs and Chinese Not Admitted' Sign: Legend, History and Contemporary Symbol." *China Quarterly* 142 (June 1995): 444–466.

Bloom, Leonard. "Transitional Adjustments of Japanese-American Families to Relocation." "The American Family and Its Housing," special issue, *American Sociological Review* 12, no. 2 (April 1947): 201–209.

Bonacich, Edna. "A Theory of Ethnic Antagonism: The Split Labor Market." In *From Different Shores: Perspectives on Race and Ethnicity in America,* 2nd ed., edited by Ronald Takaki, 139–148. New York: Oxford University Press, 1994.

Buell, Raymond Leslie. "The Development of Anti-Japanese Agitation in the United States." *Political Science Quarterly* 37, no. 4 (December 1922): 605–638.

Chan, Sucheng. "The Exclusion of Chinese Women, 1870–1943." In *Entry Denied: Exclusion and the Chinese Community in America, 1882–1943,* edited by Sucheng Chan, 94–146. Philadelphia: Temple University Press, 1991.

Cheng, Lucie. "Free, Indentured, Enslaved: Chinese Prostitutes in Nineteenth-Century American Sexual Borderlands." In *Sexual Borderlands: Constructing an American Sexual Past,* edited by Kathleen Kennedy and Sharon Ullman, 131–157. Columbus: Ohio State University Press, 2003.

Endo, Russell. "Japanese of Colorado: A Sociohistorical Portrait." *Journal of Social and Behavioral Sciences* 31, no. 4 (Fall 1985): 100–110.

Fiset, Louis. "Thinning, Topping, and Loading: Japanese Americans and Beet Sugar in World War II." *Pacific Northwest Quarterly* 90, no. 3 (Summer 1999): 123–139.

Guglielmo, Thomas. "'NO COLOR BARRIER': Italians, Race, and Power in the United States." In *Are Italians White? How Race is Made in America,* edited by Jennifer Guglielmo and Salvatore Salerno, 29–43. New York: Routledge, 2003.

Hale, Sondra. "Edward Said–Accidental Feminist: Orientalism and Middle East Women's Studies." *Amerasia Journal* 31, no. 1 (2005): 1–5.

Hansen, Arthur A., and David A. Hacker. "The Manzanar Riot: An Ethnic Perspective." *Amerasia Journal* 2, no. 2 (Fall 1974): 112–157.

Hayford, Charles W. "Chinese and American Characteristics: Arthur H. Smith and His China Book." In *Christianity in China: Early Protestant Writings*, edited by Suzanne Wilson Barnett and John King Fairbank, 153–174. Cambridge, MA: Harvard University Press, 1985.

Holloway, Lynette. "Re-enslaved: How African-American Bondage Came Back after Emancipation." *Humanities* 34, no. 2 (March-April 2013): 38–41.

Huang, Jianli. "Umbilical Ties: The Framing of Overseas Chinese as the Mother of

Revolution." In *Sun Yat-sen: Nanyang and the 1911 Revolution*, edited by Lee Lao To and Lee Hock Guan, 75–129. Singapore: Institute of Southeast Asian Studies, 2011.

Hunt, Corinne. "The Chinese Miners of Gilpin County." *Colorado Gambler* 3, no. 24 (August 18–31, 1994).

Jung, Moon-Ho. "Coolie." In *Keywords for American Cultural Studies*, edited by Bruce Burgett and Glenn Hendler, 64–66. New York: New York University Press, 2007.

Karlin, Jules Alexander. "The Indemnification of Aliens Injured by Mob Violence." In *Anti-Chinese Violence in North America*, edited by Roger Daniels. New York: Arno Press, 1978.

Karthikeyan, Hrishi, and Gabriel J. Chin. "Preserving Racial Identity: Population Patterns and the Application of Anti-Miscegenation Statutes to Asian Americans, 1910–1950." *Asian Law Journal* 9, no. 1 (January 2002): 1–40.

Lee, Jennifer, and Min Zhou. "The Success Frame and Achievement Paradox: The Costs and Consequences for Asian Americans." *Race and Social Problems* 6, no. 1 (March 2014): 38–55.

Lee, Rose Hum. "The Decline of Chinatowns in the United States." *American Journal of Sociology* 54 (March 1949): 422–432.

Leonard, Stephan J. "The Irish, English, and Germans in Denver, 1860–1890." *Colorado Magazine* 34, no. 2 (1977): 126–153.

Lim, Christina M., and Sheldon H. Lim. "In the Shadow of the Tiger: The 407th Air Service Squadron, Fourteenth Air Force, CBI, World War II." *Chinese America: History and Perspectives* (1993): 25–74.

Mieder, Wolfgang. "No Tickee, No Washee." *Western Folklore* 55, no. 1 (Winter 1996): 1–40.

Mei, June. "Socioeconomic Origins of Emigration: Guangdong to California." *Modern China* 5, no. 4 (October 1979): 463–501.

Mackinder, Halford J. "The Geographical Pivot of History." *The Geographical Journal* 23 (April 1904): 421–437.

McKee, Delber L. "The Chinese Boycott of 1905–1906 Reconsidered: The Role of Chinese Americans." *Pacific Historical Review* 55, no. 2 (May 1986): 165–191.

Métraux, Daniel A. "Jack London and the Yellow Peril." *Education about Asia* 14, no. 1 (Spring 2009): 29–33.

Muller, Eric. "Betrayal on Trial: Japanese American 'Treason' in World War II." *North Carolina Law Review* 82 (June 2004): 1759–1798.

———. "The Japanese American Cases: A Bigger Disaster than We Realized." *Howard Law Journal* 49, no. 2 (2006): 417–474.

Okihiro, Gary Y. "Japanese Resistance in America's Concentration Camps: A Re-evaluation." *Amerasia Journal* 2, no. 1 (Fall 1973): 20–34.

Ou, Hsin-yun. "Mark Twain, Anson Burlingame, Joseph Hopkins Twichell, and the Chinese." *ARIEL* 42, no. 2 (April 2011): 43–74.

Ourada, Patricia K. "The Chinese in Colorado." *Colorado Magazine* 29, no. 4 (October 1952): 273–284.

Peffer, George Anthony. "Forbidden Families: Emigration Experiences of Chinese Women under the Page Law, 1875–1882." *Journal of Ethnic History* 6, no. 1 (Fall 1986): 28–46.

Perrigo, Lynn. "The Cornish Miners of Gilpin County." *Colorado Magazine* 14 (May 1937): 92–101.

Phan, Peter. "Familiar Strangers: The Fourteenth Air Service Group Case Study of Chinese American Identity during World War II." *Chinese America: History and Perspectives* (1993): 75–108.

Roskelley, Richard W. "The Japanese Minority in Colorado following Evacuation." *Agriculture in Transition*, Proceedings of the Western Farm Economics Association annual meeting (1944): 259–265.

Said, Edward W. "On Flaubert." In *Orientalism: A Reader,* edited by Alexander Lyon Macfie, 108–110. New York: New York University Press, 2000.

Schonberger, Howard. "Dilemmas of Loyalty: Japanese Americans and the Psychological Campaigns of the Office of Strategic Services, 1943–45." *Amerasia Journal* 16, no. 1 (1990): 21–38.

Skeldon, Ronald. "Reluctant Exiles or Bold Pioneers: An Introduction to Migration from Hong Kong." In *Reluctant Exiles? Migration from Hong Kong and the New Overseas Chinese,* edited by Ronald Skeldon, 3–18. Armonk, NY: M. E. Sharpe, 1994.

Spence, Jonathan. "Western Perceptions of China from the Late Sixteenth Century to the Present." In *Heritage of China: Contemporary Perspectives on Chinese Civilization,* edited by Paul S. Ropp, 1–14. Berkeley: University of California Press, 1990.

Sperber, Murray. "*Chinatown* 'Do as Little as Possible' Polanski's Message and Manipulation." *Jump Cut: A Review of Contemporary Media* 3 (1974): 9–10.

Tanaka, Kei. "Japanese Picture Marriage and the Image of Immigrant Women in Early Twentieth-Century California." *Japanese Journal of American Studies* 15 (2004): 115–138.

Tang, Irwin A. "The Chinese Texan Experiment." In *Asian Texans: Our Histories and Our Lives,* edited by Irwin A. Tang. Austin, TX: The It Works, 2007.

Taylor, Sandra. "Interned at Topaz: Age, Gender, and Family in the Relocation Experience." *Utah Historical Quarterly* 59, no. 4 (1991): 380–394.

Ts'ai, Shih-shan H. "Reaction to Exclusion: The Boycott of 1905 and Chinese National Awakening." *The Historian* 39, no. 1 (November 1, 1976): 95–110.

Wang, Xi. "The Chinese in Denver: A Demographic Perspective, 1870–1885." *Essays and Monographs in Colorado History* 12 (1991): 37–58.

Webster, Helen. "The Chinese School of the Central Presbyterian Church of Denver, Later Known as The Oriental Mission." *Colorado Magazine* 40, no. 1 (January 1963): 57–63, and 40, no. 2 (April 1963): 132–137.

Wei, William. "Americans First: Colorado's Japanese-American Community during World War II—An Interview." *Colorado Heritage* (Winter 2005): 18–20.

———. "Five Generations in Colorado: An Interview with the Descendants of Chin Lin Sou." *Colorado Heritage* (Autumn 2002): 14–16.

———. "History and Memory: The Story of Denver's Chinatown." *Colorado Heritage* (Autumn 2002): 3–13.

———. "Hmong American Youth: American Dream, American Nightmare." In *Generations of Youth: Youth Cultures and History in Twentieth-Century America*, edited by Joe Austin and Michael Nevin Willard, 311–326. New York: New York University Press, 1998.

———. "Representation of Nineteenth-Century Chinese Prostitutes and Chinese Sexuality in the American West." In *Enduring Legacies: Ethnic Histories and Cultures of Colorado*, edited by Arturo Aldama et al., 69–86. Boulder: University Press of Colorado, 2011.

———. "Sex, Race, and the Fate of Three Nisei Sisters." *Colorado Heritage* (Autumn 2007): 2–17.

———. "'Simply a Question of Patriotism': Governor Ralph L. Carr and the Japanese Americans." *Colorado Heritage* (Winter 2002): 3–15.

———. "The Anti-Chinese Movement in Colorado: Interethnic Competition and Conflict on the Eve of Exclusion." *Chinese America: History and Perspective* (1995): 179–197.

———. "The Internment of Japanese Americans in the United States." *Everyone's War* 8 (Autumn/Winter 2003): 52–58.

———. "'The Strangest City in Colorado': The Amache Concentration Camp." *Colorado Heritage* (Winter 2005): 2–17.

Wong, Cara, and Grace Cho. "*Jus Meritum*: Citizenship for Service." In *Transforming Politics, Transforming America*, edited by Taeku Lee, S. Karthick Ramakrishnan, and Ricardo Ramirez, 71–88. Charlottesville: University of Virginia Press, 2006.

Wong, K. Scott. "The Transformation of Culture: Three Chinese Views of America." *American Quarterly* 48, no. 2 (1996): 201–232.

Wortman, Roy T. "Denver's Anti-Chinese Riot." *Colorado Magazine* 42, no. 4 (Fall 1965): 275–291.

Wu, David Yen-ho. "The Construction of Chinese and Non-Chinese Identities." In *The Living Tree: The Changing Meaning of Being Chinese Today*, edited by Tu Wei-ming, 148–166. Stanford, CA: Stanford University Press, 1914.

Yu, Henry. "Edward Said, Dispeller of Delusions." *Amerasia Journal* 31, no. 1 (2005): 67–70.

———. "Reflections on Edward Said's Legacy: Orientalism, Cosmopolitanism, and Enlightenment." *Journal of the Canadian Historical Association/Revue de la Société historique du Canada* 17, no. 2 (2006): 16–31.

BOOKS

Abbott, Carl, Stephen J. Leonard, and Thomas J. Noel. *Colorado: A History of the Centennial State.* 4th ed. Boulder: University Press of Colorado, 2005.

Abelmann, Nancy, and John Lie. *Blue Dreams: Korean Americans and the Los Angeles Riots.* Cambridge, MA: Harvard University Press, 1995.

Ahmad, Diana L. *The Opium Debate and Chinese Exclusion Laws in the Nineteenth-Century American West.* Reno: University of Nevada Press, 2007.

Andrews, Thomas. *Killing for Coal: America's Deadliest Labor War.* Cambridge, MA: Harvard University Press, 2008.

Arrington, Leonard J. *Beet Sugar in the West: A History of the Utah-Idaho Sugar Company, 1891–1966.* Seattle: University of Washington Press, 1966.

Asahina, Robert. *Just Americans: How Japanese Americans Won a War at Home and Abroad.* New York: Gotham Books, 2007.

Ashbury, Herbert. *The Barbary Coast.* New York: Pocket Books, 1957.

Atwill, David G., and Yurong Y. Atwill. *Sources in Chinese History: Diverse Perspectives from 1644 to the Present.* Upper Saddle River, NJ: Prentice Hall, 2010.

Ambrose, Stephen E. *Nothing Like It in the World: The Men Who Built the Transcontinental Railroad, 1863–1869.* New York: Simon and Schuster, 2000.

Archdeacon, Thomas. *Becoming American: An Ethnic History.* New York: Free Press, 1983.

Athearn, Robert G. *The Coloradans.* Albuquerque: University of New Mexico Press, 1976.

Bancroft, Caroline. *Gulch of Gold: A History of Central City, Colorado.* Denver: Sage, 1958.

Barth, Gunther. *Bitter Strength: A History of the Chinese in the United States, 1850–1870.* Cambridge, MA: Harvard University Press, 1964.

Beshoar, Barron B. *Out of the Depths: The Story of John R. Lawson, a Labor Leader.* Denver: The Colorado Labor Historical Committee of the Denver Trades and Labor Assembly, 1942.

Blum, John Morton. *V Was for Victory: Politics and American Culture during World War II.* New York: Harcourt Brace, 1976.

Borton, Hugh. *Japan's Modern Century: From Perry to 1970.* 2nd ed. New York: Ronald Press, 1970.

Brodkin, Karen. *How Jews Became White Folks and What That Says about Race in America.* New Brunswick, NJ: Rutgers University Press, 1998.

Brown, Ronald C. *Hard-Rock Miners: The Intermountain West, 1860–1920.* College Station: Texas A & M University Press, 1979.

Buruma, Ian, and Avishai Margalit. *Occidentalism: The West in the Eyes of Its Enemies.* New York: Penguin, 2004.

Butler, Anne M. *Daughters of Joy, Sisters of Misery: Prostitutes in the American West, 1865–1890.* Urbana: University of Illinois Press, 1985.

Chan, Sucheng. *Asian Americans: An Interpretive History.* Boston: Twayne, 1991.

Chang, Gordon H., ed. *Morning Glory, Evening Shadow: Yamato Ichihashi and His Internment Writings, 1942–1945.* Stanford, CA: Stanford University Press, 1997.

Chang, Sidney H., and Leonard H. G. Gordon. *All under Heaven: Sun Yat-sen and His Revolutionary Thought.* Stanford, CA: Hoover Institution, 1991.

Chicago Japanese American Historical Society. *REgenerations Oral History Project: Rebuilding Japanese American Families, Communities, and Civil Rights in the Resettlement Era, Chicago Region.* Los Angeles: Japanese American National Museum, 2000.

Chua, Amy, and Jed Rubenfeld. *The Triple Package: How Three Unlikely Traits Explain the Rise and Fall of Cultural Groups in America.* New York: Penguin, 2014.

Christopher, Renny. *The Viet Nam War/The American War: Images and Representations in Euro-American and Vietnamese Exile Narratives.* Amherst: University of Massachusetts Press, 1995.

Clearfield, Elaine Abrams. *Our Colorado Immortals in Stained Glass.* Denver: Mountain Bell, 1986.

Cohen, Lucy M. *Chinese in the Post-Civil War South: A People without a History.* Baton Rouge: Louisiana State University Press, 1984.

Coolidge, Mary Roberts. *Chinese Immigration.* New York: Henry Holt, 1909.

Creel, Ann Howard. *The Magic of Ordinary Days.* New York: Viking Penguin, 2001.

Daniels, Roger, ed. *Anti-Chinese Violence in North America.* New York: Arno Press, 1978.

———. *Asian America: Chinese and Japanese in the United States since 1850.* Seattle: University of Washington Press, 1988.

———. *Coming to America: A History of Immigration and Ethnicity in American Life.* 2nd ed. New York: Perennial, 2002.

———. *Concentration Camps: North America, Japanese in the United States and Canada during World War II.* Malabar, FL: Krieger Publishing, 1981.

———. *Guarding the Golden Door.* New York: Hill and Wang, 2004.

———. *Prisoners without Trial: Japanese Americans in World War II.* New York: Hill and Wang, 1993.

Dinnerstein, Leonard, and David M. Reimers. *Ethnic Americans.* 3rd ed. New York: Harper and Row, 1988.

Dower, John W. *War without Mercy: Race and Power in the Pacific War.* New York: Pantheon Books, 1986.

Engelhardt, Tom. *The End of Victory Culture: Cold War America and the Disillusioning of a Generation.* New York: Basic Books, 1995.

Espiritu, Yen Le. *Asian American Panethnicity: Bridging Institutions and Identities.* Philadelphia: Temple University Press, 1992.

Fujita, Stephen S., and David J. O'Brien. *Japanese American Ethnicity: The Persistence of Community.* Seattle: University of Washington Press, 1991.

Fukuyama, Francis. *The End of History and the Last Man.* New York: Avon Books, 1992.

Fussell, Paul. *Wartime: Understanding and Behavior in the Second World War.* New York: Oxford University Press, 1989.

Gebhardt, Jürgen. *Americanism: Revolutionary Order and Societal Self-Interpretation in the American Republic.* Translated by Ruth Hein. Baton Rouge: Louisiana State University Press, 1993.

Glenn, Evelyn Nakano. *Issei, Nisei, War Bride: Three Generations of Japanese American Women in Domestic Service.* Philadelphia: Temple University Press, 1986.

Gulick, Sidney L. *American Democracy and Asiatic Citizenship.* New York: Charles Scribner's Sons, 1918.

———. *The American Japanese Problem: A Study of the Racial Relations of the East and the West.* New York: Charles Scribner's Sons, 1914.

Guglielmo, Jennifer, and Salvatore Salerno, eds. *Are Italians White? How Race Is Made in America.* New York: Routledge, 2003.

Guterl, Matthew Pratt. *American Mediterranean: Southern Slaveholders in the Age of Emancipation.* Cambridge, MA: Harvard University Press, 2008.

Gyory, Andrew. *Closing the Gate: Race, Politics, and the Chinese Exclusion Act.* Chapel Hill: University of North Carolina Press, 1998.

Harvey, Robert. *Amache: The Story of Japanese Internment in Colorado during World War II.* Lanham, MD: Taylor Trade Publishing, 2004.

Hafen, LeRoy R., ed. *Colorado and Its People: A Narrative and Topical History of the Centennial State.* 4 vols. New York: Lewis Historical Publishing, 1948.

Higham, John. *Strangers in the Land: Patterns of American Nativism, 1860–1925.* New York: Atheneum, 1974.

Hing, Bill Ong. *Making and Remaking Asian America through Immigration Policy, 1850–1990.* Stanford, CA: Stanford University Press, 1993.

Hunt, Michael H. *The Making of a Special Relationship: The United States and China to 1914.* New York: Columbia University Press, 1983.

Hurt, R. Douglas. *The Great Plains during World War II.* Lincoln: University of Nebraska Press, 2008.

Hogan, Richard. *Class and Community in Frontier Colorado*. Lawrence: University Press of Kansas, 1990.

Hohri, William Minoru. *Repairing America: An Account of the Movement for Japanese-American Redress*. Pullman: Washington State University Press, 1988.

Hornby, William H. *Voice of Empire: A Centennial Sketch of the Denver Post*. Denver: Colorado Historical Society, 1992.

Horsman, Reginald. *Race and Manifest Destiny: The Origins of American Racial Anglo-Saxonism*. Cambridge, MA: Harvard University Press, 1981.

Hosokawa, Bill. *Colorado's Japanese Americans: From 1886 to the Present*. Boulder: University Press of Colorado, 2005.

———. *Nisei: The Quiet Americans*. Rev. ed. Boulder: University Press of Colorado, 2002.

———. *The Thunder in the Rockies: The Incredible Denver Post*. New York: William Morrow, 1976.

Ichihashi, Yamato. *Japanese in the United States: A Critical Study of the Problems of the Japanese Immigrants and Their Children*. Stanford, CA: Stanford University Press, 1932.

Ichioka, Yuji. *The Issei: The World of the First Generation Japanese Immigrants, 1885–1924*. New York: Free Press, 1988.

Ignatiev, Noel. *How the Irish Became White*. New York: Routledge, 1995.

Isaacs, Harold R. *Scratches on Our Minds: American Views of China and India*. Armonk, NY: M. E. Sharpe, 1958.

Iriye, Akira. *The Origins of the Second World War in Asia and the Pacific*. London: Longman, 1987.

Irons, Peter. *Justice at War: The Story of the Japanese American Internment Cases*. New York: Oxford University Press, 1983.

Iwata, Masakazu. *Planted in Good Soil: A History of the Issei in United States Agriculture*. Issei memorial edition. 2 vols. New York: Peter Lang, 1992.

Jansen, Marius B. *The Japanese and Sun Yat-sen*. Stanford, CA: Stanford University Press, 1954.

Johnson, Susan Lee. *Roaring Camp: The Social World of the California Gold Rush*. New York: W. W. Norton, 2000.

Jung, Moon-Ho. *Coolies and Cane: Race, Labor, and Sugar in the Age of Emancipation*. Baltimore: John Hopkins University Press, 2006.

Kaplan, Robert D. *The Revenge of Geography: What the Map Tells Us about the Coming Conflicts and the Battle against Fate*. New York: Random House, 2013.

Kawakami, Kiyoshi Karl. *Asia at the Door: A Study of the Japanese Question in Continental United States, Hawaii, and Canada*. New York: Fleming H. Revell, 1914.

———. *The Real Japanese Question*. New York: Macmillan Company, 1921.

Kimmel, Michael. *Angry White Men: American Masculinity at the End of an Era.* New York: Nation Books, 2013.

Kimura, Yukiko. *Issei: Japanese Immigrants in Hawaii.* Honolulu: University Press of Hawaii, 1988.

Kitano, Harry H. L. *Japanese Americans: The Evolution of a Sub-culture.* 2nd ed. Englewood Cliffs, NJ: Prentice-Hall, 1976.

Kitano, Harry H. L., and Roger Daniels. *Asian Americans: Emerging Minorities.* 3rd ed. Upper Saddle River, NJ: Prentice Hall, 2001.

Kwong, Peter, and Dušanka Miščević. *Chinese America: The Untold Story of America's Oldest and Newest Community.* New York: New Press, 2005.

Lai, Eric Yo Ping, and Dennis Argelles, eds. *The New Face of Asian Pacific America: Numbers, Diversity, and Change in the 21st Century.* San Francisco: AsianWeek and UCLA Asian American Studies Center Press, 2003.

Lamm, Richard D., and Duane A. Smith. *Pioneers and Politicians: 10 Colorado Governors in Profile.* Boulder, CO: Pruett, 1984.

Lee, Rose Hum. *The Chinese in the United States of America.* Hong Kong: Hong Kong University Press, 1960.

——. *The Growth and Decline of Chinese Communities in the Rocky Mountain Region.* New York: Arno Press, 1978.

Lydia H. Liu. *The Clash of Empires: The Invention of China in Modern World Making.* Cambridge, MA: Harvard University Press, 2004.

Loewen, James W. *The Mississippi Chinese: Between Black and White.* 2nd ed. Prospect Heights, IL: Waveland Press, 1988.

London, Jack. *The Strength of the Strong.* New York: Macmillan, 1910.

Luibhéid, Eithne. *Entry Denied: Controlling Sexuality at the Border.* Minneapolis: University of Minnesota Press, 2002.

Lyman, Stanford. *Chinese Americans.* New York: Random House, 1974.

Ma, L. Eve Armentrout. *Revolutionaries, Monarchists and Chinatowns: Chinese Politics in the Americas and the 1911 Revolution.* Honolulu: University of Hawaii Press, 1990.

MacKell, Jan. *Brothels, Bordellos, and Bad Girls: Prostitution in Colorado, 1860–1930.* Albuquerque: University of New Mexico Press, 2004.

Mann, Ralph. *After the Gold Rush: Society in Grass Valley and Nevada City, California, 1849–1870.* Stanford, CA: Stanford University Press, 1982.

Marchetti, Gina. *Romance and the "Yellow Peril": Race, Sex, and Discursive Strategies in Hollywood Fiction.* Berkeley: University of California Press, 1993.

Martelle, Scott. *Blood Passion: The Ludlow Massacre and Class War in the American West.* New Brunswick, NJ: Rutgers University Press, 2007.

Martin, Ralph G. *Boy from Nebraska: The Story of Ben Kuroki.* New York: Harper and Brothers, 1946.

Matsumoto, Toru. *Beyond Prejudice: A Story of the Church and Japanese Americans.* New York: Friendship Press, 1946.

Matsumoto, Valerie. *Farming the Home Place: A Japanese American Community in California, 1919–1982.* Ithaca, NY: Cornell University Press, 1993.

May, William John, Jr. *The Great Western Sugarlands: The History of the Great Western Sugar Company and the Economic Development of the Great Plains.* New York: Garland, 1989.

Mazower, Mark. *Governing the World: The History of an Idea, 1815 to the Present.* New York: Penguin, 2012.

McClellan, Robert. *The Heathen Chinee: A Study of American Attitudes toward China, 1890–1905.* Columbus: Ohio State University Press, 1971.

McCunn, Ruthanne Lum. *Thousand Pieces of Gold.* Boston: Beacon, 2004. First published 1981.

McGovern, George S., and Leonard F. Guttridge. *The Great Coalfield War.* Boulder: University Press of Colorado, 1972.

McKee, Delber L. *Chinese Exclusion versus the Open Door Policy, 1900–1906: Clashes over China Policy during the Roosevelt Era.* Detroit, MI: Wayne State University Press, 1977.

Mercado, Nestor, Elnora Minoza-Mercado, and Alok Sarwal. *Voices from Colorado: Perspectives of Asian Pacific Americans.* Denver, CO: Mercado Information and Business Services, 2008.

Miller, Stuart Creighton. *The Unwelcome Immigrant: The American Image of the Chinese, 1785–1882.* Berkeley: University of California Press, 1969.

Millis, Harry A. *The Japanese Problem in the United States.* New York: Macmillan Company, 1915.

Mitter, Rana. *Forgotten Ally: China's World War II, 1937–1945.* Boston: Houghton Mifflin Harcourt, 2013.

Monnett, John H., and Michael McCarthy. *Colorado Profiles: Men and Women Who Shaped the Centennial State.* Niwot: University Press of Colorado, 1996.

Morgan, William Michael. *Pacific Gibraltar: U.S.-Japanese Rivalry over the Annexation of Hawai'i, 1885–1899.* Annapolis, MD: Naval Institute Press, 2011.

Moy, James S. *Marginal Sights: Staging the Chinese in America.* Iowa City: University of Iowa Press, 1993.

Nakano, Mei T., with OKAASAN by Grace Shibata. *Japanese American Women: Three Generations 1890–1990.* Berkeley, CA: Mina Press, 1990.

Ninkovich, Frank. *The United States and Imperialism.* Malden, MA: Blackwell, 2001.

Okada, John. *No-No Boy.* Seattle: University of Washington Press 1976.

Okihiro, Gary Y. *The Columbia Guide to Asian American History.* New York: Columbia University Press, 2001.

Otsuka, Julie. *The Buddha in the Attic.* New York: Vintage Book, 2011.

Parkhill, Forbes. *The Wildest of the West*. New York: Henry Holt, 1951.

Peffer, George Anthony. *If They Don't Bring Their Women Here: Chinese Female Immigration before Exclusion*. Urbana: University of Illinois Press, 1999.

Perkins, Robert L. *The First Hundred Years: An Informal History of Denver and the Rocky Mountain News*. Garden City, NY: Doubleday, 1959.

Persico, Joseph E. *Roosevelt's Secret War: FDR and World War II Espionage*. New York: Random House, 2001.

Pfaelzer, Jean. *Driven Out: The Forgotten War against Chinese Americans*. New York: Random House, 2007.

Portis, Charles. *True Grit*. New York: Overlook Press, 1968.

Prasso, Sheridan. *The Asian Mystique*. New York: Public Affairs, 2005.

Pruitt, Ida. *A Daughter of Han: The Autobiography of a Chinese Working Woman*. Stanford, CA: Stanford University Press, 1945.

Quan, Robert Seto. *Lotus among the Magnolias: The Mississippi Chinese*. Jackson: University Press of Mississippi, 1982.

Robinson, Greg. *After Camp: Portraits in Midcentury Japanese American Life and Politics*. Berkeley: University of California Press, 2012.

——. *By Order of the President: FDR and the Internment of Japanese Americans*. Cambridge, MA: Harvard University Press, 2001.

——, ed. *Pacific Citizens: Larry and Guyo Tajiri and Japanese American Journalism in the World War II Era*. Urbana: University of Illinois Press, 2012.

——. *A Tragedy of Democracy: Japanese Confinement in North America*. New York: Columbia University Press, 2009.

Roediger, David R. *Working toward Whiteness: How America's Immigrants Became White, The Strange Journey from Ellis Island to the Suburbs*. New York: Basic Books, 2005.

Roosevelt, Theodore. *The Works of Theodore Roosevelt*. 16 vols. New York: Charles Scribner's Sons, 1906–1910.

Said, Edward W. *Orientalism*. New York: Vintage, 1979.

Sandmeyer, Elmer Clarence. *The Anti-Chinese Movement in California*. Urbana: University of Illinois Press, 1939.

Saxton, Alexander. *The Indispensable Enemy: Labor and the Anti-Chinese Movement in California*. Berkeley: University of California Press, 1971.

Schiavo, Giovanni. *Four Centuries of Italian-American History*. New York: Vigo Press, 1954.

Schrager, Adam. *The Principled Politician: Governor Ralph Carr and the Fight against Japanese Internment*. Golden, CO: Fulcrum, 2009.

Sherlock, Tom. *Colorado's Heathcare Heritage: A Chronology of the Nineteenth and Twentieth Centuries*. Vol. 1, *1800–1899*. Bloomington, IN: iUniverse, 2013.

Secrest, Clark. *Hell's Belles: Prostitution, Vice, and Crime in Early Denver, with a*

Biography of Sam Howe, Frontier Lawman. Rev. ed. Boulder: University Press of Colorado, 2002.

Smith, Arthur H. *Chinese Characteristics.* 4th ed. New York: Fleming H. Ravell Company, 1894.

Spector, Ronald. *Eagle against the Sun: The American War with Japan.* New York: Vintage, 1985.

Sterner, C. Douglas. *Go for Broke: The Warriors of World War II Who Conquered Germany, Japan, and American Bigotry.* Clearfield, UT: American Legacy Historical Press, 2008.

Stoddard, Lothrop. *The Rising Tide of Color against White World-Supremacy.* New York: Charles Scribner's Sons, 1920.

Stone, Wilbur Fiske, ed. *History of Colorado.* 5 vols. Chicago: S. J. Clarke Publishing Company, 1918–1919.

Storti, Craig. *Incident at Bitter Creek: The Story of the Rock Springs Chinese Massacre.* Ames: University of Iowa Press, 1991.

Tamura, Linda. *Nisei Soldiers Break Their Silence: Coming Home to Hood River.* Seattle: University of Washington Press, 2012.

Takahara, Kumiko. *Off the Fat of the Land: The Denver Post's Story of the Japanese American Internment in World War II.* Casper, WY: Western History Publications, 2003.

Takaki, Ronald. *Strangers from a Different Shore: A History of Asian Americans.* Boston: Little, Brown, 1989.

Tang, Irwin A., ed. *Asian Texans: Our Histories and Our Lives.* Austin, TX: The It Works, 2007.

Terkel, Studs. *"The Good War": An Oral History of World War II.* New York: Pantheon, 1984.

Tong, Benson. *Unsubmissive Women: Chinese Prostitutes in Nineteenth-Century San Francisco.* Norman: University of Oklahoma Press, 1994.

Treat, Payson J. *Japan and the United States: 1853–1921.* Stanford, CA: Stanford University Press, 1928.

Uchida, Yoshiko. *Picture Bride: A Novel.* Flagstaff, AZ: Northland Press, 1987.

Ueda, Reed. *Postwar Immigration America: A Social History.* Boston: Bedford/St. Martin's, 1994.

Van Sant, John E. *Pacific Pioneers: Japanese Journeys to America and Hawaii, 1850–80.* Urbana: University of Illinois Press, 2000.

Weglyn, Michi Nishiura. *Years of Infamy: The Untold Story of America's Concentration Camps.* New York: William Morrow, 1976.

White, Richard. *"It's Your Misfortune and None of My Own": A New History of the American West.* Norman: University of Oklahoma Press, 1991.

Whiteside, Henry O. *Menace in the West: Colorado and the American Experience with Drugs, 1873–1963*. Denver: Colorado Historical Society, 1997.

Whitney, James A. *The Chinese and the Chinese Question*. 2nd ed. New York: Tibbals, 1888.

Williams, Frederick W. *Anson Burlingame and the First Chinese Mission to Foreign Powers*. New York: Charles Scribner's Sons, 1912.

Wilson, Robert A., and Bill Hosokawa. *East to America: A History of the Japanese in the United States*. New York: William Morrow, 1980.

Wong, K. Scott. *Americans First: Chinese Americans and the Second World War*. Cambridge, MA: Harvard University Press, 2005.

Wu, William F. *The Yellow Peril: Chinese Americans in American Fiction, 1850–1940*. Hamden, CT: Archon Books, 1982.

Wyman, Mark. *Hard Rock Epic: Western Miners and the Industrial Revolution, 1860–1910*. Berkeley: University of California Press, 1979.

Yamashita, Bruce I. *Fighting Tradition: A Marine's Journey to Justice*. Honolulu: University of Hawaii Press, 2003.

Yoo, David. *Growing Up Nisei: Race, Generation, and Culture among Japanese Americans of California, 1924–49*. Urbana: University of Illinois Press, 2000.

Zhu, Liping. *The Road to Chinese Exclusion: The Denver Riot, 1880 Election and the Rise of the West*. Lawrence: University of Kansas Press, 2013.

DISSERTATIONS, THESES, AND UNPUBLISHED PAPERS

Arntson, Jessica Natsuko. "Journey to Boulder: The Japanese American Instructors of the Navy Japanese Language School (1942–1946)." Master's thesis, University of Colorado, 2003.

Chang, Stephanie. "Side-by-Side: Japanese Americans and Colorado, 1941–1945." Undergraduate honors thesis, University of Denver, 1996.

Committee of 100 and Harris Interactive. "Still the 'Other?': Public Attitudes toward Chinese and Asian Americans." New York: Committee of 100, 2009.

Heimburger, Christian. "Life beyond Barbed Wire: The Significance of Japanese American Labor in the Mountain West, 1942–1944." PhD diss., University of Colorado, 2013.

Holsinger, Paul M. "Amache: The Story of the Japanese Relocation in Colorado." Master's thesis, University of Denver, 1960.

Kwon, Eunhye. "Interracial Marriages among Asian Americans in the U.S. West, 1880–1954." PhD diss., University of Florida, 2011.

Lee, Catherine. "Prostitutes and Picture Brides: Chinese and Japanese Immigration, Settlement, and American Nation-Building, 1870–1920." Working Paper 70,

Center for Comparative Immigration Studies, University of California, San Diego, February 2003.

Lurie, George. "A Legacy of Shame: The Story of Colorado's Camp Amache." Unpublished paper, 1985.

May, William John, Jr. "The Great Western Sugarlands: History of the Great Western Sugarlands." PhD diss., University of Colorado, 1982.

Miyagishima, Kara Mariko. "Colorado's Nikkei Pioneers: Japanese Americans in Twentieth Century Colorado." Master's thesis, University of Colorado at Denver, 2007.

Rudolph, Gerald E. "The Chinese in Colorado, 1869–1911." Master's thesis, University of Colorado, 1964.

Shinozuka, Jeannine Natsuko. "From a 'Contagious' to a 'Poisonous Yellow Peril'? Japanese and Japanese Americans in Public Health and Agriculture, 1890s-1950." PhD diss., University of Minnesota, 2009.

Sieg, Kent G. "The Chinese Community in Park County, as Indicative of the Chinese Experience in the Western Mining Areas." Unpublished student paper, University of Colorado, Boulder.

Zhou, Xioyan. "Qing Perceptions of Anti-Chinese Violence in the United States: Case Studies from the American West." Master's thesis, University of Wyoming, Laramie, 2008.

GOVERNMENT DOCUMENTS

Bernstein, Joan Z. et al., Members of the Commission on Wartime Relocation and Internment of Civilians, and Angus Macbeth, Special Counsel. *Personal Justice Denied: Report of the Commission on Wartime Relocation and Internment of Civilians.* Washington, DC: US Government Printing Office, 1982.

Colorado Bureau of Labor Statistics, Second Biennial Report, 1889–1890. Denver: Collier and Cleveland Lithography Company, 1890.

Compendium of the Eleventh Census, 1890. Washington, DC: Government Printing Office, 1892.

A Compendium of the Ninth Census, June 1, 1870. Washington, DC: Government Printing Office, 1872.

A Compendium of the Tenth Census, June 1, 1880. Washington, DC: Government Printing Office, 1883.

DeWitt, John L. *Final Report: Japanese Evacuation from the West Coast, 1942.* Washington, DC: Government Printing Office, 1943.

Executive Documents, 47th Congress, 1st Session, 1881–82, v. 1, Foreign Relations, no. 1, pt. 1, 2009. Washington, DC: Government Printing Office, 1882.

"House Joint Resolution for the Encouragement of Chinese Immigration into

Colorado Territory." In *Second Session Laws, Colorado Territorial Legislature.* Central City, CO: David C. Collier, 1870.

McCook, Edward M. "Message to the Colorado Legislature, January 4, 1870." In *Council Journal of the Legislative Assembly of the Territory of Colorado, Eighth Session.* Central City, CO: David C. Collier, 1870.

McNaughton, James C. *Nisei Linguists: Japanese Americans in the Military Intelligence Service during World War II.* Washington, DC: Department of the Army, 2006.

"Report of State Medical Inspection of Chinese." In *Sixth Report of Colorado State Board of Health, November 15, 1900 to November 30, 1902.* Denver: Smith-Brooks Printing Company, 1902.

Smith, James T. *Eighth Biennial Report of the Bureau of Labor Statistics of the State of Colorado, 1901–1902.* Denver: Smith Brooks Printing Company, 1902.

Statistics of the Population of the United States. Vol. 1 of the Tenth Decennial Census. Washington, DC: Government Printing Office, 1883.

Statistics of the Population of the United States. Vol. 1, part 1 of the Eleventh Decennial Census. Washington, DC: Government Printing Office, 1895.

U.S. Census Bureau. American FactFinder.

U.S. Immigration Commission. *Immigrant in Industries.* Part 25, *Japanese and Other Immigrant Races in the Pacific Coast and Rocky Mountain States.* Washington, DC: US Government Printing Office, 1911.

Wright, Carroll D. *A Report on Labor Disturbances in the State of Colorado, from 1880 to 1904, Inclusive, with Correspondence Relating Thereto.* Washington, DC: Government Printing Office, 1905.

INDEX

Cheng-lu (film character), 114

Cheng, Lucie, 97, 106

Chennault, Claire L., 256, 259

Chenoweth, Edgar, 224

Chin, Edward L., 256–57, 257*fig.*, 258, 273–74

Chin Lin Sou (pioneer), 76–83, 77*fig.*, 256–57, 272, 303n48; commemorative window for, 81–83, 82*fig.*, 159; family of, 78–79, 79*fig.*

Chin Poo (Chen Liangpu), 68–70, 85–86, 87–88, 301n14

Chin, Vincent, 287

Chin, Wa, 39*fig.*

Chin, Wawa, 272–74

Chin, William ("Willie," son of Chin Lin Sou), 78–79, 79*fig.*

Chin, William C. (grandson of Chin Lin Sou), 256–58, 258*fig.*, 273–74

China Mary. *See* Ah Yuen ("China Mary")

China Polly. *See* Bemis, Polly ("China Polly")

China-US sex trade, 99; *tongs* and, 100–101, 105–6. *See also* Chinese prostitutes

Chinatown (Polanski film), 66–67

Chinatown, concepts of, 10, 64–67, 72

Chinatown in Denver: customs in, 84–89; decline of, 95–96, 129*fig.*; downtown redevelopment and, 70–73; early residents of, 46–47, 73–76; enforcement of Geary Act in, 145–46; as ethnic conclave, 67–70, 71; first "mayor" of, 76–83, 77*fig.* (*see also* Chin Lin Sou); founding of, 37–38; gender ratios in, 73, 83–84, 105; as imagined community, 64–67; impact of race riot on, 68, 95, 134; location of, 67–68, 69–73; media

depictions of, 65–67; ousting of Chinese from, 70–73; prostitutes in, 65, 98 (*see also* Chinese prostitutes); rival factions (*tongs*) in, 68–70; services and shops in, 73–76; traits of Chinese and, 72–73, 81, 92–95; white fantasies about, 64–66. *See also* Denver, Colorado; Denver race riot

Chinatown, in New York, 110

Chinese American soldiers: contributions of, 253, 255–56; number of, in World War II, 273; postwar reception of, 259, 270–74; stories of, 256–59, 336n10

Chinese Americans: certificates of residence and, 144–45; as culturally deficient, 60–63; differentiation from Japanese, 195–96; exclusion of women and, 106–17; gender ratios and, 73, 83–84, 104–6; number of, in Colorado, 96, 285–86; self-perceptions of, 273–74; war effort and, 255–59, 336n10; white construction of traits of, 83, 92–95. *See also* Chinatown in Denver; Chinese pioneers

Chinese Characteristics (Smith), 178–80

Chinese Exclusion Act (1882): expansion to Japanese, 148–50, 167–69; Geary Act and, 144–45; renewal of (1902), 147–49, 167–68; signing of, 141; Sinophobic incidents and, 141–44, 142*fig.*

Chinese funerals, 88–89

Chinese-Italian War, 55–57

Chinese medicine, 74

Chinese Mutual Protective Association, 69, 70, 95

Chinese New Year, 70, 84–86

Chinese pioneers, 36*fig.*; gold rush and, 35–36; hurdles for women and, 109; local hostility to, 38–39; in other

Romance" article, 98–101, 102–3; race
riot and, 139

Denver Evening Post, 152

Denver Inter-Ocean, 48

Denver Miners' Register, 46

Denver Post: anti-Japanese stance of, 11,
150, 225, 232, 279; Carr and, 211; Chinese community and, 92–93, 94

Denver race riot (1880), 129*fig.*; Chinese
women and, 117–18; churches and,
90–91; civil authorities and, 131–32;
compensation of victims of, 135;
diplomatic tensions and, 137–41;
impact on Chinatown, 68, 95, 134;
instigation of, 126–30; interventions
by Denverites and, 90–91, 117–18,
133–34, 135; murder of Look Young
and, 132–33; political responses and,
134–35; prosecution of rioters and,
135–37; reconstruction of, 130–35,
312n22; role of *Rocky Mountain News*
and, 123–25; roots of, 120–23; Sinophobic speeches and, 125–26; white
behavior in, 128–30

Denver Times: Chinatown and, 65; intermarriage and, 112; race riots and,
128, 130

DeWitt, John L., 195–96, 199, 200, 203,
214, 227

Dickinson, Thomas, 47*map,* 149*map*

diplomatic tensions: anti-Chinese incidents and, 137–41, 146; anti-Japanese
incidents and, 169–71, 174; treaty violations and, 26, 108, 140–41, 169–70.
See also Pacific War

discrimination against Asians: equality clause in League of Nations
Covenant and, 184; growth of Asian
population and, 286; Japanese propaganda and, 226–27; Loving v.

Virginia (1967) decision and, 284–85;
protests against, 261–62; public condemnation of, 270–71; racial prejudice as root of, 8–12; resistence to,
11–12, 156–57, 211–15, 218, 279–80. *See
also* anti-Asian incidents; anti-Asian
sentiment; immigration policy;
racial prejudice

Domoto, Wakako, 208

Douglass, Frederick, 31

Dower, John W., 177, 192

DuBois, W. E. B., 296n21

Easton, George, 158

Ebert, Roger, 115–16

economic conditions. *See* labor shortages; organized labor; Panic of 1873

Eisenhower, Milton S., 216

Empress of China (ship), 21

English language classes, 90

entrepreneurship: in Chinatown, 73–76;
Chinese miners and, 34, 48, 78;
"Harry" Hokazono and, 157–59;
Japanese businesses and, 155–57, 275;
Japanese farmers and, 160–62

ethnic enmity, 54, 59, 112, 167. *See also*
racial prejudice

ethnic solidarity: interethnic rival-
ries and, 56; Japanese Americans
and, 156–57, 161, 242–44. *See also*
Pan-Asianism

eugenics theories, 188–89

European immigrants: Chinese-Italian
War and, 55–57; in Denver, 68; Denver race riot and, 130; ethnic enmity
and, 54, 59, 112, 167; Japanese as similar to, 152; number of, 22; perceptions of, 44–45; relations with Asian
immigrants, 6–8, 162–63; return rate
of, 44. *See also* Italian immigrants

Gompers, Samuel, 147

Gow, Charles, 38*fig.*

Gow, Katsuto K., 276*fig.*

Gozawa, James, 278–79

Graetz, Friedrich, 142*fig.*

Graham (Denver physician), 137

Granada Pioneer (Amache newspaper), 225, 229, 235; Shitara sisters affair and, 243, 244

Granada Relocation Center in Colorado (Amache concentration camp). *See* Amache concentration camp

Grant, Ulysses S. Grant (US president), 41

Greater East Asia Co-Prosperity Sphere, 193–94

"Greatest Generation," 253–54. *See also* Chinese American soldiers; Japanese American soldiers; World War II

Greeley, Colorado, 69, 159, 160, 201. *See also* Weld County

Greenwald, Maggie, 114, 115–17

Guglielmon, Thomas A., 55

Gulick, Sidney L., 153–54

Gung Heung. *See* Bemis, Polly ("China Polly")

Gutstadt, Hermann, 147

Hagberg, Gene, 223

Haider, Heinrich, 241–42, 246–47, 248, 249

Hall, Frank, 48

Hall, Willis, 155–56

Halliday, H. F., 243–44

Hamilton, Colorado, 55

Hancock, Winfield S., 117, 121

Harris, E. L., 81

Harrison Narcotics Act (1914), 94

Hart-Celler Act (1965), 283–84, 285

Harte, Bret, 87

Hathaway, Henry, 4

Hawaii: Asian immigration and, 5, 22, 28, 151, 152, 171; concentration camps and, 200, 262; Japanese in, 151, 152, 187–88, 198; military recruits from, 262, 265. *See also* Pearl Harbor, attack on

Hay, John, 73, 147–48

Hayes, Everis A., 169, 170

Hayes, Rutherford B. (US president), 138

Hayford, Charles W., 178

health concerns, and the Chinese, 71–73, 109

Heart Mountain concentration camp (Wyoming), 203, 213, 215, 217

Hickey, George C., 134

Hillel the Elder, 17

Hino Tetsuji, 176

Hip Sing Tong (Chinatown *tong*), 68

Hitt, Robert R., 144–45

Hmong, 284. *See also* "boat people"

Hoar, George Frisbie, 141

Hok Yop Tong (Chinatown *tong*), 98

Hokazono, Naoichi ("Harry"), 81, 82*fig.*, 157–59

Holy Cross Trail (Leadville newspaper), 54

Honda, Mike, 327n19

Hong, Charlie (Liu Laohong), 37*fig.*

Hoover, J. Edgar, 199

Hop Alley, 64–66

Hop Yop Tong (Denver *tong*), 98

Horsman, Reginald, 7

Hosokawa, Bill, 158, 160, 254, 260, 331n92

Huerfano County, Colorado, 175*fig.*

Hughes, Charles Evans, 192

Huntington, Samuel P., 180

118, 153; Chinese immigration and, 36, 69, 70, 76, 294n19; Chinese women and, 98, 99, 109, 118; resistance to camps and, 212, 213; school segregation in, 169–71; sex trade and, 98, 99. *See also* Six Companies

San Luis Valley, Colorado, 159, 161, 201, 203

San Luis Valley Vegetable Packers, Inc., 161

San Toy (musical comedy) boycott, 70

Santa Fe Railway, 300n81

Satow, Masao, 327n20

Sawyer, Lorenzo, 107–8

Sayer, Judge, 100

Schmitz, Eugene E. (San Francisco mayor), 170–71

school segregation, for Asian children, 169–71

Schumacker, E. L., 137

Secrest, Clark, 306n90

Seiver, George F., 81

Select Committee to Investigate the Interstate Migration of Destitute Citizens (San Francisco), 212–13

Seuss, Dr. *See* Geisel, Theodor Seuss

sexuality. *See* China-US sex trade; Chinese prostitutes; stereotyping

Shallee, George E., 127

Sherman, Ethel N., 240

Shigekuni, Tom, 221

Shigeta, James, 114

Shinsekai Shimbun (San Francisco newspaper), 159

Shitara sisters affair, 237–52, 239*fig.*; characterization of, 238–41; Creel novel on, 250–52; democracy on trial and, 244–56; as forgotton story, 237–38; POW escape and, 241–42; public reaction to trial of, 242–44;

sentencing in, 249–50; treason trial in, 246–56

Silicon Valley, 284

Silver and Gold (student newspaper), 225

Silverton boycott (1902), 147–48

Sims, J. Marion, 109

Sing Lee, 132

Sing, Leo Latt, 112–14, 310n45

Sing Quong, 145

Sino-American trade, 20–22

Sinophobia: alien land laws and, 45–46; automaton imagery and, 177–80; Chinatown and, 67, 95–96; Chinese Christians and, 91–92; Chinese miners and, 49–50, 53–59; Chinese pioneers and, 38–39; coolieism and, 30–31, 34; economic conditions and, 52–53; election of 1880 and, 125–26; impact of exclusion laws and, 141–42; interethnic rivalry and, 58–59; intermarriage and, 110–17; opium and, 306n90; prior to Chinese immigration, 22; prostitutes and, 119. *See also* Chinese Exclusion Act; Denver race riot

Six Companies, 6, 78, 89, 98, 122, 137, 146

slavery, 30–31, 107, 108. *See also* coolieism

Sloane, Harry, 70

Smith, Arthur H., 87, 178–80

Smith, Joseph Emerson, 85

Smith, Nels, 216

Social Darwinism, 62

Sodhi, Balbir Singh, 288

Sopris, Richard (Denver mayor), 131

South Pueblo Banner, 75–76

Spangler, Michael, 131–32

Sperber, Murray, 66–67

THE SCOTT AND LAURIE OKI SERIES IN ASIAN AMERICAN STUDIES